Out of MANY,
ONE

Out of MANY,
ONE

Obama and the Third American Political Tradition

RUTH O'BRIEN

*With a Foreword by
Thomas Byrne Edsall*

THE UNIVERSITY OF CHICAGO PRESS

CHICAGO AND LONDON

Ruth O'Brien is professor of political science at the Graduate Center, CUNY. She is the author of several books, including *Bodies in Revolt* and *Crippled Justice*.

The University of Chicago Press, Chicago 60637
The University of Chicago Press, Ltd., London
© 2013 by The University of Chicago
All rights reserved. Published 2013.
Printed in the United States of America

22 21 20 19 18 17 16 15 14 13   1 2 3 4 5

ISBN-13: 978-0-226-04159-9 (cloth)
ISBN-13: 978-0-226-04162-9 (paper)
ISBN-13: 978-0-226-04176-6 (e-book)

Library of Congress Cataloging-in-Publication Data

O'Brien, Ruth, 1960– author.
    Out of many, one: Obama and the third American political tradition /
Ruth O'Brien; with a foreword by Thomas Byrne Edsall.
      pages cm
    Includes bibliographical references and index.
    ISBN 978-0-226-04159-9 (cloth: alkaline paper) — ISBN 978-0-226-
04162-9 (paperback: alkaline paper) — ISBN 978-0-226-04176-6 (e-book)
    1. Obama, Barack. 2. United States—Politics and government—2009–
3. Political science—United States—History—21st century.   I. Edsall,
Thomas Byrne, writer of added commentary.   II. Title.
    E907.027 2013
    973.932092—dc23   2012048348

♾ This paper meets the requirements of ANSI/NISO Z39.48-1992
(Permanence of Paper).

Dedicated to Fred O'Brien

Husband, Parent, and Editor

*who inspired the revisions for the book (and my family),
making them both together,*

better, and whole again

Contents

Foreword

Thomas Byrne Edsall

While there have been a number of journalistic accounts of the Obama presidency, in *Out of Many, One: Obama and the Third American Political Tradition*, Ruth O'Brien gives us one of the first full-length studies. Her evaluation stakes out new ground in what surely will be a long and extended debate.

O'Brien portrays Obama as instituting an impressive series of policy ruptures: deemphasizing the privileges of white Christianity, bolstering the standing of gay and transgender citizens, and generating a "commons"—an interconnected terrain where "local, state, national, transnational, and global governmental and nongovernmental actors can tackle a substantive public policy problem from a multitude of intersecting and crosscutting perspectives." Stated more comprehensively, O'Brien contends that Obama "seeks to transform the face of the American middle class, stripping it of its white, male, Anglo-Saxon, Christian, heterosexual, affluent suburban connotations." Obama embodies a new political perspective, embracing "a collaborative approach that recognizes the interdependence and interconnectedness of all Americans."

Central to Obama's governing ethos is a deliberative approach—a "democratic experimentalism," an "interactive compliance"—that O'Brien sees as embodying a "third American political tradition." She argues:

> Unlike either the strong individual-rights (or civil liberties) state or the strong welfare state, this third tradition is premised on forging alliances and on collective goodwill. Rather than operating in an absence of good faith and trust, with individuals suing to enforce their civil rights, Obama emphasizes human dignity and potential, not material potential, in a cosmopolitan collectivity of shared, yet shifting, alliances. The third tradition is not a belief that you have the freedom to live your life unfettered by the state or any organization—it is not the cowboy image. Nor is it equality of opportunity maintained by the state through regulation—a nursemaid or nanny state that helps individuals. Instead, Obama seeks to build human potential by emphasizing freedom, equality of opportunity, and earned egalitarianism as we press on toward ever-new frontiers. The relevant image is pioneers depending on one another in a wagon train—in a collectivity.

O'Brien persuasively demonstrates that Obama holds a key position in an intellectual tradition that places him alongside major figures in political philosophy: Spinoza, Foucault, Arendt, Alinsky, Dewey, Du Bois, and Niebuhr. To these figures, as well as to the president, "power is not inherently negative or repressive, but has the potential to become a positive, productive force."

In O'Brien's view, Obama's most profound challenges leading up to and in the aftermath of the 2010 election are rooted in race. She sees Obama's policies as stripping away "the assumption of whiteness," and she makes the case that Obama does not substitute blackness for whiteness, but rather "difference for whiteness." A few pages further on, O'Brien is declarative: "Race explains the limits on Obama's success as a leader."

At the same time, Obama's most profound commitment is to the middle class. Obama's reform strategy is directed at enabling membership in, and mobility toward, the middle class, only indirectly targeting the needs of the poor and working class.

The Tea Party, O'Brien writes, was key to the Democratic defeat of 2010, and that wing of the conservative movement "sees Obama for the threat he poses—against white privilege and supremacy, or simply whiteness. . . . Obama threatens American society—not by passing more civil rights legislation or even by righting wrongs, but by stripping back the white veil covering the American state, economy, and society."

More generally, Obama's economic policies hew toward the center and are not "in direct support of poor and working-class people displaced by global corporatism. His economic reforms work within the confines of corporate capitalism . . . polishing and softening the edges of only some of the sharpest consumer practices. . . ." O'Brien is clearly disappointed in what she terms Obama's "save-Wall-Street-first approach" to economic recovery policies. Nonetheless, *Out of Many, One* takes the position that the forty-fourth presidency has already generated a transformative legacy: "While Obama's legislative accomplishments have been historic . . . he may have succeeded in something even bigger, something every presidential candidate promises but few before Obama could accomplish. . . ." He has deputized the "middle-class citizenry instead of building a stronger federal state ruled largely by elites and experts," thereby "changing the way Washington works."

O'Brien makes a compelling argument that Obama, with his emphasis on "fluidity and multiple identities," has already instituted a new framework for deliberative democracy, promoting the individual's sense of "efficacy and empowerment," turning institutions into communities in which, as Harry Boyte describes, "citizens are given *more* authority and *wider* opportunities for participation."

O'Brien brings forward evidence that Obama's commitment to feminist norms has allowed the germination of new directions in American foreign policy. His appointment of Anne-Marie Slaughter, for example, as State Department director of policy planning from 2009 to February 2011 has led to the emergence of an ideology within foreign policy elites, now populated in part by women, of what Slaughter sees as "power-with" as opposed to "power-over"—"power-with" defined as "relational, horizontal, and collaborative." O'Brien quotes Slaughter: Power-with is "the phenomenon we are witnessing in so many different places—the networked, horizontal surge and sustained application of collective will and resources."

O'Brien excoriates Obama's conservative political opponents for the "controlling images" and stereotypes they have disseminated. "They represented Obama as a 'thug,' the shiftless watermelon-loving, rib-eating wastrel, the 'pimp,' the 'gangster,' the 'snob' or 'uppity' one who does not keep to his assigned 'place'. . . the raging 'ranter' who plays 'the race card' as an excuse or diversion. . . ." She is deeply angered that that Fox News termed Michele Obama, the Princeton- and

Harvard-educated lawyer who has been married to Obama since 1992, "Obama's baby mama."

Obama as president has acted as a counterweight to this direction in American politics, espousing and exemplifying a "multicultural version of American liberalism, a wide, all-encompassing, perpetually changing philosophy of inclusion." In Obama's own words, being black is both "unique and universal." O'Brien believes Obama's race has served a positive purpose, just as Holning Lau argues that Obama's "hypermasculinity may have allowed [him] to speak out against the Iraq war without being dismissed as weak."

O'Brien ends her book with a question to which we do not yet have an answer: "How strong is the scaffolding upholding Obama's state?" She answers in a surprisingly lyrical mode:

> Obama embraces the adage that we are all snowflakes, every one unique; but as each flake falls and lands on a sidewalk or in a drift, its motion and position indicate the snow's direction. While the snowdrifts alter traffic patterns among people walking, driving, skiing, sledding, or falling, there is no "good" or "bad" direction. It depends upon the person's perspective. It is random. Obama withholds or brackets all judgment. . . . There is no controlling or orchestrating or determining what happens when the snowdrift blows left, right, or sideways. And there is no point in anticipating if, like a snowflake, we drift ahead or blow backward.

O'Brien sees Obama as embodying a positive anti-positivism, or, as she puts it, "Obama has faith in the absence of faith, but embraces the pursuit of perfectibility and the futility of looking for purity. . . . Unlike most Americans, Obama believes in 'hell on earth' but demonstrates little faith in heaven on earth."

No matter who wins in 2012, O'Brien believes that "Obama will still have made great strides . . . in improving the functioning and responsiveness of government." She concludes, however, that Obama will have to await "a Joshua of his own to get the people fully involved and guide them across the last river that lies in front of them."

A truly original book, *Out of Many, One* will persuade and enrage. O'Brien has emerged as a fearless proponent of a presidency for which she makes the strongest, most daring, and most provocative case. She has stated her argument without flinching. In doing so, she challenges us all to rethink Obama's significance in the present and for the future.

Acknowledgments

Many people deserve to be acknowledged for helping me finish this book. First mention goes to my editor at the University of Chicago Press, John Tryneski. This was not our first project together, so I knew how much fun working with him could be. John's enthusiasm fostered an environment of scholarship as conspiracy that started with his initial jest about "Baruch and Barack" and never ended. The manuscript's anonymous readers rendered insights that were simply superb. Giving so generously of their time, they drew up detailed reports that helped me make this a much better book. Rodney Powell gave quiet support at key times. Norma Sims Roche's close and exacting reading of the text was also enormously helpful.

Colleagues and friends who read the initial draft of the book also made important contributions, especially Stephen Amberg. He not only invested a lot of time in reviewing the manuscript and making thoughtful comments, but also wangled an invitation for me to deliver the keynote address at the "Obama: Year One" conference at Copenhagen Business School, an event that was quite fruitful in refining my thoughts. Similarly rewarding was Gerald Berk's invitation to air my ideas on the third political tradition before his colleagues at the University of Oregon. Chloe Atkins, Ira Katznelson, Judith Grant, and Carol Nackenoff gave me challenging criticism. Mark Blasius,

Nancy Hirschmann, Eileen McDonagh, and Anne Norton sent me off in productive theoretical directions after some long phone calls. Martha Fineman, Jill Norgren, and Karen Orren were very inspiring and helpful as mentors. Brad MacDonald's insight is greatly appreciated in helping me puzzle through a key theory concept. Martha Campbell, Nadine Cohen, Natalia Dolzhanskaya, Cate Da Pron, Susan Martin-Marquez, Marta Lauritsen, and Arlene Stein have been supportive friends. And I greatly appreciate Thomas Byrne Edsall's wonderful foreword.

The CUNY Graduate Center has given me tremendous support, in terms of both time and research funds, for which I gratefully thank President William P. Kelly and Provost Chase F. Robinson. Vice Provost and Dean Louise Lennihan has been immensely encouraging and supportive, and a terrific friend. Bouncing around ideas about Obama with my graduate students was a stimulating sport, particularly when played with Flannery Amdahl, Fanny Lauby, Gerry Martini, Aaron Shapiro, and Joshua Sperber.

My family grounds and sustains me. Max, fifteen, unwittingly gave me one of the biggest compliments in asking for a copy of the manuscript that kept cluttering our mutual computer workspace. Theo, at thirteen, presents a different type of encouragement, continuing to interpret all things Obama as nifty despite my insistence on discussing this subject at the dinner table. My sister Liz gave me some good feedback. I had fun conveying the argument to Fred's family, particularly the lively and inquisitive minds of his mother and father, Ruth and Harold Schwarz. And finally, I dedicate the book to Fred, my husband, who showed his unflagging support by editing the manuscript three times and giving me blocks of time to spend alone while he took care of the boys, and whose love, compassion, and ever-endearing consideration and thoughtfulness have filled my life, and that of our sons, with unexpected riches. Our coming from diametrically opposed vantage points forced me to think more fully, and proved to be surprisingly stimulating. I would not have finished this project without Fred's inspiration.

1 In the Beginning: Locke, Rousseau, and Two Political Traditions

American political thought has been dominated by two contrasting traditions. The first is that of a minimal, weak state supporting neoclassical capitalism and imbued with strong individual rights, as seen, for example, in George W. Bush's "ownership society." The second is that of a relatively strong welfare state with regulatory capitalism, as starkly exemplified by Franklin D. Roosevelt's New Deal. In this book I will argue that Barack Obama, as candidate and then as president, represents a radical departure from both these traditions—that, in fact, his rhetoric and his actions have revitalized a third, latent but nonetheless potent, tradition in American politics. This third tradition privileges neither the individual nor the state. Instead, it promotes interaction, interconnectedness, and interdependency between the two.

To young people in the United States, the twenty-first-century American nation-state reflects no single political tradition. The relatively strong welfare state, which the Republicans have long condemned, is particularly hard to comprehend.[1] It is manifested as a myriad of overlapping states that scholars have best described as a hybrid, hidden, or submerged.[2] Yet even these adjectives capture at best a snapshot, a specific law or public policy, but not the whole nature of the relatively strong welfare state.

The welfare state that stems from the second political tradition can vary greatly, depending upon what service is being delivered: the mail, a driver's license, a loan. American youth go to the privatized post office; the locally run, state-administered Department of Motor Vehicles (the DMV); the privately or publicly run college or university's financial aid office, doling out federally guaranteed state and federal student loans; or the state-run Department of Homeland Security office, issuing passports for travel abroad from a county seat, a municipality, or a privatized post office.

All of these overlapping government offices both embody and symbolize what the American nation-state *is* in juxtaposition to the strong welfare nation-state found in Europe. What kind of hybrid it is—and how a state, federal, or local office is hidden or submerged—keeps evolving along with the perpetually changing institutional configurations that shape and reshape public policies *and* political identities in a recurring loop. In short, it's complicated. The American welfare state is a behemoth, not a benevolent guardian, let alone a savior.

When the American nation-state stopped guaranteeing welfare rights, thus reversing a policy that leftist activists from the 1960s onward have advocated, it did not just "end welfare as we know it," as President Bill Clinton said at the signing ceremony.[3] It also embroiled the American state and society in a different type of conflict about political identities as well as social and economic or redistributive domestic and foreign public policies. As political institutions and identities shifted, most notably with welfare reform in 1996, it became harder for the tail end of the baby boom and the echo boomers to regard the relatively strong welfare state in a positive way.[4]

Combining the relatively strong welfare state with the ownership society, welfare rights morphed into the "marriage cure." Yet this cure was not instigated by one political party. Nor did it occur under one regime, in one political time, or across an era or epoch. It reflected a bipartisan consensus of Republicans and Democrats that imposed their upper-middle-class, white, Anglo-Saxon, Christian, heterosexual morality about the nuclear family on "single" moms and "deadbeat" dads.[5]

It is this behemoth that Barack Obama knew needed reforming. Obama referred to his campaign and election as "Organizing for America," but it would be more accurate to say that he reconceptualized and reframed fundamental beliefs and values in the United States that are making and shaping political institutions *and* political identities. Obama embodies a new political perspective, embracing what could be called a collaborative approach that recognizes the interdependence and interconnectedness of all Americans, for better or worse. In neither his 2008 campaign rhetoric nor his actions after taking office did Obama distinguish between the private, the public, and the social spheres. Rather than having the state regulate society, or having society freed from state regulation, Obama advances a collaborative state and market and promotes a fully encompassing social sphere, or a collectivity.

Unlike either the strong individual-rights (or civil liberties) state or the strong welfare state, this third tradition is premised on forging alliances and on collective goodwill. Rather than operating in an absence of good faith and trust, with individuals suing to enforce their civil rights, Obama emphasizes human dignity and potential, not material potential, in a cosmopolitan collectivity of shared, yet shifting, alliances. The third tradition is not a belief that you have the freedom to live your life unfettered by the state or any organization—it is not the cowboy image. Nor is it equality of opportunity maintained by the state through regulation—a nursemaid or nanny state that helps individuals. Instead, Obama seeks to build human potential by emphasizing freedom, equality of opportunity, and earned egalitarianism as we press on toward ever-new frontiers. The relevant image is pioneers depending on one another in a wagon train—in a collectivity.

Pioneers, No Cowboys or Nursemaids

Obama's frontier more closely resembles the French Enlightenment borderlands of the Pennsylvania Alleghenies, as described by J. Hector St. John de Crèvecoeur, than the western Rockies, as emblazoned in American memory and myth by Frederick Jackson Turner at the end of the nineteenth century. Writing in 1782, Crèvecoeur, a French immigrant farmer, described Americans as part of a "new race," built on the pioneer principle of creating one's own wealth by tilling the wilderness. These frontier farmers had escaped the "prejudices and manners" of the *ancien régime.* "They wanted America to be the exception—the exception to the corruption and licentiousness of Versailles' court life." Romanticized, they hoped for peace and prosperity and expected the state to facilitate "stability, tranquility and political liberty."[6]

A state facilitating the freedom of hardworking frontier men, women, and children, behaving responsibly and without privilege or corruption, interprets and mediates that freedom, not of just one, but of the entire "asylum." It is not the myth of independence, but more the wagon train, more the village, and it is not the individual *or* the state, but the interaction between the two, that facilitates freedom, promotes equality of opportunity, and mediates earned egalitarianism. The state neither protects individuals nor shelters society as an organic whole. Instead, the state both mediates and facilitates growth—both the organic growth of the individual and that of the individual within her social context—and therefore the collective that populates the United States.

In addition to the founding French frontier tradition, Obama's political vision includes a third, lesser-known, and harder-to-fulfill reformist and radical tradition of small-*d democratic* progressivism. First, it is *democratic* progressivism because of the power instilled in the people—the *demos*—that Obama hopes can be made more deliberative. Second, it is *middle class*, because an overwhelming majority of Americans aspire to be part of this middle class. Like Theodore Roosevelt, a progressive Republican, and most Democratic presidents thereafter, Obama sees the middle class as more of an ideological construct than a demographic category. It embodies hope as an aspiration.[7]

Obama's progressivism is not in direct support of poor and working-class people displaced by global corporatism. His economic reforms work within the confines of corporate capitalism, polishing and softening the edges of only some of the sharpest consumer practices of a proprietary global capitalist market that most Americans believe lacks legitimacy, and some consider corrupt. Obama supports consumer reform as an antidote to Wall Street excess. He advances a middle-class perspective of incremental change made by those who already participate. Obama is a middling, middle-class economic reformer at best, not a radical, whose policies only indirectly help the poor and the working class.

One aspect of Obama's moderate middle-class progressivism, however, is radical. He seeks to transform the face of the American middle class, stripping it of its white, male, Anglo-Saxon, Christian, heterosexual, affluent suburban connotations. He downgrades the "city on a hill" language of John Winthrop, the idea that the United States is a "Christian nation," substituting the civic religion of Alexis de Tocqueville. As a nation of joiners, all Americans—single African American mothers, gay married fathers, white soccer moms residing with their children in rural, urban, and suburban areas—are part of Obama's expansive spatial, physical, and virtual visions of an aspiring middle class.

In Obama's view, neither these individuals nor their nuclear and extended families can survive alone in the twenty-first-century global economy. Obama made inclusivity and interconnectedness paramount during the 2008 election and vital to his administration and reelection efforts. The critical consideration is whether a family, any kind of American family, adopts the middle-class ideal as an aspiration.[8] "Our country is some kind of mongrel that is spiritually a chameleon," poet and *New York Daily News* columnist Stanley Crouch writes, "but always remains a bastard."[9]

Obama's political platform showed the voting public that equality and freedom could be relational and reciprocal in the United States. Freedom could not be found alone, nor could equality (or equality of opportunity) be secured singularly. Depending on and being accountable to one another, Obama proclaimed, is essential to the American individual, society, market, and state in the twenty-first century. It is part of their democratic existence. "I believe deeply that we cannot solve the challenges of our time," Obama said, "unless we solve them together."[10]

Obama's campaign for reform was fresh. He imagined a nation that embraced the interdependence, equality of opportunity, authenticity, and freedom of its people. Obama envisioned how the United States could profit from what this book calls a democratic pragmatist notion of mutual inclusivity and survivability or what Spinoza calls self-obligation. All American citizens should have both the autonomy to determine their own needs and the right to self-preservation.[11] So do citizens in other sovereign nations. Building on the basis of "shared reliance," Obama cast equality of opportunity, earned egalitarianism, and freedom as mutually inclusive constructs that foster a give-and-take among all parties. The state wields its power not to dictate, but to mediate and facilitate; it helps its citizens forge voluntary, shifting alliances.

The Collaborative State

What makes Obama's platform part of a third tradition is that his notion of "change" creates a new vision of American politics. His is *not* the public-interest progressive reform perspective practiced by Teddy Roosevelt a century ago. Nor does he advance a watered-down version of communitarian social contract theory that sees the state as "the solution," a central concept that other progressive eras have held in common.

To Obama, as to a significant part of the American youth, the state manifests itself as a bureaucracy, one in which a citizen stands in long lines and fears that the civil servant behind the counter could get one digit of her Social Security number wrong, plunging her into a mistaken-identity nightmare. Obama rejects the rigidity of the social welfare state. To be sure, he accepts regulation, but he does not believe that building governmental institutions constitutes liberal reform, as it did in the Progressive Era, the New Deal, and the Great Society.

Put differently, Obama does not seek a European social welfare state "lite." The state is not the savior. No institution can come to the rescue, only people—people helping themselves as they help others. What is important is not that the state provide health care, nor that the state make health care private, but that the individual must buy into health care and that health insurance companies must reform their actuarial practices. The individual takes; the state mediates and facilitates, moderating proprietary capitalism through consumer reform. Obama governs the state, the market, and society with social technology. "In the bush or somewhere up in somebody's mountains, we assume—or hope," writes Crouch, "that there are people whose sense of life has not been totally encroached on by the boxed, electronic shadow world of television or the Internet universe in which cyberspace seems as real to many as God, angels and heaven are to an atheist."[12]

Three Merged and Spinning Spheres, More Planet than Public Space

Obama relies on social technology to merge the public, the private, and the social spheres. Yet this should not be confused with the public space carved out by the second tradition of the relatively strong social welfare state. Obama does not collapse the public and the private spheres. Merging the three spheres is not similar to the social rights that we associate with the post–World War II democratization in Europe that underlies the EU.[13] These spheres are better thought of as planets with intersecting orbits.

Explaining how the social welfare state expanded its conception of citizenship, the oft-quoted T. H. Marshall argued that strong welfare states in Europe gave, and should continuing giving, their citizens political, economic, *and* social rights after World War II. Some historians and sociologists studying American political development (APD) and political scientists informed by sociology initially incorporated Marshall's notion of *universal* social rights into their work on social welfare states, societies, and citizenries as a benchmark for the United States to aspire to, or conversely as a reform that represented a disappointing compromise. These descriptions of social welfare states, particularly those done from a comparative perspective, developed across political time or in distinct regimes or eras, cultivating a citizenry that got more and more "civilized" or reformed, becoming a mixed economy, and thereby stymieing real economic and political change.[14] Marshall's strong social welfare state itself followed a teleological path or trajectory. The citizens composing societies in the EU battled and gained, first, human rights, which later included civil rights; second, political rights or suffrage; and finally, social rights.[15]

This sociological view of APD cast doubt upon American exceptionalism by explaining how citizens in the United States participate, promoting (or not) their own self-interests. The most promising recent work in this vein incorporates sociology *and* social theory. It does not merely collapse the public and the private spheres, but recognizes how formal and informal units, like the family, are political institutions, and as such, foster differences between and among formal *and* informal groups, and particularly peoples with different, and often vulnerable, identities.[16]

This book recognizes that Obama's merging of the private, the public, and the social spheres does not mean that he gives American citizens the traditional social rights and obligations that come with the European strong social welfare state, or the EU. It does not advance the idea that social rights are housed in a social sphere. It relies on social theory to make a nonlinear and nonteleological argument in APD that features social technology. It rests development on a perspective of history cast as time, agency, and contingency that is articulated best by blending Hannah Arendt and Jean Baudrillard.[17]

For the democratic progressivism of the third tradition to be effective, the state, the market, and society must be *performative*. The state and its active citizenry must foster and facilitate political participation that produces public policies that are progressive, not regressive. When Obama intersects and merges parts of the public, the private, and the social spheres, he focuses not on production but on *consumption* in the state, the market, and society. The president does not maintain that progress vanishes, as neocons claim. Globalization did not end history any more than Cold War liberalism ended ideology.[18]

Obama recognizes the reach of an interconnected and interdependent market, state, and society in what political theorist Benjamin Barber called McWorld in the mid-1990s and what cultural studies professor Toby Miller called "creepy Christianity" after 9/11. Miller reminds us of Attorney General John Ashcroft pulling blue drapes over Lady Justice's breasts in an attempt to restore the "majesty of law" and Under Secretary of Defense Paul Wolfowitz returning over half a million military berets made in China after 9/11. Obama realizes the "significance" of Cokes, curtains, berets, and burgers. He understands the dangers associated with turning french fries into "freedom fries." And Obama knows that hope cannot create change in the absence of authentic political participation.[19]

This underscores how an all-encompassing and all-encroaching social sphere, as Arendt notes, has its perils. It outlines Obama's critique of American hegemony; and at the same time, it highlights hope for Americans and shows how Americans can become good global citizens. Obama's vision of globalism recognizes how all three spheres spinning simultaneously can collaborate and/or collide. A collaborative state, market, and society can be cooperative while having pockets of resistance that put political institutions and peoples of different identities in collision. Obama seeks an effective, enlarged social sphere free from resistance that incorporates the public and the private spheres. But this third political tradition can produce change for its *demos*, and hope for generations in the future, if and only if its citizens cooperate and actively participate in constructive civic action.

Given all the terms for world markets and societies—globalization, globalism, global commons—an enlarged social sphere that cultivates collectivities is a double-edged sword. Small-*d* democratic progressivism depends on its *demos* participating in politics. In other words, in a deliberative democracy, citizens must be good (i.e., participate and deliberate). Eventually, they must produce good deeds (by participating with enough integrity and authenticity to produce results that match the dreams and hopes of a representative democracy). And the deliberative citizens of this state, market, and society must be perceived as being fair or acting and behaving well (not being corrupt or corruptible). Obama's vision of good governance at home and abroad depends on authentic political participation, nudged or held in line by social technology that depends on defaults. Civic action cannot afford to produce, and reproduce, power inequities that can be regarded as unfair or, worse, corrupt. Nor can this action create public policies that perpetuate political, economic, and social inequities, like income and education inequalities or gaps. Governance is only as good as the people populating and participating in the commons.

A New Exodus?

This collaborative approach can be seen in many areas. Like Bill Clinton and George W. Bush before him, Obama supports faith-based initiatives, but, unlike Bush, he believes that the extensions of the state they create must be rooted in American values (i.e., with no exclusions). Catholics cannot hire exclusively Catholics, and Mormons can-

not hire only from their own faith, to help the poor and serve the needy
in their neighborhood or congregation. Nor can these extensions of the
state do any proselytizing. Obama's faith-based initiatives give secular
groups the same role as religious ones, making room for nonbelievers
to serve the community. His aim is simply to facilitate "those organizations that want to work on behalf of our communities, and to do so
without blurring the line that our founders wisely drew between church
and state."[20]

This decision against embracing the state does not mean, however,
that Obama swings to the pendulum's other side. He does not adopt
the classical American liberal perspective—emphasizing individual autonomy and accepting a self-regulating or free market. Obama rests his
faith in people and believes the state should help them achieve their potential. This Democratic president does not accept the liberal premise
underlying Lyndon B. Johnson's Great Society—the premise that gave
the poor and disadvantaged what Republicans later called an "excuse"
for life. Obama does not privilege experts who attribute the problems
of vulnerable people to societal ills. Each and every one of those people
must be accountable and accept personal responsibility.

Obama insists on implementing public policy programs that promote individual responsibility. He believes in accountability. Talking
about fatherhood and the African American community, Obama says
men must take "full responsibility for [their] own lives." In his view, this
involves "demanding more from our fathers, and spending more time
with our children, and reading to them, and teaching them that while
they may face challenges and discrimination in their own lives, they must
never succumb to despair or cynicism; they must always believe that they
can write their own destiny."[21]

Obama expects the beneficiaries of reformist public policies to pull
their own weight. At the same time, these policies must be as inclusive
as possible. Health care, for instance, must be available to everyone,
though this does not mean that everyone will subscribe. Obama advocates policies that are universalizing, but he does not offer universal
entitlements. The irony of the constitutional battle over health care is
that Obama did not initially advance an individual mandate.

To do so, Obama pools resources. He insists on "binding our particular grievances—for better health care, and better schools, and better
jobs—to the larger aspirations of all Americans—the white woman struggling to break the glass ceiling, the white man who's been laid off, the
immigrant trying to feed his family."[22] Obama's ideas about equality of
opportunity, responsibility, accountability, inclusivity, and universalism

reflect a very different conception of progressivism, one based not on economic reform, but rather on consumer reform.

Obama not only balances freedom with equality of opportunity, but also introduces a third term to this third tradition. A right and duty to participate can be earned by citizens who choose to act. All citizens retain the right to vote, but those who choose to participate in the deliberative process underlying democracy must be willing to do their homework. They need goodwill. They must be honest and authentic. They must cultivate and foster dialogue and promote public reason. Obama throws earned egalitarianism into the deliberative democratic mix.

This type of progressivism is not built on the thought of either the classical liberal John Locke or the communitarian social contract theorist Jean-Jacques Rousseau. It is neither liberal nor communitarian. It promotes neither negative nor positive freedom. It uses no negative night watchman and erects no positive social welfare state. Instead, it employs social technology.

Wolves Circling Wagon Trains

Democratic progressivism emanates from ideas articulated most comprehensively and with greatest consistency in a third doctrine: that espoused by the seventeenth-century religious thinker and philosopher Baruch Spinoza, whose principles can be found in the American political thought of John Dewey, Saul Alinsky, W. E. B. Du Bois, Reinhold Niebuhr, and Hannah Arendt.

In Spinoza's view, the state, the market, and society create the context in which the individual can *become* free. Going beyond survivability, an interdependent state and society help the individual pursue her potential or, in Spinoza's words, her "perfectibility." It is about "a more perfect union," as Obama titled a 2008 speech. Two heads are stronger than one.

Spinoza replaces the Hobbesian maxim underlying individualism, that "man is a wolf to man," with "man is a god to man." While some people act like wolves, attacking others for their own gain, Spinoza emphasizes that other people behave like gods or saviors, helping their peers not out of altruism, but for their own preservation and perfectibility. And Obama echoes this principle: working together, he says, "ordinary people can do *extra*ordinary things."[23]

Locating the character of Obama's vision in Spinoza, or in the modern American iterations of Spinoza—as found in the thoughts of Dewey, Alinsky, Du Bois, Arendt, and Niebuhr that compose this third tradition—is not to say that Obama has read the work of these American political thinkers. Yet there is some causality here. According to David Remnick and Obama himself, he did read Alinsky, Du Bois, and Niebuhr.[24]

Obama's democratic progressivism exhibits the same faith in the power of the people, and upholds the same belief that self-interest is transformative, as the writings of all of these political thinkers did. It maintains that truth and knowledge are socially constructed, and it suggests that everyone is interdependent. "Interconnectedness," Obama said, "now spans the globe." We live in an "interdependent and interconnected world."[25]

Obama's democratic progressivism spurns the idea of pitting public interest against self-interest. "We all have a stake," Obama insists, "in each other's success." He dismisses a belief in absolute truths and challenges the myth of autonomy while questioning whether the strong social welfare state represents the solution. Each person can understand and discover her own self-interest instead of relying on experts within state institutions to do so.[26]

Obama's democratic progressivism differs greatly from Teddy Roosevelt's or Walter Lippmann's public-interest progressivism, which trusts in experts, embraces the public interest, and advances Americanization. Obama heeds Jane Addams's warnings about cold, detached "experts" who place themselves outside, and above, the lives of the people they serve. As historian Daniel Rodgers observed, the roots of such detachment grew rapidly with the growth of the secular state before World War I. American graduate students studying in Europe were fired with reformist zeal to tame the destructive market forces that had moved Addams and others of their progressive generation. But these students adopted a model of "scientific objectivity." They envisioned public policymaking in private consultation with political leadership, far removed from public involvement.[27]

Survival Can Be Social

Obama upholds what could be described as the survivalist part of the American political tradition. He believes in the frontier. Instead of advancing the particular interest of the farmer, the rancher, or the miner, he promotes the interest of all the families on the pioneer wagon train that perpetually moves forward, yet does not represent a teleological march of progress.[28]

No one should try "to fool Mother Nature." No one, in other

words, can do it alone. Obstacles such as a winter storm impose limitations that no individual—no matter how fast, strong, or smart—can surmount alone.

The so-called abstract individual, who underlies individualism and is one of the basic assumptions behind classical liberalism and capitalism, is a red herring. Instead of invoking this imaginary device, Obama refers to interdependence and interconnectedness and argues that individual responsibility must be seen in the context of a collective of shared yet shifting alliances. He believes in pooling resources as a way to find universalizing solutions for our many collective problems—problems, however, that reflect the concerns of those in the aspiring American middle class, not the poor or the working class.

What Obama's perspective on democracy shows is his steadfast belief that it must be open and tolerant of all peoples—peoples of different races, ethnicities, religions, genders, and sexualities. But this is not to say he supports identity politics. To the contrary, he rejects identity politics because it typologizes by placing different peoples in separate boxes. He spurns identity politics because it creates permanent minorities, rather than the shifting majorities he prefers; because of the resentment that minority politics generates among those in the majority; and because it diminishes what makes an individual distinctive or unique. Obama believes in universalizing peoples and universalizing problems, and the best way to achieve this is with those who are in, or aspire to be in, or consider themselves in the middle class. They all harbor a middle-class sensibility.

Leadership: Of Wolves and Men?

Placing Obama's vision in historical context, I suggest, helps us better understand not only his administration's accomplishments but its failures as well. It is hard to forge alliances, rally collectivities, and take the pragmatic course without being called an opportunist. The flip side of the win-win is the lose-lose.

During the midterm elections of 2010, Obama was characterized as having a lose-lose presidency: he made virtually no inroads against a unified Republican opposition while also failing to form alliances with congressional liberal Democrats and progressive voters. His primary constituency—the youth—went back to college. Hosting a town hall meeting targeting the youth using Viacom networks MTV, BET, and CMT, Obama fielded one critical question after another as twenty-year-olds aired their dissatisfaction with his administration.[29] The Obama campaign, with its "unprecedented efforts to mobilize young people and minorities, along with significant reinforcements from liberal groups, produced the most diverse electorate in history and the youngest since 1992." But "the drop-off [in turnout] from 2008 to 2010 was especially stark."[30]

Thus the paradox of Obama's first two years: while legislatively he accomplished so much, politically he achieved little. His goal of governing on the basis of democratic progressivism—not even getting the *demos* to deliberate, but simply getting them involved—presents Obama with his greatest challenge. To be sure, he did his best to facilitate discussion in his many, "many summits—on fiscal responsibility, faith organizations, health care." The difficulty of eliciting public participation is an inherent weakness of any deliberative democracy. "The lack of participation and involvement in decision making," said Obama. "That's part of the change I've talked about." "There's a need to recognize what we have in common, a sense of empathy with each other in order to come to some basic agreements." In Obama's view, a "social" state, or one that facilitates and mediates, must also encourage or induce its citizens to participate. They must want to *earn* that egalitarianism.[31]

Tradition One: Umpires and Night Watchmen—The Classical Liberal Default, or the Minimal State

Most mainstream political scientists in the United States consider American freedom and equality—as well as the individual, the state, and society—to be mutually exclusive concepts. Either they regard individual autonomy as paramount, or they advance the needs of the state and society first. Citizens can pursue individual self-interest or the public interest, but not both. These scholars regard the American state in the same way that Louis Hartz did—as a liberal state influenced by the philosophy of John Locke, who privileged the individual over the state and society.[32]

A so-called Lockean state, or classical liberalism, also makes private property sacrosanct, privileging capitalism. "That was his property which could not be taken from him where-ever he had fixed it." "The reason why men enter into society," Locke writes, "is the preservation of their property."[33]

Locke's philosophy accentuates human rationality. It supposes that people behave in a way that is consistent with, or based on, reason or logic. "The state of nature has a law of nature to govern it, which obliges everyone: and reason, which is that law, teaches all mankind, who will but consult it, that being all equal and independent, no one ought to harm another." Each individual has agency and choice, and her'choice is dictated by reason. That, for classical liberalism, is human nature.[34]

This is not to say that everything is dependent on human action; natural rights exist and are also inherent in human nature. Each human being has the right to life, liberty, and private property. But natural rights are not contingent on human actions; they exist no matter what. A natural right is categorically different from a juridical or legal right that has been enacted, implemented, and enforced by a government. Of the three natural rights, however, only private property is "well set, by the extent of men's labor."[35]

Liberalism has many incarnations and appears at different times, but in no nation did it take greater hold than in the United States. Nearly a century after the Glorious Revolution and the English Bill of Rights, Locke's *Second Treatise* influenced the drafters of the Virginia Bill of Rights, who wrote, "All men are by nature equally free and independent, and have certain inherent rights, of which when they enter a state of society they cannot by any compact deprive or divest their posterity: namely the enjoyment of life or liberty with the means of acquiring and possessing property." One month later Thomas Jefferson penned the Declaration of Independence, including the pursuit of happiness among its "unalienable rights." The date 1776 also witnessed the publication of Adam Smith's *The Wealth of Nations*, marrying representational democracy with mercantilism and later with capitalism. The rule of law protected the sanctity of private property, defined now as prosperity and happiness.

Today's incarnation of classical liberalism in political science is still best translated by Louis Hartz. A political scientist by training, Hartz critiqued consensus historians writing after World War II. He maintained that all individuals are rational, self-interested actors. Consensus historians agreed that the Cold War had room for only one ideology—American liberalism—a view captured succinctly in the title of Daniel Bell's well-known book *The End of Ideology*. As Paul Roazen wrote about his mentor, Hartz "wanted to use Locke as a symbol for a brand of political thought that could illuminate political reality."[36]

In Hartz's view, the American liberal tradition takes human nature into account. Society is the sum of all traits and qualities shared by its members. Rational actors act alone, though in concert. It is a sum rather than a community or a collective. Nonetheless, such a society establishes a social contract that creates a government.

Were it not for this contract, a government would not exist. The government is an artificial entity built to protect natural rights, one of those now being referenced as "happiness." "The world had moved away from the Calvinist austerity of the seventeenth century into the more cheerful hedonism of the eighteenth century."[37] The American government shifted from rights to laws. Political philosophers on the Left and the Right, ranging from Jeremy Bentham to David Hume to Edmund Burke, translated natural rights into positive laws, or natural rights into natural laws. But regardless of the nomenclature, it was laws that sustained the state and protected its citizens under representative democracy.[38]

All individuals are concerned first and foremost about maintaining their own advantage and maximizing their well-being. But to accommodate everyone and to provide security, each citizen has to surrender some of her liberty. How much liberty must be lost to maintain an orderly civil society governed by a liberal state operating under a rule of law? The basic principle, simple to state but difficult to enforce, is that all people must be free to pursue whatever they like, so long as they do not harm another person or stop her from pursuing what she prefers. "No one ought to harm another in his life, health, liberty, or possessions."[39]

Citizens relinquish some freedom, in other words, granting this artificial state authority to enforce their legal rights, in lieu of securing a night watchman. On duty, the state umpires all conflicts. Constitutional constraints, natural laws, and positive laws dictate what constitutes interference. The government, however, must be careful not to draw lines too heavily, or the people might reassert their freedom, toppling or overturning it. With all citizens acting alone but in concert, and pursuing their own preferences without interfering with one another, a well-ordered society arises, based on the rule of law.

When this society is highly civilized, an invisible hand emerges, dictating economic relations premised on the same assumption of the individual maximizing her self-interest. Classical liberalism believes that people pursuing their own self-interest have high moral character, and that a whole society of people with such high moral character needs no state regulation: "Everyone as he is bound to preserve himself, and not quit his station willfully, so by the like reason, when his own preservation comes not in competition, ought he as much as he can to preserve the rest of mankind, and not unless it be to do justice on an offender, take away or impair the life, or what tends to the preservation of the life, the liberty, health, limb, or goods of another." No night watchman or umpire is needed because law is used to settle civil disputes. Citizens voluntarily stick to their legal rights and respect constitutional constraints.[40]

Such a self-regulated society, however, is not a community or a collective. It lacks a common good. Society and the state have no identity of their own, for in a classical liberal state and society, citizens remain the unit of analysis, not the collective or the community. Each person is an abstraction. Only after first recognizing the individual unit can we envision how a group of individuals comes together, and then how these groups merge, forming the river of a civil society.

What Locke, whom Hartz considered the chief architect of classical liberalism in the American liberal tradition, outlined is called a negative state. Constitutional constraints and legal rights, personified as a night watchman guarding the periphery, ensure that no person harms another. Each individual is autonomous.[41]

The concept of negative liberty recognizes the difference between internal and external constraints, whereas positive liberty does not. As Isaiah Berlin described it, negative liberty embodies the idea of being free *from* constraints. When two people exercise their freedom and collide, the state recognizes them as adversaries and adjudicates the dispute in criminal or civil court.[42]

Tradition Two: For Goodness' Sake

Intellectual historians balked at Hartz's characterization of the American liberal tradition, even if it was a critique. The new wave of social historians, who began populating the academy in the 1960s, saw Hartz as emblematic of "consensus" history, notwithstanding his role as critic. This political scientist, they cried, writing during the McCarthy era, rendered a distorted view of political history with his emphasis on American exceptionalism.[43]

Yet social historians too were a product of their time—not the New Deal generation, but a generation that did not believe in the individual as *the* unit of analysis. Freedom was not to go it alone. Freedom was not to be gotten alone. Freedom was found in the community. Frustrated that the New Deal had not gone farther, they reinvented a romantic view of the world.

Intellectual historians steeped in either social history or the history of ideas brought what I call the second tradition of American political thought into political science. Historians such as Gordon Wood and J. G. A. Pocock did this via the term "republicanism." Before capitalism emerged in the 1830s, they argued, the philosophies of Hume, Montesquieu, and Machiavelli had influenced the framers during the creation of the American Republic. Hume, a Scottish Enlightenment follower of Jean-Jacques Rousseau, inculcated a new type of republicanism that emphasized the public good rather than making individual self-interest predominant. The founders' fear of corruption, what is more, planted an Americanized version of virtue in the Constitution and helped rationalize and justify westward expansion.[44]

For historians, time bound the republican roots buried in American history. Unlike political scientists, few historians stuffed, boxed, and wrapped more than a decade or two into any one tradition. And introducing the public good into an otherwise individualistic perspective in American politics helped political scientists create a new field—American political development (APD)—around the refutation of the explanation for the relative absence of a nation-state.[45]

Influenced by the theories of Max Weber as well as by Walter Dean Burnham's work on the two-party system, Theda Skocpol, Stephen Skowronek, and Karen Orren, among others, refuted Hartz's thesis that the absence of a history of feudalism explains the absence of socialism, or at least a strong social welfare state, in the United States.[46]

And just after social historians turned away from institutions, they brought "back in" the "American state." In the 1980s APD revived "the state" as a term worthy of study, following Wood and Pocock and other social historians who had put the United States in comparative context. Students of APD questioned why the United States lacked the type of vigorous social welfare state found in Germany, France, or the Netherlands, one that derived from and helped foster a close-knit socioeconomic and political community.[47]

The social welfare state that these students of APD hankered after was the gold standard: the Scandinavian state. Is there any public good buried in policy programs in the United States? An ideal social welfare state would use its strength to create public programs that would help and encourage citizens to participate more fully in the community, or at least participate minimally as clients of social services. As cited earlier, Marshall said that the strong social welfare state provides political, economic, and *universal social rights*. Extending universal social rights requires a mixed economy rather than a free market.[48]

Historians debate whether it was the Scottish Enlightenment or Machiavelli's idea of virtue that influenced the creation of the American state and Andrew Jackson's frontier state. I suggest, however, that students of APD, policy history, and theory tacitly rely on the assumptions underlying Rousseau, who is credited with creating a social contract that depends on a positive state that advances universal social rights. As Rousseau writes in *The Social Contract*, "Each man, in giving himself to all, gives himself to nobody; and as there is no associate over whom he does not acquire the same right as he yields others over himself, he gains an equivalent for everything he loses, and an increase of force for the preservation of what he has." This more full-bodied account of the state, or lack thereof, forms the basis of the second tradition in American political thought.[49]

Rousseau provides the counterfactual—the road not taken, in path-dependency literature—more fully than the historians tracing how Machiavelli or the Scottish Enlightenment influenced specific moments in American history. What good is it to defend your civil liberties if you're out on the street, uneducated, or unable to take care of yourself?[50] The state has a responsibility to intervene.

Positive liberty is best characterized as helping a citizen have the freedom *to do* something. "Since men cannot create new forces, but merely combine and control those which already exist," Rousseau writes, "the only way in which they can preserve themselves is by uniting their separate powers in combination strong enough to overcome any resistance, uniting them so that their powers are directed by a single motive and act in concert."[51] This kind of night watchman does not just prohibit; he also helps people by giving them the goods and services they need. Traditional demands for universal health care, for instance, rest on a positive conception of liberty. A person cannot be free unless he or she is healthy; therefore, the state should provide health care. Eradicating an individual's internal constraints is invasive. External constraints do not penetrate society as deeply as internal constraints do. With internal constraints, the state tells a person what to do.

Legal and political history has illustrated the greatest irony of individualism, as articulated by Alexis de Tocqueville: that pursuing freedom from external constraints accentuates the similarities rather than the differences among people. "Individualism proceeds from erroneous judgment . . . it originates as much in deficiencies of mind as in perversity of heart." Negative liberty does not foster difference. Women who succeed at work, for instance, do so on male terms. They must act like white men, since white men served as the model for the first unit of analysis, setting norms and standards that cannot be violated. The night watchman does not disturb the status quo.

Lifting the barriers that kept women from entering the workplace does not mean they will feminize it by changing its culture if all it does is free them from external constraints. "Individualism is of democratic origin, and it threatens to spread in the same ratio as the equality of condition." Internal constraints must be imposed as well. As Tocqueville adds, "individualism, at first, only saps the virtues of public life; but in the long run, it attacks and destroys all others and is at length absorbed in downright selfishness."[52]

But students of APD knew well that alleviating internal constraints as a positive state is intrusive and is opposed to basic American political values. The dilemma associated with positive liberty is that it depends on what political theorist Nancy Hirschmann describes as a Rousseauian trap, second-guessing who needs what. "He shall be forced to be free; for this is the condition which, by giving each citizen to the nation, secures him against all personal dependence." It is a politician or a bureaucratic expert who determines the needs.[53]

APD and the Social Welfare State "Lite"

The progressives were responsible for beginning the American state—not simply the Interstate Commerce Commission, as historian Gabriel Kolko, and later Skowronek, describe, but also the Bureau of Labor Statistics, the Food and Drug Administration, and the federal-state program of workers' compensation. Meanwhile the federal judiciary began instituting progressive reform in the *Lochner* era, which also included the Brandeis brief in *Muller v. Oregon*. We cannot forget that these progressive programs were responsible for the first round of Americanization, and that many of them propagated eugenics.[54] The right-wing Zionist Israel Zangwill, for instance, popularized the Progressive Era's "melting pot" coercive Americanization theme in his 1908 play *The Melting Pot*. The play suggested that the United States should be dominated by one culture, "a fusion of all races," or what cultural anthropologists, sociologists, and geographers later called "Anglo-conformity."[55]

The Progressive Era, lasting from the early 1890s until 1919, ended with an excess of expert and state control. "American" English and basic political and social ideologies, intended to create a pliable workforce and ensure certain political leanings, were force-fed to the foreign-born. Public schools began instructing immigrant children about how to practice "proper" Anglo-Saxon traditions and encouraged them to take their lessons home to educate their parents and grandparents.

Expanded state power, with elites determining the needs of "others," followed by oppression constitutes a pattern in the United States. Some scholars of APD, such as James Morone, have turned this pattern into a morality cycle that swings from sinners to saviors—creating an "us and them." Whether the United States can be neatly explained as a Victorian or Puritan state, the needs-slipping-into-oppression dialogue has much resonance.[56]

Experts Plus Needs Get People to Run for the Exit

Scholars are not the only ones who have noticed this cycle. Beginning in the 1940s, the political foes of universal health care consistently managed to undermine the debate by inflaming the American cultural fear of needs and experts. Conservative critics picked up on the idea that liberals wanted what the European Left got, and they painted the liberal penchant for the public good, in keeping with a Rousseauian second tradition, as a means of maintaining the stranglehold of the first tradition. "As soon as this multitude is so united in one body, it is impossible to offend against one of the members without attacking the body, and still more to offend against the body without the members resenting it." The idea that the individual would surrender any of her autonomy was an anathema. To prevent this, conservatives introduced the notion of needs into the debate, a notion antithetical to American political values and beliefs.[57]

If needs are to be determined, there must be trust. Progressives, conservative critics claim, assume that people are, by nature, good. People can be saved from themselves. Benevolence reigns. Interpreting Rousseau from the standard or mainstream perspective, the Enlightenment showed how society had evolved, overturning Hobbes's and Locke's arguments about the "state of nature." "Nature makes man happy and good," Rousseau claims, "but society depraves him and makes him miserable."[58]

While society creates the general will for such a public good, it is the sovereign alone who dictates the political agenda. The sovereign knows what matters to society overall. And the sovereign knows how to protect the whole. As society develops and becomes more complex, it transforms into a civil society. Legal institutions emerge, staffed by magistrates or experts, who manage the division of labor and private property that the laws address. During the heyday of the European social welfare state in the 1960s and 1970s, *experts* became the embodiment of the modern-day "sovereign."

Society degenerates, according to Rousseau, only when everyone starts competing with one another while simultaneously depending on one another to fulfill their basic political, social, and economic needs. This situation creates a "double pressure" or double squeeze that threatens everyone's survival and freedom. Some citizens must therefore subordinate their needs to those of other citizens to ensure that society and the state do not collapse. Rousseau writes, "In place of the individual personality of each contracting party, this act of association creates a moral and collective body, composed of as many members as the assembly contains votes, and receiving from this act its unity, its common identity, its life and its will."[59]

Dependent on a sovereign, and later on impartial experts on the social welfare state who anticipate every citizen's needs, balancing one against another on the basis of merit, Rousseau's state must be run with benevolence. But benevolence "smacks of paternalism." It is constraining, but most of all, benevolence is easily described by opponents of a strong social welfare state as anti-American. Benevolence rubs against the grain of the American notion of self-reliance. This type of civil society and state does not free its citizens from second-guessing. It undermines the American can-do pragmatic spirit. Rhetorically associating reform with the second tradition helps the GOP, moderate Democrats, and whatever industry is affected to defeat attempts to create a stronger social welfare state.[60]

"In the Jungles of Civilization the Evolution Is Always Downward"

American political history is rife with programs that were founded in the name of the public good or the public interest but later caused great consternation. Faced with shifting scientific and cultural emphases on matters such as heredity and environment, biology and culture, and free will and determinism, progressives developed eugenics. As historian Mark Pittinger points out, the progressives thought the working poor were "in peril of sinking" into the "social layer currently styled the 'underclass.'" An anonymous female reformer wrote that in the "jungles of civilization the evolution is always downward—from man to beast, to reptile, and to that most noisome of living creatures, the human worm." Not surprisingly, hereditary traits got absorbed into academic analyses of poverty.[61]

A social Darwinist socialist twist even existed. In her classic book on the history of social science, Dorothy Ross argues that progressive social scientists operated "at the intersection of history and nature, seeking to capture both the concrete particularities of experience and universal natural forms, both the changing shape of modern society and an unchanging dynamic at its core." The public good—not the social welfare state—had an underbelly to it, an underbelly of trampling on the poor.[62]

This tradition was not confined to the Progressive Era. To be sure, the patronizing, or paternalizing and maternalizing, aspect of substantive justice peaked in the Progressive Era, with experts knowing what was best for the downtrodden within American society. But it also constituted a large part of the ethos underlying the Great Society, as we will review in chapter 6. The APD literature corrects the illusion of the absence of an American nation-state. But in their enthusiasm, more historians, like Pittinger, than political scientists have documented the excesses of the American state, particularly if these political scientists focus on political reform to the exclusion of culture and economics.[63]

A Map of the Book; a Chart for the Future?

Barack Obama rejects both the night-watchman state and the nanny state. He does not accept the individual/society dichotomy. Nor does he accept the state/capital dichotomy. And he casts aside the public/private distinction. The individual, the state, and society are interdependent. Capitalism and the state are interwoven and codependent. One cannot operate without the other. Relying on what the next chapter will describe as Hannah Arendt's critique of capital, Obama believes the marketplace must be pushed back and the state must facilitate the well-being of the individual within society.

Chapter 2 shows that the character of Obama's vision springs from a contemporary interpretation of Baruch Spinoza's ethics that can be credited with breaking these binary oppositions between the individual and the state, the state and capital, and the public and the private. The intellectual basis of Obama's vision, however, is not premised on causality. I do not claim that Obama was familiar with Spinoza, followed Alinsky, or read Dewey or any other authors or activists. Rather, Obama's vision reflects the third, lesser-known, and harder-traveled perspective of small-*d* democratic progressivism. This vision represents a significant departure from both the Republican ownership society (the so-called minimal state) and the Democratic attempt at the welfare state or FDR's New Deal (the so-called strong welfare state).

Chapter 3 reviews Obama's emphasis on difference and his rejection of identity politics, and it reveals how universal he is with his anti-universalism. It sets forth the policies Obama supports that have gotten less notice than his larger legislative achievements, but are still vital because they challenge the underlying American character of our Weberian roots and the implicit belief in Christianity as an inherent part of the Protestant work ethic. First, it explains why Obama supports a reversal of the forty-year war on drugs. Second, it shows how Obama spurns the "just say no" policies from the 1980s preaching abstinence and chastity in sex education. And third, it describes how Obama supports turning sexuality into a protected class under civil rights law.

The book argues that these significant public policy reversals show how strongly Obama manifests his support of *difference* and puts *equality first*. While Obama relies on the middle class as his vehicle for reform, it is not a middle class of white, suburban, Christian heterosexuals. Instead, it is a middle class the Tea Party fears. Obama supports a middle class that includes persons of any race, ethnicity, or sexuality, as long as they accept generic American values that balance equality and freedom and embrace earned egalitarianism. To be sure, the president believes in the nuclear family, but a family that professes its support of aspirational values and characteristics—namely, competition born out of difference and real equality, not normalcy or whiteness.

Chapter 4 examines Obama's crowning legislative achievements: financial regulation, health care, and the stimulus package. Looking at this legislation as a glass half full (rather than half empty, as many progressive Democratic pundits do), this chapter argues that when viewed in light of its primary goals, the legislation was a success, particularly given the contentiousness of Congress. Passage of health-care reform alone should be enough to establish Obama's successful legislative leadership.

Obama's success can also be seen in the administrative state he built within his notion of regulatory reform. All three major pieces of his legislative agenda, and his plans for regulatory reform, reflect what I call the Spinozan stakeholder state and society. The stakeholder state and society is not new. It does not regulate its subjects in a way reminiscent of the New Deal, but neither does it deregulate, as in Republican attempts to dismantle the New Deal state, starting with Reaganomics. Instead, Obama expanded an existing administrative structure replete with social technologies that instill reform. He participated in an already-existing congressional legislative trend of passing public policies that are deliberately kept sketchy, leaving those details that are too partisan for Congress to get bogged down in to executive branch governance. Elizabeth Warren's influence on the Consumer Financial Protection Bureau is an example of this, as is the concept of negotiated rulemaking in administrative law.

Chapter 5 outlines Obama's foreign policy as another example of his universal anti-universalism as well as his belief in difference. *E pluribus unum*—"Out of Many, One"—gets transformed, in Obama's vision of multilateralism, into "Out of One, Many." Obama does not support Bush's policy of "spiteful unilateralism" or Bush's attempts to democratize other nations.[64] For the same reason, he does not back human rights as much as Democrats with a progressive agenda had hoped. Obama adopts inclusivity and an ontology of difference similar to Gilles Deleuze's interpretation of Spinoza.

Chapter 6 discusses the biggest question for most Obama watchers: How did this win-win candidate and successful legislative leader become a lose-lose Democratic Party leader (though still retaining potential for a second term)? Before examining race as a social construction, manifested most clearly by a new concept of discrimination called "scripting," I juxtapose my argument with the dominant one in scholarship and in the elite press. What has become the standard explanation, offered by Theda Skocpol and Lawrence Jacobs as well as by political journalists such as Jonathan Alter, suggests that Obama's difficulties stem from a combination of his personal leadership failures and the well-known structural and foundational problems of American parties and institutions (such as bicameralism, federalism, and sectionalism). According to these interpretations, Obama erred by, for example, giving too few speeches to rally his base, and he failed to create a "narrative" to offset those structural and foundational obstacles.

By contrast, my book argues that the Foucauldian construct of race provides a better explanation of Obama's perceived failures as a legislative and party leader. It argues that the disappointment of the old New Deal coalition and the progressive Democrats was, and potentially remains, the most debilitating aspect of race. Their expectations can be located in the Democratic Party's transformation in the 1970s and 1980s, when it abandoned the urban poor.

Chapter 7 concludes the book with an evaluation of Obama's leadership. It adopts a deliberative democratic lens, rather than a racial one, to assess Obama's leadership successes and failures. Did he promote public reason and instigate deliberation during the debates about health care, and immigration, and education? The chapter reveals that he applied his own inductive logic of congruence and consilience to all three of these debates. It also explores how both Race to the Top and Obama's implementation of Bush's No Child Left Behind Act created productive or effective forms of diversity and inclusion. Obama is working hard to narrow the education gap correlated with race, ethnicity, location, and income. Finally, the chapter discusses how two different social movements—the Tea Party and Occupy Wall Street—reacted to some of Obama's public policy reforms. These movements could be symptoms of Obama's historic success or failure as a leader. Occupy Wall Street has had less impact than the demonstrators who displaced dictators in the Middle East. The Tea Party's emergence as a social movement that has already started governing is the most telling evidence of how threatening Obama has been to the religious faction within the GOP, a faction that became its electoral base beginning in 2000. Much of Obama's social and moral legislation champions diversity, or privileges diversity and differences that challenge the "normate," though he never frames it that way. The emergence of a conservative social movement like the Tea Party was a natural response to a president like Obama, the most radical part of whose agenda it addresses most closely.

2 The Third Political Tradition—Reclaiming the Frontier: Wagon Trains, Pioneers, and Deputies, but No Cowboys or Nannies

Barack Obama referred to his campaign and election as "Organizing for America." What he meant by "organizing" came from his experience as a community organizer, which is to say someone who reframes existing fundamental American beliefs and values so that members of the community can discover for themselves the need for reform. This reform manifests a cultural change and calls for civic action. For Obama, this change reflected the shift in the United States from the myth of self-reliance to mutual reliance. Obama's vision embodies a third political tradition that recognizes the interdependence and interconnectedness of all Americans. He seeks a state that would forge alliances and create stakeholders who would huddle and help out the state like the members of a pioneer wagon train—with the motto "one for all and all for one."

In Obama's view, the social sphere, equated by Hannah Arendt with the Greek *agora*—the marketplace—has increasingly encroached on the private sphere. Arendt explains the "recent trend of making what is private become public." As one contemporary political theorist, Trevor Norris, explains, Arendt "outlines the modern ascent of the activities of the private realm or the *oikos* into the public realm." She does so, however, as part of a critique of capitalism and modernity. Arendt's philosophical distress stems from the loss of the public sphere as the *agora* was hollowed out. Once expanded, the *oikos*— the social sphere—or the household identified with women rather than men in the *agora*—cannot be easily retracted. Obama's vision of politics recognizes this and takes into account the encroachment. He flips it around. Rather than limiting or bolstering it, Obama merges the *agora* with the *oikos* as a critique of consumer society that uses social technology. Obama merges the private, the public, and the social spheres.[1]

Do the Spheres Collaborate or Collide?

How Obama weds the *agora* and the *oikos* departs from early studies in APD, namely, pre-1989 ones that take the comparative sociological perspective on citizens and American exceptionalism, implying that the relatively strong welfare state should be "Europe-lite." As explained in chapter 1, Obama's view of an enlarged and encroaching social sphere differs from the space universal social rights gained in European social welfare states like France or Germany. Indeed, the social rights Europe has tried to bestow upon its citizenry since 1989, particularly the EU, have been met increasingly with popular resistance and mixed success.[2]

Social rights are not housed in the social sphere that contains informal groups, such as those grouping vulnerable peoples, or ethnicities, or political identities. Burdened with teleology, as explained earlier, T. H. Marshall's construct of a citizen, let alone a global citizen, no longer captures the relatively strong welfare state and society post-1989 and post-9/11. This construct lacks authenticity. After 9/11, the United States did not begin stripping away the social rights of its citizens, as happened in Europe, particularly on the Continent. Why? These rights never existed in the first place.

While many European social welfare states gave their citizens "economic welfare and security" after World War II, the United States always offered little security. To Marshall, after these strong social welfare states gave their citizens these securities, the next step was to bestow upon them "the right to share to the full in the social heritage and to live the life of a civilized being according to the standards prevailing in the society."[3] Beginning in the 1990s, some sociologists studying American political development incorporated Marshall's notion of social rights into their definitions, making the American welfare state aspire toward becoming a European welfare state despite the scars of slavery.[4]

Europe—particularly the Scandinavian countries, and including the Low Countries, such as the Netherlands and Belgium—became the benchmark of the American relatively strong nation-state being *unexceptional*. Some APD scholars disputing American exceptionalism retained Marshall's teleological overtones by adopting his notion of political, economic, and social citizenship, and some of their scholarship contained a normative edge suggesting that the United States should emulate these nations with a strong social welfare state. Crossing through three distinct thresholds—first gaining human rights, then securing political rights, and finally heralding social rights as the private and public spheres collapsed—gave many European citizens in the ever-expanding EU false dreams and high hopes that some critics contend have recently come crashing down, given the Muslim question.[5]

By contrast, this book does not advance the idea that the social rights cushioning identity groups are housed in a social sphere or setting. To do so, it injects social and literary theory or cultural studies, not just sociology, and makes a nonteleological argument about American political development. It adopts the comparative perspective, recognizing that some strong welfare states in Europe have become neoliberal or Americanized over the last thirty years. Indeed, their postwar democratization and the creation and rapid expansion of the EU and its marketplace increasingly expose the cracks and contradictions inherent in how they make and shape the public policies that deliver social rights that were riddled with identity inequalities given the differences between the secular, white French, for instance, and the religious, ethnic Muslim French.[6]

By relying on the political theory of Hannah Arendt and the social theory of Jean Baudrillard, this book relies on a different notion of history, sidestepping the normative underpinnings of American exceptionalism that favor the United States becoming a European lite state and a society infused with secularism.[7] Historical institutionalism and political identities are better described with a theory of agency, time, and contingency that is inherent in the third American political tradition that is deontological, privileges the *demos*, and upholds a toleration for different beliefs and values, including but not limited to religion.

Obama spurns a teleological notion of political time, or development as progress. This chapter will show how Obama envisions hell, but not heaven, on earth, and this can best be found in Arendt's and Baudrillard's descriptions of the social sphere, though this must be distinguished from social rights, and European secularism and universalism undergirding them. Baudrillard himself—being influenced by the semiotics of Gilles Deleuze, Jean-François Lyotard, Michel Foucault, Jacques Lacan, and Jacques Derrida—spurns the teleological grasp of history that some sociologists in Europe or the United States impart in the political development studies. These social theorists' understandings of history, of religion, of gender, of the body, of sexuality, and of consumerism loosely lumped together in cultural studies best capture Obama's notion of Spinoza and the third political tradition.[8]

When Obama marries the public, the private, and the social spheres, he concentrates not on production but on consumption, and he understands the dangers affiliated with this merger. Obama does not equate political and economic development with a march toward civilization. It does not necessarily constitute progress. There is no teleological trajectory, no end of ideology, history, or modernity.

Nor is the absence of progress the end of modernity, as neoconservatives, such as Francis Fukuyama, claim. Globalization did not end history, any more than Cold War liberalism ended left/right ideologies. Obama recognizes the perils associated with an interconnected and interdependent state, market, and society. What happens when people—deliberative citizens—do not participate in politics at home or abroad?

This merger—or recognizing the wedding of the public, the private, and the social spheres—stems from Obama's critique of the United States' hegemonic position in the interconnected, interdependent global state and society. How the United States behaves, and how the United States is perceived as behaving, provides the answer to good governance at home and security abroad.[9]

Doing Good Governance

To understand how Obama's vision extends and enlarges the social sphere, this book locates earlier thinkers who share his fundamental ideas. It makes no claim of causality. Obama knew some of these political thinkers well, as many of his biographers observe, but not necessarily all of them. Nonetheless, Obama can be identified with existential political thinkers, starting with Baruch Spinoza, who, first, recognize critical theory, knowledge, and power; second, create an ontology of *doing*; and third, emphasize subjectivism, spurning norms, universals, or absolute truths, and teleology.

Obama does all of these things while trying to foster an adversarial democratic forum for a reintegrated and reenergized citizenry in an enlarged social sphere that spurns the "normate." Obama's vision is consonant with, and can best be translated by looking at, the critical and existential political thought of Hannah Arendt, John Dewey, Saul Alinsky, and W. E. B. Du Bois as sifted through a Spinozan perspective. Chapter 5, on Obama's foreign policy, shows how Reinhold Niebuhr's anti-universalism also influences him. Obama underscores how American security depends not just on the United States trying to "do good," but also on its being perceived by the global citizenry as being, and doing, good, or better put, as "behaving well" abroad.[10]

What unites all these political thinkers is the belief that the individual, society, the market, and the state should combine, cooperate, and collaborate to limit the extent to which the social sphere, under the influence of social technology, determines policies that shape the public and private spheres. The private, public, and social domains, they all argue, are intertwined and interdependent and cannot be untangled.

The solution for Obama is not less entanglement, but more. As one theorist explains, "Deliberation is a process through which people grapple with the consequences of various public problems." Economics Nobel laureate Elinor Ostrom writes of "polycentric governance systems . . . where citizens are able to organize not just one but multiple governing authorities at different scales." Ostrom, a political scientist and a member of the so-called interdisciplinary Bloomington group, combined deliberative democracy and behavioral social science, particularly behavioral economics, arguing that "the Bloomington principles are *political* in the citizen-centered sense of politics descending from the Greeks—free action by distinctive agents who engage with each other to address common problems and shape a common world."[11]

In Obama's view, the nation-state should facilitate and protect an active, responsible citizenry, thereby elevating a social sphere over the private and public spheres. He follows the Bloomington principles of the commons, which, "positing horizontal interactions among diverse agents, valorize the self-directed action at the heart of participatory democracy."[12] This type of deliberative democracy turns institutions into "communities" in which "citizens are given *more* authority and *wider* opportunities for participation." These citizens earn egalitarianism by finding "robust ways to deliberate, learn, and work across differences." Following the principles of Dewey and Arendt, or civic work and action, this type of deliberative democracy involves "communities and groups in sustained problem-solving efforts which create rich learning cultures," which then follow Alinsky in "often integrating themes, methods, and concepts of organizing." The facilitative state works "*with* other citizens, rather *on* them or *for* them."[13]

The operative words here are *facilitates* and *mediates*. This means that the state creates public policies that make an action, or a process, easy, or easier. It is relative, not absolute. Facilitation is about movement—promotion, helping someone move forward, providing assistance.

Mediation means that no side wins, but that no side or perspective will be shortchanged or overpowered by the other perspectives except by the rules of engagement—persuasion. To mediate means that the state comes up with common solutions for the collective. Such a state represents a departure from either a traditional social welfare state, which provides substantive goods and benefits, or a minimal state, which protects procedural rights or due process. State facilitation and mediation is categorically different from a state providing something (substantive due process) or a state protecting the right to something (procedural due process). To argue that the state facilitates assumes a definition of a state that involves all parties who agree on a common goal. They cross the frontier together.

Separate Spheres and the Gender-Bender Turnaround

Obama inherited a United States of America in which the separations between public and private, between individual, state, and society, and between the free market and the state-regulated market have long since dissolved and crumbled. Even the dominant economic theory—namely, neoclassical capitalism—has been chipped away and eroded and is now referred to as "rational economics." The University of Chicago—once the church professing capitalist and neoclassical capitalist doctrine—is being shaken by an alternative doctrine: behavioral economics.[14]

No longer focusing on self-interested, rational actors, behavioral economics studies the irrationality of actors and the unintended policy consequences of that irrationality. Its practitioners seek to determine why people do what they do. They no longer judge or analyze behavior (though those practicing behavioral economics in the social sphere aspire to profits); instead, they study it. What behavioral economists have discovered is a series of odd and counterintuitive correlations created by the combination of markets and public policies, such as that between the rise of women's reproductive rights and the decline in murder rates among the poor in urban neighborhoods.[15]

Studying the collective consequences of irrational behavior in the social sphere provides behavioral economists with ample evidence of how the American culture has changed. First the Moral Majority and now the Tea Party movement have protested these cultural changes. These movements hark back to a time that few Americans would find appealing—a time of one-car garages, when women stayed home with children, when people of color lived in segregated neighborhoods and went to segregated schools. They seek villains to blame for this cultural transformation, which emanates not from the political or the private spheres, but from the all-pervasive social sphere.

Despite their efforts, neither the Reagan nor the Bush administrations managed to end abortion or gay and lesbian rights or restore the nuclear family. Republican rule did not stop free-market television from creating and producing Murphy Browns, Simpsons, Wills, or Graces. "Democrats were day-trading, Republicans were divorcing," as Mark Lilla succinctly put it.[16] Out of government, parts of the Moral Majority—largely white, upper-middle-class and working-class heterosexual Christian men—triggered the ferment that today underlies the Tea Party movement, expressing their dismay, discontent, and disgruntlement with hegemonic cultural change. But this change is not isolated in, or restricted to, the private, the public, or the social sphere.

A fringe movement like the Tea Party casts Obama as an antihero. And Tea Parties may score more victories, such as Supreme Court rulings or state laws that regulate American morality, like those curbing a woman's right to abortion—described in 2012 as the "war on women." But neither this movement nor a conservative Supreme Court nor "red state" legislatures can turn back the cultural clock to the white, segregated, gendered, Christian 1950s, no matter how romanticized a picture they paint for voters. It is doubtful that public opinion will rebound enough to support public policies from the postwar period of white male heterosexual dominance, giving more than lip service to fundamental "American" values such as God, universal truth, heterosexuality, and the nuclear family.[17]

War on Women: The Agora/Oikos Collapse

Obama campaigned on all of this—though he addressed the positive, not the negative, side of these issues. Neither a child of the sixties nor a baby boomer, Obama appealed more to the youth, African American men and women, white women, and urbanites (including the gay and lesbian coalition) than to white middle-class or upper-middle-class heterosexual men. Obama is now trying to navigate this cultural chasm, captured by the phrase "the war on women," without getting caught in any Left/Right, black/white, gay/straight, male/female, public/private, or individual/state binaries or ruts. Despite being accused of conservatism, he relies on behavioral economists more than neoclassical or rational ones, and even within the G8 and the G20, he opposes austerity.

Obama tries to govern from the middle, and by consensus. He insists that the middle class, not the poor or the working class, is the aspiring engine of reform. But this middle is not one born of bourgeois individualism, normalcy, or the bell curve. Obama's version of the middle class does not reflect "the" demographic statistics—either an average or a median—of two parents with 2.2 children and a two-car garage. Rather, it is shaped by complex cultural conflicts and juxtapositions within the black working and middle classes. It is a middle class in which women can be strong (in terms of work and salaries), men absent, and grandparents overwhelmed, all while a resegregated society simultaneously inculcates and stymies racism and feminism. It is a complex, partially racist and sexist society where families cannot afford to have women leave the workforce, be they white or African American, upper class or service sector/working class or poor.

Obama's middle class reflects an interactive age in which the state and the individual are locked into perpetual political reaction to a *social sphere* dominated by a global economy. It's an interconnected age in which Obama's vision, and some of his successful public policies, are trying to curb the excesses of the social sphere by reinvigorating its citizenry in a more adversarial and participatory democracy.

What does participatory democracy look like to Obama? Like Dewey, he holds the pragmatic belief that democracy is "more a matter of culture than politics." Equality and freedom are expressed not just externally and politically, but through personal participation in the cultivation of "a shared culture." The operative words that capture the inner workings of such a democracy are consensus, process, and continual transformation. Its culture reflects the dynamic of an interconnected and interdependent world undergoing constant transformation. Yet unlike the great upheavals of the past, this transformation is neither teleological nor frozen in time. There is no perfect storm, no Hollywood ending. It's about ongoing change that can be shaped by democratic inquiry, process, and method.[18]

Binaries Be Gone

This book argues that Obama reflects a third political tradition, called *democratic progressivism*. The 2008 election and the first three years of his presidency showed how Obama tapped into this third tradition in American political thought, one that shows how people can count on one another. This tradition constitutes a departure from mainstream political science and social and intellectual history. And it represents a rupture in the Left/Right continuum that is often invoked in campaign rhetoric in the United States.[19]

This third tradition accepts Walt Whitman's "indomitable optimism." And it agrees with historian James Kloppenberg that "for the sake of historical accuracy as well as democratic renewal," the grassroots interpretation of American history should not be dismissed as "un-American" and discounted. Yet Kloppenberg's argument about democratic renewal does not go far enough, for this intellectual historian's small-*d* democratic, bottom-up approach does not fully capture the American spirit or ethic of reciprocity.[20]

Couched between the classical liberal tradition and the communitarian tradition, Obama's democratic progressive tradition straddles the middle. This middle position, however, should not be confused with the mixing of black and white to create gray. It is not a politics of consensus. It is not solely rational. It is neither liberal nor conservative—it defies Left/Right categorization. In Obama's view, the interdependence of the multitude in its impact on American democracy represents the third political tradition. America's citizens are all tied up together. In a nation that rewards autonomy and independence as no other wealthy nation does, Obama underscores the interdependence or interconnectedness of the individual, the state, the market, and society—wrapped up in an all-encompassing social sphere.[21]

An Interactive Age

Obama's vision represents a philosophical tradition in the United States that was embodied by one of the first philosophers to reject metaphysics or the Cartesian mind/body duality: Spinoza. While on one level, those Spinozists, hereafter called *democratic progressives*, value power and argue that self-interest is transformative, they do not believe in the autonomy of the individual.

On another level, these democratic progressives (or middle-class populists) cannot be categorized as Rousseauians. They see citizens within the state and society as causally related or interdependent. They believe that politics should dictate markets, not the reverse. But they promote a collective (wherein lies the multitude) instead of a community. This multitude is not bound or wedded to a community that harbors its own traditions, beliefs, and values. The collective that democratic progressives envision in the United States lacks a distinct identity that would resemble a national identity in the European strong social welfare state. Instead, it is a collective of forged alliances based on a set of American ideals, many of which are about process rather than rights.

What is more, offering a Spinozan interpretation of the individual, the state, and society reveals how American thinker Dewey and American activist Alinsky took into account individual and collective responsibility and rewarded initiative and mutual self-reliance. Obama's 2009 inaugural address advanced "a new era of responsibility." He builds reforms based on social technologies.

This new era of responsibility distrusts a government motivated by benevolence. Neither Dewey, Alinsky, nor Obama believes one person can, or should, *care* for another. Nor do they have faith in an objective truth. In their view, neutral experts within national state institutions cannot govern impartially, since the public interest cannot be peeled apart from individual self-interest. They have a "habit of respecting and building local people's agency and power, a commitment to supporting people in doing for themselves what only they can do, a belief that people together are stronger and wiser than any of us standing alone."[22]

Seeing truth as socially constructed, Spinoza, Dewey, and Alinsky place their power in the people. There are no absolute truths, no natural laws, no invisible hands guiding the economy. People can discover what is in their self-interest without the help of experts. But it is not always rational.

How do people make these discoveries? By being empowered. Like the Deleuzian Spinoza, Foucault, Arendt, Alinsky, and Dewey believe that power emerges out of interactions among agents and that it exists only when used and flexed. Power must be exercised. In their view, power is not inherently negative or repressive, but rather has the potential to become a positive, productive force. For Foucault, power is positive *and* productive, whereas Alinsky, Arendt, and Dewey equate action with power and go even further, arguing that it constitutes the domain of politics itself. All five political thinkers concur that power can be nefarious, but that it does not have to be. Power can be strategic, a means to an end, but is not necessarily so.[23]

To fully understand power as Obama envisions it, we must distinguish it from its close cousins—strength, force, authority, and violence. Unlike strength, Arendt argues, power is not the property of an individual, but of a plurality of actors joining together for some common political purpose. She does not associate force with power either. Force is natural, whereas power must emerge from collective engagement; it is a human creation. And finally, unlike violence, power is based not on coercion, but rather on consensus and rational persuasion.

Power appears in its most positive incarnation when it fosters solidarity. This is a type of power that is consensual, concerted, and reciprocal. Power is, therefore, a condition of both agency and subjectivity. It is the legitimacy derived from the initial getting together of people, from the original pact of association that establishes a political community; it is reaffirmed whenever individuals act in concert through the medium of speech and persuasion. Power is sustained not by material factors, nor by economic or bureaucratic or military actors, but by the power of common convictions that result from a process of fair and unconstrained deliberation. Power can only be stored—it exists only as potential that is actualized when actors gather for political action and public deliberation. In Arendt's words, "Power is what keeps the public real." It is "the potential space of appearance between acting and speaking." It "springs up" between people "when they act together and vanishes the moment they disperse." It lies at the basis of every political community and is the source of legitimacy of political and governmental institutions. "It is the people's support that lends power to the institutions of a country, and this support is but the continuation of the consent that brought the laws into existence to begin with."[24]

As they adapt to their environment, individuals evolve and can become accepting and enlightened, which makes them more open to and tolerant of their peers within a collective that strives for the same thing. To come together, they must support, but not judge, one another. "All political institutions are manifestations and materializations of power; they petrify and decay as soon as the living power of the people ceases to uphold them." The collective helps a dynamic among citizens, society, and the state to survive and can even make it flourish.[25]

Neither Positive nor Negative Rights: Homespun Spinoza

Isaiah Berlin's dichotomy of negative and positive liberty has no place in this environment. Freedom is not found "from" the state. The state is not an umpire that protects our civil liberties and, for the rest, leaves its citizens alone. Nor is freedom gained by "doing something" or "getting something," such as the universal health care that strong European social welfare states provide. Freedom must be secured *through* the state. It is similar to education, or to an Internet connection, which is tested for speed, efficiency, and quality. Freedom is the conduit, the process.

The state must facilitate and mediate to promote the freedom of both the individual *and* society. Society is what is unique here. "The state retains its usefulness," explains political theorist Warren Montag, only as long as people are able through "collective existence to do and think more than they could alone." "At its most elemental level," Obama similarly stated, "we understand our liberty in a negative sense. As a general rule we believe in the right to be left alone. . . . But we understand liberty in a more positive sense as well, in the idea of opportunity and a subsidiary of values that help us realize our opportunity—all those homespun values Benjamin Franklin first popularized . . . [that] express a broader confidence that so long as individual men and women are free to pursue their own interests, society as a whole will prosper."[26]

While it has less of a footprint in the United States than the Lockean tradition, this Spinozan vision fits well with American political culture. Although radical, this democratic progressive vision contains a state and society that can be homegrown. Self-interest, initiative, innovation, pragmatism, tolerance, inclusivity, and responsibility are political values found in the United States that underlie such a Spinozan state, market, and society. These values, moreover, are grounded in more than the state and society; they are embodied in the individual pursuing the American dream. "And what binds us together," said Obama, "what makes us an American family, is that we stand up and fight for each other's dreams."[27]

A Spinozan vision makes self-interest the catalyst or engine of change. Self-interest helps close the divide between the individual and society by coupling equality with interdependence. A Spinozan state finds freedom by discovering the mutually inclusive interests of an individual and society. American political renewal, as Obama describes, should revolve around cultivating and inspiring those "who see their own self-interest as inextricably linked to the interests of others." What is good for the individual can be good for society, and vice versa. Built on interdependence—an interdependence that depends on equality but *fosters* freedom—the Spinozan state, market, and society help reinvigorate the American dream and make citizens earn egalitarianism. "We have lost the understanding that in a democracy, we have mutual obligation to one another—that we cannot measure the greatness of our society by the strongest and richest of us," said Michelle Obama, as she echoed her husband's notion of mutual self-interest.[28]

Expanding the Social Sphere, Not Social Citizenship

Since the 1990s, Spinoza's thought has been increasingly associated with politics, not just with religion. His ideas engage both classical liberalism and communitarian theories of politics, yet they establish a unique political order that suits neither camp. On the one hand, Spinoza echoes John Locke and Thomas Hobbes by validating self-interest. He considers an individual's obligation to herself sacrosanct. But then Spinoza spurns one of the most basic premises underlying Hobbes's and Locke's classical liberalism: that an individual can be autonomous. In Spinoza's view, no one can survive on her own, out in the cold.[29]

On the other hand, Spinoza makes his political theory communitarian by injecting the idea of interdependence. His notion of interdependence, however, is distinctive. It lacks one of the foundational principles underlying most, if not all, communitarian theories: that one individual cares for another. Like Hobbes and Locke, Spinoza discards the communitarian's notion of benevolence. He dismisses the proposition that people can see past their own self-interest and care for one another. There is no public good. There is no public interest. In Spinoza's view, an interdependent group of like-minded individuals can act collectively *and* maintain their own self-interest. People come together for reasons of survival rather than benevolence.

What Spinoza does is to make self-interest transformative. Not being autonomous, individuals apprehend their interests in context with each other; they can know their interests only by virtue of interaction. Seeing self-interest as what changes people helps Spinoza demonstrate how a mutually inclusive collective can operate. In other words, it is the interactions between, and among, self-interested individuals that count. After all, every person occupies a unique position in the world. Individuals dwell in a specific time and place, and they maintain certain social, economic, and cultural positions, which give them multiple, overlapping, and fluid identities.

When individuals interact, they must each secure something. An interaction is no abstraction for Spinoza. Interactions exist on both a practical and a material level. If one observes these interactions, she can see that the individual is not autonomous. People recognize each other, they acknowledge each other, and they rely on each other. At the same time, all people are first obliged to themselves, and it is only because self-obligation is sacrosanct that interactions between and among people are authentic, or can reflect their true self-interest. Being true to oneself helps one become true to one's neighbor.

Spinoza does not stop at demonstrating how interactions maintain our survival. An interdependent collective, not individuals acting autonomously, forms a state that offers security and freedom. And what gives people hope about Spinoza's theory is that a state and society helps them pursue their potential, or, as he puts it, their "perfectibility." To thrive, the state and society must encourage its citizens to strive and earn their place at the deliberative democratic table. Freedom means more than fulfilling our physical needs. It feeds our soul. It requires individual accomplishment and fulfillment that society acknowledges and applauds. Each person will know what she wants and pursue it.[30]

The Irony of the Identity-less Who Like Difference and Being "Different": Obama and Du Bois

Obama's 2008 campaign rested on the idea that he was not about his black identity. Identity is essentialist. Based on the essence of an individual—who that person *is*—identity is a fixed, static, and constant concept. Our identity is not fluid or in flux. Rather, we are motionless. Identities are stagnant, immobile, and inactive, and by being inert, they force others to react. In part this reaction stems from acknowledging what value the culture assigns to each identity. Assigning value breaks identities into a hierarchy or a tree of hierarchies, with different branches characterized and categorized as higher or lower, lesser or better than one another.

In the 1960s and 1970s, identity politics caught hold as a way to challenge the dominant identity—white, heterosexual, Anglo-Saxon, Christian, male—and helped redefine American liberalism, making it more inclusive. Activists contested the so-called marginalization of identities such as being African American, a woman, or an African American woman. They fought for de jure protection from discrimination by passing civil rights laws. Rev. Dr. Martin Luther King Jr. made American liberalism more expansive, freeing it of its original hypocrisy. Over the decades, liberalism came to include more and more marginal groups. Civil rights restored and promoted liberalism, as King described, not only for African Americans, but for all Americans.

Once a marginal group assimilated, however, it could no longer be distinct or come to a boil. Supposedly part of a melting pot, identity groups were free of any assigned value, at least in the political arena. But in keeping with American liberalism, these groups also accepted the idea of separate spheres: the public, the private, and the social spheres.

Obama rejects this notion of identity politics. He dispenses with a rigid categorization of separate spheres or domains, particularly since the public and the private come at the exclusion of the social. Nor does he accept the idea of the self and the other. On the one hand, Obama rejects the idea of assimilation—and the universal values it instills. He is not King, a civil rights supporter who upheld the Christian value of universal human rights. Nor does he agree with critics of white supremacy about hegemony. Obama does not accept that the white, Anglo-Saxon, Christian male identity must remain the "default" identity.

Obama is not an essentialist. He believes in difference, advancing a pragmatic belief in the lack of any universal truth that would define an African American identity or any identity. Like Gilles Deleuze, who in turns relies on Spinoza, Obama promotes a philosophy of difference that is rooted in a transcendental empiricism and pragmatism but is eminently practical. His philosophy of difference, moreover, is an experimental philosophy in that it explores how to avoid subsuming difference to the identity of concepts or to the play of categorical opposition. Obama employs a philosophy of difference that goes beyond the opposition of categories such as black and white or the private and public spheres.[31]

All of this is premised on an Arendtian, Foucauldian, Madisonian notion of power. Power is not bad. Interest is not bad. It is how one wields power that matters. What one does with power determines whether it is negative and repressive or positive and productive. Obama, as a grassroots community organizer, understood the here and now, or the art of the possible.

Ideas as Tools and the Pragmatics of Race: Obama, Dewey, and Du Bois

For pragmatists like Du Bois and Obama, ideas themselves are tools. Ideas are instruments to be used for interacting with and capturing "the forces, facts, and tendencies that define our environing state of affairs." Ideas build new frameworks or provide alternative perspectives. The whole point of pragmatic inquiry is to clarify previously indeterminate situations. Du Bois, a Deweyan pragmatist, did this with his concept of race in the service of perfectionism and in the grip of a chastened, meliorist sensibility.[32]

Obama shares this vision of an ontology and ethic of difference and pragmatism. Evidence of this vision can be found in Obama's identification with Du Bois's view of the contextual nature of racial identification, or the mechanizations of racialization. According to Du Bois, this context makes the concept of race do double duty. First, it shows how we can reconcile racialism with Du Bois's recognition of hybridity and impurity. Races are contingent features of certain social landscapes. And second, because racialism is contingent, they need not be part of the infrastructure of the cosmos.[33]

The social units that emerge, composing races, are not groups per se. Members of a race need not share good intentions, or even awareness

of a common relation to processes of racial formation. Du Bois suggests that these units can best be characterized (in the words of Paul C.
Taylor) as "probabilistically defined populations." To classify someone
within a race is to identify her with those who are similarly situated.
They have the same social conditions, such as wealth, health, and education. And it is these social conditions, or what Du Bois calls "mechanizations of racialization," that assign deeper meaning to bodies and blood-
lines than race itself.

While race is real or a physical fact, the mechanizations of racialization are socially constructed. These mechanizations can be taken apart
piece by piece, reexamined, and then reconstructed. In the 1940s, for
example, black people had to abide by Jim Crow laws in Georgia. This
social practice brought into being certain institutional facts that an individual could ignore only at her own peril. You could violate Jim Crow
laws, insisting you are white, but all the while knowing legal authorities
and citizens alike would see you differently.[34]

Veils

In *The Souls of Black Folk*, Du Bois purposely makes the visibility of the
object of ethnographic inquiry problematic by locating African Americans behind a veil. On the one hand, this invisibility is partly a function
of racism that erases and objectifies the "Other." They sit in the back of
the bus. On the other hand, this invisibility gives the Other the agency af-
forded with a refusal—a refusal to be materialized within the dominant
culture and a desire to remain extraneous to or unclassified within the
material order. It is the tension, the juxtaposition, that counts.[35]

Du Bois had no doubt that people could transcend the race line. But
they could not do it alone. A Herderian nationalist, Du Bois argued that
individuality was expressed in terms of broad social structures and that
these structures created bonds between the social units. It was what connected Du Bois to other black people.

Du Bois spoke of a twin sacrifice. It did not involve merely ceding
the possibilities of self-realization to the constraints of white supremacy. That sacrifice had to be paired with a contingent manifestation of a
deep fact of philosophical anthropology: the gap recognized by Dewey,
Hegel, Herder, and others between "abstract individualism" and "articulated individuality."[36]

Du Bois determined the "color line" in relation to the contested terrain between the spiritual and the material. He launched a fundamental
challenge to the methodological and ideological strategies of positivist

science by constructing an alternative model of black leadership based on the figure of the seer. This seer has a spiritual doubleness, quite different from Booker T. Washington's troubling oneness that corresponded to the materialism of the age.[37]

Contrary to allegations made by some of his African American critics, Obama does not promote the theory of whiteness. Speaking at the same 2004 Democratic National Convention at which Obama gave the speech that pushed him onto the national stage, Al Sharpton argued that racial reconciliation should involve reparations. For Sharpton and Cornel West, among others, race is paramount. They equate racial transcendence with an erasure of some of four-plus centuries' worth of injustices committed against African Americans. What they deemphasize, however, is how Obama's position echoes Du Bois's dynamic—his philosophical and psychological "double consciousness." Influenced by both the American transcendentalists and the existentialists regarding what it is to be African *and* American, Du Bois underscored the "twoness" of racial discourse: "two souls, two thoughts, two unreconciled strivings, two warring ideals in one dark body."[38]

Obama magnifies this consciousness. It is not just a doubling, but possibly a tripling (gender), a quadrupling (sexuality), or a quintupling (disability). Simply put, he accentuates the fluidity and multiplicity of our identities and the uniqueness of our experiences. What Obama promotes is individuality—not identity. And the term "individuality" captures the distinctness of all people—their being and their existence or experience, their minds and their bodies. Obama remains unburdened by binaries or Cartesian dualism. And, like Dewey, Obama offers hope by promoting cooperation or harmony that stems from what some scholars call the "utilization of difference." No ranking groups of people as primary, secondary, or tertiary—it's the relationship or dynamic between the different individuals within the groups that matters.[39]

Traveling the Last 10 Percent: Obama and Joshua

In *The Audacity of Hope*, Obama recounts how he devoured books like those of Du Bois, searching for his own identity. He is even more self-conscious about the leaders who shaped him—melding Abraham Lincoln and Martin Luther King Jr. One hundred years apart, both these leaders gave moral depth to politics. They sought a "beloved community," or what historian Thomas Sugrue calls common ground and a shared purpose. Obama came to "a single, powerful, and conventional reading of modern American history . . . that reinforced a grand narrative of racial reconciliation, an account of America moving inexorably toward racial equality, or, as Obama put it in his most famous speech, 'toward a more perfect union.'" For Obama's generation, racial conflict remains an unfinished journey as it enters a new stage of reconciliation. In his view, they need only travel a final 10 percent of the way. Speaking on the anniversary of "Bloody Sunday" in Selma, Alabama, where forty-two years earlier state troopers beat and brutalized activists marching across the Edmund Pettus Bridge, Obama said, "The previous generation, the Moses generation pointed the way. They took us 90 percent there. We still got that 10 percent to cross over to the other side."[40]

This final 10 percent, according to Obama, depends on Americans' discovering their common beliefs as well as the values of initiative, self-reliance, and mutual reliance and responsibility. "If cousin Pookie would vote, get off the couch and register some folks and go to the polls, we might have a different kind of politics. . . . We have too many children in poverty in this country and everybody should be ashamed . . . but don't tell me that it doesn't have a little to do with the fact that we got too many daddies not acting like daddies. Don't think that fatherhood ends at conception."[41] Obama scolds his generation—his entire generation, not just African Americans—for not recognizing their debt to the civil rights movement, which allows all Americans to let African Americans squander their new freedoms, their opportunities. This is what he seeks to change.[42]

Standing "on the shoulders of giants," Obama recognizes his debt and the debt of his generation. But American reform must now be symbolized not by Moses's struggle for liberation, but rather by Joshua's struggle to consolidate Moses's gains. Distancing himself from racism and confrontations with white people, "Obama positioned himself as the heir to King and the civil rights movement," writes Sugrue, "but also as part of a vanguard of black politicians who jettisoned a now untimely and divisive sense of racial grievance and embraced mainstream, 'middle-class' values (which many commentators interpreted as 'white'), rather than appealing to race consciousness."[43]

It is not just that Obama sanitized King, Sugrue writes, so that he can now embrace middle-class values. Obama goes much further. He melds King and Du Bois, turning middle-class values into a belief structure that embraces difference or all identities universally. No longer racially conscious, Obama rejects the underlying white, heterosexual notion of normalcy as well. In his view, all identities count; identity politics counts, but it is an identity politics premised on the universal appeal of difference. Americans are forever crossing a new frontier. This explains why, as will be shown in chapter 3, Obama is the first president to offer passports to the transgendered community.[44]

Power of the People: Obama and Alinsky

How do we capture this dynamic? The philosophy that best captures Obama's type of community organizing is pragmatism—a pragmatism informed by Spinoza, not Locke or Rousseau. Indeed, sociologists in the Chicago school of pragmatism trained Saul Alinsky, the most prominent community organizer and the leader Obama studied and cited as most influential in his days as an organizer in Chicago. John Dewey and William James, the fathers of American pragmatism, held great sway over those University of Chicago sociologists.[45]

Headed by Albion Small, the Chicago school of pragmatism represented a "philosophical methodology built upon an awareness of the emergent nature of reality, wherein experience was viewed as a laboratory where theories and practices were continually experimented with and their validities tested." Such a perspective on "truth" and "knowledge" made Dewey a critic of knowledge "for its own sake." Knowledge, an asset, must be put to good use.[46]

Alinsky's community organizing incorporated this perspective from pragmatism. He followed no rigid principles; there was no theory for theory's sake. Instead, Alinsky argued that community organizing must be idealistic *and* realistic at the same time. Decades earlier, James had described Dewey's leadership the same way. Dewey believed in "real thought and a real school." "Truth and meaning were socially constructed concepts emerging within communal inquiry," as Lawrence Engle explains in an article about the close ties between Alinsky and the Chicago school of pragmatism. Pragmatism "in and of itself was continually subject to the self-corrective processes of democratic life."[47]

Action shaped ideas. For this reason, pragmatists rejected religious fundamentalism, with its emphasis on faith and strict adherence to abstract ideals. Some pragmatists even went so far as to equate "parochial evangelism" with pure science. Both fundamentalism and science suffered from being too detached from reality. They were also both rigid and static.[48]

Given this interpretation of truth and knowledge as well as action and ideas, Dewey and the pragmatists could be called critical theorists. Community organizers, Alinsky insisted, should never abide by ironclad principles. Organizers could not fixate on an ideology for themselves, nor could they consider the ideology that governs the state and society to be fixed. They should critically analyze all ideologies, viewing them less as principles and more as norms designed within a specific context that reflects a particular constellation of power.

Dewey and Alinsky exercised subjective causal analysis. In their view, the state, harboring its specific principles, should recognize those principles for what they really are—norms. Norms, moreover, must be placed in context. They reflect the environment.[49]

The American environment, the American culture, and American beliefs and principles all shaped these norms. They fostered reform. In Alinsky's view, American political culture did not contain any "seeds for revolution," only for reform. Organizing was a way of fixing specific problems and building a culture. Obama called the narratives he collected "sacred stories."[50]

Political LSD

Obama agrees with Alinsky's view that the chance of a revolution ever occurring in the United States is remote. Reform, homespun reform, represents the only way of achieving change in the United States. Tracing how Obama's perspective on Alinsky changed, David Remnick quotes Jerry Kellman, one of Obama's first mentors, who trained him to undertake the United Neighborhood Organization, saying, "That's Alinsky. It's all self-interest. Very hard nosed. What is their self-interest and how to use it to organize." Kellman urged Obama not to waste time on Alinsky's books, *Reveille for Radicals* and *Rules for Radicals*, but to focus instead on the nexus between self-interest and power. First an organizer gets a community to recognize its own self-interest, then the organizer engages people so that they form their own leadership. Those leaders must be homegrown, though the organizer can go so far as to teach them how "to analyze power" and will even offer them lessons in public speaking. Remnick concludes that Obama's "being a community organizer helped him create a black community."[51]

Obama's experience organizing on Chicago's South Side shaped him, and he departed from his intellectual guru in believing that both electoral politics and governing are worthy of pursuit. While this explains why Obama left Chicago for Harvard Law School, it also explains why he came back. Obama turns Alinsky's argument around. Neither electoral politics nor government at any level can create great political change without community organizing, he argues in a piece for *Illinois Issues* titled "Why Organize? Problems and Promises in the Inner City."[52]

Alinsky's response to the radicals who sought revolutionary change in the 1960s was telling. He thought those radicals had it all wrong—it was wrong to use violence, wrong to insist on black power, and wrong to abandon electoral politics. Real change must be instilled from *within*, not without, the American political system. Real, lasting change should bolster, build, and expand electoral participation. "When you start telling me you can't have any revolutionary changes by working within our structured institutions, that you've got to get rid of the whole society, tear it down, burn it down or something—then from where I sit this is just political LSD."[53]

Alinsky believed that violence, particularly on behalf of black power, would result in state repression that could kill the movement. "Now the society's method of dealing with this," he said, "will be repressive"— and this type of repression would be destructive. Alinsky warned the radicals that repression creates polarization that alienates everyone and ultimately defeats the activists and their cause. "There's a difference between just being an ethnic group seeking power to participate as normal individuals in an ongoing society, and it's another thing when an ethnic group is also radical in its politics and begins to have revolutionary overtones. It means it doesn't want just to participate in that society; it's looking for radical change in that society." The youth should expand the electorate. They must have faith that electoral politics can lead to change.[54]

In Alinsky's view, electoral participation cures political alienation. While enjoying his greatest success in the 1930s and 1940s, Alinsky insisted that the poor had to get involved in politics, and that by their very involvement, they would see what power they held and would therefore fight for reform. Political participation begets more political participation. This, to him, was community organizing. Indeed, one of Alinsky's "rules for radicals" was "never do for others what they can do for themselves!" He empowered people.[55]

Obama expresses a similar conception of efficacy and empowerment. The person, the body, the corporeality, is not an end in herself. She is not the unit of analysis. Obama dismisses individualism but advances individuality. Each person must pursue her full potential. This means that the individual is the subject of analysis, though within the context of the collective.

Obama crosses the liberal/communitarian divide by recognizing politics as power and making it relational or social. He rejects the individualism underlying classical liberalism, disputing the idea that individual autonomy is either natural or preferable. It isn't. It's cold out there. Obama realizes that alone, a person lacks power. People help each other to gain power. It is a relationship. Or, as he relays, "No person is an island."[56]

To thrive, a state and society must encourage its citizens to reach for their potential. Freedom means more than supplying our physical needs. It requires individual accomplishment and fulfillment that society acknowledges and applauds. Each person must know what she wants and pursue it. People are emboldened and empowered. As Obama maintains, "Americans don't want a handout, they just want a real chance to go to college." "We welcome success stories here in America. We admire those who have climbed to the top of the ladder. We just need to be sure that the ladder doesn't get taken away from the rest of us. We want a system based on fairness—not special favors."[57]

The power necessary for "change" emanates both from a group's individual members and from the collective weight of these members. Unlike a community, a collective must find and develop its principles on the basis of consensus. The principles created by such a consensus are not fixed. As was true with the pragmatists, action must be informed by theory and theory informed by action. Democratic progressivism represents an ongoing, perpetually evolving experiment, so community organizers must be flexible and adapt to each situation. Society is "in a never ending process of flux." It is in "an unending competition and conflict of interests." A society, and any collective within it, is fluid. Identities are ever changing. Change was the only constant Alinsky and the pragmatists recognized. In Obama's view, the "genius of this nation" is that "America can change."[58]

Dreamers Disdained

Obama disdains reformers "who preferred the dream to the reality, impotence to compromise." He does not prefer the dream to reality. He is a can-do man. Obama, like Alinsky and the pragmatists, holds little regard for following principles at the expense of action, or for reformers who are painted into corners by their principles. Obama left community organizing because he wanted a "long-term vision" that this type of activism could not provide. He had a greater chance of being less marginal as a mainstream politician than as a community organizer, though he knew that being an effective leader meant learning the art of compromise.[59]

The criticisms of African American activists, public intellectuals, and academics who claim that transcending race reifies "ideologies of innocence and positive self-presentation" or constitutes an "erasure of race" cannot be substantiated by Obama's campaign speeches or his Senate record. Obama does not make whiteness the starting and ending point.

Whiteness is not "normal." Nor does he champion the middle class—as a class. To be sure, Obama starts from the center, which in part accounts for his electoral success as the first African American president. He seeks reform rather than revolutionary change. But Obama's emphasis on fluidity and multiple identities creates a standardless standard—or no standard.[60]

Obama does not want a color-blind country to "jump off," but rather a colorful one that brings new hope to American democracy. Like his second memoir, *The Audacity of Hope*, Obama's most complex and controversial speech on race was aptly titled so as to capture the subtlety of his dynamic argument: "A *More* Perfect Union." Obama takes in, in equal measure, the past and the future: the explanation and the solution; the horror and the hope; the individual, the group, and the individual within the group. It's a dynamic, kinetic, ever-changing, relational conception of American politics.

Unlike the sixties radicals, Obama heard Alinsky and unwittingly recognized the challenge of building a collective that would promote the individual's sense of efficacy and empowerment. He spoke of a "belief that our destiny will not be written for us, but by us." Obama believes in working within the American political and economic system, not in singling out black power, which is why he fought for universal reforms that are not race or gender specific. He places great faith in the individual and in what makes each person unique. Being part of a collective in a community organizing effort or a political campaign, rather than a composite, means that each member retains her uniqueness.[61]

Obama embraces difference. He transcends race. We may have "different stories," Obama says, "but we hold common hopes." He rejects individualism and embraces individuality, as Dewey did. In the American context this has great meaning. If the individuality of each group member is to be accepted, then everyone in the group must practice tolerance. While Obama's perspective has been classified as a grassroots organizer's view of power and politics, this book shows that his worldview goes further, given his belief in difference and tolerance—a belief system that fosters individuality.[62]

Obama goes beyond Alinsky and other community organizers by recognizing how the individual operates within a group dynamic. Obama defines the relationship in terms of the individual, society, and the state, not just the individual versus the establishment. He makes it dynamic. By so doing, he promotes difference and tolerance more than Alinsky and most community organizers, who privilege identity, power, and empowerment. He also believes in long-term vision—and, like Dewey and

Arendt, makes self-interest an ideal, not an immediately obtainable concrete goal.[63]

Recognizing difference means that no one, no matter how well intentioned, can dictate another's needs. The people must decide for themselves. Obama rejects identity politics, and he conflates individuals and groups so as to give them each agency—but he never lets anyone or any group off the hook. "He links the suffering of others to his own fate," explains rhetorician David Frank, "displaying a rhetorical model of empathy necessary for transformation." In his address to the 2004 Democratic National Convention, Obama turned all identity groups into a composite: "There is not a black America and white America and Latino America and Asian America; there's the United States of America." Obama unites all Americans because he "*nests* the traumas of slavery and racism with those suffered by American workers lacking a living wage and affordable health care, the bigotry faced by gays and Arab Americans, and an America in the wake of 9/11."[64]

A Different Ontology: No Philosopher-President

Obama subscribes to a different ontology and a different ethic: We are defined not by who we *are*, but rather by what we *do*. Deleuze too, like Spinoza, subsumed philosophy into ethics—it is the "theory of what we do, not what we are." Deleuze's ambition was to make "thought" ethical.[65]

Deleuze distinguishes ethics from morality, rejecting the latter. He characterizes morality as built on a belief in universal truth. Instead of morality, Deleuze opts for ethics, which are descriptions of how to behave. Yet Deleuze's ethics, like those of Spinoza, constitute an alternative to a morality, one that can function as a system of judgment.[66]

What makes traditional morality unethical, according to theorist Zygmunt Bauman, is that moral principles stem from extrapolating our present experience under the influence of our desire for progress—for a better future. Moral principles appeal to the supposedly free choice of subjects who are not encumbered by economic, social, or psychological pressures. Yet these subjects are disembodied, rational agents. They are abstractions.[67]

In such a world of disembodied agents, the rule governing moral encounters constitutes the true relationship between these parties. It is an agent's relationship to a rule, not to all other free subjects. When one agent encounters another subject, the cause or target of the action "is but a pawn moved around the chessboard of rights and duties," explains Bauman.[68]

Morality is therefore unethical or unjust, because in creating relationships between rules and agents, it dehumanizes people. Put differently, it can be described as a reversal of Platonism. Reversing Plato—who privileges thought or reflection over action, the mind over the body—does not merely invert all oppositions. It does not privilege the body over the mind or action over thought. Instead, this reversal reveals a plane of immanence as the unity of humanity and nature, or subject and object.

Unlike morality, Deleuzian ethics are partial, merely correlating acts of thought with acts of the body. Correlating these acts constitutes a relationship between subjects, not a rule and a subject in contradistinction to the other—the opposing subject. In Deleuze's materialism, a body is both a physiological and a social institution. Instead of trying to isolate thought from economic, social, cultural, and psychological determinants, this ethic recognizes immanent thought as culturally conditioned.[69]

Deleuzian ethics mirror what pragmatists claim about the role of inquiry and practice. The pragmatic method claims an experimental basis for its emphasis on continuity and commonality, thus rejecting the claims of skeptics and others that the primary features of human life are difference, discontinuity, and incommensurability.

Dewey, for example, distinguishes between ontological Truth (the nature of truth) and epistemic validity (the test of truth). In his view, logical theory is rendered subservient to metaphysical and epistemological preconceptions, so that interpretation of logical forms varies with underlying metaphysical assumption. He argues that the principles of logic are not a priori principles. Those principles are fixed in advance of inquiry, but the principles of logic are "generated in the very process of control of continued inquiry."[70]

Dewey coins the term "synechism" to reconcile and unite his doctrine of absolute chance or fallibilism with the real necessity that is the backbone of his logical realism. In *Logic*, Dewey insists that we inquire because we have doubts. When these doubts are removed or allayed, our inquiry ends. Doubts make us feel uneasy and unsettled; when our doubts are settled, we have genuine belief or knowledge.[71]

To determine whether our ideas are reliable and worthy of action, we must look at how we warrant our assertions. Since we are fallible, contextual human beings, the only truths we have access to are derived through our own error-prone, yet self-correcting, procedures. In other words, our logical forms are developed from within our own contextuality. We call knowledge or truth "warranted assertability."[72]

Instead of being binaries based on static identities, conjunctions and disjunctions are correlative within a broader context. The self is neither the subjective modernist self nor the fragmented and ineffectual self that one finds in postmodernist literature. The pragmatic self is an individual that exists as an individual only in relation to the connections and communities that enable it to be so. It is an agent who acts "within a nexus of thick social-behaviorist" ethics.[73]

It's the Situation: Neither Rational, Irrational, or Emotional Views

An ethic rests on a situational view of morality, as opposed to a Kantian or utilitarian one. It is based on context, moving away from rules or moral absolutes and into particular contexts in which the pertinent question is what a "good" person would do in a given situation. Under a situational ethic, "the process of growth, of improvement and progress, rather than the static outcome and result, becomes the significant thing . . . the end is no longer a terminus or limit to be reached. It is the active process of transforming the existent situation. Not perfection as a final goal, but the ever-enduring process of perfecting, maturing, refining is the aim in living. . . . Growth itself is the only moral 'end.' "[74]

Pragmatists argue over what they call inquiry as a method or a practice.[75] Dewey's philosophical inquiry called for experimental methods to resolve moral and political problems. From time to time, he wrote, an "intelligent furthering of culture" requires that "we take them off, inspect them, and then criticize them."[76]

Deleuzian, Deweyan, and Spinozan ethics all share an emphasis on subjectivity, though not on absolute subjectivity. Rather, these ethics rely on what could be described as a "qualified" relativism, which made the possibility of uniqueness universal without descending into chaos. Relativism is defined as viewing reality as a function of human belief and truth as a function of human practice.

The problem with this formulation, to someone who seeks clear direction, is that if all truths are relative to the individual and to the time and place in which she acts, then the logical result is that nothing can be proved right or wrong, or as critics often argue, "anything goes." Yet the concept of universal truth itself involves five elements of uncertainty. First, whenever someone makes an assertion, she presupposes some standard. Second, different people have employed incompatible standards in making assertions about the same subject matter. Third, sometimes those differences in standards are ultimate. Fourth, where the third element of uncertainty obtains, it is nonsense to speak of one set of standards as correct. Fifth, and hence, a decision to accept or reject some fundamental standard, to the extent that it lies within our power, must of necessity be arbitrary. It is the abandonment of fixed criteria or a fundamental standard that creates subjectivism.[77]

But qualified relativism within pragmatism does not abandon fixed criteria. Although culturally bound, philosophical assumptions can still affect inquiry. Inquiry involves people becoming "situated knowers" who recognize that philosophical assumptions are culturally bound. Situated knowers compensate for our cultural embeddedness. They can help fight our natural predisposition toward closed-mindedness by expanding our horizons and including others in our conversations, creating an all-inclusive critical discourse.[78]

The ontology and philosophy of difference advanced by Spinoza, Deleuze, and Dewey rests on qualified relativism. Pragmatism does not support "anything goes." As Dewey describes, it allows room for an "unjustifiable hope and for a groundless but vital sense of human solidarity." Dewey makes no differentiation between ideas and principles, and he suggests that we assess ideas according to their ability to further the purposes of some individual or group. In this way, truth is redefined as correctness.[79]

Physics and Politics: Obama Comes to Arendt's Table

How do individuals and groups come together? While vague, Spinoza's term "common notions" describes the situation in which one person encounters another whom she is compatible with, or relates to, on a fundamental level and can therefore interact with. The idea of common notions sheds light on Spinoza's account of group formation in civil society. When a collection of individuals have "notions in common," it pulls them together, creating the basis for their interaction.[80]

Spinoza illustrates this concept by describing a "physics of bodies," painting a graphic picture of how they relate and interact: "Man, I say, can wish for nothing more helpful to the preservation of his being than that all should so agree in all things that the Minds and Bodies of all would compose, as it were, one Mind and one Body; that all should strive together, as far as they can, to preserve their being; and that all, together should seek for themselves the common advantage of all." In Spinoza's view, society can be characterized as a multitude of bodies in motion. These bodies lump together and unite, fueling the idea that two can be twice, or thrice, as powerful as one. A society emerges when one individual's power is aligned with that of the collective. Unity is needed, and self-interests are served, with no conflict between the two. The individual and the collective are mutually reinforcing and mutually reinvigorating. They constitute a dynamic. They cause a minor activity explosion.[81]

The challenge for Spinoza is to show how these bodies or individuals can and do unite around their collective self-interest. Like animals, people have appetites. As a result, they seek out what advances or enhances those appetites. People remember how they satisfied their appetites earlier and therefore, he maintains, can do so again in the future. They have memories. Distinguishing between "good" and "bad" appetites, Spinoza shows how members of society determine their likes and dislikes (or what he calls "aversions").[82]

Almost as vague as "common notions," the term "aversion" explains how people try to reproduce "joyful passions" that they experienced in the past, particularly when encountering another person. This is the glue that sticks people together. The same motivation for two is the motivation that can unite all—the state and society. It's all about compatibility.

Spinoza envisions a state that connects emotion—the imagination and joyful passions—to reason and adequate knowledge. To achieve this state, Spinoza prefers a democracy to all other forms of government. But because of his emphasis on reason and passion, consensus building and difference, Spinoza promotes a type of democracy that is more deliberative than representative. Deliberation occurs, moreover, within groups that interact with the state, rather than within society at large.[83]

Arendt also believes that this dynamic represents citizens seeking their commonalities: "contingent articulations of differing positions, always conditioned in the presence of others," writes feminist literary theorist Katherine Adams in a pivotal piece that rearticulates Arendt's notion of self-interest. "Interests are not produced by material context alone," this feminist elaborates, "but by perception of position within it." Like Spinoza, Arendt calls for imagination: "Through deliberation, action, and reflection, members of a group or potential group not only can discover that their underlying interests differ from their previous preferences, but also, by creating themselves anew, can create new interests."[84]

Deliberative Democracy: Shifting Collectivities and Sandy Alliances

Just as pragmatism is not tantamount to individualistic subjectivism, in which anything goes, neither is it partial to collective subjectivism. Ideas cannot be determined and assessed by voting: there is no thumbs-up or thumbs-down. Inquiry must be conducted and arguments constructed, which together constitute a discourse.

When this happens, disagreement can ensue. A qualified relativist can object to ideas propounded by her community as long as she is prepared to defend her disagreement on grounds the majority accepts. While most people will find a ready-made framework for this disagreement within their social environment, thereby limiting their scope and perspective, some people will construct a new framework that induces others to join.

The law provides us with the best analogy for the community and discursive practices. Those administering a legal system will not tolerate a rival legal system established within their jurisdiction, but they will accept disagreements from within. Relativists need be no more tolerant than others, and in fact they have special reasons for being intolerant: if argument is impossible, coercion becomes especially attractive. Feminist authors Katherine Adams and Barbara Thayer-Bacon, among others, envision a fallibilistic universe that is open to a pluralistic universe in need of embracing inclusion of others to avoid subjectivism or dogmatism.[85]

Coalition discourse occurs when people can co-articulate difference and commonality. Instead of viewing differences and commonalities as polarities, they should be recognized as mutually nourishing conditions. By disrupting the normative fantasies of a unified, a priori subjectivity and universal truth, interest-based discourse facilitates political interactions that neither rely on sameness nor reify difference to the exclusion of connection. To achieve this, we depend on negotiation among divergent identities, voices, histories, and desires. Self-interest seeks to enlarge material advantage and expand power to maintain and preserve the self.[86]

Coalitions seek ways to address differences without reifying them. Cross-difference negotiation accommodates diverse truths and centers their constitution in material culture. Differences cannot become static, but must remain fluid.

First, a member of a coalition must be willing to take positions as a subject of her desires and perceived needs—it is about speaking a "self." This self is interested on its own behalf, as with Obama and the healthcare debate.

Second, a coalition "requires a high level of critical, skeptical interest in that desiring self—its unity and stability." Its members must interrogate their own positionality from within. Only then can they transform the coalition, ensuring that it remains in flux.

This twofold practice of self-interested discourse—honesty with others and with oneself—is performed in the context of a desire for alliance and justice. This practice adds a radicalizing element to coalition discourse and is similar to a pluralistic conception of pragmatic inquiry. Dewey portrays it as engaging in perpetual inquiry and process without having any preset notion of norms, values, or beliefs.

The radical mestiza queer activist Gloria Anzaldúa engaged in this practice when she tried forging alliances without subordinating differences. She showed that interest in the indeterminacy of selfhood grants the "mestiza queer" awareness of the shifting, situational nature of her differentiation from others and helps her to explore, engage, and enter into alliances.[87]

Similarly, Susan Stanford Friedman's book *Mappings* exposed narratives of relationality that helped destabilize the absolutes of difference and sameness within coalitions. "It is relationality or relational positionality," she writes, "that posits identity as situationally constructed and defined and at the crossroads of different systems of alterity and stratification." She creates axes to map or find these "situationally-constructed identities, such as sexuality."[88]

Diane Fowlkes goes further with her notion of "material intersubjectivity." Anzaldúa's perception of oneself and others as different and complex leads to the crucial recognition that oppression acts on subjects in multiple and overlapping dimensions. The fight against domination thus becomes a more complex fight requiring coalitions to organize around multiple aspects of identity to work on interlocking oppressions.[89]

Consider, for example, Du Bois's veil and Obama's mixed identity. It all comes down to questioning or challenging a singular notion of a unified subjectivity. Relational discourse requires four steps. First, it must remain open to processes of revision. Second, revisions must be constituted within overlapping material contexts. Third, an ability to exceed and to disrupt the sameness/difference binary must remain constant. And finally, a resistance to the notion of a priori subjectivity (and the public/private binary) must undergird it. Adams calls it being "grounded in thingness of identity and inter-relationships." She seeks discursive modes that move beyond difference.[90]

Similarly, James Madison believed that interest was integral to representative democracy, but he posed it against a *telos*, or end, of national unity. Factionalism divided people into parties and infused them with animosity. This mutual animosity "rendered them more disposed to vex and oppress each other than to cooperate for their common good." In Madison's view, the only way to reach a consensus about the public good is for someone to transcend her self-interest and become disinterested. The public good, as a universal, does not exist.[91]

Madison disputes the ideal of civic virtue—or of an abstract or universal public good. The very term "disinterest" differs categorically from a universal public good in that it holds sway or creates fluidity and flux. The civic republican binarism of interest and disinterest changes into an opposition.

Self-interest is not juxtaposed with the public interest. Self-interest is not inimical to political processes and cohesion. Jane Mansbridge described contemporary interest-based politics as a type of adversarial democracy in which fundamentally conflicting interests compete. An interest-based model is built on antagonistic forces that cultivate and harbor irresolvable differences. A disinterest-based model is one in which associations create a transcendent and unified condition of sameness expressed through rational consensus on common good.[92]

A Generation of Generators: Undermining Norms and Customs

Like the Lockean interpretation of the American state and society, a Spinozan interpretation bolsters cultural beliefs and values long held in the United States about how to obtain freedom and practice equality. Spinoza describes a state that represents a departure from the old European social welfare state. But instead of basing an American liberal state on individualism, liberty, and private property, a Spinozan interpretation challenges traditional European social and cultural hierarchies in a different way, by using equality and collective power to gain freedom.

Rather than balancing freedom and equality of opportunity, as the Lockean interpretation does, a Spinozan interpretation uses the power that *emanates from equality to secure freedom*. This power makes the United States exceptional in that it promotes the cultural values of initiative, innovation, pragmatism, tolerance, and responsibility. It fosters an open and inclusive society, rejecting the closed communities and bounded national identities that are still prevalent in Europe, despite the European Union's founding.[93]

Obama, who is no romantic, nonetheless understands how easily an open society can be corrupted. By a matter of degrees, or shades of gray, rather than absolutes, "self-reliance and independence," he explains, "can transform into selfishness and license." He shores up his democratic eye with his pragmatic or technocratic one—mixing efficiency with technology through path-of-least-resistance thinking.[94]

Giving all individuals equal amounts of power underscores their reciprocity. Only by understanding their interdependence can they liberate themselves. Only by emphasizing the role that power plays among equals can they find freedom. Why? Spinoza's notion of freedom requires mutual action and cooperation, not competition. It involves a give-and-take between, and among, equals. It is made manifest by people pitching in to accomplish or achieve something. Obama, too, relies on a theme that emphasizes cooperation rather than competition: "In this country, our grand experiment has only worked because we have guided the market's invisible hand with a higher principle. It's the idea that we are all in this together. From CEOs to shareholders, from financiers to factory workers, we all have a stake in each other's success because the more Americans prosper, the more America prospers."[95]

For Lockean conservatives, by contrast, the state and society prosper without interference from the ever-present, yet supposedly invisible, hand of free-market capitalism. Politics and economics cannot be separated any more than a private and a public sphere can be called distinct. Freedom means exerting power and control over our lives. Life cannot be limited to separate spheres or arenas. Freedom stems both from being liberated from external constraints *and* from having the license to *do* something. There is little juxtaposition between external and internal constraints with Spinoza and Obama. Individuals must retain their agency, for example, with freedom of speech and freedom of association. The Nobel laureate Amartya Sen illustrates how this would work in less wealthy nations than the United States or Europe with what he calls the capabilities approach in *Development as Freedom*.[96]

But freedom does not mean independence. It does not mean autonomy. Spinoza's notion of interdependence includes the idea that when one person exerts power and control, it affects another's power and control. This is not to say that an umpire prevents one person from crossing the line. Freedom is gained and captured more like territories; it depends upon your perspective, or where you are standing on a Friedman-like "map." It is complex and always changing, never static or stationary like an umpire. Nor is it as intentional as dressing someone up in an umpire's uniform. It is less intentional than that. It is not just about the crossing of lines, since all exertion has an impact. Spinoza sees these lines and the collective as a "physics of bodies."[97]

In Spinoza's view, the axiom later attributed to capitalism or supply-side economics—that a high tide lifts all boats—is not restricted to the economy. It describes the collective as well. Moreover, as one boat docks, its speed determines how much the other boats rock and sway. It's the mass or physics of the bodies in the boats that counts.

Writing long before capitalism emerged in the 1830s in the United States, Spinoza does not separate economics from politics. He would have had difficulty explaining how economics, as such a vital part of life, could be viewed as distinct from the other parts of a collective. As Arendt later explained, economics is the social sphere—the *agora* or the marketplace—for men in ancient Greece, whereas women could only participate in the economy as consumers. For them, economics appears in the *oikos* when they acquire purchasing power by buying products, services, and goods to run their households. Obama reflects this contemporary tension with his critique of capitalism via consumer reform. Arendt explains the "recent trend of making what is private become public." As political theorist Trevor Norris describes, Arendt "outlines the modern ascent of the activities of the private realm or *oikos* into the public realm." She does so, however, as part of a critique of both capitalism and modernity. Arendt's philosophical distress stems from our loss of the public. The *agora* has been hollowed out. This literal "gathering place" or "assembly" no longer represents the polis's heartbeat. It is no longer the center of all athletic, artistic, spiritual, and political life of the city since the emergence of consumerism and materialism.[98]

Following his theme of cooperation, Obama explains that he "gets it." He realizes the significance of Cokes and burgers. As he says,

> We have not come this far because we practice survival of the fittest. America is America because we believe in creating a framework in which all can succeed. Our free market was never meant to be a free license to take whatever you can get, however you can get it. And so from time to time, we have put in place certain rules of the road to make competition fair, and open, and honest. We have done this not to stifle prosperity or liberty, but to foster those things and ensure that they are shared and spread as widely as possible.[99]

Indeed, Obama relies on the "high tide" analogy to explain two fundamental reasons behind his universalizing political strategy. First, this analogy explains why he does not mind getting into "trouble" for standing up against identity politics and why he supports universal solutions to the collective problems in the United States. Second, envisioning high tides helps us understand why Obama makes the middle class, as opposed to the poor or the working class, the protagonist of his political reform story.

The axiom that a high tide lifts all boats not only applies to external restraints that limit the individual's freedom; it applies to internal restraints, even subconscious ones, as well. Freedom means liberating individuals from their so-called demons. But, unlike Rousseau and other communitarian thinkers, Spinoza does not accept "second-guessing": experts do not assess and determine what constrains an individual and then diagnose how she can avoid or overcome these constraints. It's up to each individual to understand and triumph over her own limitations. She must retain power and control over her life; she must discover her self-interest. After all, if there is no absolute truth, how could anyone but the person receiving services understand her own interest?[100]

For Spinoza and Obama, the obligation to oneself is sacrosanct. But self-obligation is not the same as autonomy because it constitutes a duty, not a right. It is not an entitlement. It contains responsibility. Spinoza makes us accountable to ourselves because only by taking this responsibility can we know how to help a collective. Obama articulates the same sentiment: "Our communal values, our sense of mutual responsibility and social solidarity, should express themselves not just in the church or the mosque or the synagogue; not just on the blocks where we live, in the places where we work, or within our own families; but also through our government."[101] By taking your obligation to yourself seriously, you will be taking your obligation to others seriously. It is the emphasis on duty buried within Spinoza's notion of self-obligation that is the key. This is where the nexus of mutual self-interest resides.[102]

To be sure, everyone has basic needs that must be met. Yet no one is as special or as distinct as we make ourselves out to be. No one has a constant and stable set of needs that can be anticipated fully by the state. Everyone's needs change. Fulfilling the needs of a collective, therefore, is like putting together a puzzle with missing pieces. It's a puzzle that cannot, and should not, ever be finished. But as more individuals participate, bringing their own pieces to the table, the puzzle picture grows.

Obligations do, however, help shape expectations, even if only the expectation that each individual will help put together the puzzle. What freeing individuals from their internal constraints and meeting their mental and physical needs involves is fulfilling these expectations. And expectations are set as much by norms and customs as by physical and material needs. In times of need or scarcity, a great leader manages expectations as much as she manages resources.

A large part of being freed from external and internal constraints is having the capacity to transform cultural norms and customs. A Spinozan state, market, and society rely on power and equality to alter existing norms and customs and change expectations. They are in flux. It is a process. Expectations should not become constant. In Spinoza's view, an ever-changing spectrum of expectations displaces the universalisms that restrict our political identities, preventing expectations from becoming assumptions. They should not be anticipated to the extent that they become entitlements; expectations must not become hardened.

Practical Problems: Discovering Self-Interest

It is difference or heterogeneity, not homogeneity, that makes Spinoza's state, market, and society unique—different people, different contexts, or contingency. And it is Spinoza's ideas about embodiment that help us imagine an equitable society. Using an opaque concept he calls "sociability," Spinoza presents a bottom-up model of political power that embraces cultural, ethnic, religious, and sexual diversity.[103]

A nation without demographic homogeneity depends on difference. Tolerance begets difference. Difference fosters the kind of freedom that furthers our self-preservation and helps us strive toward self-perfection. Spinoza accepts difference by practicing tolerance, though it is a type of tolerance that does not free people from accountability. Spinoza successfully mixes and matches the strengths of classical liberal and communitarian traditions while jettisoning their weaknesses by recognizing individual reason and passion. Spinoza's monism, in contrast to Cartesian dualism, presumes that the individual has a right to exhibit and express her reason and passion. As a result, he argues that those individuals who have different physical, emotional, and mental strengths and vulnerabilities form a collectivity, in which they depend on one another. The individuals within this collectivity seek each other out because they can best secure their needs by utilizing their power as a group. Power, not benevolence, remains central to the state and society. But this power must be wielded to promote tolerance and difference so that individuals can strive toward self-perfection.

This approach turns freedom into something that is not individualistic, but a quality of the collective. Freedom is a kind of security. This is not to say, as feminist theorist Moira Gatens points out, that the collective as a whole can be absolutely free. We're always "becoming free, and the most we can attain is a degree of freedom." Spinoza associates the state with the pursuit of freedom. "This pursuit is not about the striving for self-preservation through reason," writes the contemporary political philosopher Georg Geismann, "but even more about the striving for self-preservation *of* reason itself. Reason is not reason as imposing laws (of freedom) but reason as recognizing laws (of nature)."[104]

Accountability happens as the collectivity sets itself to rights. Bad social, economic, and political institutions and structural configurations are collectively repaired and remedied through collective understanding.

By collective understanding, Spinoza means something akin to deliberation—deliberation based not only on reason, but also on passion.[105]

Creating a nonjudgmental or tolerant state and society does not mean that no one is to blame for bad outcomes. Spinoza understands the difference between a wise person and a fool. Human beings have the capacity for reason, but they also have the capacity for passion and desire. A wise person or official follows reason; a fool is governed more by his ability to pursue desire. Despite this discrepancy, Spinoza blames neither the wise person nor the fool for following his instincts toward self-preservation. The question is how those instincts became part of the human condition.

Spinoza does not believe in "oughts." A wise person "ought" to know better, whereas a fool cannot. Having a society that does not blame its state does not mean that its members should refrain from judgment. On the contrary, Spinoza insists on understanding. He wants to understand the structures that promote the incentives that help the individual and society discover what programs are, or can be, mutually inclusive. Indeed, reforms depend on acquiring a full understanding of cultural norms. In Spinoza's view, it is economic, social, and political institutions that can produce a "bad situation" in need of correction.[106]

Performing: Passion and Power

If people were guided solely by reason, Spinoza argues, they would by nature always be in agreement. But passion also motivates people. It complicates matters as, among other things, people make enemies. To help them restrain and repress their appetites, and to provide them with greater protection and the ability to strive for perfection, the state must have authority. Giving the state this authority, however, does not unconditionally oblige the people to follow it. Nor must they abandon their rights. To be sure, Spinoza maintains that "in order . . . that men . . . live harmoniously and be of assistance to one another, it is necessary for them to give up their natural right." Citizens surrender part of their natural ability, and people pledge their willingness to try to restrain themselves, but this is not to say that their natural rights cease in a political order.[107]

Theoretically, once members of civil society seek a state's help in acquiring self-preservation and self-perfection, there are no checks on its power. The state has the right to rule however it sees fit. It can exact the death penalty for little cause. But practically, a state cannot, and will not, do this. Experience shows that a capricious state is a short-lived state, causing its own downfall. In contrast to social contract theory, the government forms when, as Gatens and Lloyd explain, institutional forms "congeal." Members of society normalize the coalescing state as they realize the utility of having state apparatuses resolve their "inevitable disagreements."[108]

Spinoza's theory of knowledge—his epistemology—is intertwined with his "physics of bodies." While moral responsibility is neither needed by the state nor attributed to its citizens, Spinoza claims, as Arendt would do later, that all social, economic, and political goods must be shared, or that they are public in nature. Spinoza is not a philosopher of right who considers natural right as tantamount to self-preservation and therefore predominant. Instead, the principle that goods are public directs the entire potential of all people. In Hobbes's view, the natural state of men is discord, which makes the state a necessity for peace and security—a necessity for reasons of right. Spinoza is much more comprehensive than Locke, Hobbes, or Rousseau. Connecting his ethical and political thinking to his metaphysics, Spinoza creates a physics of bodies, which is to say that people are determined by the laws of their specific nature, not by universal laws of human reason. They have unique and concrete needs.[109]

In Spinoza's view, while politics is about power, it is not about raw power. It is not hand-to-hand combat, but power put in context, or relational power. Eating, for example, involves destroying one body to feed another. This is not to say that Spinoza advocates the survival of the fittest. He does not mean that might makes right. Instead, Spinoza's identification of right with ability or power excludes guilt, which he goes so far as to view as an ineffective emotion that can obstruct reason. For an example of a Spinozan society and state, consider *Madagascar*, an animated movie in which the animals escape from Central Park Zoo and feel guilty about wanting to eat one another. Common notions arise when one individual encounters another with whom it is compatible. A lion does not belong with zebras who want to escape being eaten. Lions can consort with tigers, cheetahs, and jaguars, whereas zebras can live in peace with antelope, gazelles, and deer. Zebras, however, cannot play with their predators.[110]

Critical Collectives

When Spinoza spurns universal truths, deeming our judgment to be all in the eye of the beholder, he makes morality subjective. A society resolves itself around the principle that the more virtuous people are, the more power they have. People seek harmony as a means of enhancing their power. But Spinoza's moral philosophy is a theory of praxis, not a theory of obligations or duties. The word *ought* has no meaning for him; he maintains that norms motivate us and determine our actions. Utility and efficiency represent the key in evaluating and accessing these norms; questioning their moral validity is not part of the equation.[111]

What Spinoza gathers is not so much an assessment, or a justification and an assessment, as an analysis and a causal explanation. He acts more like an anthropologist than a theologian, observing, understanding, and accepting human nature. Spinoza designs maxims for actions based on empirical knowledge of human nature. Unlike either classical liberals or communitarians, Spinoza dismisses utopian ideals.[112]

Spinoza argues that people cannot escape their society, nor can they escape their embodiment. As finite, rational beings of flesh and blood, they make demands on the state for self-preservation. But unless we know what makes people tick, who they are, how they behave in accordance with their capacity for reason and passion, we cannot know how to help one another. Spinoza uses a mechanism of nature so that we can know one another and therefore help one another.[113]

Self-preservation, however, is not enough. People also seek self-perfection. Just as virtue has little to do with morality, Spinoza's notion of self-perfection has little to do with morality. Rather, self-perfection constitutes Spinoza's notion of striving. It is a "going-after," not an achievement. It's the open-endedness that counts, the journey rather than the destination.

Although he was a theologian, Spinoza would be better described as a social scientist who pursued causal analysis. Not hung up on justice or rendering judgments, Spinoza long predates Machiavelli, Tocqueville, Nietzsche, Weber, and Arendt in their powers of observation and their abstention from value judgments. They promote the power of causal analysis and logical conclusion, or cause and effect. It is not "the richness of the empirical basis" as much as the "clear awareness of its necessity" that matters. This principle was best paraphrased by E. E. Schattschneider as "who gets what, when and how."[114]

Spinoza, characterized as the first critical theorist, understood causal analysis. An optician, Spinoza understood that all visions depend on the eye of the beholder. In his view, the state and society, harboring their specific norms, must be placed in context; it's the environment that counts. Societies are not sealed; rather, they converse with one another.

Perceiving your society through the glasses of another is therefore invaluable. For instance, Americans may find female circumcision objectionable, whereas Somalians might find locking up grandparents in nursing homes far away from their grandchildren shameful.[115]

American Values, Spinozan Style

What makes Obama's interpretation of the state and society simultaneously Spinozan and distinctly American is its emphasis on individual responsibility, inclusivity, initiative, pragmatism, innovation, and tolerance. All six of these concepts that compose American political culture share one thing—their dynamism, or fluidity, or lack of constancy. American political culture involves movement, drive, and progress. It focuses on forging alliances and on moving ahead. It's a right to a process—not a right to something. This culture does not include a sense of entitlement to anything other than a procedure, a phone call.

Initiative, pragmatism, innovation, and tolerance are part of the American penchant for originality. Americans enjoy riding the cutting edge or being "top gun"; this can be seen in our technology. Yet Spinoza's notion of progress is not tantamount to truth. Americans prefer edges and tops to marches forward in Western history. While Americans favor progress, this does not mean, as Spinoza would argue, that they see progress as linear. Nor is it steeped in universalisms from the Enlightenment. Spinoza's idea of originality is at once unique *and* subjective. It is out there on the top of a cliff and yet never falls. And he insists that it is easier for two people (or the multitude) than for one to find the cliff.[116]

Two strains—the emphasis on procedure, and progress rather than universalism—run deeper in the United States than in other wealthy nations. Human rights represent an excellent example. The fact that there is always an opportunity, a chance, a belief in equality of opportunity exposes what Americans mean by universal values—that they are procedural, not substantive. The right to due process takes precedence over substantive issues such as providing everyone with food and shelter.[117]

Spinoza's notion of originality remains central to American interdependence. One innovation leads to another, and it's all about placing something in context—inventions and technology as well as political ideas. Spinoza believes in historical contingency. No one and nothing emerges in a vacuum. Spinoza's notion of originality depends on two interrelated variables: someone's behavior, and where within the collective it occurs. Where does one dwell? How does that dwelling shape one's perspective or behavior? Innovation, after all, means discovering things or ideas that we, the users, shape, thus turning them into new creations.[118]

Initiative includes an individual's drive or ambition to embark on bold new adventures. She is ready to take a journey, but an interdependent society, again, must place her journey within a context. The journey is relational. Bumping into others sends one off in different directions. Wading through a mass of bodies in New York's Penn Station alters one's straight path to the train platform.[119]

Meanwhile pragmatism counts on American ingenuity—that is, adapting what already exists into something new. It is spontaneity and contingency; it casts aside universal principles. It frees Americans from stodgy beliefs, or a constant and closed set of cultural values. People come up with practical solutions after studying the consequences of their actions. John Dewey rejected absolute truths, since all concepts are socially constructed and must be set in context with the person who framed them.[120]

Like pragmatism, tolerance rejects universalism. Practicing tolerance means recognizing and respecting other ethnicities, religions, sexualities, and cultures aside from our own, all of which can upend our own beliefs or the truths we may have held about our own identity. "At the core of American experience," writes Obama, is "a set of values that continue to stir our collective conscience; a common set of values despite our difference; a running thread of hope that makes our improbable experiment of democracy work." Tolerance indicates a willingness to recognize and respect others' differences. It's inclusive. It promotes diversity. It accepts differences. It upends things. And it is disturbing, particularly when others' beliefs, such as fundamentalism in Islam and Christianity, are antiliberal.[121]

Obama's expression of religion has not been antiliberal. When Obama denounced and then distanced himself from Rev. Jeremiah Wright in March and April 2008, commentators from the Right, not the mainstream or the Left, associated him with black liberation theology, or the belief in the divine for African Americans as the starting point for uniting the world's dispossessed, liberating them from the white demons. Obama argued that that African American anger, while justified, should be understood, and could be soothed through what religion professor Curtis Evans called the "burden of black religion."[122] This is not to say that Obama supported separatism. He never substituted white oppression for God, Jesus, or the Gospel, as editorials from the Right claimed.[123]

But Obama takes a more nuanced position. To be sure, he credited the "Black Church" with playing a pivotal role in addressing racism during the civil rights era. Black liberation theology stems from the racial turmoil of the sixties and seventies, and Obama attended Wright's church for over a decade. But according to biographer David Remnick, Obama told Wright, "I need a faith that does not put other faiths down."

Mark Kruglik, a friend of Obama's from his early days in Chicago, goes further. Obama saw Wright's Trinity Church as a "power church," or a church with a power base in the community. "You can't interpret what Obama does," Kruglik said, "without thinking of the power factor." Obama never believed in the divine for African Americans at the expense of other Americans or expressed support for Jim Cone, the founder of black liberation theology. Obama universalizes the African American experience of racism, extending it to all other Americans, in "A More Perfect Union," emulating Lincoln and King. The speech shows his faith not in integration, but in the integration of all identities.[124]

There is no denying that cultures sitting side-by-side rub off on one another. They can be infectious. For this reason, homogeneous cultures like those in France or Germany find diversity dangerous, even frightening, if they are intolerant or antiliberal. Diverse cultures influence mainstream culture, and, conversely, mainstream culture influences diverse cultures. The impact one culture will have on another cannot be anticipated, let alone contained, confined, or repressed.[125]

Obama, by contrast, equates universality of oppression with infectiousness. Experience, good or bad (racism or liberation), can be transferred from one group to another—whether it be race or religion.

Power within the equality necessary for interdependence is a prerequisite for promoting American freedom. It's not the balance between freedom and equality of opportunity that matters; it's the power. Democratic progressives emphasize the power of the American people. They return the United States to its radical roots. The same nation that made the rule of law sacrosanct, after all, gave juries—not elected representatives, judges, or bureaucratic experts—the power to deliberate and decide their peers' fate.

But to rekindle this radicalism, Obama returns the United States to the precapitalist frame of mind that gave birth to its eighteenth-century ideals of popular sovereignty. The people, not the market, should offer the state its legitimacy and authority. Only *through* the state can the people have equality and find freedom.[126]

The Necessity of Inclusivity: Civic Action and Public Work

The people, however, cannot be viewed as part of a mass or "mass politics." Obama takes a *narrative* view of a human being. Each and every person has her own story, and by recognizing the difference, the subjectivity, the individuality of each individual's story, Obama dismisses the positivism underlying most theories of politics that regard people as standard units that make up a mass, or undifferentiated parts of a community. As an organizer in Chicago, Obama called the narratives he collected his "sacred stories." "I learned that everyone's got a sacred story," he said, "when you take the time to listen."[127]

In Obama's view, governing, like organizing, involves bringing people together to tell their stories. Those stories help us deliberate, because in telling our stories and listening to those of others, we discover that we face similar challenges and can find common goods.

A consistent theme of Obama's value and belief structure is the significance he places on listening and relaying shared experiences. As we will note in chapter 3, Obama nominates federal judges on the basis of diversity. What their diversity brings is not the essence of their identity, but rather their empathy, an understanding of what it is like to struggle in the United States. It is not their identity, but rather their experience, that he seeks.

As we will see in chapters 3, 4, and 5, Obama governs like an organizer, turning institutions into communities. In his view, the state facilitates and mediates dynamic interactions. The organizing world refers to these interactions as "one-on-ones." And indeed, Obama creates these "one-on-ones" wherever he can—in permanent institutions like the federal judiciary or in temporary ones that seek change and reform, such as G8 summits, town hall meetings, or conciliatory meetings with Democrats and Republicans alike about health care, financial regulation, or climate control.[128]

3

Thinking in Threes: Diversity, Destruction, Redemption, and Social Policy Ruptures

Like John Dewey and other twentieth-century democratic progressives, Barack Obama emphasizes cooperation, not conflict, though his is a cooperation born of competition incited by inclusivity, diversity, and difference. Obama relies on inquiry, but he calls this process "reconciliation," invoking the "truth and reconciliation" peace process established in South Africa. Reconciliation is not a "compromise." Instead, it involves reestablishing ties or working out differences while staying mindful of discrepancies in *power*, and then arriving at a conclusion based on commonalities that all parties can accept after hearing painful truths.

"Each member of the household should do his own part faithfully," Dewey wrote of family life, "in cooperation with others." Dewey believed, in contemporary Harry Boyte's deliberative democratic words, that "everyday productive work taught habits of cooperation, responsibility, productive outlook. It also meant a deep connection with the world." The progressives understood cooperation to be an integral part of interdependence. They recognized that each person's strengths and weaknesses differed, making cooperation like piecing together a never-ending puzzle. It involved a process of finding where people fit in together to make a whole, all the while knowing that the whole is based on different, distinct, and yet unequally shaped parts.[1]

The creative aspect of reconciliation stems from Obama's emphasis on difference and the inherent value of inclusivity and diversity, or the "value-added" concept of difference. Diverse peoples, holding different basic assumptions, harboring different beliefs and values, cooperate and compete, producing an open but stimulating environment, or a never-ending process of inquiry that creates ever-evolving public policies based on perpetually changing norms. Sound dizzying?

Obama's first public attempt at underscoring the common ground between Republicans and Democrats was not a "we are all Americans" speech made by a victor in hopes of appeasing the vanquished. Rather, it was a "points of commonality" or "shared values" speech. In his 2004 address to the Democratic National Convention, Obama said, "The pundits like to slice-and-dice our country into Red States and Blue States. . . . But I've got news for them. . . . We worship an awesome God in the Blue States, and we don't like federal agents poking around in our libraries in the Red States." Here Obama does not proclaim that his party's ideology is *the* American ideology, nor does he pander to the bipartisan public. Unlike most politicians who give speeches about unity and bipartisanship while practicing partisan politics, he seeks to discover, and then *do*, what we have in common.[2]

Obama's notion of unity is not only procedural (a means to an end), but also substantive (an end in itself). Obama looks for the mutually inclusive interests of each side, just as Baruch Spinoza, the first critical theorist, did, as described in the previous chapter. In part this is because Obama does not value fixed principles over action. He is multidimensional, offering a kaleidoscope of principles and presenting a spectrum and array of actions. Obama's position on abortion illustrates this. "When we open up our hearts and our minds to those who may not think precisely like we do or believe precisely what we believe—that's when we discover at least the possibility of *common ground*. . . . So let us work together to reduce the number of women seeking abortions, let's reduce *unintended pregnancies*. Let's make adoption more available. Let's provide care and support for women who do carry their children to term." In Obama's view, all forms of action, not simply abortion, should be explored, initiated, and facilitated by the American state.[3]

In seeking common ground, Obama fully pleases neither pro-choice nor pro-life advocates. He focuses on how unintended pregnancies affect both women and children, albeit in a multitude of different intersecting, interconnecting, and interdependent ways. Not all women are the same. Not all teen girls are the same. Not all children are the same. Not all pregnancies are the same. Obama focuses on how unintended pregnancies can be avoided. Their being unintended (not just unplanned) makes this issue multidimensional and complicated *and* creates the most fertile common ground. Provisions in the Affordable Care Act, executive action in implementing the No Child Left Behind Act, the actions of the White House Office of Faith-Based and Neighborhood Partnerships, regulations from the Department of Health and Human Services, and enforcement of civil rights on the basis of gender and sexuality, this chapter shows, have put the GOP, particularly its Christian coalition, on the defensive about the "war on women" that Obama claims the party instigated. And with both Obama and the GOP trying to gain ground, a historic battle over the separation of powers has occurred. The president and the Supreme Court are redefining the public and private spheres, particularly the role religion plays in the United States.[4]

Reproductive Rights and Redemption

Obama's position in this battle showcases his views about power, inclusivity, individuality, and difference. He does not equate unintended pregnancies with "accidents." He holds the sanctity of life dear. And the war on women must be opposed so as to ensure the best action for women and children. Obama fights for balancing their right to survival and their right to aspire toward perfectibility. He creates a state that mediates zero-sum conflicts.

Further, the common ground underlying the prevention of unintended pregnancies can be equated with Spinoza's belief in sociability. That is, Obama does not just turn reproductive rights into a reactive reelection issue that defines what American morality is. He challenges the Republicans' attempts to locate reproductive rights in the private sphere. Obama believes these rights should be housed in an all-encompassing social sphere. In other words, Obama "domesticizes" abortion on a local, regional, state, national, and international scale, turning it into a critical voting issue for the Democrats, though not without issuing ample private and public warnings to all parties who want to deprive women of their reproductive rights.

The president reassured all the key players upon first taking office— faith-based organizations, religious groups, identity groups, and members of the scientific and medical communities as well as groups promoting a pro-growth economy—that he will fight for the separation of church and state. Obama believes in civic religion. He practices tolerance. And he supports secularism. He does not believe that the United States is solely a Christian nation.

Obama is redemptive himself, in that he learns from his mistakes, not just his successes. In social, domestic, and foreign policy, as this book shows, he has no problem wielding the power, authority, and control associated with the White House. Where does the president's belief in redemption and righteousness stem from? Good governance must rest not on benevolence, nor on any inherent goodness in humankind, but rather on the collective power of all Americans striving for survivability *and* perfectibility. American citizens have rights and obligation to themselves, or what Spinoza calls self-obligations. They must retain the freedom to preserve themselves in body and in mind, as well as the right to aspire toward the American dream, though it remains elusive. A state, a society, and a market must be built on people's understanding of their interdependence, or the idea that they are riding on a wagon train, rather than riding alone as cowboys, or traveling with the help of a nanny, in the form of a strong social welfare state.

This chapter describes Obama's reaction to this purported failure to protect women and children from *un*intended pregnancies when they have abortions that could have been avoided. He hopes to make unplanned—or what he calls unintended—pregnancies preventable or avoidable. By so doing, Obama turns reproductive rights from a so-called moral issue into a civil rights/civil liberties/state sovereignty/religious/economic/foreign policy issue that is polarizing at home and abroad. It reflects the president's attempt to redefine the role of religion, particularly Christianity, in the United States. Just as the American state and society have become increasingly secular, and the global community has become more divided about the separation of church and state in response to the rise of religion in the late twentieth century, Obama is making the United States less exceptional by promoting a cosmopolitan conception of civic religion.

A New Culture War? Secularism vs. Fundamentalism

By turning reproductive rights into a litmus test in a battle over freedom of religion and the powers of the executive branch—all decided by the judicial branch (namely, the Supreme Court)—Obama faces a separation-of-powers conflict that could be pivotal for the Democratic Party. Obama has turned a long-standing zero-sum conflict about morals—abortion—into a broad, potentially coalition-building one, giving the Democrats the chance to take the offensive, instigating a new set of "culture wars." Unlike the culture wars of the 1980s and 1990s, this set could help Democrats rather than Republicans. It could behoove Obama Democrats to defend women and children from the "war on women." It is the president's public policies—social, domestic, and foreign—that support vulnerable peoples as they defend women, their offspring, and all the vulnerable under their care, including young adults who immigrated to the United States without documents as children. Obama extended amnesty by executive order to 800,000 of these young people.[5]

This book argues that Obama has taken the offensive by carving out a unique position against neotribalism. When comparing various types of fundamentalism—Christian, Islamic, and Judaic—most people focus on the differences among them. To be sure, honor killings are not the same as denying women their reproductive rights. Yet while these differences in kind are stark, this book appropriates the term *neotribalism* as a means of concentrating on the primary assumption that religious fundamentalisms share: patriarchal rule performed in a re-enlarged private sphere. "Why extremists always focus on women remains a mystery to me," said Secretary of State Hillary Clinton. "But they all seem to. It doesn't matter what country they're in or what religion they claim. They want to control women."[6]

Getting the public sphere to limit a woman's autonomy regarding her reproductive capacity or killing her for sullying the family's name are both the results of neotribalism. There is a "trifecta of sex, death, and religion," as Mona Eltahawy writes in "Why Do They Hate Us? The Real War on Women Is in the Middle East." The extended family—the tribe—reestablishes the primacy of the patriarch. After all, the nuclear or extended family is governed by one of the three dominant world faiths or religions, all of which have fundamentalist branches that are premised on patriarchy. In the United States, religious organizations, primarily Christian ones such as conservative Catholic dioceses and evangelical churches, declared the war on women, hoping to push reproductive health back into the private domain. The lawsuits they instigated against the Obama administration, according to *Washington Post* columnist E. J. Dionne, do not reflect the views of the majority of either Catholics or Protestants, provoking him to call for a "Catholic Spring."[7]

Making reproductive health, including abortion, *private* puts women and their offspring, or their future offspring, in a position like the two mothers King Solomon was called on to mediate between. Whether the religion challenging their right to public protection is Islamic, Judaic, or Christian does not matter. By accepting an expanded definition of religious freedom under the conservatives' interpretation of the Religious

Freedom Restoration Act (RFRA) of 1993, the United States would be promoting patriarchal rule. If a Catholic hospital heals the poor and refuses to give contraception to women or perform abortions with federal government funding, a central tenet of this religious belief—patriarchal rule—has become public. If a parochial school fires a woman teacher who teaches not religion, but all subjects, to her students and yet has no protection for having a debilitating disability, then the federal government has sanctioned a discriminatory workplace on the basis of religion. All this undermines the United States' long-established public policy of gender *neutrality* that exists in all fifty states as well as the laws of the nation-state. Put simply, if Obama does not battle against these religious organizations' imposing their private beliefs on the larger Christian and non-Christian populations who rely on their services, given the dearth of public ones, the United States has reasserted the patriarchal rule that ended in the 1980s.[8]

Why call this tribal? It is tribal because the resurgence of religion in the 1970s and 1980s and the subsequent culture wars were transnational. Three main religions—Christianity, Islam, and Judaism, with all their fundamentalist offshoots and branches—have been trying to get governments to re-privilege the private sphere on regional bases. Some regions within the Middle East and North America, to name a few, do not respect state sovereignty. As the domain of the private sphere expanded, religion placed women, children, and the vulnerable in more jeopardy of repression and violence. Some states in the United States—and some nation-states across Europe, the Middle East, Asia, and Africa—have tolerated violence against women and children, or, worse, given impunity to those who commit it.

While nation-states in the Middle East, Africa, and Asia tolerated murder in the form of honor killings and bride burnings, Christian fundamentalists and Catholics in the United States tried to reverse the rights of women and children. Meanwhile progressives, including feminists in the United States and Europe, opted out of, or lost ground in, the private-public debate by relying on multiculturalism. "Resist cultural relativism and know that even in countries undergoing revolutions and uprisings, women will remain the cheapest bargaining chips," writes Eltahawy. "You—the outside world—will be told that it's our 'culture' and 'religion' to do X, Y, or Z to women. Understand that whoever deemed it as such was never a woman." Obama, being cosmopolitan and a proponent of civic religion, does not support multiculturalism to the extent that it limits the rights of women and children to the private sphere.

Rather, Obama facilitates state action that promotes what Spinoza calls human sociability.[9]

Obama's public policies composed what this book calls a meditator state. Whether this mediator state supports civil rights in terms of the sexuality of gays, lesbians, and transgendered people, as described in this chapter, or reproductive rights under the Affordable Care Act, as described in chapter 4, it limits the scope of the private and public domains and instead builds a larger social sphere. This social sphere can provide safety for women and children. It does not allow a Christian priest, an Islamic mullah, or a Jewish rabbi to deprive them of their dignity, rights, or autonomy. Obama reasserts a separation of church and state. He does not allow religion to encroach on the public sphere by herding women, children, and those who do not reflect the "normate" back into a private domain controlled by their husbands, their fathers, and their brothers. To put it positively, Obama expands the social sphere as a means of curbing patriarchal rule.[10]

Having reproductive rights as a trigger point—or acting in reaction to the GOP in Congress and the conservative Supreme Court—gives Obama the capacity to test the limits of the American public's interest in practicing tolerance, promoting inclusivity, and facilitating freedom rather than concentrating on divisive red/blue state policies. It was religious organizations like the Catholic Church and evangelical churches that brought their issues before the American judiciary, making the Roberts court step up and protect religious freedom.[11]

Obama supported the twin principles of "faith and work" when he worked as a community organizer. Nonetheless, he may be the first president to contain the role that Christianity plays in this increasingly secular nation by arguing that religion be restricted to "a matter of belief." To be sure, belief can be practiced in private. But by relegating it to the private sphere of each individual, rather than a family, an extended family, a hospital, or a school, Obama ensures that fathers and father figures cannot restrict their wives, daughters, or sons from asserting their autonomy and achieving their full capacity.[12]

Know Thyself

A second theme in this chapter, following Obama's stand against neo-tribalism, is his belief that self-interest is transformative. By exploring all forms of action, people gain different perspectives that could alter their thinking. If one person explains how an interaction benefits the other person, that person may indeed support it. Obama tries to demonstrate that people "need" physical, mental, or emotional sustenance, such as a fetus needing the shelter of a womb, a child needing physical shelter, or a parent needing health care. Obama's emphasis on needs is different from opportunism, in which one exploits circumstances, ignoring one's own ethical constructs. It reflects Obama's belief in pragmatism instead. In the absence of fixed truth, it is all about the process or inquiry. Obama believes the state and society must help people help themselves. His is a cosmopolitan civic religion, a type of redemption that emphasizes personal responsibility and accountability, similar to St. Augustine's idea that it is "the very perfection of a man, to find out his own imperfections."

Pragmatism advances the idea that truth and knowledge are social constructions. Dewey perceives values as encapsulating or articulating an attempt to find common ground. For Dewey and Obama, the creation of common beliefs, values, and assumptions (an active process) is essential to political progress. Affirming shared understandings helps us address problems that have become entrenched in partisanship.

According to Dewey and Obama, "values" are faithfully applied to the facts before us, while ideology overrides whatever facts call theory into question. In his speech accepting the presidential nomination in 2008, Obama explained, "I know there are differences on same-sex marriage, but surely we can agree that our gay and lesbian brothers and sisters deserve to visit the person they love in the hospital and to live lives free of discrimination." Obama's values embody faith, tolerance, and inclusion, not faith and Christian values based on intolerance and exclusion.[13]

In 2009 Obama struck the same inquiry and shared values chords in his inaugural address. He did not see the individual as separate or apart from the community, but as a product of it. In Dewey's view, the social world made the individual viable. Obama argues that finding common ground is the only way to move forward—and that common progress is the best measure of individual progress. Just as Dewey is criticized for his naïve perspective, Obama is criticized for his search for "what works, what is valued, and what brings the good." But unlike Dewey, Obama cannot be accused of being innocent or naïve, given his emphasis on the Hebraic Bible and Augustine and his belief in hell on earth.[14]

Social Technologies and More Voices in an Extended and Enlarged Agora/Oikos

A third and final theme in this chapter is how Obama builds Arendt's and Baudrillard's contemporary political theory and social theory critiques of consumerism into deliberative democracy. While Obama relies on pragmatism, he is building on Arendt's notion that the *agora*, or marketplace, has spilled over, running into every aspect of life, including the *oikos*, or household. By pushing it back through a consumer conception of contingency and political agency, Obama regulates the *agora/oikos*, creating more avenues for the individual to deliberate within democracy. Obama's state facilitates public policies, like health-care reform and financial regulation, that promote the well-being of its citizens, whether they are in the public, the private, or the social sphere, by involving them—in this case, by making them healthy or financially literate.

Obama's state is neither a nanny state, with experts telling its citizens what to do, nor a night-watchman state that waits until one side impinges on the other before acting. It incorporates Spinozan sociability in a global understanding of good governance: the state, the market, and the society facilitate not private or public action, but social action.

The combination of his middle-class focus with domestic policies that are redistributive—like his health-care reform, financial regulatory reform, and stimulus package—has created a myriad of misunderstandings about Obama. During the campaign, journalists and pundits described Obama as a neoliberal, a market centrist, a market liberal, and even a University of Chicago Democrat, while others called him a grassroots radical. Still other political commentators claim that his support for Reaganomics, however partial, reveals nothing deeper than a "postpartisan veneer."[15] This book has shown that Obama has been misunderstood, in part, because he subscribes to a complex, dynamic Spinozan perspective on the state, society, and the individual that defies Left/Right or state/individual categorization. Obama is not conservative, liberal, or radical.[16]

Obama is a progressive, a middle-class reformer who rejects a static conception of normalcy, and by so doing collapses the distinct private and public spheres into a social sphere. He is not a bourgeois reformer, but a reformer who accepts difference. Unlike that of many nineteenth- and twentieth-century progressives, Obama's progressivism does not fault the *demos*, as did many state-oriented progressive reformers who relied on the expert elite. He condemns trickle-down economic policy and tax cuts for the wealthy, but he does not condemn wealthy people, instead inverting a traditional formulation: "When that dream of opportunity is denied to too many Americans, then ultimately that pain has a way of trickling up."[17]

Obama embraces not the exploiters, nor the most exploited, but those in the middle, in what he calls the "middle-class squeeze." Obama is that

rare progressive who objectifies who and what has squeezed the middle
class, then strives toward making them take responsibility through consumer reform. Working within the American value structure, Obama
describes progressivism in terms of redistributive reform for the middle
class: "A strong middle class can only exist in an economy where everyone plays by the same rules, from Wall Street to Main Street." Redistribution of wealth is generally viewed as a radical policy, yet Obama
describes his reform as repairing rather than tearing down the establishment. He characterizes redistributive reform as restoring freedom, since
it gives individuals more power and choice—for example, it gives them
full information about credit products. Here, as in so many other areas,
Obama supports self-reliance and mutual reliance.[18]

Middle-Class Aspirations for All

Reform of capitalism through consumerism is a type of reform that benefits the solid middle class, with its belief in individual responsibility and
hard work, alongside business accepting its responsibilities and engaging
in fair practices. Like the progressive reformer Teddy Roosevelt, Obama
humanizes capitalism. Putting faces on his reforms, Obama initially
described the beneficiaries of his policies as the average Joe and Jane with
two average children, not specifying their ethnicity or race. And capital-
izing on the "war on women," the White House went so far as to create
a computer-generated composite of a female, named Julia, who gives her
perspective on how the Obama administration has benefited her across
her life span, from three to sixty-seven years old. Mocked by many, it
nonetheless revealed how Obama tags his own administration's achievements. Obama showcased how his policies help females from cradle to
grave, as well as their offspring. He denies class by putting everyone
either into the middle class or among those aspiring to join it, without condemning capitalism per se. And, as will be shown further in this
chapter, he expands our notion of family, defining it by virtue of reproductive capacity or sexuality, not sex or gender.[19]

    Obama realizes that the American middle class, being ubiquitous,
does not perceive itself as a class. In a society in which the working
class, the working poor, the upper middle class, and even the wealthy
all consider themselves part of the middle class, Obama showed keen
understanding by promising tax relief for working and middle-class
families at his first White House press conference. In terms of both reforms and rhetoric, Obama tapped into a strong sentiment that, as sociologist Kevin Leicht has said, the middle class "is in crisis and decline."

"Between wages that have been stagnant since the middle of the 1970s and government policies that are weighted exclusively in the direction of the wealthy," Leicht explains, "the only thing that has been holding up most of the American middle class is access to cheap and easy credit." To explore this issue, Obama had Vice President Joseph Biden's White House Task Force on Middle Class Families examine "everything from access to college and child- and elder-care issues to business development and the role of labor unions in the economy."[20]

Obama's emphasis on the middle class, however, is more aspirational than redistributionist. This is the class that all Americans aspire to be part of; specifically, it represents the goal of his greatest constituency—the youth. Prospects for graduates have been declining for a decade, and Obama's "greatest challenge," journalist Joel Kotkin writes, "will be to change this trajectory for Americans under 30, who supported him by two to one."[21]

To Obama, the middle class is more than an income range: it also represents a set of values associated with American democracy. According to historian Jennifer Goloboy, the term "middle class" was not used in the United States until the 1830s or 1840s. What the term described at that time was a social and economic class that was diligent, frugal, self-restrained, and optimistic. A century earlier, Benjamin Franklin's *Poor Richard's Almanac* adages regarding thrift and sobriety had captured the essence of this class.[22]

The emergence of the middle class explains the success of the American democratic experiment. As sociologist Teresa Sullivan says, "A large middle class, especially one that is politically active, tends to be a kind of anchor that keeps your country from swinging back and forth." Long viewed as promoting political, economic, and social stability, middle-class values "tend to be very good for democracy." "In America the middle class has been a lifestyle, a certain way of life," writes Demos senior fellow Jennifer Wheary.[23]

Obama's middle-class progressivism not only supports American democracy, but also, because it has come into play during a global economic crisis, makes growth its primary means of economic reform. "Talking about the middle class is the closest that American politicians and maybe Americans are willing to go to emphasize the fact that we have growing inequality in this country," states political scientist Jacob Hacker. Relaying the statistics himself, Obama said: "For the top one hundredth of one percent, the average income is now $27 million per year. The typical CEO who used to earn about 30 times more than his or her workers now earns 110 times more." A Pew Research Center study suggests that "fewer Americans now than at any time in the past half-century believe" they are part of the middle class. And "if the trend of rising inequality continues," Obama argued, "it's estimated that a child born today will only have a 1 in 3 chance of making it to the middle class." "When middle-class families can no longer afford to buy the goods and services that businesses are selling," Obama said, featuring his global growth agenda, "it drags down the entire economy, from top to bottom."[24]

First Lady Michelle Obama gives this perspective more of a personal narrative. "I am always amazed at how different things are now. . . . When I was growing up, my father—as you know, a blue-collar worker—was able to go to work and earn enough money to support a family of four, while my mom stayed home with me and my brother. But today . . . people can't do it—particularly if it's a shift-worker's salary like my father's." Elaborating his wife's point, Obama said, "Long before the recession hit, hard work stopped paying off for too many people. Fewer and fewer of the folks who contributed to the success of our economy actually benefited from that success."[25]

Elizabeth Warren: Obama's People's Lawyer?

Following law professor Elizabeth Warren's logic about the crisis of the middle class, Obama believes the economy should grow to expand the class's size. Obama gave Warren more voice in portraying the problem than he gave to any other public intellectual or policymaker other than his White House economic team. Warren characterized the scope and nature of the crisis along with her daughter, Amelia Warren Tyagi: "For quite some time, we've had a sizable minority of the middle class under enormous strain and on the verge of crisis." The problem, however, is not excessive consumerism, as some conservatives argue: "Middle-class families are [not] rushing headlong into financial ruin because they are squandering too much money on Red Lobster, Gucci and trips to the Bahamas." This impression, Warren and Tyagi demonstrated, is a "rock-solid" myth.[26]

Clearly persuaded by their argument, given his own emphasis on the aspirational aspect of the middle class and his emphasis on redistribution during the 2008 campaign, Obama gave Warren the chance to tackle this class crisis with legislation. Warren chaired a congressional panel overseeing the $787 billion financial bailout of 2009. When it came to financial reform, Warren, having authored the pivotal piece "Unsafe at Any Rate" in 2007, showed that as consumers, Americans needed protection from the excesses of capitalism, and that as citizens, they should be safeguarded from proprietary global capitalism, including political corruption practiced in other nations.[27]

Warren's consumer reform does not fault the principles underlying capitalism. Instead, it uses regulation to ensure that they remain true. Warren and Obama believe that citizens' primary problem is the lack of information that they need to make decisions. As will be reviewed in the following chapter, the Dodd-Frank Wall Street Reform and Consumer Protection Act established a new agency, the Consumer Financial Protection Bureau (CFPB). And on September 17, 2010, Warren became the first person proposed to head this new federal agency that embodied Arendt's notion of the *agora*, though she failed to be confirmed.[28]

The Bureau (without a Hoover)

In the face of conservative opposition to Warren, Obama passed her over and appointed her right-hand man, Richard Cordray, to head the CFPB. Although he did not address her opponents' outrage, Obama showed his support by turning the appointment into a demonstration of how he stood for consumers, or white, middle-class suburban moms like Warren, who work hard at balancing their checkbooks in these austere times: "Building on efforts to cast himself as a protector of the middle class, the President portrayed Mr. Cordray as his hand-picked protector of consumers."[29]

Known for his confrontational style, Cordray had already called attention to the mortgage abuses of a Countrywide Financial lender "by covering his front lawn with small plastic 'loan' sharks." The CFPB announced its plans to revamp mortgage disclosure forms, which had long confused prospective home buyers, soon after Warren officially left office. But the bureau, more bark than bite, announced it would look for other financial-form "tricks" and would scrutinize credit card forms, ensuring that big banks cannot rely on teams of behavioral psychologists to intentionally design misleading documents.

Yet to progressives of all stripes, the bureau was a disappointment. Poised to "pick its battles," the bureau was vulnerable to both GOP and progressive Democratic attack. Conservatives, by definition, oppose the bureau's pro-growth agenda, whereas two camps within the progressives battle about it. Progressive critics Robert Reich, Paul Krugman, and Joseph Stiglitz condemn Obama for supporting the pro–Wall Street speculation economic policies of Robert Rubin, Lawrence Summers, and Timothy Geithner, which they claim do not achieve growth.

How then can the bureau protect the public, as Warren, Cordray, and Obama promised with their pledge to provide all-encompassing middle-class consumer relief? Reich, Krugman, and Stiglitz are all outsider critics, whereas Summers and Geithner are not. Geithner is unlikely to remain Obama's secretary of the Treasury for a second term. He was resistant to the bureau since its institutional inception, since he and Warren were at opposite ends of the ideological spectrum. What makes all of this "deliberative" is that the federal regulatory process, with its notice-and-comment period, opens the enforcement process up to public-interest groups and consumer advocacy groups, along with competing business groups. But this is not to say that Obama supports middle-class consumerism at the business community's expense. Instead, he supports negotiated rulemaking that involves nudges balancing consumer interests with those of business. Unlike the Great Society, Obama's reforms emphasize settlements over lawsuits, and unlike the New Deal, they stress the adoption of voluntary measures over increasing quasi-judicial scrutiny.

The Obama administration also deputized individuals who work in the financial sector by creating a whistleblower provision. At the same time, it gave consumers access to start blowing whistles outside the industry. Within months of the Consumer Protection Act's enactment, hundreds of consumers had lodged complaints with the bureau, mostly about mortgages.[30]

The Consumer Protection Act required nearly four hundred regulations to be issued. "The federal rulemaking process is arguably as important to regulated companies as the initial legislative process that led to the Act itself," wrote one journalist. A regulation is deemed "economically significant" if it will cost over $100 million in any one calendar year. All regulations exceeding this threshold are sent to a behavioral social scientist and law professor from the University of Chicago: Cass Sunstein, who heads the Office of Information and Regulatory Affairs (OIRA). The 100 million bucks stop there, before the federal government—or the bureau—can submit the "regulatory rule" to the *Federal Register*. If the financial industry objects to a regulation, it, like all regulated industries, can either demand an administrative appeals tribunal or ask the federal judiciary to hear how the federal government's actions will supposedly harm the economy.[31]

The Obama administration opens the regulatory process to individual citizens more than ever before. It also gives state and local officials—as well as public-interest, industry, and consumer advocacy groups—access to that process. They can pursue complaints and help design regulations—or help determine the "rules" to dictate the direction of "future" complaints. While the perils of quasi-judicial-agency politics and public policymaking are well known and have been summed up in two words—capture theory—the Obama administration has created a new bottom-up role for individual activists and consumer advocates and for those who reside in the communities most affected by regulations. There is even a local role, as will be shown in chapter 4, so the states are very much part of this regulatory decision-making process. In the worst case, they can go public with their complaints.[32]

A Greek Oikos/Agora for Consumer/Citizens

Obama's consumer protection program also manifested Arendt's conception of the *agora* in the sense that he did not confine his redistributionist ideas to financial regulation, stimulus packages, and budgets. Rather, he wove them into all his domestic policies, particularly the Affordable Care Act. The central theme of these policies is regulation and management, not alleviation, of the excesses of the domestic and global marketplace. It is consumerism, or a consumer movement, that believes that individuals—acting as a collective—accept their rights and responsibilities, but the basic principle that individuals and enterprises drive the marketplace remains. There is no surplus value. The system is not premised on exploitation. The market works—as long as individual consumers receive full information about the products they purchase. It corrects what makes capitalism vulnerable to corruption: the tendency of business to withhold full information from individual consumer/citizens.

The consumer-oriented, correcting-the-market theme was first promoted during President-elect Obama's transition. Just two days after his election, Obama and Rahm Emanuel, whom he later appointed as his chief of staff, started working with Democratic congressional leaders on a stimulus package to ensure that it included "more jobless benefits, food stamps, aid to financially strapped states and cities, and spending for infrastructure projects that keep people at work."[33]

Once in office, he expected that Biden's task force would provide more evidence of the middle-class crisis. Speaking about the task force, Jared Bernstein, Biden's chief economist, said the group had "a different target" than the recently enacted $787 billion economic stimulus plan. "Its goal is to make sure that once the economy begins to expand again, middle-class families will reap their fair share of the growth, something

that hasn't happened in recent years." But Obama generated little reform that has had great effect on the economy before 2010, and arguably 2012.[34]

More George than June: A Diverse Middle Class

But what most separates Obama from all the presidents who preceded
him is not his emphasis on middle-class consumerism as economic reform, despite Jesse Jackson calling out Newt Gingrich's racial slur when
he called Obama the "food stamp President."[35] Rather, it is the fact that
when he discusses the middle class, one should not assume it is embodied
by a couple who are white, heterosexual, and Christian with two children and who reside in the segregated suburbs. To Obama it is as much
about Bill Cosby playing Heathcliff in the Huxtable family, and George
in the Lopez family, as it is about June Cleaver in the *Leave It to Beaver*
television family.

While restoring the middle class is the centerpiece of Obama's policy
platform, his policies also change the face of this class. He opens it to all
races, ethnicities, and sexual orientations. There is "no doubt" that, as
Obama describes, he sees friends, families, and children of gay couples
"thriving." On Father's Day in 2011, Obama announced that families
headed by same-sex partners could rear their children well. "Nurturing
families come in many forms, and children may be raised by a father and
mother, a single father, two fathers, a stepfather, a grandfather or car-
ing guardian."[36]

Obama instructed his administration to reinterpret the Family Medical Leave Act (FMLA) so that same-sex partners would have the same
rights as opposite-sex partners. They should have the same (read equal)
right to take care of their nuclear families, giving care "to their partner's
children." Caregiving takes precedence over, or should be considered
tantamount to, biology, ensuring that same-sex couples "bond" with
their children.[37] Obama also supports equal adoption rights for members of the lesbian, gay, bisexual, and transsexual (LGBT) community
and has urged states to treat same-sex couples with "full equality *in* their
family and [*under*] adoption laws."[38]

Finally, Obama supports the Uniting American Families Act (UAFA).
This little-known and little-publicized legislation offers same-sex *binational* couples the same "rights and obligations as married couples in our
immigration system." According to the 2000 census, 36,000 binational
same-sex couples reside in the United States.[39]

In an even more controversial move, the Obama State Department started issuing passports to transgendered people. Little news appeared about this other than "negative" news: an editorial in the conservative *Washington Times* condemned Obama's notions of diversity and inclusivity, saying that his "administration has ramped up programs intended to reshape conceptions of the family. When it comes to moral values, it is clear that radical leftists are driving the agenda."[40]

Obama downplays the race, sexuality, or ethnicity of anyone in the middle class, or any other class. He rejects identity politics on philosophical grounds, as discussed in the previous chapter, and sees middle-class values as a component of the positive quality of difference. Obama does not describe the lack of opportunities for the poor or working class in terms of groups or group identities. "This time we want to talk about how the lines in the Emergency Room are filled with whites and blacks and Hispanics who do not have health care; who don't have the power on their own to overcome the special interests in Washington, but who can take them on if we do it together."[41]

Well aware of the correlations between poverty, gender, and race as well as the correlations between voting, poverty, education, and race, Obama nonetheless dwells little on them. "We want to talk about the men and women of every color and creed who serve together, and fight together, and bleed together," Obama proclaims, "under the same proud flag." Obama criticizes tax policy as unfair, health-care policy as unfair, and the lack of higher-education opportunities as unfair, but exactly who causes the unfairness remains nameless and faceless.[42]

In Obama's view, all Americans must strive "to realize that your dreams do not have to come at the expense of my dreams; that investing in the health, welfare, and education of black and brown and white children will ultimately help all of America prosper." But he does not name names. Obama does not speculate as to who, or what groups or identity groups, within the United States can be considered accountable for causing the middle class to shrink. He insists that the middle class is us—all of us. Obama therefore maintains the idea that the American dream remains within everyone's grasp, though he recognizes that it is elusive, and that fewer and fewer people will be likely to have this dream materialized. The middle class—the very fabric of American democracy—is shrinking, and he argues that this affects all, not just those groups of people who can be classified in terms of identity politics. He does not underscore who remains responsible for locking anyone out of the middle class. And yet Obama knows that this class is still predominately white or mainline

Protestant (meaning those northern and midwestern churches dominant from the colonial era until the early 1900s) and suburban.[43]

For reasons both philosophical and political, then, Obama creates an impersonal type of progressivism with no villain and no establishment. There is no class conflict, no masses versus the elite, no "us versus them," no brown and black versus white. Instead, Obama describes a culture and the behavior of individuals within it, identifying "the real culprits of the middle-class squeeze" as "a corporate culture rife with inside dealing, questionable accounting practices, and short-term greed; a Washington dominated by lobbyists and special interests; economic policies that favor the few over the many." He universalizes the middle class, placing great significance on different races within it and, by accepting diversity of all kinds, tries not to ignite the fears of what some astute critics call the "normate."[44]

Jumping the Gun—Transitions

Obama anticipated making the most basic departures when he began to govern as the head of the executive branch. "A team of four dozen advisers, working for months in virtual solitude, set out to identify regulatory and policy changes Obama could implement soon after his inauguration." Relying mainly on lawyers, Obama's preelection team came up with a list of approximately 200 regulatory actions and executive orders that he would rescind the moment he stepped into office. The incoming president planned "to move fast on high-priority items without waiting for Congress."[45]

Even more exceptional was that on October 20, 2008, in anticipation of governing the executive branch, Obama spoke directly to federal employees at seven agencies. He outlined precisely how his practices would differ from those of George W. Bush. Obama tailored "his message to a federal audience" by "tapping into many workers' dismay at funding cuts and workforce downsizing in the Bush years."[46]

And indeed, during his first week in office, Obama took the first steps toward closing the detainee camp at Guantanamo Bay, Cuba, and banned questionable methods of interrogating suspected terrorists. He issued an executive order permitting states to impose more stringent automobile emissions standards. Waiting a day to commemorate the *Roe v. Wade* anniversary, Obama rescinded the so-called Mexico City policy, which banned the use of American funds outside the United States to perform abortions, provide information or counsel about abortions, or lobby for legalizing abortion. Obama instituted a new ethics rule curbing the revolving door of governmental employees leaving office to work on K Street or become lobbyists. He opened up all archival documents from past administrations, made it easier for unions to organize and collect dues, and issued a stay on any last-minute Bush administration regulatory orders.[47]

By February 5, 2009, Obama had revamped the White House Office of Faith-Based and Community Initiatives, renaming it the Office of Faith-Based and Neighborhood Partnerships to reflect his emphasis on grassroots groups and collective change. What is more, he considered atheism a faith. This met with great protest. But little did these protesters anticipate that what this book describes as neotribalism, extending the war on women to reproductive freedom in the United States and abroad, would carry this conflict into potentially perilous judicial waters despite the federal courts' conservatism.[48]

Wresting Power from the Courts

Just as quickly as Obama started signing executive orders, he moved to diversify the federal judiciary. Unlike many civil rights leaders, Obama emphasized the "popular branches" of government—Congress and the presidency—instead of the courts. In the 1940s and 1950s, with the president and Congress taking little action on civil rights and women's rights, liberals had sought redress from the courts, and when Earl Warren became chief justice in 1953, legal liberalism became manifest in judicial activism. As Supreme Court reporter Jeffrey Toobin describes, "Liberals believed that the Constitution should be read expansively, and that the Supreme Court should recognize newly defined rights—the right, say, to attend an integrated public school, or, later, the right to choose abortion." But in Obama's words—words that echo the ideals underlying "truth and reconciliation" mediation principles exercised in South Africa—the "law is also *memory*; [it] records a long-running conversation, a nation arguing with its conscience."[49]

In the 1960s conservatives from the GOP's moderate and right wings, as well as civil libertarians, stood behind what they called "judicial restraint." On procedural grounds, these conservatives argued that federal judges must stop rendering decisions that political officials in the elected parts of the government are supposed to make. Of course, these conservative advocates knew how unlikely it was that the elected branches would take action on abortion or on protecting civil rights.

Obama disagrees. Thinking the judicial era has run its course, and knowing that the elected branches can now act on these "moral" issues,

Obama joins a chorus of liberals who now call for judicial restraint. Being president of *Harvard Law Review* in 1991 meant that Obama could take any clerkship in the country. "I asked him to apply to clerk for me," said Abner Mikva, a former federal appeals court judge. "I was a feeder. At the time, I was sending clerks to work for Brennan, Marshall, Stevens, and Blackmun. I don't have any doubt that Obama would have gotten a Supreme Court clerkship if he wanted one." But Obama chose not to take a clerkship.[50]

Instead, Obama moved back to Chicago, where he joined a small law firm, started teaching law at the University of Chicago, and laid the groundwork for a political career in an era when most progressives chose the academy and radicals went into punk rock music. "He had decided at that point to go back to work in the community that he had worked in as a community organizer," said Cassandra Butts, a law school classmate of Obama's who now serves as his deputy White House counsel. As Mikva remembered, "He wanted to go back to Chicago, and he wanted politics to be part of the mix." Showing the power of his conviction, Obama chose not the prestige or the intellectual challenge of the courts, nor the quiet of academia, but rather defending civil rights in a law school classroom *and* seeking elected office in the state and national legislative branches before running for president.[51]

So it is not surprising that Obama embraces *political* activism instead of *judicial* activism. Obama's ambitious legislative agenda, combined with his stated devotion to judicial restraint, reveals the consistency of his thought in supporting the elected branches, particularly the executive branch, which after all has a great deal of authority in its legitimate role of implementing laws. Obama wanted to create a more participatory type of deliberative democracy that courts cannot, and do not, provide. "You start with the premise that the political branches are the first line of defense of constitutional rights," law professor Jack Balkin said. "If you think that health care is a very important right that people should enjoy, you think that the best way to enforce it is for Congress to pass a law and the President to sign it. This is a very different model from the late sixties."[52] It is also a very different model from the 1980s.

More generally, Obama hopes to move beyond the categories of judicial activism and restraint. Both sides, Balkin argues, now claim to embrace restraint and eschew activism. Yet this does not mean that Obama has abandoned his capacity to shape the federal courts. The president had advisors working on how to accomplish this long before his election. No matter how restrained they may be, the federal courts rule on federal rulemaking. Obama would therefore not pass up the opportunity to shape this bench by diversifying it.[53]

Not 99 or 1 Percent: The New 71 Percent

Months before his election, Obama asked Preeta Bansal, a former solicitor general for New York State and then a law partner at Skadden, Arps, to concoct a plan to transform the federal judiciary by diversifying it. In a series of memoranda, she calculated how many vacancies would open, surveyed the professional and ethnic backgrounds of those who sat on the bench already, and drew up a comprehensive list of candidates Obama could consider.[54]

Before 1977, "minuscule numbers" of ethnic minorities, very few women, and practically no African Americans sat on the federal bench. Thirty-five years later, 84 percent of lower court judges remained white (presumably straight) men. Hoping to diversify the courts in accordance with Bansal's plan, Obama began extensive outreach efforts. To increase the pool of applicants, Obama did not follow the conventional path of nominating only judges. "We are looking for experiential diversity," he explained, "not just race and gender. We want people who are not the usual suspects, not just judges and prosecutors but public defenders and lawyers in private practice."[55]

The Obama administration reached far outside the halls of the judiciary, talking with minority and women's groups to see whom they could recommend. "They hoped to 'negotiate the selection gauntlet,'" one law professor relayed, going so far as proposing "that officials and their panels adopt special initiatives to recommend persons of color and women."[56] Obama counted on these new federal court judges to be "norm generators." With their differences, they would displace the straight white male norm, the perspective that had become standard.[57]

Only 29 percent of the federal court judges Obama appointed in his first two years in office were white, presumably straight, men. Obama explains his privileging diversity and inclusivity in terms of "empathy," or the language of caregiving. One could assume, he argues, that this type of judge has "struggled" in life. "We need somebody who's got the heart, the empathy, to recognize what it's like to be a young teenage mom, the empathy to understand what it's like to be poor or African American or gay or disabled or old—and that's the criterion by which I'll be selecting my judges." This is the international language of truth and reconciliation and memory, and the domestic language of an ethic of care, found first and largely in feminist political and feminist legal theory, and increasingly in different theories about identity, such as queer theory or theories of the body.[58]

Obama's definition of diversity first remedies systemic discrimination by federal court judges seated by presidents in the past.[59] Second, by the process of including all those groups symbolized by their exclusion in the past, it does the reverse. It creates a new process of symbolizing their inclusion. And finally, it opens up the judicial decision-making process, ensuring that all voices are heard. And more voices—be they voices of African Americans, Africans, Mexicans, or Hispanics—are valuable, since they have different perspectives. And more voices, in high and low tones, of women who are also African American or Mexican, or gay white men, and even gay African men, should be heard or registered in such a chorus. Obama is "the first president," wrote one law professor, "to rely exclusively on the theory of substantive representation to justify his diversity policy for the federal courts." Substantive representation is qualitatively different from equal- or same-treatment representation. It is similar to the comparable-worth doctrine in pay equity cases, or the anti-universal idea of truth in European and African truth and reconciliation tribunals.[60]

Diversity and Inclusivity Trump Truth and Ideology

In keeping with Obama's preference for diversity over ideology or partisanship, Sonia Sotomayor caught Obama's eye when Justice John Paul Stevens announced his retirement. First appointed to the bench by a Republican, George H. W. Bush, Sotomayor was neither a law professor nor a legal theorist who would fall prey to accusations of being too radical or too ethnic. Being single and without children, she also avoided the day-care dilemma. Most importantly, her style of judicial rendering was conservative. With a few exceptions, Toobin wrote, her opinions "stuck closely to the facts of each case. 'Her judicial philosophy was to follow the rule of law, apply it in each case,' [an] official said." She avoided grand jurisprudence statements. " 'She was not going to be painted as an ivory-tower judge, but a real-world judge,' the official continued. 'I don't think that she has an ideology—that's what was so great about her.' "[61]

Nonetheless, critics of Obama's judicial appointments saw the selection of Sotomayor as reverse racism. Trying to paint her with the same brush that got Bill Clinton to reverse his support for Lani Guinier, Pat Buchanan argued that Sotomayor "is a quota queen. . . . In her world, equal justice takes a back seat to tribal justice." Buchanan was not alone.

"He didn't pick a post-racial candidate," said Abigail Thernstrom, a leading conservative scholar on race. "She's a quintessential spokesman for racial spoils." But Obama had done his nomination homework, and members of his administration responded fast, denouncing Sotomayor's critics for their poor *choice* of words. "I'm sure she would have restated it," Obama himself said baldly. "But if you look in the entire sweep of the essay that Sotomayor wrote, what's clear is that she was simply saying that her life experiences will give her information about the struggles and hardships that people are going through—that will make her a good judge."[62]

The accusations of reverse racism stemmed from Sotomayor's contentious decision on an appeal by white male firefighters in New Haven, Connecticut. "She believes in, preaches and practices race-based justice," Buchanan wrote. "Her burying the appeal of the white New Haven firefighters, who were denied promotions they had won in competitive exams, was a no-brainer for her." Scarcely any Democrats rose to Sotomayor's defense on the New Haven case, except to say that she had followed existing precedent.[63]

Yet Obama persisted in calling Sotomayor "a non-ideological and restrained judge" whose opinions "reflect a keen understanding of the appropriate limits of the judicial role." Most Democrats concurred, likening her judicial modesty to that of Chief Justice John Roberts when he was up for confirmation in 2005. And to a large extent, the use of conservative language by Sotomayor and her allies during the confirmation process showed that the progressive agenda in the court is not the same as it once was. On the sensitive subject of affirmative action, Sotomayor, along with her Democratic supporters, gave no more than what Toobin called a "tepid defense of the use of racial preferences in affirmative action, another traditional liberal cause."[64] But, as we will see in chapter 6, the high-water mark for Supreme Court support of civil rights, especially equality of outcomes or results, was in 1971, nearly forty years earlier.

Kagan, Team Players, and Popcorn

Elena Kagan's appointment was much less contentious, though no less significant for Obama. Kagan, a white single woman from a secular Jewish background, knew how to fight "like a man." She was a "team" player, which is cultural code for "she works well with white, straight men." Before becoming solicitor general, Kagan had worked well with Obama's former constitutional law professor, Laurence Tribe, and with Lawrence Summers. As the calls for Kagan's recusal from challenges to the Affordable Care Act revealed, she emailed Tribe in March 2010 to say, "I hear they have the votes, Larry!! Simply amazing."[65]

Obama appointed Kagan, as the story goes, because of her great gift in bringing people with diverse ideas, lineages, and backgrounds together. The president hoped she would be a ballast, helping derail the conservative Supreme Court chief justice John Roberts, also known for his charm, sense of humor, and ability to get people with strong ideas to recognize the value of other (i.e., not their own) perspectives. Kagan and Roberts were both immensely skilled power brokers or consensus seekers who did not propagate narrow ideological positions or stand rigidly behind their own dicta. Unlike Obama, however, these two did not mind getting sullied by everyday rough-and-tumble politics. They stood not above, but rather under, the radar, or stood side by side as umpires, facilitating and mediating conflicts like corporate attorneys who never sought litigation, but instead encouraged their clients to settle their cases.

David Remnick reported that Tribe had influenced Obama's worldview more than any other professor at Harvard. More professors came to Washington from Harvard than from Princeton, though many of them, like Secretary of the Treasury Timothy Geithner, had connections with both of these Ivy League institutions. Obama, Remnick implies, knew that his destiny would lead to the White House. "A modern would-be politician, particularly a Democrat like Barack Obama, arrives at Harvard Law School keenly aware that the law school—its students and faculty—provided much of the brainpower for the New Deal, the New Frontier, and the Great Society."[66]

Obama left Harvard Law School with a reputation for being able to stand above the fray as a consensus seeker. Obama chose to work not with the radical critical legal theorists or the conservative law-and-economics types, but rather with a progressive civil libertarian. Tribe, "by almost any standard, among the most brilliant scholars of constitutional law of his, or any other, generation, a dazzling mind engaged in issues of political significance," had a disappointing job in the Obama administration as "senior counsel for access to justice." Indeed, since quitting this post in June 2010 after telling people he felt "largely invisible," Tribe, whom his friends knew to have a "big intellectual and a healthy ego," and who also taught Chief Justice John Roberts, has been doing what some advisors in the White House feared—he "stray[ed] from his assigned lane" after leaving this job, when Obamacare was before the Supreme Court.[67] While the nation was in suspense, Tribe told reporters he had predicted not just the conclusion, but the rationale behind his other student's—Roberts's—decision. "I predicted before the decision that it would come out in favor of the Affordable Care Act, and that the chief justice would probably, as I said on the air on a couple of stations, conclude that it was a tax. That didn't surprise me." He was right.[68]

Yet Remnick did not anticipate this behavior from the law professor he labeled a civil as opposed to a civic libertarian. He argues that Obama preferred academics embroiled in politics and administrative academics skilled at the art of negotiation over professors who propagated scholarship based on original ideas, their own ideologies, or even consistent substantive content:

> Almost from the start, Obama attracted attention at Harvard for the confidence of his bearing and his way of absorbing and synthesizing the arguments of others in a way that made even the most strident opponent feel understood. Once, at a debate over affirmative action with the staff of the *Harvard Law Review*, Obama spoke as if he were threading together the various arguments in the room, weighing their relative strengths, never judging or dismissing a point of view. "If anybody had walked by, they would have assumed he was a professor," Thomas J. Perrelli, a friend of Obama's who went on to work in his Justice Department, said. "He was leading the discussion, but he wasn't trying to impose his own perspective on it. He was much more mediating."

Obama earned this reputation because of his "earnest, consensus-seeking style." It was not the depth of his ideas, but the process, that earned Obama his first presidency, as the president of *Harvard Law Review*.[69]

Remnick claims that Obama's style "became a source of joking among his friends. A group would go together to the movies and tease Obama by imitating his solicitude: 'Do you want salt on your popcorn? Do you even *want* popcorn?'" What Remnick downplays is Obama's Deweyan lineage, which follows the logic of congruence and consilience as described in chapter 2.[70] Obama does not seek consensus, but rather consilience or common goods—goods that two or three or four sides can agree are in the common's best interest. It is about the best, not the only. It is not about a universal truth, but an ethic of care.[71]

Unlike Jeremy Bentham, Obama does not believe that the greatest number of people should constitute the superior solution. He is not a utilitarian or a consequentialist. This is not the "best." There is no such thing as the "best and the brightest." No group, no number of people are the best, let alone the peak of the triangle of merit, or even better informed than non-superior people. He does not support statistics, averages, or even the concept of "being bourg"—the bourgeoisie. Obama does not propagate the culture-of-poverty argument, or the subculture-of-poverty argument, that there are everlasting cycles of poverty.

Obama supports the polar opposite of this type of thinking, no matter how many pundits like Remnick call him an elitist. Obama condemns the culture of supremacy—underlying what Rosemarie Garland-Thomson named the "normate," or what would more accurately be defined as the subculture of supremacy. Obama does not agree with statistics—the average—finding the bell curve. Obama's definition of the middle is "aspiring." That is, Obama does not think we have even gotten there yet, but yet there is no there, there.

Bentham is different in advancing statistics that further the theory of whiteness (read culture of supremacy, defining what is supreme by what is the color white). He contests the subculture that participates in the cycle of a so-called "meritocracy" based on "bad faith" or inauthenticity. The meritorious, or the people who are the "best," the "most deserving"—as neo-Victorians and neocons alike say when referring to the cult of prosperity—are defined in these terms as white, male, heterosexual, not necessarily Anglo-Saxon, but Judeo-Christian or believers in the Hebraic Bible or the Old Testament.

To be sure, we should not practice exclusivity or reverse discrimination, but we must practice inclusivity and diversity. Obama's idea is that inquiry *is* process, process *is* inquiry, or the journey *is* the journey, and that great ideas don't trickle up or come from the bottom up. The notion that ideas and perspectives can emerge from random and contingent sources exists for Obama. He suspends the idea that ideas necessarily have to be moving in step with Western civilization's march forward. It's *all* relative; it's qualified. That is, Obama adopts a position of qualified relativism, or what could be portrayed as perspectivism or mapping. It all depends upon what the person's perspective is or where or if they are "standing on the wrong side of history."[72]

Standing, mapping, or perspectivism does not mean Obama throws the proverbial baby of history out with the bathwater. Like the timeline on Facebook, people, places, events, and even full and thumbnail face photographs help one cultivate and compose her perspective, and can, in the collective, inform and dictate one's actions over, in, and across political time or history. Not surprisingly, given his complicated yet cosmopolitan upbringing, Obama does not share the same optimism as most people in the United States. One reporter observed that "hell experts—and yes, there are scholars who spend this life studying the next one—

say the underworld has been losing favor for some time." Belief in "what lies beneath" has been diminishing in the United States. In a 35,000-person sample, the Pew Forum on Religion & Public Life found that 74 percent of Americans say they think there is a heaven, "where people who have led good lives are eternally rewarded," while just 59 percent believe in hell.[73] "They believe everyone has an equal chance, at this life and the next," said Alan F. Segal. "So hell is disappearing, absolutely." "Hell is for nonbelievers, and most Americans don't believe there are nonbelievers next door, even if their religion is different."[74]

Many of Obama's domestic and foreign policies substantiate the critical race theorists' foundational idea that the *intersection* between race, law, and power must be studied. No matter what Remnick argues to the contrary about Obama's tendency toward consensus—the middle—a compromising or a settling, Obama supports Tribe's civil liberties and critical race theory interpretation of the American Constitution.

Remnick overstates Tribe's influence. More importantly, he downplays and understates the perspective of Tribe's longtime Harvard Law School colleague Martha Minow, as well as her father's tutelage of Obama in Chicago before he won a seat in the Senate.[75] Minow, like Obama, emphasizes difference *and* inclusion in her book titled *Making All the Difference: Inclusion, Exclusion, and American Law*. She is a human rights lawyer and advocate for racial and religious minorities, women, children, and persons with disabilities. In 2009 she stepped into Harvard Law School dean Elena Kagan's shoes when Kagan became Obama's solicitor general. And despite her liberal or progressive leanings to the left of Tribe, Obama put her on the long list for the Supreme Court nominees in 2010 for what became Sonia Sotomayor's seat.[76]

Partiality, Not Neutrality; Universality, Not Impartiality;
Let's Mediate Just the Facts, Please

What does seem odd about Remnick's description of Obama is that this wannabe "prince" faced criticism from academics on the Right for being disrespectful of the law. "Obama has nothing much he wants from the courts," Richard Epstein told Toobin. "He wants them to stay away from the statutes he passes, and he wants solidity on affirmative action and abortion. That's it." Epstein is the politically and methodologically conservative legal scholar who was interim dean of the University of Chicago Law School when Obama taught there. A leader of the law-and-economics movement, Epstein is locked in battle with behavioral economists and behavioral social scientists such as Cass Sunstein, the former University of Chicago law and political science professor who is a minimal-state advocate and believes in critical race theory from a critical-liberties perspective. By becoming Obama's "regulatory czar," Sunstein received a better job than Larry Tribe.

Obama's form of deliberative democracy, like his transformation of the federal judiciary, is premised on the diversity principle. Obama embraces universality of means or benefits over particularity. He does not want to divide the nation into zero-sum factions or constituencies. But he also mixes universalizing benefits with a rejection of neutrality. Obama privileges "having perspective." Put simply, perspective trumps neutrality, as long as there is an array and a spectrum or multidimensionality in terms of perspective.[77]

Neutrality is simply whiteness, creating a standard and then denying it is such. Nowhere is this better seen than in the conservative attempt to appropriate John Rawls's notion of "public reason" for conservative purpose. Obama's Spinozan lineage, with his belief that power is wielded on the basis of survivability and perfectibility rather than benevolence, is at the heart of the issue of the American spirit or the ethic of reciprocity in the United States.[78]

What is more, Remnick's, and others', interpretation of the American spirit or ethic is heavily gendered—something feminists such as all the Marthas (Minow, Nussbaum, and Fineman) challenge, as does Anne-Marie Slaughter, former Harvard Law professor and director of Princeton's Woodrow Wilson School of International and Public Affairs, along with progressives like Sunstein who practice behavioral social science and economics, and my own previous work on Spinozan governance. These progressives agree on some basic assumptions underlying an ethic of care, the capacities or capabilities approach, and a theory of needs based on ethics rather than morals. These approaches underemphasize causality while taking into account all people's needs—not just those discovered or premised on reason. These theories take into account citizens' rationality and emotionality as well as their mental, intellectual, and physical needs, capabilities, and capacities.[79]

Obama believes that diversity brings in many different perspectives, none of which are neutral and none of which are superior, and all of which can be measured and balanced. Diversity means partiality, but given the competition for different perspectives, the partiality is fair, because it serves an important purpose. As mentioned earlier, affirmative action can be cast along class lines, which, given the correlation between race and class, would have about the same effect as affirmative action for an immutable characteristic like race. Universal solutions that privilege perspective over neutrality, and an understanding that this perspective is not neutral but rather partial, reflects the best practice of a deliberative democracy that champions difference and creativity over sameness and conformity to potentially repressive bourgeois values.

The same idea of universality, but not impartiality or neutrality, can be seen in a different Obama forum: the reconciliation process. In addition to departing from forty-year policy paths like the war on drugs, Obama practices a type of political strategy that he calls reconciliation, in honor of the "truth and reconciliation" process initiated in South Africa. As with all these programs, Obama's notion about how to universalize goes back to his Democratic National Convention speech: It is important not to blame, not to moralize, but to solve the problem. To work it out with inquiry and process, but to solve it—to find the idiosyncratic aspect of the issue, given our common values, and resolve the conflict. This is also why diversity is a positive value. Only by making difference something positive can people solve problems creatively and therefore be effective. The difference must be framed as value added, not subtracted.[80]

A Question of Norms

In an attempt to find common ground without "feelings," as teen pregnancy researcher Rebecca Maynard concludes, Obama suggests that one individual consider another individual's perspective. Eschewing universal truths or moral judgments, they must try to understand each person's particular situation. Representative thinking helps individuals judge. Each person takes into account other opinions as she formulates her own opinion. This helps them to distinguish or to judge a plurality of opinions. "Very, very few curricula," Maynard elaborated, "say, 'God will strike you dead if you have sex,' or, on the abstinence-plus side, 'Just go have fun, and don't think about the consequences.'"[81]

Inclusivity does not count without a full range of voices being heard loudly. Belonging to a socially dominant group transforms one's status as a citizen. It gives one privileges. As so much feminist work on male privilege and critical race theory shows, belonging to a dominant group distorts both one's moral ontology and one's moral epistemology.[82] Members of the dominant group attribute their privilege and power to "real, natural differences." This only reinforces the inequities in power and, as explained earlier, it means no more "unknown privileging" can exist.

Interests must be named. As radical legal feminist Catharine MacKinnon elaborates, "an equality question is a question of the distribution of power."[83] Equal treatment must be accompanied by an equal distribution of social power. Without this power, members of a subordinated group stand little chance of being either equal or free. "Equality as sameness is a gendered formulation of equality," writes political theorist Wendy Brown in *States of Injury*, "because it secures gender privilege throughout, naming women as difference and men as the neutral standard of the same."[84]

All deliberative democracy theorists argue that inclusion is vital to ensure that this type of government gains and maintains its legitimacy. As political theorist Iris Marion Young explained, "the normative legitimacy of democratic decision depends on the degree to which those affected by it have been included in the decision making processes and have had the opportunity to influence outcomes." Understanding a promise of equality and giving equal consideration to all views facilitate participation. When all those governed by collective decisions have helped in making the decisions, they often accept them as binding.[85]

Spinoza offers a fluid conception of society in which different people select different associations of like-minded people and then seek harmony. There is nothing hierarchical about their associations. But most importantly, they question prevailing norms. To do this, the federal government does not call any constitutional convention where millions deliberate. Nor do opinion polls rate norms. Rather, the legitimacy of a deliberative democracy can be found in the character of the reasons justifying the laws that govern a state and society. The decision-making process must be inclusive and not privileging of any few. It is the dynamic of the relationship between the individual, the state, the market, and society that bestows legitimacy.[86]

Dynamic, Deliberative, Regenerative Democracy

Obama anticipates a similar dynamic. Like Spinoza's idea of sociability, this dynamic can be characterized as a free-flowing relationship. That is, the "relatively informal and fluid networks of opinion" circulating within the public sphere help to influence the governmental agencies responsible for creating and enforcing laws and public policies. Put differently, those deliberating in the democracy must have the capacity to underwrite or destabilize collective outcomes that the government oversees and implements. Or, as political theorist John Dryzek argues, democratic legitimacy is exemplified by discursive legitimacy and reciprocity. It is achieved "when a collective decision is consistent with the constellation of discourses present in the public sphere, in the degree to which this constellation is subject to the reflective control of competent actors." When all parties believe that the norms of social cooperation are fair, they are more willing to abide by them.[87]

Deliberative democracy particularly suits the United States, not just because of deliberative democracy's emphasis on inclusion, legitimacy, and reciprocity, but also because of its predilection for freedom of association, tolerance, and mutual and self-reliance. This type of democracy does a better job than simple vote counting of making sure that all voices have a chance to be heard and taken into account. A vast amount of literature shows that majorities rarely represent minority interests because the state either co-opts or represses minority views. To maintain their viability in the political arena, minority groups are often forced to dilute their messages or start championing symbolic rewards the state gives them. Dryzek argues that many minority groups do better without formal state representation.[88]

To achieve real change, Dryzek argues, reformers must apply pressure from a position outside the state. In his view, the deliberative democratic process demonstrates that votes are "largely epiphenomenal, functioning mainly as markers of the prevailing balance." Disaffected populists in the United States, Dryzek argues, should not seek to enter and capture the American state; instead, they should continually confront the state.[89]

(Painful) Truth and Reconciliation

Like the truth and reconciliation practiced in South Africa, Obama's notion of reconciliation accepts power relationships and promotes difference. It does not advance the idea that citizens must compromise; it's not about mixing black and white to create gray solutions. Forgiveness results from "truth telling." That is, it not only recognizes differences but embraces the intractability of those differences (which form, and will continue to form, different perspectives), knowing that over time the varying memories of events could re-create the conditions ripe for another apartheid or genocide. Hence it is better to forgive but *not forget*, so that a collectivity, such as those peoples struggling to recover from civil war or ethnic cleansing, will always remember and the events will not recur when conditions are ripe again. To reconcile, the truth must be told, and this truth recognizes the power and domination of one group over another.

None of the truth and reconciliation dialogue comes from a liberal construct or vocabulary. The South African conception of reconciliation succeeds, defusing nationalism and the dangers associated with tribalism, if the collective—all parties—can achieve and practice forgiveness. Truth and reconciliation is a radical construct in that it is premised on the concept of power and domination instead of enlightened self-interest, consensus, or compromise.[90]

Truth and reconciliation is a pragmatic but not an opportunistic forum. It promotes perpetual dynamic learning on the basis of diversity, all the while embracing collective forgiveness on the basis of recognizing and trying to adjust imbalances of power among peoples. Obama's and Eric Holder's type of truth and reconciliation involves "speaking the truth" about race. Initially, Obama supported the attorney general's quest for truth telling and honesty about race, but then he reversed his position. In practice, truth telling becomes problematic. Instead of focusing on contentious issues like reparations for slavery, it is liberating and reenergizing.

More importantly, Obama's emphasis on reconciliation helps explain how and why he challenges whiteness. Yet instead of putting whiteness under a public policy spotlight, he invites to the table other performers, who receive their own light. Bringing diverse political players to the table changes what is on the table. Obama understands this by virtue of having always been the outsider at every table. Instead of objectivity, neutrality, formality, and principle, Obama is for inclusivity, universality, pragmatism, partiality, and perspective.

These two conceptual juxtapositions yield dramatically different results. Truth and reconciliation applied to domestic public policies "racinates," rather than *de*racinates, them. Only by accepting the power and domination behind whiteness can you have healing. It is akin to diversity in turning black into a good color, in contrast to the denial (read denigration) of the absence of color (read golden baby, not colorless baby).

From Different and Differing Perspectives

A bench whose composition essentially reflects America instills greater public confidence. The president stresses diversity because it yields multiple benefits. For instance, people of color and women often help other judges understand and decide complex issues respecting certain questions, such as abortion and discrimination, and hold different, valuable perspectives in fields such as criminal procedure and employment law. Obama's minority and female nominees might increase the court's ideological diversity, as a number of them seem to favor the ideas of a "living Constitution" and empathy, but he deemphasizes ideology per se. Persons of color and women may also help limit the racial, gender, and other types of bias that afflict the judicial process.[91]

The shift from discrimination to diversity, and from blackness to whiteness, makes civil rights more of a threat. Originally created to decouple the problem of discrimination from its solutions, diversity creates more of a threat to those who wittingly or unwittingly promote whiteness. Diversity is no longer a corrective, but something that benefits everyone, whereas traditional affirmative action programs evoke images of slavery and demand that people acknowledge and assume responsibility for this country's history of racial oppression (a responsibility that many people are loath to accept because they feel that they and their ancestors have done nothing wrong). At the very least, affirmative action programs may arouse feelings of fatigue, guilt, defensiveness, and anger and bring to mind concerns about racial preferences, quotas, merit, stigma, and reverse discrimination, among other things.[92]

By contrast, diversity, lacking any remedial element, evokes a different image, one that is inherently inclusive. Not just black people or white people, but all people, profit from diversity. And why stop with race? Diversity calls to mind a host of factors connoting difference, including class, race, gender, age, disability, geographic origin, sexual orientation, artistic talent, and athletic ability. Obama's policies on a range of issues, from college affordability to the anti-obesity initiative, showcase his commitment to working on issues of importance to the African American community without framing them specifically as black issues. In this way, Obama has long sought to define himself as something other than a traditional legal liberal.

"Organizing America"

Obama no longer looks to the courts to enact his agenda, but instead relies on his popular branch to wield power with pluralities—pluralities of political subjects or agents. He applies Saul Alinsky's organizing techniques not to the working class, from which he is estranged due to their mechanization of race, but to the middle class. Dewey's community is "wherever there is conjoint activity whose consequences are appreciated as good by all singular persons." Obama adopts Spinoza's notion of two heads being better than one and takes it to a new level, a level that is all relational, all situational, all contextual—but one that all must be joined to and in permanent flux.

For Dewey, it is not enough to say that we spurn the public good. Equally important is that we are not altruistic. We do not try to make others happy to increase our own happiness. Yet at the same time, we cannot be happy alone. Obama repeats this language everywhere. Our happiness cannot even be conceived of as separate from that of others. Our state of interaction, our state of interdependence, means that the right choices—or choices based on good ethics—make both our own lives and the lives of others more fulfilling. Dewey believes that the moral self must empower others so that as many of us as possible can become involved in activities that make people's lives happier and more meaningful. Happiness leads to "effectiveness in enabling others to achieve happiness through social action." This is not the goal of one's behavior, as in altruism, but a by-product of pursuing one's self-interest.[93]

In pragmatic terms, this process is called "meliorism." Meliorism suggests that a citizen's situation improves, and her circumstances get better, through human involvement. "It rests on the idea that life will not get better but that it can get better in ways in which people handle specific obstacles before them." This concept shows how Dewey's idea of a community entails creating a successful democratic relationship between individuals and groups.[94]

Dewey envisioned group membership not unlike Aristotle or Hegel, as something innate. Individuals are born into groups, and individual responsibilities to groups must then be fulfilled according to the individual's capacity. This is not to say that one specific group exists for an individual to identify with as a result of their birthright. Rather, there is a plurality of groups—family, academic, professional, civic religion, recreational, ethnic, gendered—and the level and nature of one's participation in them will vary over time.

Obama phrases all of his reform this way. For both Dewey and Obama, "interacting flexibly" is a condition of democratic groups. The state must therefore never act in any way that represses group members. Individual action within groups enriches our lives, creating "a wider orbit of activity for individuals." The democratic ideal contains a multiplicity of perspectives acting in concert. It depends on the maintenance of a true pluralism of group loyalties, on which emerge heterogeneous "publics," rather than one homogeneous public. There is no public good and no republic: only different individuals, in different groups, with different perspectives.[95]

Drawing on Deleuzian and Spinozan ethics, Arendt's *vita activa*, Du Bois's deconstruction of racial mechanization, and Dewey's insistence on a plurality of perspectives, Obama asks American citizens to reach beyond bipartisan discussion. Inquiry—the process of acquiring knowledge while eschewing universal truths—offers us the means of adjusting for our own limitations, correcting our standards, improving the warrants for our assertions, and recognizing the role of power and privilege in epistemological theories. An inclusion of pluralistic voices becomes a criterion for judging what we count as "knowledge," and "knowledge" becomes a process of knowing that is in need of re/adjustment, correction, and re/construction. This process is premised on qualified relativism.[96]

Vita Activa: *The State Facilitates Action*

For Obama, power is not in the office, and power is not in the people. The power to effect change is in our interdependent relationships—in the structure and the will of the people. Obama does not want the person in office to transform things, and this does mean that the power is derived from the people. The president tries to give more voice to the people as he tries to make democracy more responsive and more vibrant. The state must be responsive to groups. The state facilitates action.[97]

Dewey describes inquirers as members of social communities who must appeal to the experiences of their fellow community members for confirmation and correction of their individual results. He cultivates a "transactional view of selves-in-relation-to-others." Pragmatists compensate for the embeddedness of each individual by embracing pluralism. Due to their focus on knowledge in relation to power, they specifically seek to include in that pluralism those who have been silenced and marginalized, those who are outsiders to the mainstream discourse.[98]

As an African/white Hawaiian who spent his formative years in Indonesia, Obama agrees with Dewey that the more other voices are included, the more each of us can trust that we have considered all available information and can hope to make a sound judgment. People are social beings formed in relation, and those relations will cause people to be formed in certain ways and not in others. Our knowledge is partial, not neutral and objective. And our knowledge, being partial, will limit the possibilities of knowing. Feminist Jane Flax points out that "thinking is a form of human activity which can't be treated in isolation from other forms of human activity, including the forms of human activity which in turn shape the humans who think."[99]

Like Rousseau with his general will, or Marx with his proletarian rule, Dewey pinned his faith on the fact that true democracy was as yet unattained: "The prime condition of a democratically organized public is a kind of knowledge and insight that does not yet exist." "We are born organic beings *associated with others* . . . we are not born members of a community." Yet sheer associative activity is endemic to human life. Dewey understood that the impetus toward community arises when individuals desire more than such basic associations.[100]

Individuals are content with the cooperative alliances they form in forging the frontiers of their cultures. It is when their cultures reach a certain degree of complexity that individuals desire deeper relations. Dewey's community is "wherever there is conjoint activity whose consequences are appreciated as good by all singular persons."[101]

The difference between notions of community endorsed before and after Dewey is that post-Deweyans maintain a pervasive sense of dissatisfaction with institutional means of recovering individuality. When Dewey speaks of the public, his words are of process, of transformation, of undergoing. Obama echoes all these terms.

An American state and society could be premised on deliberative democracy that advances Spinoza's notion of creating mutually inclusive goals for the individual and society, given a state's emphasis on social, political, and cultural inclusion, legitimacy, and reciprocity. Democratic politics, as collective deliberation, beats lone thought. A deliberative democracy could wrest power away from those who rig the rules—capital, special interests, and political parties—by questioning the norms that guide them.[102]

People and Their Problems—Drugs

Americans who embrace the Puritan heritage (white, Christian, heterosexual)—many of whom are members of the Tea Party—squirm at and protest the concept of diversity.[103] Understanding how threatening diversity can be, Obama emphasizes his middle-class progressivism instead. This makes his reform seemingly less critical of the establishment, because the bourgeoisie embody the establishment, which he wants to open to all Americans—including immigrants from the Middle East, African Americans, and Hispanics.

Knowing well the politics of resentment, Obama turns consumer reform into a restoration effort targeted at the middle class—one that is aspirational and economic—instead of redistribution or reconstruction for the poor and working classes. He cannot afford to be seen as a champion of the poor, or of people of color. Instead, he seeks the middle, trying to defuse the politics of resentment first articulated by Richard M. Nixon, who suggested challenging the supremacy of African Americans by hyphenating all Americans. To restore American freedom in a nation that fears radical change is no small feat, but Obama does not stop there. He

also underscores the values of inclusivity, tolerance, and difference, emphasizing that these are part of the American heritage of political values
and beliefs that is also solidly middle class.[104]

A White War on Drugs

Nowhere can this shift be seen better than in the small but essential
changes in emphasis made by Attorney General Holder and drug czar
Gil Kerlikowske when together they ended the forty-year-old so-called
war on drugs. President Nixon declared it a war in the early 1970s, and
every president thereafter supported it, with Ronald Reagan and George
W. Bush stepping it up. Crime became racialized. The 100-to-1 sentencing disparity between crack and powder cocaine told it all.[105]

Some call the last forty years an era of "mass incarceration of African
Americans" that gave law enforcement an excuse to harass Americans
who have committed no crime besides being black. "The most common
but faulty reasoning for racial profiling is that blacks commit a disproportionate share of crime," writes Laura J. Khoury. "When criminalness
and blackness become synonymous, the practice of surveillance becomes
completely normal."[106]

The American population constitutes "only 5 percent of the world
population but has 25 percent of its prisoners." Moreover, "48 percent
of the prison population is black—four times their proportion in the population."[107] Michelle Alexander, a former ACLU lawyer who had clerked
for Supreme Court Justice Harry Blackmun, shores up these statistics and
offers more in *The New Jim Crow: Mass Incarceration in the Age of Colorblindness*, a scholarly work that became a crossover book given how
much media attention it received. "The United States now has the highest
rate of incarceration in the world, dwarfing the rates of nearly every developed country, even surpassing those in highly repressive regimes like
Russia, China and Iran. The racial dimension of mass incarceration is its
most striking feature," writes Alexander. "No other country in the world
imprisons so many of its racial or ethnic minorities. The United States
imprisons a larger percentage of its black population than South Africa
did at the height of apartheid." Khoury, and all the scholars who have
been publishing these types of statistics for over twenty years, must have
been pleased when the issue finally gained public notice. Ira Glasser, who
had served as ACLU executive director, had also called it "The New Jim
Crow" a decade earlier, but it gained little public attention.[108]

After decriminalizing African Americans, Obama then sought a drug
policy based on what works: prevention and treatment. The Obama

administration retains the policy's facelessness, though the demographic it targets is white and middle class. He removes the African American faces, which account for 85 percent of all crack-cocaine defendants.[109]

With the passage of California's trendsetting "three strikes" law in 1994, the United States became the "world champion" of incarceration. Mass incarceration, social scientist Anthony Bottoms maintains, is best described as "populist punitiveness." Similarly, Arie Freiburg calls it "penal populism," a term that captures "an emotional, non-rational, expressive trend" in the mid-nineties. "Politicians tapp[ed] into [penal populism] . . . using for their own purposes, what they believe to be the public's generally punitive stance." The penal populist movement reflected the public's distrust in the government's use of experts.[110]

"Long-standing patterns of racism and racial distrust in American political culture," Albert W. Dzur argues, are other "contributing factors," such as criminal offenders receiving their "just deserts." But to Obama, the "war on drugs" is "not about a culture war. It's not about a battle over 'Are you harsh, or are you permissive?'" Arguing that the war on drugs has been an utter failure, Obama instigated "clear steps we can do that will continue to make the problem smaller and make it stay small."[111]

To begin addressing the racial injustices underlying the criminal justice system, Obama signed the Fair Sentencing Act and the Second Chance Act into law. Long needed, the Fair Sentencing Act reduces the 100-to-1 sentencing disparity between powder and crack cocaine. Once the law passed, the Obama administration started pushing the U.S. Sentencing Commission to rewrite its guidelines so that they could be applied retroactively, hoping to release 5,000 prisoners early, until the Roberts court intervened. Then came the Second Chance Act, which funded programs that helped coordinate state and local reentry services.[112]

The Obama administration changed the face of crime, the underclass, and the underworld, but all with the idea that it is not about being white, but rather about using drugs. It is the *doing*, or engaging in criminal behavior, not the *being*, or the essence of any group, as in racial profiling that targets African Americans for "driving while black" (DWB). The fact that there is an acronym for this, as one scholar claimed, speaks volumes.[113]

Suburban Drug Abuse

The Obama administration's new emphasis on drug enforcement focuses on white, middle-class drug abusers and prescription drug abuse, which the drug czar declared to be his top priority because it is at "record levels." In 2008 prescription painkillers such as Oxycontin, Vicodin, and methadone caused almost 15,000 people to die. This was a threefold increase in prescription drug abuse deaths since 1999.[114]

Rather than criminalizing drug abusers, the Obama administration seeks treatment. Of the approximately 25 million substance abusers in the United States, only approximately 2 million receive any form of treatment. The Obama administration hopes to triple the number, making drug addiction treatment part of the primary health care system. In a variant of the attention paid to the "crack baby" syndrome, the Obama administration is funding studies of babies born with prescription drugs in their systems.

Not a Christian Nation, After All

Not only does Obama disturb the normate by stripping crime of the colors black and brown, he also outrages conservatives by declaring that the United States is not a Christian nation. Obama is the first president to debunk John Winthrop's "city on a hill" image of a chosen people. "We do not consider ourselves a Christian nation or a Jewish nation or Muslim nation," Obama said in Cairo in his first major foreign policy speech. Rather, the United States is a "nation of citizens who are bound by ideals and a set of values."[115]

The percentage of Americans who consider themselves Christian has shrunk dramatically over the last twenty years. Since 1990 the percentage of Americans declaring no religious preference has nearly doubled. This is particularly true of the youth. Knowing this, in 2009, Obama decided against having the White House honor the National Day of Prayer. White House press secretary Robert Gibbs said that while Obama would sign the annual proclamation to recognize the day, he would not do as past presidents did by honoring the day with a service. "Prayer is something that the president does every day," Gibbs explained. "I think the president understands, in his own life and in his family's life, the role that prayer plays." Again, Obama faced the ire of religious conservatives.[116]

Separation of Church and State

In its first year Obama's Office of Faith-Based and Neighborhood Partnerships kept a low profile. The first president ever to refer to "non-believers" in his inaugural address began seeking more involvement from the youth in 2011, when he announced the President's Interfaith and Community Service Campus Challenge. "At Agnes Scott College, a small Presbyterian school in Atlanta, Georgia," an official stated, "students and local Christian, Jewish and Muslim faith community leaders are teaming up to address educational inequity in urban schools." "Interfaith service impacts specific community challenges, from homelessness to mentoring to the environment, while building social capital and civility . . . [and] can unite people of all faiths."[117] Whereas George W. Bush had made hiring the most controversial aspect of his faith-based program by allowing religious organizations receiving governmental grants and contracts to hire workers on the basis of religion, as outlined in a 2002 presidential directive and a 2007 Justice Department memo, the Obama administration championed inclusivity, diversity, and difference.

The Bush administration policies caused a stir, particularly since several organizations, most notably the Salvation Army, had been caught using their faith to justify their policy against hiring gay people. "This issue has been controversial," law professor Ira Lupu said, "because it raises a direct conflict between two opposing viewpoints on church-state relations." "If organizations can't hire staff that share their mission, they will quickly lose their mission." Blogger Michael Sean Winters argued that "if the government chooses to give funds to a Catholic organization because of the services it provides, that does not mean the government should be entitled to tell us whom we can hire."

Challenging this view, other groups argued that "hiring on the basis of religion is discriminatory and that the government should never subsidize such discrimination." Blogger Maureen Fiedler, host of the public radio show *Interfaith Voices* and a member of the Sisters of Loreto religious community, takes a different perspective. "If one is hiring a drug counselor, or someone to run a soup kitchen or a job-training office," she said, "it's a neutral job—religiously speaking—and there is no reason to discriminate on the basis of religion. In fact, since such salaries are paid with tax dollars, there is every reason not to discriminate." Lupu offers the underlying reason for all this contention: homophobia. "One of the deep undercurrents [of the issue] is a gay-rights question," he maintains. "That's what's been driving the more heated politics of it."[118]

Hoping to scuttle what they perceived as Bush's discriminatory directive, the moment Obama took office, a coalition of fifty-eight religious, educational, civil rights, labor, and health groups urged Attorney General Holder to direct the Office of Legal Counsel to review and withdraw the 2007 Justice Department memo permitting belief-based hiring. They maintained that this memo is based on an "erroneous" interpretation of the 1993 Religious Freedom Restoration Act (RFRA) that "threatens core civil rights and religious-freedom protections." RFRA, as they described, maintains that the federal government may not "substantially burden" a person's free exercise of religion "without compelling justification." The burden is misplaced on the state, not the religious organization.

Obama responded by forming an advisory task force, composed of people with diverse views on church-state matters, to review the regulations. But by 2011, the Obama administration had shifted the burden back to these religious organizations, rendering a very narrow definition of religion. Even the Chicago organization that a young Obama once directed, the Developing Communities Project, defines its purpose as being "faith and works," which the president is now ignoring, complained one conservative newspaper. "Florence Nightingale, Mother Teresa," this editorial continued, "the Salvation Army, or any modern-day good Samaritan would not be religious" under this definition. The RFRA guarantees "freedom of worship," or a private faith, rather than "freedom of religion," which includes engaging the public. Only governmental and secular groups can heal the sick, feed the hungry, or bind the broken-hearted unless religious organizations elect to follow federal laws.[119]

Secularism

Obama's position on inclusion, difference, and civil rights protection has been consistent. In a June 2006 speech titled "A Call to Renewal," he said, "I do not believe that religious people have a monopoly on morality, I would rather have someone who is grounded in morality and ethics, and who is also secular, affirm their morality and ethics and values without pretending that they're something they're not. They don't need to do that. None of us need to do that." This issue, however, takes a back seat to the question of whether faith-based groups can discriminate on the basis of sexuality and still collect governmental funds.[120]

To Obama, religious groups, secular grassroots community groups, or public-interest advocacy groups all represent an avenue for practicing deliberative democracy. Rather than disbanding the Office of Faith-Based Initiatives, he expanded it, making it more inclusive. Facing criticism from all sides, Obama took a cautious approach by issuing an executive order that seeks the Justice Department's opinion on a case-by-case basis, and then used this order as leverage in an attempt to broker a "sensible conscience mandate."[121]

The Obama administration knew that the Supreme Court would, and will continue to, weigh in, giving a very expansive definition of the role of religion in the United States. In October 2011 a unanimous Supreme Court reinforced the so-called "ministerial exception" permitting religious organizations the freedom to hire and fire ministers, or those who perform ministerial duties, without having to follow federal employment laws, such as antidiscrimination laws. The case involved Cheryl Perich, a teacher at a religious school, who asked for standing to sue her employer for discriminating against her under the Americans with Disabilities Act Amendments Act (ADAAA). While most of what Perich taught was secular, she had some religious responsibilities. Arguing that the ministerial exception should be disavowed altogether, the Obama administration insisted it should determine on a case-by-case basis when religious employees should be under its jurisdiction. As one critic put it, "This would mean that, in every future case, a court—and not the church—would decide whether the church's reasons for firing or not hiring a minister were good enough." But the Roberts court ignored Obama, ruling unanimously that the ministerial exception applied, making the ADAAA, a federal antidiscrimination statute, inapplicable.[122]

Obama flipped the original intent of the Office of Faith-Based Initiatives on its head, and he renders a very narrow interpretation of religious freedom in the United States. He believes in civic religion, not in religious organizations performing state actions without heeding federal laws. Like governmental contractors, both secular and religious groups and organizations must follow national laws if they accept governmental funding. When the president adopted this position, his critics denounced him for doing nothing less than redefining "religion, which not only steps on a basic liberty but a basic understanding of religion's role in society."[123]

Round two of the historic separation-of-powers battle between the Roberts court and the Obama administration is explained in the next chapter, which covers the Affordable Care Act. But for the purposes of this chapter, with regard to Obama's concentration on civic religion and opposition to neotribalism, the Catholic community ignored Obama's sensible conscience mandate in forgoing their opportunity to "opt out," allowing insurers to take the heat for abortions performed in their hospitals. What became clear by 2011 was that the Obama administration would dole out preemptions and exemptions on a case-by-case basis as it executes and implements the Affordable Care Act, the No Child Left Behind Act, and civil rights laws such as the ADAAA, arguing that "religion is primarily a matter of belief" and that, as a belief, it should be constrained to the private sphere.

Obama's interpretation of the separation of church and state is that freedom of religion applies solely to "groups whose primary purpose is the inculcation of religious values and who primarily serve their own members." This interpretation has outraged many religious organizations, since they do "far more than simply teach their tenets or minister to the faithful." Over forty Catholic churches and dioceses are suing Obama, since in the United States their schools, hospitals, and soup kitchens in churches "help and heal others based on one's spiritual convictions." As a conservative editorial opined, "For Christians especially, the call to serve and heal others is not separate from their understanding of God's infinite love for humanity and the command to love one another." But Obama has remained steadfast in his belief in civic religion: If these religious organizations wish to serve and heal nonbelievers for the state, they must follow the laws of the nation-state.[124]

Obama has been consistent. Contrary to what some conservatives charged, Obama did not reverse his position as outlined in his 2009 inaugural address about faith. "For as much as government can do and must do, it is ultimately the faith and determination of the American people upon which this nation relies." Conservatives, however, mistook his belief in faith and work, which is found in all religions, and which underlies his own support of civic religion, for the support for one religion—Christianity. Meanwhile the pitch and tone of the rhetoric increased in advance of the Supreme Court's decision about the Affordable Care Act, with Bishop Salvatore Cordileone of Oakland saying there is reason to fear Obama's "despotism." Other religious figures revived an image of a cowboy with a rifle and a crucifix, all while some Catholic bishops and priests called for a protest they dubbed a "Fortnight for Freedom," ending on July 4, 2012.[125]

Civic Religion

Obama has a very complex understanding of the roles of the church and state. The only religious values that belong in a democracy, in his view, are those that can be translated not into a universally appealing set of Christian values, but into a *plurality* of religious values. These values are not to be confused with universal values, because Obama renounces *one* truth. He speaks of truths. To him, religion is about becoming. It captures striving, or a human being's quest for perfectibility. What is more, the only type of religion that should influence governance is that which is founded on reason and argumentation, not on blind faith. Obama advances what one scholar describes as a cosmopolitan version of civic religion.[126]

Three religious traditions exist in the United States—liberal secularism, religious nationalism, and civic religion—each purporting to incorporate the "proper" relationship between religion and politics. Liberal secularism envisions a clean separation between the church and the state, whereas religious nationalism seeks their reunification. Until 1981, no president spoke the language of religious nationalism. Most referred to Christianity, and to God, but it was a unitarian God. Then, in 2001, George W. Bush introduced "God talk," marking a new turn in politics toward evangelicalism or a Christian nation.[127]

Before taking office, Obama made it clear that he rejected the idea of a Christian nation, opting instead for a Tocquevillian civic religion. That is, Obama believes religion mediates a "partial separation" of church and state, and can produce constructive "tension" with the state by balancing individual autonomy with the common good. Most importantly, Obama's vision of civic religion relies heavily on responsibility—the responsibility of the individual, the state, and society.[128]

Nowhere did Obama express his version of cosmopolitan civic religion more clearly than in his 2009 inaugural address. Unlike members of the evangelical Christian Right, who advance eternal principles about religious authority and tradition, Obama favors a tradition consonant with social justice, particularly civil rights, that stems from an individual's efforts at perfectibility. It is "a language of becoming, of change as we strive to understand the injunction that the arc of the universe is long but that it bends toward justice." Through ancient texts and modern voices, Obama maintains God is "still creating." God challenges us to change not just our own lives, but also those lives in the world around us. As a result of God still creating, Obama maintains, "the future remains undetermined."[129]

Obama mixes reason and religion, believing in the integrity of both religious and scientific methods. He maintains that, through argument and argumentation, both methods can be productively harmonious and conflictual. Obama demands a rapprochement between the two. In "A Call to Renewal," Obama insisted it is a "mistake" to overlook the "power of faith in people's lives." In his view, it was time to "reconcile faith with our modern, pluralistic democracy." Religion can help produce truths, Obama suggested, "based on realities that we all can apprehend." Obama points to Talmudic reasoning, or the agonistic and dialectical practices of Judaism that accept the "arguing with God" tradition instead of relying on intuitive perceptions, mystical revelation, or proofs that nonbelievers cannot access.[130]

This explains why religious believers can and must translate their concerns into generic, rather than religion-specific, values. If I am opposed to abortion for religious reasons, for instance, and hope to ban its practice, I cannot be persuasive by underscoring God's will. Religion should enter the public square and be persuasive only if I explain why abortion violates some principle that is accessible to people of all faiths and to some with no faith at all. Obama expressed the same sentiment to a global audience when he spoke in Cairo in 2009. Obama identifies the actions that different religious traditions take to achieve translation of specific traditions into general values.

Hell on Earth

What religion does most for Obama is to identify "the sacred responsibility for others." Indeed, this was what attracted Obama to the church in the first place. Trinity, Obama's church in Chicago, practiced a prophetic theology that equated responsibility with seeking transformation and liberation. It emphasized the welfare of others, all the while highlighting the indeterminacy of the future.

Obama explored another aspect of responsibility in Reinhold Niebuhr's theology. Niebuhr tempered Christianity's idealism with an analysis of power and evil. He saw evil intertwined in human motivation. Niebuhr disagreed with many theologians who believed that social institutions accounted for the primary source of injustices. Concentrating on the limits of human influence, stressing its ironies and its paradoxes, Niebuhr insisted that evil can come from within. Obama told a reporter, "I take away [from Niebuhr] . . . the compelling idea that there's serious evil in the world, and hardship and pain. And we should be humble and modest in our belief we can eliminate those things." In finding evil within the individual, Niebuhr tethered Christianity's prophetic and optimistic impulses to a tragic view of human nature. It is this tragic view that accounts for Obama's emphasis on interdependence. Obama pairs social, political, and economic responsibility with individual responsibility. They are all blended, interconnected, and interdependent.[131]

At the same time, Obama does not believe that anyone is "purely one thing." Obama enacts Edward Said's observation that "labels like Indian, or woman, or Muslim or American are not more than starting points, which if followed into actual experience for only a moment are quickly left behind. Imperialism consolidated the mixture of cultures and identities on a global scale. But its worst and most paradoxical gift was to allow people to believe they were only, mainly, exclusively, white, or Black, or Western, or Oriental." Obama believed that his own identity was "black and more than black." And, as mentioned earlier, Obama viewed the struggle of African Americans as "at once unique and universal."[132]

But Obama identifies with Joshua instead of Moses, perpetuating the myth of exodus. In his March 4, 2007, address in Selma, Alabama, Obama declared that his generation was "called to be the Joshuas of our time, to be the generation that finds our way across this river." Obama did so as a means of distancing himself from some of the positions taken by the Moses generation of Martin Luther King and Jesse Jackson.

What is most distinctive about Obama's religious view (and also extends to his worldview) is how he renders paradoxical interpretations. His view is what literary theorist Stanley Fish calls "more paratactic than hypotactic . . . [resembling] the prose of the Bible given its long lists and serial 'ands.'" "Of course," Fish adds, "no prose is all one or the other." Obama builds his responsibility theme by using consilient and congruent reasoning. This type of reasoning, as explained in chapter 2, means that different lines of argumentation converge on the same conclusion (convergence) and that by induction, one can "leap to" the generalization (consilience). Obama uses convergence and consilience to bring a composite audience into agreement with a more general value or ethic. For him, nothing is more persuasive than the call for responsibility.[133]

Convergence and Consilience: Obama's Inductive Reasoning

Convergence and consilience are inductive rather than deductive thinking, as it unfolds through juxtapositions of opposites that lead us to a new frame of thinking or a new perspective. Obama juxtaposes the government with the free market, for instance, or national security with civil liberties. He transcends binary thinking, holding, for example, that "we reject as false the choice between our safety and our ideals."[134]

Obama reframes binary oppositions, as mentioned in the previous chapter, resisting the laws of noncontradiction and identity. "The appeal of Obama's take on identity, often misunderstood as an attempt to move 'beyond race,'" writes rhetorician David Frank, "is in its interrogation of accepted thinking about race." But it is not an attempt to move beyond race. Rather, just as he believes in pragmatism, Obama believes that God is still working in the world. People are still "in process." It is this emphasis on process that gives all believers and nonbelievers access to truths and shows that those truths advance first and foremost a sacred responsibility to others. For this reason, Obama embraces religion's more austere side—the one related to law, order, and right, rather than the softer side related to love.[135]

Obama makes use of dissociation in the face of dialectical opposites, breaking "free of all topical assumptions." Some scholars believe that Obama's dissociation reflects his attempt to "remodel reality by re-envisioning the relationship between philosophical pairs" so he can avoid "false choices." Obama creates a new frame that removes or re-duces the influence of an incompatibility. As mentioned earlier, when Obama said in his 2007 speech at the Jefferson-Jackson dinner in Des Moines, Iowa, that he did not want "to pit Red America against Blue America, I want to be the President of the United States of America," he was enacting a dissociation seeking to "remodel" the American percep-tion of identity from division into unity.[136]

Obama has resisted dissociation with the same intention of creating a sense of "unity" out of racial division. In *Dreams from My Father*, Obama describes "Joyce," who, like him, was biracial, but refused to ac-knowledge that she was black. Both Obama and Joyce rejected the one-drop rule, but Obama criticized Joyce for not claiming her blackness. He condemned her attempt to move "beyond race." A multiracial iden-tity that did not acknowledge the unique history of African Americans, or any minority group for that matter, would fold them into the white, dominant culture. So as not to suffer this loss, Obama identifies himself as black, white, and African American.[137]

Obama's treatment of binary oppositions with dissociative strategies, his embrace of paradox, and his complex understanding of the contra-dictory impulses of human nature call for a rhetorical strategy that links particular truths to a broader set of values or ethics. He bridges not a universal truth, but truths held by some to a more generally accepted set of principles held by others.[138]

Convergence and consilience also help Obama frame the United States as a nation characterized by its patchwork heritage, one of "Chris-tians and Muslims, Jews and Hindus—and non-believers." In his 2009 inaugural address, Obama rejected the religion/atheism divide, recognized three Abrahamic religions, and became the first president in American history to recognize the Hindu religion. It follows the Euclidian necessary *and* sufficient logic found in Spinoza's pantheism, or an acceptance of all gods that literary and social theory as well as social philosophy made accessible by coining the term "cosmopolitan."[139]

Relying on a cosmopolitan notion of civic religion to frame his Cairo speech to combat Orientalism, or the idea of Western superiority, Obama notes that Islam has always been a part of the American narrative. Like Lincoln's attempt to rewrite the Constitution in the Gettysburg Address by making equality a founding principle of the Federalists, Obama rewrites the American immigrant story to make it our current story. He anchors America's identity, past and present, in religious pluralism, not in its Anglo-Saxon Christian lineage. Obama underscores the cultural, linguistic, and geographic diversity of American citizens, making this diversity so expansive that civic religion accepts both religion *and* atheism.

Religious pluralism creates a jumbling, or "jumping together," of different and divergent religious traditions around a shared principle of responsibility. "Obama developed the responsibilities of the citizen and affirmed the role of soldiers who were fighting in foreign nations or who had died in service to their country. He built to a second climax in the [inaugural] address with illustrations of selfless citizens providing unrewarded assistance to others, announcing that the traditional values of honesty and hard work were old, and that there was a great need for a new era of responsibility, which he argued was the price and promise of citizenship."[140]

In his 2009 inaugural address, Obama vested humans with agency, holding that the past can yield to progressive change: "Men and women and children of every race and every faith can join in celebration across this magnificent mall." Obama gave voice to the language of being represented by Rick Warren's invocation as well as to the second perspective voiced by Joseph Lowry's benediction, reflecting the language of becoming.[141]

"The arc of the universe is long, but it bends toward justice," is Rev. Dr. Martin Luther King Jr.'s phrase, one that Obama utters fondly and often. God calls people to "shape an uncertain destiny." This notion of uncertainty, as will be shown in chapter 5, does not merely pervade Obama's belief in religion and politics, as well as other aspects of domestic politics, but also accounts for the humility within his foreign policy. Obama's notion of civic religion challenges the Bush doctrine that heralds the future of the United States in terms of our dominance and our triumph. Obama promotes multilateralism.[142]

Finally, Obama's notion of civic religion challenges American nativism. Republican Newt Gingrich, for instance, believes that American citizens cannot be citizens of the world. "What if [Obama] is so outside our comprehension, that only if you understand Kenyan, anti-colonial behavior, can you begin to piece together [his actions]? That is the most accurate, predictive model for his behavior." Gingrich is right in that Obama is cosmopolitan. Comfortable with other countries and cultures, Obama rejects nativism in the United States. Conservatives, however, keep propagating the wrong-headed idea that nativism is pro-Americanism. During his run for the GOP nomination, Gingrich and his wife Callista produced and co-starred in "A City Upon a Hill: The Spirit of American Exceptionalism." No matter how many fact check-ers debunked the debunkers, or commentators called foul, arguing that Obama's critique of American hegemony and support for religious toler-ance is not equivalent to anti-Americanism, "conservatives nevertheless are on a tear to save American exceptionalism, or at least their view of it, from the likes of Obama."[143]

Obama's vision of civic religion is not rooted in Western civiliza-tion. Yet it is premised upon a version of Christianity that is wide and welcoming. It did not grow out of the Enlightenment or English natural law, but it is tolerant and inclusive of all peoples who accept this faith. Obama situates civic religion in the Hebraic Christian tradition. Obama places God beyond the reach of the nation-state. In telling the story of America, he retells the journey of its origins by describing the pain endured by those who helped found and develop the country. Americans are therefore citizens of the United States *and* the world, and they are responsible for themselves and others.[144]

Sex and Sexuality

Obama's universal anti-universalism also extends to sex education of minors. Demonstrating that drug abuse is a general problem, not just a black one, and stripping the United States of its claim to a Christian lineage were not enough for the president. Obama also began fund-ing school sex education that promotes safe sex, not just so-called abstinence-only programs. He funded programs that could demon-strate—in large, randomized trials that follow rigorous methods of test-ing—that they effectively prevent pregnancy and sexually transmitted disease. Unlike abstinence-only education, safe sex education does not offer minors morals. It represents an education program that offers no values of chastity, but promotes public health. Safe sex education acknowl-edges the facts that an overwhelming number of teenagers have sex and should therefore use protection to prevent disease and pregnancy.[145]

Obama is undoubtedly aware of the correlations between sex, sex education, unwanted pregnancy, and race. He replaced the discontinued

abstinence programs with a new teenage-pregnancy-prevention initiative to curb the 400,000 teen births every year. Administered by
the newly established Office of Adolescent Health (OAH) within the
Department of Health and Human Services, it funded existing programs
by following the "Race to the Top logic" established by the Department of Education. "This administration and this Congress have made
a historic investment in preventing teen pregnancy," said Bill Albert,
chief program officer at the National Campaign to Prevent Teen and
Unplanned Pregnancy.

Obama undoubtedly knows that seventeen states would have sent his
mother to prison for twenty years for violating the law forbidding inter-
racial marriage when she became pregnant with him. Obama's parents
participated in a post-pregnancy marriage. Obviously his mother and father did not regret his birth, but Obama was aware of this delicate situation. Not until 1967, when Obama was five years old, were "miscegenation laws" declared unconstitutional.[146]

The Obama administration also came down in favor of allowing
faith-based groups to receive federal monies, but not if they discriminated
against vulnerable populations, such as those not practicing heterosexuality. Obama refuses to enforce the Defense of Marriage Act (DOMA)
on the grounds that it promotes discriminatory actions on many different levels of governance. He came out unequivocally in support of gay
rights when he instructed Attorney General Holder not to enforce the
DOMA. Holder informed the media that "he and President Obama had
determined—after an extensive review—that the law's key section is unconstitutional. 'Given that conclusion,'" Holder added, "'the President
has instructed the Department not to defend the statute' in court."[147]

On this issue, too, Obama seeks support from public opinion. He
changed with the culture. Just five years ago, a journalist wrote in 2011,
"support for gay marriage barely topped a third of all Americans. Now,
53 percent say gay marriage should be legal." What is more, this shift
is "'very consistent with a lot of other polling data we've seen and the
general momentum we've seen over the past year and a half,' said Evan
Wolfson, president of Freedom to Marry, a leading pro-gay-marriage
group. 'As people have come to understand this is about loving, committed families dealing, like everyone, with tough times, they understand
how unfair it is to treat them differently.'"[148]

In 2012 Obama took the symbolic step of supporting marriage between same-sex couples. One month later the First Circuit U.S. Court
of Appeals decided that DOMA's denial of equal treatment of same-sex
couples legally married in states that permit it makes DOMA unconsti-

tutional. Both decisions appeal to the Supreme Court's swing vote, Justice Anthony Kennedy, by relying on the 1996 Supreme Court precedent *Romer v. Evans*, which says that animus toward gays is not a legitimate reason for government to discriminate, rather than asserting that there is a fundamental right for homosexuals to marry. "There's no question that this [decision] is in concert with the president's views," said law professor Suzanne Goldberg, who hears DOMA's "death knell."[149]

Pooling Problems or Harm Reduction

The rhetorical context that Republicans and social-welfare-state Democrats create juxtaposes the individual (read credit or blame) with society (read patronizing help or sharing). But Obama believes the American state, market, and society need not be limited to these binaries. Society need not subsume individual values and norms. The individual need not be sacrificed as the self dissolves into the society. Having a state that does not blame its citizens is not the same as refusing to judge them or make them accountable.

We can imagine how public goods can be universalized by the pooling of resources, but doing so does not necessarily mean pushing for universal public goods. Universalizing involves the process of making a policy widespread. It is the making, not the principle, that counts. It is how many people a public policy covers that counts. Pooling particularly takes care of the middle class and the poor, but not because we care. It is not propelled by benevolence; it is fueled by economy. Universalizing or pooling while suspending judgment helps the poor not by providing them with opportunities, but rather by purchasing goods.[150]

Under pooling, buying benefits in bulk is cheaper than buying them on an ad hoc basis. Preventing diseases, illnesses, and injuries is cheaper than using emergency care. Providing good high schools, colleges, and technical schools costs less than building prisons or handing out welfare.

Pie and Privileges: Obama Spurns European Social Welfare Lite

To better understand pooling or universalizing in the frontier state, one must compare it with the strong European social welfare state. Aside from Britain, most European nation-states give every citizen a specifically sized slice of pie. The trick is getting invited to the table: you must be born European to sit there. It is a sense of entitlement that creates a community that helps its citizens see the bottom line or the notion of social justice underlying the European social welfare nation-state.

Americans lack any such cultural sense of entitlement. The native-born have few more privileges than those born abroad. Rhetoric about entitlement falls flat because it goes against our political homogeneity. It also goes against the American power structure.[151]

The United States also lacks the ability to suspend judgment. The Republicans blame individuals for their own problems, and this explains how little funding goes to the poor. Whereas Europeans see the poor as unfortunate, Americans hold them personally accountable for their plight. Meanwhile the Democrats blame society, sometimes relieving its citizens of responsibility. They look to big government for solutions. A new progressive vision, however, would benefit from putting an end to blame altogether.

Spinoza's ideas about self-preservation fit in with the American political beliefs and values described above. By pooling resources, Obama can build a state and promote a market that creates incentives for individuals to follow that bolster society. Pooling resources, moreover, is an idea not owned by the Right or the Left. Instead of venturing on the Right/Left or Locke/Rousseau or classical liberal/social liberal divide, pooling mixes and matches motives and outcomes that are distinctively American. This idea emphasizes efficiency and looks at outcomes. It creates a bottom line without romance.

Necessary and *Sufficient: Interdependency Based on Survivability*

For Obama, initiative and self-reliance still count. Initiative sparks more initiative. He proposes, for instance, policies that harness "the ingenuity of farmers, and scientists, and entrepreneurs to free this nation from the tyranny of oil once and for all." It sometimes takes the initiative of only one person to clear a path out of the wilderness. Yet initiative is not enough. Following mathematical logic of necessary and sufficient, Obama insists that it is necessary and sufficient to have initiative and self-reliance, thereby creating a productive type of mutual reliance or completing the Three Musketeers cry of "all for one and one for all." Everyone is interrelated and interdependent, often facing the very same limitations in life.[152]

Obama believes in relational power. He views Americans as an interdependent mass. We are bound together. Obama refers to this as interconnectedness. This term is overarching, as he speaks of the "interconnected world of this new century" in terms of the economy, the environment, war, and globalism, among other issues.[153]

Obama emphasizes relationality with the state and society, but he does not see it as built on benevolence, as mentioned earlier, which is why no one should tell a teenager to practice abstinence or determine that only heterosexual couples can be married by the state. It is not that people care for each other; as Obama said in Cairo, unlike most European nation-states, Americans do not have a community united by a common religion or a national heritage. Rather, they take care of one another, as Dewey argues, because it increases their own chances of survivability. Two heads are smarter than one. During a winter storm, two bodies pressed together are warmer than one.[154]

Being tied together does not mean that this mass constitutes an organic whole. Nor does advancing tolerance mean that there is no mass. The second fundamental principle that Obama adopts is that while a group of reform-minded citizens should step forward, it should be a group not imbued with its own identity. For Obama, a group constitutes a collective, not a community. He honors the American tradition of having no common nationality, racial or ethnic identity, or religion. Presenting his own experience as evidence of his conviction, Obama said, "I have brothers, sisters, nieces, nephews, uncles and cousins, of every race and every hue scattered across three continents."[155]

For Obama, the absence of a community means that Americans are a collectivity that is better described as a compilation of individuals pulling together in pursuit of a common goal, though one devoid of a substantive set of values and beliefs.[156] The group is not defined by the essence or the political identity of its individual members, unlike turn-of-the-twentieth-century Republican and Democrats, many of whom advanced Americanization, or a substantive value behind being American, or the post–World War II Cold War liberals purporting democratization or the medicalization of gay, lesbian, or transgendered people (LGBTers).[157] "I will value your contribution to this country and I will do what I can to encourage it," Obama explains, "because I understand that how well you do is inextricably linked to how well America does."[158]

Power, Benevolence, and Responsibilities

The power necessary for "change" emanates both from the individual members of a group and from the collective weight of those members. Unlike a community, a collective must find and develop its principles on the basis of consensus. The principles created by such a consensus are not fixed. As the pragmatists argue, action must be informed by theory and theory by action. For these reasons, democratic progressivism represents an ongoing, perpetually evolving experiment. Community organizers must be flexible and adapt to each situation. Society is "in a never ending process of flux." It is in "an unending competition and conflict of interests." Change was the only constant Alinsky and the pragmatists recognized. To Obama, the "genius of this nation" is that "America can change."[159]

Why did Obama choose to work in Alinsky's type of community organizing? Not only did he believe that people can change, but he accepted (and accepts) Alinsky's and Spinoza's belief that the communitarian view expressed by Rousseau is naïve and romantic, since it lacks a theory of power. They all condemn the communitarians for placing the individual and the community in opposition. In Spinoza's view, it is the state that helps people preserve and perfect themselves, and by so doing offers hope, security, and freedom. It is not that man cares for man—we are not by nature benevolent—but that man must band together with man for survival. There is power in numbers. And with each number being equal, or each individual having an equal share of power, cooperation and consensus, not conflict, cements the state and society. During his career as a community organizer, Obama adopted a similar position: "His community organizing work has taught him the realities of power based negotiation, in which the status quo is always supported by strong and vocal forces that must be overcome to accomplish change."[160]

For Spinoza, Alinsky, and Obama, the state is not an umpire to whom we surrender our authority so that it can maintain peace. Nor is the state a nanny who gets us to behave well by demanding our obedience. The state cannot persuade us to comply "for our own good." Rather, the state is a powerful entity that derives its legitimacy from the people it governs. To be sure, the state is a necessity. But rather than blowing whistles or making us do what is good for us, the Spinozan state strives toward creating norms that help its citizens achieve their potential. We may never achieve our potential, but that's the point: it's the striving, the journey of becoming on a wagon train, that counts.[161]

But how do you create a society whose members can strive toward their potential without believing in benevolence? You do so by abandoning morality and abstaining from judgment. A state authority need not be moralistic or, if it fails to achieve a certain type of morality, hypocritical.

First, the Spinozan state does require moral or benevolent leaders. Because political leaders, like everyone else, are susceptible to corruption, Spinoza suggests that those leaders be placed in an organizational configuration that does not rely on their "good" character. In Spinoza's view, a state that depends on a human being's good faith is an unstable state. To be self-sustaining, a state must not rely on leaders who can be led astray by either reason or passion.[162]

Second, Spinoza frees citizens of moral responsibility. This is not to say that citizens are free to act however they please; when something goes wrong, the state simply says, "This has to stop, and in order for it to stop we have to intervene." But the act and its effects are what elicit the state's response, not the actor. State authorities are not saying, "You are the site of evil through your exercise of freedom, so you must be punished." A Spinozan state and society lack moralistic judgments, though without releasing their members from liability or accountability. When something goes awry, both the rulers and the ruled seek reform, as in other types of states; the difference is that this reform is blame-free and collective.

Citizens may not be held morally responsible, but they can still enjoy collective redemption, as Obama refers to it. Both Spinoza and Obama believe that responsibility is always a collective matter—it cannot be attributed to either the individual or society. The individual blame/societal constraints binary should not exist. Both individual and society seek— in Obama's words—"collective solutions." Obama has faith in mutual reliance, collective solutions, and collective redemption.[163]

Spinoza's emphasis on collective responsibility and Obama's notion of collective redemption correspond well with the unique American penchants for accountability and tolerance. Spinoza does not believe that the individual self should be dissolved into society. Few sacrifices should be made. But how can a state ask for no individual sacrifice and yet maintain a collective identity based on tolerance? How can the state keep pushing the envelope? The one-word answer is *difference*.

United States of Sameness?

Spinoza's individual, state, and society are premised on difference rather than sameness. By contrast, classical liberals make the individual paramount. As Alexis de Tocqueville observed in the nineteenth century, American individualism promotes sameness. Ironically, he noted, individualism constitutes a novel expression that gives birth to egotism or selfishness. Rather than seeing selfishness as a virtue, as the GOP does, Tocqueville considered it a "passionate and exaggerated love of self." Individualism blights the "germ of all virtue," sapping the "virtues of public life," or what we call the public good. Individualism counters the European class system to good and bad effect. Everyone may indeed achieve a certain equality of condition, but it cultivates sameness as they run the selfish race alone.[164]

To be sure, classical liberalism does breed a certain amount of tolerance, with everyone recognizing another person's rights. The individual has the right to do whatever she wants as long as it does not cross the line, hindering another individual. When mixed with capitalism, however, classical liberalism turns tolerance into competition, which then guides everything. As everyone pursues their own advantage, they compete with one another, and this competition supposedly helps everyone achieve their potential. But with the line between the private and public spheres fixed, this competition also produces large discrepancies between the rich and the poor, the elite and the non-elite, and the college educated and the less educated. This marker, this line, jimmies the system. A single mother cannot compete with a working husband who has a wife at home who cleans house, picks up his dry cleaning, and takes care of the children. Yet classical liberalism explains discrepancies away not by acknowledging the line, but by attributing them solely to an individual's merit or talent. The working husband has more talent than the single mom.

The United States does not practice what radical feminists call "naming interests" or put an end to "privileged unknowing." We do not acknowledge the wife's role behind the working husband. Of her white Christian ancestry, poet and activist Minnie Bruce Pratt confessed, "We have gotten our jobs, bought our houses, borne and educated our children by the negatives: no niggers, no kikes, no wops, no dagos, no spics, no A-rabs, no gooks, no queers. . . . Jobs, houses, and education—all represented the privilege of access or were all modes of attachment that reproduce systems of privilege." To Pratt, this is American history. Obama also insists that much American excess is cultural. "What accounts for the change in CEO pay is not any market imperative. It's cultural. . . . Sometimes we need both cultural change and government action," he elaborates.[165]

But going even further is the radical feminist argument that, *in theory*, no individual should be privileged and no group can be privileged. It is not that privilege is unfair, nor that it exposes the hypocrisy of a nation supposedly founded on equality of opportunity. Rather, it's because there is no such theoretical construct as "we the people." There is "no women's movement." There is no single mother versus a traditional husband and father. This is a mirage. Each situation must be examined in its own right. Obama phrases it best with his notion of universalizing. "What would help minority workers are the same things that would help white workers: the opportunity to earn a living wage, the education and training that leads to such jobs, labor laws and tax laws that restore balance to the distribution of the nation's wealth and health-care, child care, and retirement systems that working people can count on."[166]

In Mind and Body

By rejecting the Cartesian duality and accepting monism, Spinoza and critical theorists such as radical feminists understand that our identities are in flux and therefore cannot be privileged. The divorced mom who remarries could be receiving two forms of support—the father's child support and her new husband's economic support—that help her provide better for her children than a husband and father supporting a nuclear family. Gloria Anzaldúa put this in everyday terms, stating, "This morning I looked in the mirror to see how I was (I keep changing)." Or, as Obama frames it in policy terms, "An emphasis on universal, as opposed to race-specific, programs isn't just good policy; it's also good politics."[167]

We all have "multiple identities and live in multiple, simultaneous, and overlapping contexts."[168] Hence we can engage only in groups that facilitate, not suppress, the flexibility, fluidity, and multiplicity of our complex identities. No identity should be privileged. During the 2008 election Obama used his own identity as the son of a Kansan and a Kenyan to show the intersection, the nexus, as a means of arguing against identity politics while showing that he understood the politics of identity.

Obama's victory was not because of affirmative action. Having the identity of a Kansan and a Kenyan meant something specific, but not something static; he was not looking to capture the crucial Kansan-Kenyan bloc of supporters. Critics such as Cornel West and Tavis Smiley nonetheless still criticize Obama, saying he's not "beautifully black." They think he lacks the "courage" to represent African Americans.[169] Neither West nor Smiley accepts Obama's belief that he can present a politics of difference that will be fair and just to African Americans and their lineage. West and Smiley are suspicious of a politics that accepts the fluidity of ever-changing identities as an expression of individuality.

Spinoza would consider both Locke and Rousseau idealists because they elevate the mind over the body in the Cartesian duality. Spinoza's philosophy works well with the idea of fluid identities precisely because he rejects the mind/body duality, as well as the nature/culture one and the reason/passion one. Obama too writes about these complexities—not identity, but the multiracial identities, shaped by the personal context of how and where he was raised, that created his individuality. He raises questions about nature and nurture and mixes reason with passion in describing his grandmother's fear of a black man who scared her at the bus stop. Explaining who it was and why she no longer wanted to ride the bus, his grandmother admitted, "The fella was black." And "the words," Obama said, "were like a fist in my stomach."[170]

It is not only our physical fluidity, but also the way the mind and body work in tandem, that makes a difference. In Spinoza's view, each action in the mind coincides with an action in the body, and each passion in the body with a passion in the mind. He challenges the bleak analytical empiricism and rational-choice theory that flatten out the circuits of political life that they purport to represent and explain. The mind does not dictate or control the body. Nor does the body control the mind. Not everyone has the multiracial identity of Obama, with relatives on three continents, but we all have multiple identities.[171]

Given this complexity, political actors cannot know what their citizens need without a great deal of input. People do not need a prescribed amount captured on an actuary's spreadsheet. Nor should experts inform us about what we need. In Spinoza's view, the individual's subjectivity is always a becoming, not a being. It is more akin to political existentialism than essentialism. He does not anchor everyone by categorizing or cataloguing their needs. Because everyone's identity is fluid, or in process, the only means of changing the context that does influence this process is by constructing a new one. The context can change. The context can be transformative.

Unlike that of Hobbes, who emphasizes that people exchange some of their liberty for security provided by the state, Spinoza's state helps free people by helping them get what they need. Spinoza does not derive the state's authority from either natural or legal rights. People do not give anything up. They are not accepting state authority in exchange for security. The passions that led Hobbes to believe in a war of "all against all" that only a covenant can stop are not vices. Spinoza considers these passions instead to be properties of human nature.[172]

Ethics grows out of the endeavor of the self to preserve itself. But because the self is inevitably invested in a larger world, or (better put) because it enters into compositions with other selves, the "conatus"—the embodied impetus to self-preservation—has the capacity to become extended. Yet another vague Spinozan term, the conatus shows that a person can be part of larger entity. One body overlaps with others, composing networks of contacts and connections through family, work, and the broader body politic, or what democratic theorists call a constellation of groups in civil society.[173]

As theorist Genevieve Lloyd explains, Spinoza shifts thinking about what is social and collective to an awareness of the body as it is impinged on by, or in relation to, other bodies. A commuter confident about when her suburban train departs sees another person walking toward the train station at a faster pace and adjusts her own pace. A lone bystander sees someone fall into a canal, and that person seems to be drowning. She jumps into the canal and rescues that person, forgetting her own fears of drowning. As part of a small crowd, the same bystander might not make the leap, waiting for the others to jump in, and if they are all thinking the same thing, the person in the canal might just drown. It is the context that helps shape the outcome.

Bracketing Judgment

Obama's notions about universalizing represent a similar attempt to change the context. He recognizes the "politics of resentment" for what it is—a wedge that generates and mobilizes all the animosity of the white working class. He tries to mitigate this animosity by showing how this wedge splits apart those who should be united, those who have a universal allegiance against privilege, and how its exclusivity splits and divides Americans so that they cannot achieve a meritocracy. Republicans latched on to the divide between the white working class and African Americans around issues like affirmative action. As a result, Obama wants to abandon identity politics. He wants to universalize the problems and unite the opposition against those who disguise their privilege.[174]

To do so, Americans must remember their lineage. "I believe that part of America's genius has always been its ability to absorb newcomers," writes Obama, "to forge a national identity out of the disparate lot that arrived on our shores." He takes a very nuanced position on race: "When I hear commentators interpreting my speech to mean that we have arrived at a 'postracial politics' or that we already live in a color-blind society, I have to offer a word of caution. To say that we are one people is not to suggest that race no longer matters—that the fight for equality has been won, or that the problems that minorities face in this country today are largely self-inflicted. We know the statistics." Obama realizes that none of this is so simple. Instead, he offers us a split screen:

"To think clearly about race, then, requires us to see the world on a split screen—to maintain in our sights the kind of America that we want while looking squarely at America as it is, to acknowledge the sins of our past and the challenges of the present without becoming trapped in cynicism or despair."[175]

To name privilege and to find the Republican strategy of exclusion—of keeping the riffraff out of their whites-only country clubs, for instance—Obama insists we go back to our Jacksonian roots. He insists we support the middle class. "It is through the quintessentially American path of upward mobility that the black middle class has grown fourfold in a generation, and that the black poverty rate was cut in half. Through a similar process of hard work and commitment to family, Latinos have seen comparable gains."[176]

Obama wants to create a new context in which an inclusive middle class—independent of race, independent of ethnicity—is again open to all who wash up on our American shores: "Ultimately, the most important tool to close the gap between minority and white workers may have little to do with race at all." Obama tries to take away the emotion of resentment and reunite those who will all profit from universalizing substantive policies like education or health care. "These days, what ails working-class and middle-class blacks and Latinos is not fundamentally different from what ails their white counterparts: downsizing, outsourcing, automation, wage stagnation, the dismantling of employer-based health-care and pension plans, and schools that fail to teach young people the skills they need to compete in a global economy."

Obama's Spinozan ideas about the individual's fluidity and complexity can be viewed as homespun. They reflect the American penchant toward inclusivity, meritocracy, and equality. Obama does not want African Americans and Latinos to hold on to their identity; they must escape identity politics to escape the universal problems that plague the United States in the early twenty-first century.[177]

Civic Religion Plus Rock and Roll

Obama believes the United States has undergone great change, a change that promotes difference. Max Weber understood the history of religion and culture in *The Protestant Ethic* as a history of rationalization combined with the world's increasing disenchantment with magic. These two changes, however, unfolded over two sequential stages, not simultaneously. Science, experts, knowledge, all began to trump magic and religious prophecy.[178]

Under Obama, *Wissenschaft* is waxing, while religion is waning. Religion has lost its hold in the United States. The last industrialized nation to undergo secularization, the United States faces great struggles between "Us and Them." The Moral Majority, which dissolved in 1989, and the Tea Party are rearguard social movements trying to revive an old era. As the United States has more and more of its denizens declaring that they are "not religious," it is difficult to base programs on religious beliefs, let alone base a culture on assumed shared values. Public policies will increasingly be instituted because of evidence, not norms or ideology.

As explained earlier, Spinoza counters the Hobbesian maxim that people are wolves. People are capable of helping one another. All people, and therefore all politics, are relational. Spinoza recognizes that alone, the individual lacks power. People help one another to gain power in what, in today's terms, could be seen as a constellation of groups that compose civil society. Or as Obama explains it, "We are our brother's keepers. Our sister's keepers."[179]

4

Obama Stakes the Nation: A Spinozan Stakeholder State, Market, and Society

Since the day he took office, Obama has been a transformative leader, instituting a plethora of ruptures in forty-year-old public policies—transforming the war on drugs, changing policies that privilege Christianity, and issuing executive orders and taking executive action on sex education as well as giving or bolstering rights for the LGBT community. Yet these reform efforts, which are substantively and methodologically consistent with democratic pragmatic progressivism, have not been portrayed as a type of liberalism or progressivism with Obama's name qualifying it. There are as yet no "Obama Democrats," no "Age of Obama."

Few people recognize Obama and his administration for what it is: a Spinozan stakeholder state and society that promotes civic action. It creates what some scholars call a "commons," a virtual and physical space or interconnected terrain where local, state, national, transnational, and global governmental and nongovernmental actors can tackle a substantive public policy problem from a multitude of intersecting and crosscutting perspectives. Changing the *way* we govern may be an even bigger Obama accomplishment than his many policy initiatives.

This absence of a label for Obama's era would be understandable if his ideas were foreign, fresh, or free-floating, but they are not. What is little known by the

public, though understood and accepted by Washington insiders, is that
Obama's policy platform for reform advances an existing administrative
state that actually embraces and enhances deliberative democracy even
though it represents a departure from the traditional social welfare state.
It does this by giving governmental and nongovernmental actors access
to the making of policies that are implemented within a horizontal and
diagonal federalist framework. The nation-state facilitates equality of
opportunity and earned egalitarianism for those who help influence this
interconnected whole in ways that affect its citizenry.[1]

The state that Obama advances has been given more than a dozen
names, including "collaborative governance," "decentering regulation,"
"democratic experimentalism," "responsive regulation," "negotiated
governance," "cooperative implementation," and "interactive compliance." What all these terms share is that they describe something fluid,
deliberative, inclusive, and democratic.[2]

Obama's platform for reform promotes not simply a national state
with increased federal regulatory powers, but a hybrid state that facilitates dynamic interactions among governmental and nongovernmental
players, who combine to shape regulatory reform. They are not simply
recipients helped or hindered by the reform, but participants.

The Obama administration creates a regulatory role for the federal government by promoting a new type of federalism "in service of
progressive policy." It is not the New Federalism that the conservative
William Rehnquist court and Ronald Reagan sought, with the federal
government privileging state sovereignty and the Tenth Amendment by
returning control over health, welfare, and education to the states while
reducing national funding. Obama develops what some scholars characterize as a "hybrid model of federal policy innovation and leadership,
which mixes money, mandates, and flexibility in new and distinctive
ways."[3]

The Obama administration identifies a common policy problem, such
as climate change, targets progressive options or solutions, and then gets
state, local, and even sublocal governmental and nongovernmental actors to interact from a multidimensional perspective. As in negotiated
rulemaking, these actors commit themselves to a dynamic that emphasizes cooperation rather than conflict. "Critical decisions about the
actual scope of state powers and autonomy," as one law professor
described, have been moved from Congress or the judiciary to the "halls
of agencies like the Department of Health and Human Services (HHS)
and the Department of Education." "Federal administrative agencies
have long had substantial power over the shape of nation-state rela-

tionships, but the recent regulatory developments expand that power considerably . . . allowing states to exercise genuine implementation discretion—indeed at times actively soliciting state partnerships." Governmental and nongovernmental actors on local, state, and sometimes even global and transnational levels deliberate possibilities for "deconstruction and reconstruction" of a single public policy. They suspend, bracket, or check their predictable "self-inter-ests," as Hannah Arendt describes them, at the door during the deliberative process.[4]

This type of federalism denies that governmental and nongovernmental actors must remain locked into predictable positions or patterns of rational self-interested behavior. Dynamic interaction among a diverse set of public and private actors who work horizontally and diagonally on all levels of government—international, national, state, local, and sublocal—helps them tackle large- and small-scale problems from the top down, or the bottom up, or even sideways, in a spirit of cooperation or good governance. It is a dynamic zigzag, given its multiple dimensionality in terms of the size and scale of the issue and the axis and hierarchy of access for the participants' interaction. Like negotiated rulemaking, this type of federalism spurns zero-sum decision making.[5]

Legislation increasing regulatory power, relying on negotiated rulemaking and based in part on a horizontal and diagonal federalist framework, follows a well-worn path—a third tradition in American politics. Demonstrating this in a chapter devoted to the domestic package of public policy reforms that Obama has put before Congress and the federal courts requires an archaeological road map. Obama does not build a new administrative state, but follows this third path, excavating old institutional configurations, shoring them up by interspersing old and new theoretical planks, and ensuring progressive purpose.

Navigating the Terrain

Part 1 of this chapter reviews the general theoretical planks and pillars of Obama's facilitator nation-state. It shows how he emphasizes negotiated rulemaking, deputizes third parties that promote public interest, and energizes the popular branches of government, all the while wielding the executive branch's regulatory powers when neither Congress nor the federal courts will cooperate.

Part 2 provides two examples of national regulatory reform after reviewing tenets of behavioral economics that can be crosscut with a Spinozan theory of governance. First, it presents the Obama administration's rulemaking for the Americans with Disabilities Act Amendments

Act (ADAAA). Second, it outlines the executive branch's regulatory reform of climate control when faced with Congress's reluctance to legislate.

Part 3 traces how all of this regulatory reform and rulemaking emphasis intersects with Obama's legislative legacy—the stimulus bill, health care, and financial regulation. Part 4 returns to theoretical claims, scrutinizing how this newly excavated nation-state, built on layers of states and localities, invokes civic work and civic action. Part 5 concludes the chapter by showing what Obama inspires with his Race to the Top values of inclusivity, diversity, and difference—his approach to public policies that encourage cooperation, instill competition, and generate norms that cannot be categorized as moral or universal, but are ever-changing and thereby perpetually expose the privileges associated with promoting the status quo. They reflect Spinoza's ethic that underlies good governance.

This third American political tradition promotes deliberative democracy and deputizes its middle-class citizenry instead of building a stronger federal state ruled largely by elites and experts. It opens the process not just to the parties involved—through lobbyists representing industries targeted by the regulation—but also to state, local, and sublocal officials and to grassroots and community organizers who have the public interest at heart, and it invites them all to sit at the same table. Pulling "back the curtain . . . on Obama's agenda" reveals that it is "strikingly similar to those of the biggest progressive nonprofits" and that "the White House has ensured that the left is invested in the president's success." Obama demands that all players deliberate from a kaleidoscope of perspectives, spurning the idea that self-interest is entrenched and predictable. "Inviting ideological opponents," one political journalist described, "has had the effect of neutralizing (in the case of the big health insurance providers) or shaming (in the case of the major credit-card executives) powerful interests into a more favorable stance with respect to [what] White House policy asks."[6]

Part 1: Making Indeterminate Laws?

For the last fifteen years, an administrative revolution—what one law professor calls a "Renew Deal"—has been unfolding. Now, under Obama, a new regulatory regime—a third way, reflecting a *tri*lemma—has emerged. It constitutes nothing less than a revolution in government, one as significant as the New Deal.[7]

It's not surprising that Obama capitalized on this administrative revolution, given his penchant for using the popular branches of government, rather than the judiciary, and for transforming existing structures for progressive purposes. Turning away from the courts, which no longer serve the civil rights community (as seen in the previous chapter), Obama promotes legislation that gives the executive branch vast administrative power. Bureaucratic procedures are often as dull as they are opaque, and scholars of politics may be forgiven for seeking more rewarding topics to study. But understanding Obama's vision for the regulatory process is the key to understanding Obama's reforms.

Negotiated rulemaking, the crux of this type of regime, was codified in 1990 with the Negotiated Rulemaking Act, passed by a Democratic Congress and signed by George H. W. Bush. In 1996 a Republican Congress and the Clinton administration reauthorized the law and made it permanent. Both Republicans and Democrats accepted it, since members of both parties practice what this book calls the public policy "wink-wink"—dodging blame for controversial pieces of legislation, like those concerning health care and financial regulation. Obama achieved a consensus that legislation *about* health care and financial regulation should be passed, but he could not get his own party, let alone the Republicans, to concur with the content he wanted, so negotiated rulemaking was the ideal vehicle for him.

Under Obama's system, the president, not the House or Senate, invites the first set of people to sit at the rulemaking table. Given the vagueness of the legislation and the scope of the task, this is where the rules are made that will determine governance. In soliciting input, however, he goes beyond the usual corporate leaders and lobbyists, expanding the participants to include nonprofits and public organizations. This shift is even more important than it seems, because the usual players may not be able to return to their dominance of the table after Obama leaves office. Obama's system creates a procedural practice that could be difficult to dismantle or disassemble *if* progressives accept his invitations to participate.

Administrative Federalism: Recovery, Care, and Affordable Protection. To achieve these goals, Obama relied on conservative methods, including federalism: "What is striking so far in the Obama Administration is the range of methods and the intensity of its efforts to influence state policies, budgets, and administration." The influence works both ways, as the states are given a "role in setting the content of federal regulatory standards and even overseeing federal agency performance." Climate change offers an instructive example. The Senate's recalcitrance ensured that Obama would not pass national legislation in this area, making executive branch and federalist action necessary if he was to have any impact on the environment. Fortunately, Obama had installed horizontal and diagonal federalist frameworks for all of his legislative achievements in 2009 and 2010.[8]

This type of federalism is all for progressive purposes. As Gillian Metzger explains, "States that choose to stay on the sidelines face the prospect of direct federal intervention or loss of access to substantial federal funds, and their ability to pursue their preferred regulatory (or deregulatory) strategies may be curtailed." To be sure, Obama offers the states money, but what makes this type of federalism distinctive is that he offers them control as well. In the new health insurance system, for example, states play a pivotal role, with their responsibilities ranging from creating and operating health insurance exchanges to overseeing premium rate increases to running expanded Medicaid programs.[9]

States also have increased regulatory responsibilities under the Dodd-Frank Wall Street Reform and Consumer Protection Act. The federal government now takes a restrictive approach to preemption. Unlike the Bush administration, Obama insisted that federal agencies give the "legitimate prerogatives" of the states "full consideration." That is, only if a state undermines, rather than furthers, the intent or purpose of federal legislation can a federal administrative agency preempt its action. For instance, California's attempt to be more restrictive about regulating greenhouse gas emissions will be encouraged, not discouraged, by Obama's Environmental Protection Agency (EPA). Federal regulations provide only a floor, not a ceiling, to further the administration's goals.[10]

The Facilitator State. What makes this new administrative emphasis Spinozan is that normative authority is expanded and pluralized. The state is only *a* facilitator—not an adjudicator or legislator, as it was during the New Deal and Great Society eras. The state deputizes stakeholders, or civic agents.

Under this system, questions about the capacity of the state are, as Dewey and Obama keep saying, less about its size—big or small—than about its function. What does the state *do*? Under Obama, the state enhances the capacity of its citizens to participate in political and civic life and facilitates multilateral involvement as a way of creating norms, cultivating reform, and managing what some call "new market realities."

The greatest stakeholder participation occurs, however, at the implementation stage. Congress passes legislation about controlling climate change, for instance, but the question remains, how much? The answer emerges from a series of meetings, studies, analyses, and negotiations among regulators and interested parties.[11]

This stakeholder state and society recognizes that a regulatory regime that catches an oil company polluting has failed. The EPA, for instance, sets a regulation that creates a code; an oil company exceeds that limit; and then, after years of litigation, the judiciary weighs in, rendering a ruling for enforcement. Not only is this regulatory regime burdened by costly litigation, but the litigation takes years to play out, given how cumbersome the process is. With all parties recognizing these costs, regulation got a bad name, and in the 1980s the Republicans advanced deregulation, which worked even less well.[12]

Both models failed. The traditional administrative state—what law professors call the regulatory regime model—was either under- or overeffective, never just right. It either "overlegalizes" or "juridifies" society. At the same time, regulation itself risks becoming colonized by the regulated subsystems—being politicized, or "economized," as either the public interest or the private interest in question captures the agency. What these two models describe, however, is not a dilemma, but a *tri*lemma, which can be resolved with a collective interaction of outside community groups.

Just as NGOs (nongovernmental organizations) emerged from the international politics of the United Nations, what could be called domestic NGOs should emerge and grow, rather than remaining on the sidelines. Progressives can opt in. They can participate in rough-and-tumble regulatory politics and help Obama achieve real and long-lasting progressive reform. Obama makes apathy and inaction perilous.[13]

Instituting Popular Government. During the Reagan era, deregulation—in reaction to the New Deal, the Great Society, and classical liberal-democratic social welfare states—became prevalent. The federal government started reducing its role, allocating fewer resources to administrative law enforcement. States increased their role in response.

Democrats in office, specifically Bill Clinton, did not restore the power of the old regulatory state. Yet while politicians and pundits continued arguing about big and small government, about improving regulatory reform or opting for deregulation, the players at the administrative law table began transcending Left/Right political alignments. Obama's policies reflect this twenty-first-century transformation in administrative law—resulting in a stakeholder state and society that does not render universal judgments, but is premised on survivability, or every person's right to self-preservation, in mundane everyday politics and public policy execution and implementation.[14]

The Spinozan democratic progressive (or stakeholder) all-inclusive social sphere achieves what Hannah Arendt called for in redefining state-society interactions: it encourages everyone to "go public" and create a multiplicity of stakeholders to share the traditional roles of governance. These stakeholders are "norm-generating nongovernmental actors," and the model promotes a movement downward and outward, transferring responsibilities to states, localities, and the private sector—including private businesses and nonprofit organizations.[15]

What the federal regulatory policies actually do is focus on the executive branch's everyday job: executing or implementing laws. The mundane daily implementation of a law or public policy involves negotiated rulemaking, audited self-regulation, performance-based rules, decentralized and dynamic problem solving, disclosure regimes, and coordinated information collection. Under the new rubric that this book calls a Spinozan stakeholder society, this level of implementation—what the government does—is defined by new features such as dynamic learning, process orientation, iteration, innovation, and adaptability.[16]

"Common Sense Rules of the Road." Unlike any executive before him, Obama is throwing open the doors of the regulatory process not just to leaders of organized groups, but to the general public. He's carved out a larger role for individual activists and for domestic NGOs. The executive order for regulatory reform that Obama issued in January 2011 contains a whole section devoted to a new "process that involves public participation." In his massive regulatory reform, Obama has designed something akin to Dewey's idea about how the *demos* can deliberate and participate in governance.[17]

Obama came into office with a tight and specific set of regulatory reform goals. He seeks "transparency, participation, regulatory analysis, and scientific integrity."[18] No goal seems more important to Obama, however, than public participation.[19]

Public participation represents the bedrock principle for this middle-class progressive. It is also a critical component of his Open Government Initiative, which encourages public engagement and denounces the Bush administration's rulemaking practice of undermining science and technology. In Obama's view, the Bush administration's refusal to use scientific experts shows the lengths to which it went to keep the public uninformed. Like Dewey and Arendt, Obama insists that only an enlightened public or active citizenship can pursue pragmatism or perpetual inquiry and process rather than universal truth. It is this process that helps the public deliberate and therefore participate in a real and worthy democracy. Obama achieves these goals of keeping the public informed and involved through extensive use of new media; as one expert describes it, "The single, most obvious manifestation of the congruence of these objectives in the federal regulatory process is e-Rulemaking."[20]

Anchoring the Choice Architects. Just as critical as Obama's emphasis on an informed, participating public having access to regulatory decision making was his choice of *who* could help him implement this vision. To that end, Obama appointed Cass Sunstein, from the University of Chicago Law School, as administrator of the Office of Information and Regulatory Affairs (OIRA). Obama and Sunstein are longtime friends who share a number of basic theoretical tenets and assumptions about human motives and behavior. They both emphasize a type of progressivism that promotes distributional equity and human dignity, and they both practice a type of pragmatist methodology that focuses on perpetual inquiry and win-win thinking. For Obama, Sunstein's contribution is exemplified most in his use of behavioral economics.

Behavioral economics, as explained in chapter 2, overturns one of the most fundamental assumptions behind the neoclassical economic theory that undergirds American capitalism. That is, it no longer expects an individual to be, or behave like, a rational, self-interested actor. Behavioral economics provides evidence against what Martha Fineman calls "the autonomy myth."[21]

Behavioral economics recognizes dependency, codependency, and interdependency as well as shared or mutual reliance. "Individual behavior departs from strictly rational action," law professor Ronald Mann writes, "in routine and predictable ways." How? Emotions get in the way. Or a social context can change individual and group behavior. Behavioral economists rely on cognitive psychologists to figure this out.[22]

In *Nudge*, a book Sunstein coauthored with Richard Thaler, a University of Chicago business school professor, these two advocates of behavioral science and economics advance a minimal state. The book is filled with ideas Sunstein has discussed with Obama since their time at the university. To Sunstein and Thaler, behavioral science and economics offer people better choices, though without requiring "anybody to *do* anything." A minimal state, reluctant to impose mandates and bans, is nonetheless shrewd about orchestrating people to behave well or move in good directions.[23]

Sunstein claims that Obama promotes a similar minimal state. In *The Audacity of Hope*, Obama included a proposal for retirement plans that came straight from Sunstein and Thaler's playbook. It would automatically enroll employees in retirement plans, requiring them to take action only if they choose *not* to participate. This strategy gives workers "a non-coercive nudge" toward making sounder decisions for better futures.[24]

Sunstein says that Obama "knows an astonishing amount about cutting-edge economic thinking." For this reason, he characterizes the president as a "visionary minimalist" who wants to pursue large goals in a way that offends the deepest values of as few people as possible. What is more, Sunstein reconciles this minimalist state with deliberative democracy.[25]

Deliberation engages civic action—action premised on preconditions, or a thick populism, if you will. Thin populism, as Albert Dzur, a theorist of deliberative democracy, explains, refers to oversimplifications, or simple ideas such as "good versus evil scripts." Most people do not embrace these "outlier" positions, but rather prefer to live in political gray. Dzur contrasts this with a "thick" populism of "increased democracy— not its curtailment."[26]

The idea of a "commons" or "common-pool resources" based on civic action, as propounded by the Bloomington school of "new" institutional economics led by Elinor Ostrom, posits "horizontal interactions among diverse agents" and "valorizes the self-directed action at the heart of participatory democracy." What Sunstein, Dzur, and Ostrom share is the notion that deliberative democracy does not stem from an unthinking, emotionally charged *demos*. Civic action requires an enlightened, informed, and educated citizenry, no matter how minimal or full-bodied the state.[27]

To Obama, this means that the public must also be prepared to listen. Individual citizens must be self-critical and follow the Socratic exhortation to "know thyself." Deliberative democracy "denotes a conversation among adults who listen to one another, who attempt to persuade one another by means of argument and evidence, and who remain open to the possibility that they could be wrong."[28]

Obama links the concept of deliberative democracy with Lincoln, who, in his first inaugural address, just five weeks before Southern militiamen fired on Fort Sumter, urged his countrymen, "Think calmly and *well*, upon this whole subject. Nothing valuable can be lost by taking time. If there be an object to *hurry* any of you, in hot haste, to a step which you would never take *deliberately*, that object will be frustrated by taking time; but no good object can be frustrated by it." Similarly, Obama demands deliberation. He embraces failure, or the idea of learning from one's limitations and mistakes. Obama emphasizes self-criticism and critical thinking. The president pushes for process over all other values, and by so doing he has co-opted procedures more identified with the conservative Right than with progressives.[29]

Nudges and Other Social Technologies. In Obama's view, the old Left/Right, regulation/deregulation, or big government/small government debate no longer applies. It reflects entrenched self-interests that have only hardened since the 1970s and need to be decentered, or shaken up. Upon declaring his presidential candidacy, Obama said, "I am convinced that whenever we exaggerate or demonize, oversimplify or overstate our case, we lose."

Acting with less than full information can be perilous in one's personal business just as it is in civic affairs. Indeed, one of the central premises of behavioral economics is that "people make mistakes all the time." The 2009 Credit Card Accountability, Responsibility, and Disclosure Act is a consummate example of legislation protecting people from making mistakes without being too intrusive.[30]

Credit card companies, like all corporations, try to push people into spending more money. They hire teams of psychologists and economists to study the routine, predictable ways in which people *anchor* decisions on managing their accounts in "arbitrary and irrelevant numbers." For instance, as Sunstein and Thaler report, when presented with a carefully chosen figure for minimum payment, "people will repay less than they otherwise would" and thus "incur greater interest charges." The trained professional who designs all of this, they explain, is a "choice architect," "responsible for organizing the context in which people make decisions."[31]

As a middle-class progressive reformer, Sunstein stands alongside reformers like Elizabeth Warren and Michael Barr of the Treasury Department with his hopes of informing the public. Like all these reformers, Sunstein hopes to curb American businesses from practicing a predatory and unfair type of capitalism that tries to trick consumers. But while Sunstein supports a minimal or default state, Warren prefers a citizenry that is more active than passive, and therefore she supports a state that emphasizes regulatory enforcement.

Not surprisingly, Sunstein's appointment as the United States' regulatory czar met with resistance from activists on the Right, many of whom still claim that deregulation holds the most promise for the American economy. "It's difficult," said one former Bush official, "to square the choice of an anti-regulatory scholar" as the nation's chief regulatory officer. "Obama's many, many promises for a new direction and moving forward from eight years of anti-regulatory, deregulatory misbehavior" has him appointing an "*anti*-regulatory" scholar. Only with a scholar like Sunstein could Obama change the table's entire dialogue, and therefore reform the whole regulatory process, as he pledged.[32]

Sunstein is not alone in breaking out of traditional channels. Many of Obama's choices for key positions, such as Secretary of Education Arne Duncan and Supreme Court justices Elena Kagan and Sonia Sotomayor, know how to play well with people from both sides of the ideological spectrum by emphasizing rules and procedures propounded by conservatives. As with Obama, their ideology does not limit or circumscribe them. In their search for solutions, they seek and find common ground with seemingly odd bedfellows, given their emphasis on rules and regulations. Sunstein, for instance, cochaired the Center for Regulatory and Market Studies advisory board for the very conservative American Enterprise Institute.

In Sunstein's view, regulations must be "harmonized, to help basically everybody, as in the case of the fuel-economy rule: consumers, manufacturers, breathers." Not only does Sunstein seek harmonizing—an odd word to describe decision making—but he describes a constituency unconventionally by referring to them as "breathers."[33]

By so doing, Sunstein makes the table larger and seats more perspectives—each partial, and each different. Finally, Sunstein makes one last, very unusual request. He "even asks regulators to begin considering distributional equity and human dignity" in their decision making[34]—"values that are difficult or impossible to quantify," the Executive Order states, "including equity, human dignity, fairness, and distributive impacts."[35]

Win-Win Risk Taking. To be sure, this type of non-zero-sum or win-win thinking does not always work. It is high-risk, and when it fails, the win-win usually falls flat, turning into a lose-lose. As one reporter wrote, Sunstein "became a bogeyman to both the Right," who denounce him as a "regulatory czar," *and* "the Left," who condemn him for being a "deregulator"![36] Moreover, after the Republican gains in the 2010 midterm elections, and in anticipation of Obama's reelection campaign, some progressives accused Sunstein of pandering to the middle.

Bringing diverse groups of people to the table is simultaneously a strength and a weakness, one that Sunstein and Obama share. As explained earlier, for Obama, it's a strategy, and a tactical one, but this strategy should not be confused with a philosophical compromise. Nor is it purely instrumental. Neither Obama nor Sunstein is what one calls, in common parlance, pragmatic; they cut their losses more than they compromise.

Much confusion exists about the difference between pragmatic decision making (that is, watering down or compromising one's principles to achieve a partial result) and pragmatism. Both Obama and Sunstein justify their pragmatism by professing to know no universal truths. Pragmatism to them means conducting a constant search or a perpetual inquiry and process, based on a qualified notion of relativism. And, as Sunstein explains, to achieve regulatory reform, "we also need to draw on the experience and wisdom of the American people."[37]

Part 2: Regulating Politics, Not Capturing Institutions

Some journalists have predicted what will happen to regulatory reform on a political level. As one explains, the "implicit quid pro quo is in funding: If Congress will approve money for the Securities and Exchange Commission to carry out its new responsibilities, for example, the administration will try to clear out regulatory weeds." Another journalist observed that "in some instances [during the regulatory reform process] . . . agencies went out of their way to highlight their responsiveness to industry."[38]

Spoiling for a fight, in 2011 Tea Party Senator Rand Paul produced an alternative to Obama's regulatory reform, called the REINS (Regulations from the Executive in Need of Scrutiny) Act. In 1996 Republican Speaker of the House Newt Gingrich and the Republican Senate leadership had tried to paralyze Clinton in a similar way when he introduced regulatory reform.[39]

Both before and after the 2010 elections, Obama followed his usual tough-love modus operandi, which will be further fleshed out in chapter 5. First Obama and his administration bend over backward by inviting the opposition to the table to begin a dialogue. When this strategy fails—usually as a result of partisanship, as the Republicans themselves seek public support—Obama highlights the opportunity that was squandered. The president does not so much seek compromise as clarification; he's not living in gray, but rather exposing the rift between black and white, and he is trying to find a point of reconciliation that both sides can concur on and live with. This is a meditative state. Obama well recognizes public opinion's capacity to hold court, and he knows who punishes those who are blamed for creating and perpetuating conflict.

In fact, Obama has sought transparency in another arena. Shortly after signing the regulatory reform executive order, he issued another order about governmental contractors and campaign contributions. To qualify for governmental contracts, all businesses, Obama ordered, must disclose to whom they have given campaign contributions. Again Obama threw open doors, offering the public a window into an otherwise opaque decision-making process, one that can be muddled or corrupted by the electoral process. "This isn't transparency," said one critic, "it's brute politics."[40]

Disabling the Courts—Deliberative Democracy and the EEOC. Another example of indeterminate lawmaking by Congress, and of the impact of negotiated rulemaking, is what happened when the Obama administration's Equal Employment Opportunity Commission (EEOC) issued the final federal regulations on the Americans with Disabilities Act Amendments Act (ADAAA). By 2011 Obama's EEOC had gone after the "largest number of affirmative-action violations in at least nine years . . . as it sought to boost the hiring of veterans and people with disabilities," explained a reporter.[41]

In 2008 the ADAAA passed with little public notice. Congress, with George W. Bush "looking forward to signing it," overturned the conservative Supreme Court's narrow interpretation of the Americans with Disabilities Act of 1990. Obama's EEOC took two years to determine the final federal regulations, and understandably so, considering how much input it solicited from all the participants. In the meantime, Obama had nominated very strong and expansive advocates of civil rights to direct this agency. He named Jacqueline Berrien—who had worked for the NAACP Legal Defense and Education Fund, the Ford Foundation's Peace and Social Justice Program, the American Civil Liberties Union (ACLU), and the Lawyers' Committee for Civil Rights—as chair of the EEOC.[42]

The Right expressed immediate outrage over Obama's nomination of Berrien, but he did not stop there. He also named an EEOC commissioner on a recess appointment. Georgetown law professor Chai Feldblum had been at the forefront of legal activism on behalf of expanding civil rights to include disability rights as well as LGBT rights. As one right-wing organization charged, Feldblum's appointment "signals a new level of harrassment [sic] . . . to further disrupt and destroy traditional values, economic prosperity and force bizarre sexual practices on the population over the objections of consumers and its citizens."[43]

The EEOC, having started collecting input on federal "regs" across the country, was now headed by these strong advocates for the rights of women, people of color, persons with disabilities, and the LGBT community. As the Right saw it, "Obama appointed a dangerous new head of his campaign to further destroy free enterprise and devout Christian beliefs with an avalanche of new regulations."[44]

Groups largely from the two sides—advocates in favor of expanding disability rights and employers hoping to restrict them—sent comments. The primary issue was what would be considered a disability. The 2008 legislation made the definition of a disability very expansive, overturning the very narrow Supreme Court cases that had gutted the earlier legislation. Before the ADAAA, of the 20 percent of employment lawsuits under Title I of the ADA not dismissed on summary judgment by the federal courts, persons with disabilities lost over 94 percent. Title I had no discernible impact in law.[45]

The EEOC, whose goal was to "to set forth predictable, consistent, and workable standards," considered all the comments from third parties. Not only did these comments influence the process, but the EEOC posted them all for public review, making the federal government accountable. The result of this process was a set of federal regulations that promise a dramatic increase in disability rights power in the United States. By redefining so broadly what constitutes a disability, the EEOC made the law so expansive that, as one group predicted, "most individuals over 50 years old seem likely to be covered by the ADA."[46]

As this author wrote earlier, "The definition of disability is vast, expansive, and indeed almost universal." "By recognizing the breadth of the ADA's new definition of disability, its employment provisions could undermine one of the most basic tenets of capitalism. American business rationality generally dictates that employers use profits, not human need, to determine better work conditions. By contrast, the ADA's employment provisions, which require reasonable accommodations, take into account human need. These provisions therefore have the capacity to humanize the face of capitalism."[47]

With one fell swoop, the ADAAA humanized capitalism, ensuring that employers must accommodate employees with medical conditions. They can no longer be fired for health reasons. Capitalism still exists, but now employers with more than fifteen employees must determine whether their employees have any health problems—mental or physical—

that can be accommodated. The state facilitates this problem by orchestrating the importation of public values into the new private-sector economy.[48]

The issuance of the final regulations created a firestorm of protest. Employer associations and conferences called in lawyers for workshops seeking ways to "protect" themselves from lawsuits. When the federal regulations became effective in late May 2011, a virtual panic ensued. "Strangulation by regulation" was what one blogger called it. Others called it "dangerous." And indeed, the EEOC received its largest number of disability-related grievances in 2011.[49]

Danger! No Norms Ahead. The concept of state facilitation means that the government advances no norm and exerts no authority, but rather facilitates the negotiation of an ever-changing set of norms. It solicits help from state and nonstate actors, representing not just corporate interests, but public interests as well. This approach creates public participation or deliberative democracy. Agencies like the EEOC now take into account the activists behind a broad or narrow interpretation of the law.

The stakeholder-society-and-state movement is Deweyan in its emphasis on participation, process, and a never-ending public policy journey based on perpetually changing and evolving norms. Another term for it is "organic," given its built-in ability to innovate and constantly renew itself. Put differently, it reflects a relegitimation of the legal process by shifting to a more advanced form of public, deliberative participation.

Whereas society demands flexibility and dynamism, the state offers bureaucracy and rules, with an elaborate oversight apparatus. Therefore, "policy has to be flexible and revisable to cope with an increasingly complex and volatile world." Law should recognize the new reality of "radical indeterminacy" and the "pervasiveness of unintended consequences."[50]

Technological advances and changes in market infrastructure have been conducive to these new demands for openness and "radicalized modernity." There is no ideal, no normal, no assumption of white Anglo-Saxon Christian lineage. The state facilitates administrative law—its governance—by reacting to "increasing heterogeneity." It also promotes this heterogeneity by creating "diverse sources of norms and strategies." This type of administrative law is radically open (cognitive openness), not operatively closed. "The more it is autonomous, the more it can both reference and investigate social facts, political demands, social science research, and human needs [in a way] that is ultimately self-sustaining."[51]

Pooling and Pragmatism. To Obama, most policies present a collective action problem. As journalist John Talbot elaborates, "The power of bottom-up economics is . . . that it is an economically just system that encourages everyone to work hard, to educate themselves, to be their most productive because it fairly rewards those who do so."[52] This type of bottom-up reform, or reform based upon civic consumerism, which historian Liz Cohen first associated with the post–World War II era, is the Keynesian's variant of the high-tides-lift-all-boats thinking overlying identity politics.[53] At the same time, American political beliefs promote tolerance and freedom of association and promise inclusion in a way that supports both Spinoza's and Obama's political aspirations. Tocqueville said it best: We're "a nation of joiners."[54] Additionally, everyone has the chance to remake themselves; we live in a society that emphasizes striving and accepts starting over or starting anew. None of this is to say, however, that we are a completely tolerant, inclusive society, because marginal groups lack power.

Since politics is about power, the individual is not autonomous, but must be couched in a social context. "The individual ceases to be a meaningful unit of analysis. For the power of the individual as individual, that is, as separate and autonomous, is so minimal as to be theoretically negligible." No one can afford to be alone. As Americans, Obama suggests, we value something "bigger than ourselves."[55]

Uncivil Lobbyists—Obama and Arendt. But what groups constitute civil society? They include family, social movements, and public communications media, but not lobbyists. It is these groups that transform and contest discourses in which deliberation is couched. Deliberative democracy manifests itself not so much by voting as by "democratic contestation of discourses." As political theorist John Dryzek explains, Obama promotes a "quasi-Deweyan," "integrative" model of deliberative democracy, one that seeks "what works" rather than "what's true."[56]

This contestation, moreover, must be open-ended. Contestation alters the balance of discourses, making possible the transformation of people's opinions. Collective choice arises through reasoned agreement, but this agreement is not necessarily based on common values as much as it is on politics. While different people have different beliefs and values, they can support the same ends. Tolerance is vital.

Traditional lobbyists, particularly corporate ones, corrupt the democratic process. Obama plans on using the power of the people to undermine their influence. "This year's presidential campaign witnessed unprecedented levels of online engagement in the political process," the Pew Research Center reported in 2008, adding that "more questions arise about the ability of the Obama team to translate its successful Internet political operations into new levels of engagement and activism when Obama assumes the presidency."[57] To expose the influence of lobbyists, Obama created an Internet database with campaign finance information and lobbying reports that are not only accessible but also downloadable and simple to use.[58]

Deliberative democracy depends on information, and on citizens with an "enlarged mentality" actively disseminating this information.[59] And indeed, the Obama administration opened a staggering number of portals, offering an overwhelming amount of easily digestible data and information. People can find information easily, searching on every aspect of government's federalist structure—municipal, state, federal, and global—with Data.gov. The page on communities, for instance, has portals labeled "participate, collaborate, compete," giving citizens information, access, and ideas on how to get involved or how to affect change in the government, in the market, and in American society. Not only can an individual discover what a zoning board is doing in her community down the street, and what contractor landed the job, but she can collect data on coal mining from 1985 or sign petitions in support and in opposition to many governmental projects on all three levels of governance. Obama is "giving all Americans a way to engage their government on the issues that matter to them." The Obama administration has quests to challenge or motivate individuals like the "equal futures" app contest to form an "app," or an application for an Internet platform, that "will promote civic education and inspire girls to serve as leaders in our democracy" on challenge.gov, which suggests "the public and government can solve problems together."[60]

These ideas about deliberative democracy, civil society, and contestation closely resemble what Spinoza means by common notions. Common notions arise when one individual encounters another with whom she is compatible, and together they form an association within civil society. This individual, acting in concert with a collective, then seeks self-preservation from the state.

To enhance their power, people must seek harmony. A society revolves around the principle that the more harmonious people are, the more power they have. The more groups there are in civil society that jar the norms or offer convincing contestations, the more power they have. In Spinoza's view, it is our norms that motivate us and determine our actions. How well do these norms work? How do they shape our behavior? Utility and efficiency, not moral validity, represent the key in evaluating and accessing these norms.[61]

The "How To" of Collaboration—Motivating Deliberating Publics. Recognizing this, Obama seeks reconciliation by promoting our universal experience. He underscores commonalities, but this does not mean that he advances universal values or normality. Obama commences "from these disparate traumas [and] encourages his composite audience to walk the path of commonality, and in the process," David Frank explains, Obama "offers a *rhetoric of consilience.*" What Frank means by "consilience" is that "a composite audience are invited to 'jump together' out of their separate experiences in favor of a common set of values or aspirations." Everyone jumps together—fights for a common cause—yet from a different perspective. This approach does not work with some zero-sum issues. Yet Obama's position as a community organizer trained him well. He knows what issues this approach does work with. After all, the role of such an organizer is finding how to get different peoples and groups to cooperate around their common self-interest.[62]

In 2011 Obama created the Accountability and Transparency Board, which has already exposed misspent tax dollars. How every dollar of the federal stimulus package was spent can be traced.[63] In delivering on his campaign pledge of providing data information and open access, it is an open question first as to how much political participation the Obama administration has generated. Only forty-three individuals signed up over a year to create the app for motivating girls and women to participate in the polis.[64]

And like any sunshine law or executive branch action, the data mined from these portals collected by the Obama administration makes Obama and the Obama administration—including every dollar the federal government oversees when it hands out government contracts or gives individuals, municipalities, and local and state governments monies—vulnerable to criticism.[65]

If people were guided by reason, Spinoza argues, they could be more in agreement. They are not. Passion motivates most people, causing many of them to tussle and make enemies. It is therefore more effective to find fellowship, joining with one's own. The state then helps people restrain and repress their appetites. This is not to say that they incur any unconditional obligations to the state. "In order . . . that [people] . . . live harmoniously and be of assistance to one another, it is necessary for them to give up their natural right." What they renounce is just some of their natural abilities to gain more for themselves. But tigers still consort with tigers. People must pledge their willingness to try to restrain themselves, but this does not mean their natural rights cease in such a political order.[66] While Obama has been less successful in motivating the youth, like the youth in Occupy Wall Street, to create apps and participate in initiatives, quests, and endeavors, he found municipalities, states, locals, and global citizens eager to participate in the political process.[67]

Part 3: Climate Control: Regulatory Power When Congress Refuses to Collaborate

One of the best examples of common self-interest can be found in the Obama administration's quest for climate control. This example differs from the ADAAA case in that it pulls back the curtain on the use of horizontal federalism for a progressive purpose. In 2009–2010 Environmental Protection Agency (EPA) administrator Lisa Jackson's commitment to rulemaking "produced historic standards for greenhouse gas emissions and . . . also led to aggressive limits on other forms of air pollution." Business organizations expressed their alarm, but the days of the Bush administration, in which neither experts nor scientific reasoning had any sway, were gone. Jackson had "set an active agenda and begun to restore science to the agency's decision-making processes."[68]

The federal government first began regulating air quality in 1955 under the Air Pollution Control Act, the precursor to the landmark 1963 Clean Air Act. The EPA was established in 1970 and immediately began promulgating rules and regulations to reduce pollution. The Energy Policy and Conservation Act of 1975 expanded the EPA's jurisdiction, and in 1978, Jimmy Carter expanded its jurisdiction further by requesting that it "assist the Nation and the world to understand and respond to natural and man-induced climate processes and their implications." In 1987 the Global Climate Protection Act directed U.S. leadership efforts in international climate change.[69]

Five years later, under George H. W. Bush, the United States participated in negotiations for the United Nations Framework Convention on Climate Change. In 1994, under Bill Clinton, the agreement went into effect with the United States as a member. Clinton actively participated in the subsequent Kyoto Protocol negotiations, but to no avail, since the Senate unanimously passed a resolution that the United States should not enter into any protocol that excluded two of the major emitters of greenhouse gases, China and India. As a result, Clinton never submitted the Kyoto Protocol to the Senate for ratification.

Then, under George W. Bush's leadership, the nation backtracked. Bush did not enforce existing environmental laws regulating greenhouse gas emissions. What is more, he prevented states from regulating greenhouse gas emissions on their own. The Senate also became increasingly recalcitrant, stalling all climate-control legislative efforts passed in the House of Representatives.[70]

Obama's cap-and-trade legislation faced a similarly hostile Senate, so he did what he could to work around it by giving states the go-ahead to regulate emissions and by sending memoranda to federal agencies on fuel-efficiency standards. States like California could once again take the lead in regulating air pollution. Obama's actions ensured that the federal regulations represented only the floor, not the ceiling, in limiting greenhouse gases.

Hoping to follow Europe's example, the Obama administration drafted legislation for a cap-and-trade incentive structure limiting pollution of all kinds. Obama's participation in the Copenhagen climate-control talks in early December of 2009 gave him an international stage to promote cap-and-trade legislation as well as solicit public support for environmental regulation. Yet despite great media attention, the climate-control negotiations did not go as well as environmentalists had hoped, with the main nation-states making their commitments contingent on other countries' action.[71]

With cap-and-trade legislation pronounced dead by early 2010, the EPA decided to create comprehensive regulation under the Clean Air Act. Jackson pursued the course of enhancing the agency's regulatory powers by opening up the federalist framework.

Under traditional vertical federalism, regulatory power must first settle the question of jurisdiction. The process revolves around *who*, for example, sets tailpipe emissions standards. Automobile manufacturers advocate and lobby for national standards, hoping to ensure uniformity. Their lobbying efforts have great effect in Congress, particularly in a Senate governed more by sectionalism than by ideology. Meanwhile some states, such as California, argued that the EPA should let them set their own standards if they exceed national standards. With federal power trumping state power and authority, a state must ask the EPA for a waiver. The Bush administration denied California's waiver request, preempting state action as part of its campaign to undermine efforts at climate control.

When Obama took office, he immediately reversed the Bush administration's preemption policy and directed the EPA to grant California a waiver. At the same time, he instructed the EPA to harmonize state and federal standards so that they would converge by 2012. Meanwhile states and localities, and even sublocal actors, got involved in designing fuel-efficient transportation policies, which they incorporated into their land-use planning decisions. The Obama administration awarded federal stimulus funding to conservation-friendly states, counties, and localities.[72]

Not only was the EPA planning to give states discretion, but Jackson reframed the whole question of controlling greenhouse gases. She began thinking of climate control as a single issue involving both *what* cars we drive and *how* we drive them. In April 2010 she succeeded in merging the two, as her agency and the Department of Transportation promulgated joint rules on fuel economy and tailpipe greenhouse gas emissions.[73]

Following the incentivized-negotiation principles of the cap-and-trade system, which could also be described as nudges in terms of behavioral economics, both the EPA and the DOT agreed to measure compliance with the joint rules on the basis of a calculation involving fleet average performance at the end of each model year. This calculation gave manufacturers leeway. Those that exceeded the fleet average CO_2 or CAFE standard received transferable credits, while those who fell short received debits. The rules created an incentive to conserve energy and reduce pollution.[74]

Then, in September 2010, the EPA and National Highway Traffic Safety Administration announced that they would begin establishing standards for fuel economy and greenhouse gas emissions for light-vehicle models. It also announced the EPA's establishment of a schedule for promulgating national source performance standards for greenhouse gas emissions by power plants and refineries.[75] In these ways, while failing to enact climate control on the international and national levels, the Obama administration nonetheless was able to achieve some of its goals by using its regulatory powers as well as by supporting states and local areas.

Part 4: Obama's Legislative Legacy: More Nudges—Stimulus and the American Recovery and Reinvestment Act

Compounding the EPA's efforts, another federal agency—the Office of Management and Budget (OMB)—joined in the pursuit of climate control. Obama had appointed Peter Orszag, a behavioral economist, not from academia but from Wall Street, to run the OMB. Orszag drafted the federal stimulus package—the American Recovery and Reinvestment Act of 2009 (ARRA)—stuffing it with funding for little nudges so that federal, state, and local officials would encourage climate control, sustainable growth, and educational reforms.[76]

The ARRA moved in three directions at once, advancing economic stimulus, providing program support, and offering the Obama administration political leverage for making all policy changes progressive. The issue ancillary to economic policy was what all this Keynesian spending power actually purchased. The ARRA included incentive after incentive that nudged the United States toward climate control, emphasizing conservation and cultivating green growth by, for instance, supporting environmentally sound businesses. Domestic automakers got retooling tax credits and loan guarantees, while public utilities got funds for updating the national energy grid and for research and development, particularly in renewable energy.

Long ignored by previous administrations, wind power producers received investment tax credits too. The Interior and Energy Departments began working collaboratively with relevant states, localities, and tribal governments to create an offshore wind industry capable of producing 20 percent of the nation's energy. Multiple grants were aimed at improving fuel efficiency in heavy-duty trucks and passenger vehicles. An incentive—the X Prize Foundation—was also included in the legislation, awarding over $5 million to the team that designed the best energy-efficient vehicles. Finally, Orszag's legislation encouraged innovation on the very smallest level, including grants for low-income weatherization programs and for individuals making batteries for plug-in hybrids. In January 2011 the Obama administration demonstrated that 997,000 jobs had emerged from its emphasis on green growth.[77]

A theme running through all these programs was the way bottom-up efforts under horizontal federalism capture all the differences and divergences in different economies and environments so that smaller-scale actors can respond to local conditions without the rigidity and constraint that often accompany top-down mandates. They encourage cooperation and generate creative solutions to old problems. What made the Obama administration's efforts unique was, as Robert Percival puts it, that debates about environmentalism used to focus on the question of federal versus state authority.[78] Obama has changed the game. Percival and Tseming Yang believe "global environmental law" will help American lawyers "learn about environmental governance from . . . the areas of regulatory non-compliance and environmental human rights." Making the federal government and the states *alternative* sources of regulatory authority that interact over time helps address environmental problems more effectively.[79]

Nathan Sayre has underscored how ecologists understand scale by relying on the terms "grain" and "extent." Grain determines "the finest level of spatial or temporal resolution available within a given data set," and extent captures "the size of the study area or the duration of the study." A topographic map is created, and then, within the confines of this map, governmental and nongovernmental actors can debate the comparative value of large- and small-scale climate change regulation; focus on vertical or horizontal dimensions of interactions; propose top-down, bottom-up, or mixed hierarchical schemes; and emphasize conflict or cooperation in the regulatory interactions. A public policy is constructed, deconstructed, and reconstructed. It must be continuously assessed and reassessed from these different scales, axes, and directions.[80]

Convergence—or Collapse? A Conservative Grassroots Changer? Obama believes in convergence. Several years ago, at a seminar on rebuilding community at which political scientist Robert Putnam's well-known thesis about how Americans "bowl alone" was extensively discussed, one expert said, "I don't mean he makes all conflicts go away—that would be crazy. But his natural instinct is not dividing the baby in half—it's looking for areas of *convergence*. This is part of who he is really deep down, and it's an amazing skill. It's not always the right skill, because the truth doesn't always lie somewhere in the middle. But I think at this moment America is in a situation where we agree much more than we think we do. . . . And that's why I think he's right for this time." Obama's notion of reconciliation and congruence, as well as consilience, as explained earlier, stems from his emphasis on inductive reasoning, or the logic underlying the idea of "necessary *and* sufficient." Common elements becoming congruent or pooling, like two streams of thought, converge; and as they converge, they corroborate and verify each other.[81]

Advocating for change and demanding reform, but with a reconciliatory approach built on pragmatism rather than universal values, is an odd mix. Obama understands that Americans hunger for "change." Obama's change, however, is not just a change in policy programs per se, but rather a change in the political process. To him, compromise is tantamount to reform, but this is compromise from norm-generating subjects—not meeting in the middle, but finding commonalities, as his complex horizontal and diagonal federalist frameworks also demonstrate. There is no baby to divide, as Putnam puts it.[82] Obama has placed his emphasis on the political process and promoted his unique theory of regarding reconciliation as a form of reform. At the same time, many supporters insist that he must fulfill his promise of change less by transforming the political process than by enacting concrete policy programs.[83]

When Obama seeks change, he promises the public a vital role in the process. He welcomed public scrutiny by opening the deliberative process for health-care legislation by televising a conference on C-SPAN. Is this a "dopey idea?" asked one journalist rhetorically. "I don't think so," he continued. "All presidents who achieve big change have been first-rate communicators in the theater of the presidency." As Franklin Roosevelt said, an effective president must be "the educator-in-chief."[84]

In Any and All Cases—Care: Obamacare, or the Affordable Care Act. On February 25, 2010, the C-SPAN town hall meeting on what became the Patient Protection and Affordable Care Act (ACA) got under way. Some political journalists, such as Richard Wolffe, insist it was this gathering that explains how Obama finally convinced Democrats in both the House and the Senate that the ACA could succeed. Or, as a rhetorician suggests, it also helps explain how Obama redrafted the narrative, winning more control.

A week after the town hall meeting, on March 3, Obama stood at the podium in the East Room discussing the dire need for health-care reform before an audience of intersecting layers of industry participants: nurses, doctors, physician assistants, and even insurance executives. These executives attended in response to Secretary of Health and Human Services Kathleen Sebelius's letter to the whole insurance industry, which "threatened" those who acted in "bad faith" with being excluded from the new health insurance markets opening in 2014. Obama's battle for health-care reform took another turn toward success. As one senior White House staff member said, "We needed the struggle against the insurance company. We couldn't get it done without them." The administration needed a common enemy to battle that the public identified as acting in bad faith.[85]

The Spinozan stakeholder idea revolves around collaborative governance. It encourages participation and partnership. The person in charge—the authority—is not embodied by one person or by any one identity, as explained above, and as can be seen in both the openness of Obama's regulatory schema and the horizontal and diagonal federalist framework. Even the middle class can represent the bedrock for Obama, but the size and color of this middle class—be it their religion or their race—should not be determined.

The basic principle is that governance is pluralized, made multifaceted and multidimensional. This type of governance encourages collaboration, diversity, and competition. It promotes an integration of policy domains while remaining decentralized. As stated earlier, Obama promotes policy deconstruction and reconstruction.

A Renew Deal regime practices civic republicanism and pragmatism simultaneously by engaging multiple actors and shifting citizens from passive to active roles and then back again. Increased participation permeates the many different strata of the public policy process, from legislation to the creation of federal regulations to the implementation and enforcement of those rules. When Congress and the president draft legislation in an indeterminate way, their avoidance of conflict and controversy gives the deliberating publics more power. Public-interest groups have more input into the public policymaking process, and new groups demand more access to policy processes and a role in governing social institutions.[86]

Multiparty involvement is understood as a way of creating norms, cultivating reform, and "managing new market realities." For instance, if African American children constitute the majority of children in poverty without health care, Obama believes in universalizing health care for all children in poverty. It's their lack of health care, not their identity, that creates the problem. Obama supports a politics of real equality of opportunity and difference that reflects ever-changing norms.

This is not to say that he accepts all norms. Obama does not believe in universal social services. He spurns most entitlements. He did not support universal health care for this reason. No one should have a right to health care; rather, they should have a realistic opportunity to purchase it. This means the government must make health care accessible by making it "affordable and available" for all. But it is a system that emphasizes prevention, and prevention works only when patients listen and take a role in their own health care.[87]

Making History. In 2009 the Obama administration emphasized that the United States spends more than any other industrialized nation on health care. The cost adds up to a full 16 percent of the nation's GDP, more than in the nations of Europe, for example, and even this amount does not cover everyone. The Institute of Medicine of the National Academies documented what Elizabeth Warren had been observing: 62 percent of all personal bankruptcy cases involved medical debt. Meanwhile neoconservative opposition equated Obama's plan with rationing. One conservative journalist went so far as to characterize it as "health care fascism."[88]

When on March 25, 2010, Obama signed a historic health-care law—the Affordable Care Act—it contained provisions to decrease this 16 percent of GDP. To that end, it created electronic record keeping and altered the economic incentive structure. No longer rewarded for how many patients they see or paid for specific services, doctors must now treat their patients' conditions. "Obamacare" did away with the "encounter-based, quality insensitive, fee-for-service system of compensation." It got rid of a private health-care system that "aggressively delivers massive quantities of health care services in a highly fragmented non-system, but pays little attention to whether the services in question actually contribute to health." For particularly expensive conditions such as obesity and diabetes, doctors must now practice preventive medicine, and patients must participate in their own health care.[89]

At the same time, Obama's plan no longer allows insurance companies to discriminate against people with preexisting conditions. They too must be treated. Indeed, an insurance exchange was established for individuals and small businesses, and tax credits are being extended to individuals and small companies. Finally, to identify fraud, abuse, and waste, the plan creates independent commissions or exchanges. The plan goes so far as to dictate that 85 cents of every premium dollar be spent on medical care in small-group markets and by Medicare Advantage insurers. For large-group markets the figure is 80 cents of every premium dollar.[90]

Obama's health-care reform had another function: helping him redistribute wealth. "Health insurance coverage for lower and middle-income insured Americans could be financed only through hard-fought steps to place new charges on businesses and the well-to-do." As a health-care magazine summarized, "Under the revolutionary bill, health insurance will be extended to nearly all Americans, new taxes will be imposed on the wealthy, and restrictive insurance practices will be outlawed."[91]

The Affordable Care Act also furthers Obama's notion of federalism, making state and federal responsibilities "interwoven, interdependent, and varied," as one expert noted. Federally administered subsidies and state-operated exchanges will affect each other. In many areas, who has what powers and responsibilities remains unclear. Though each of these programs balances federal and state responsibilities differently, the success of all depends on how well they coordinate with one another.[92]

Ironically, Obama did not want an individual mandate included in health care. He wanted no mandate at all. Given the division among the Democrats, he was flexible about what type of public option to include, but he "strongly believe[s] that Americans should have the choice of a public health insurance option operating alongside private plans."[93]

But the final bill represented the deal he struck with insurance companies, causing at least one person to call the law not health-care reform, but health insurance reform.[94] Obama envisioned the federal government facilitating affordable health care, not mandating it.

The individual mandate is what makes Obama's health-care reform vulnerable to being declared unconstitutional. In a federal district court, Judge Roger Vinson ruled that the entire Affordable Health Care Act was unconstitutional because of the individual mandate clause. The suit, representing twenty-six states, found that forcing individuals to purchase health insurance was not part of the federal government's powers granted in the Commerce Clause.[95]

Guns, War, and Disease. Obama won a great victory when the Supreme Court rendered the ACA constitutional. The victory, moreover, came from the of jaws of defeat. Insider information leaked about Roberts—the fifth vote in the 5–4 majority—indicated that the chief justice changed his mind during a last few grueling days of deliberation, an argument advanced further by the lack of sleep showing in his red-rimmed eyes the day the court rendered the decision, upholding Obamacare's constitutionality.[96]

The Supreme Court began limiting the federal government's power and authority—either upholding the expansive reach of the commerce clause or protecting the Eleventh Amendment on state sovereignty—until the mid-1990s, when the Rehnquist court began batting it down.[97] The redefining of the New Deal and the Great Society's federal authority began with three decisions involving guns, violence against women, and making a state university exempt from paying damages to a woman it fired who had breast cancer, which is, and is regarded as, a disability. Did the federal government have the power and authority to prevent people from packing guns in a school zone? Must a state-run hospital in Alabama comply with the federal Americans with Disabilities Act, giving a woman with breast cancer standing to stop the discrimination? And could the federal government outlaw violence against women? In all three cases, the Rehnquist court ruled no. Now, the Roberts court had a chance.

Given the media spotlight, analyses of the Roberts court and predictions of its actions abounded. Many ironies were noted.[98] The greatest irony was that Stuart Butler, author of the conservative Heritage Foundation report "Assuring Affordable Health Care for All Americans," first came up with the concept of the individual mandate, which he renounced in 2012. This idea was modeled after what many states did about car insurance, "requiring passengers in automobiles to wear seatbelts for their own protection." "Neither the federal government nor any state requires all households to protect themselves from the potentially catastrophic costs of a serious accident or illness." It only protects passengers; drivers are free to kill themselves.

Picked up then by Oregon senator Ron Wyden, a Democrat looking for health-care reform, the individual mandate found support from eighty members of the Senate, including Bob Bennett, the conservative Utah Republican. GOP 2012 candidate and former Massachusetts governor Mitt Romney supported the individual mandate as late as 2009. Earlier in 2008, Democratic contenders John Edwards and Hillary Clinton made the individual mandate one of the legislative linchpins underlying their proposals for health-care reform. "The main Democratic holdout," reports Ezra Klein, "was Senator Barack Obama," who started supporting it to pass it. "I was opposed to this idea because my general attitude was the reason people don't have health insurance is not because they don't want it. It's because they can't afford it," he told CBS News. "I am now in favor of some sort of individual mandate."

When the Obama administration supported it, however, it had the solicitor general arguing that purchasing health insurance is an economic activity. This claim generated much discussion, with the most famous quote coming from Justice Antonin Scalia asking whether, if you could require people to buy health insurance, you could "require them to buy broccoli?" This remark had court watchers remarking on Scalia's ingenuity. "The food market," the solicitor general explains, "shares that trait that everybody's in it, [but] it is not a market [like health care or being a passenger rushed to the ER in a car crash] in which your participation is often unpredictable and often involuntary."

Meanwhile, Jeffrey Toobin's behind-the-judicial-curtains book *The Oath* maintains that Roberts suddenly switched because of Antonin Scalia's politicking. Supposedly "Scalia's view of the justices as gladiators against the president unnerved Roberts." Yet Scalia is always spoiling for a fight. What remains clear is that Roberts did not appreciate Obama speaking out against the Supreme Court during his 2010 State of the

Union address, when he condemned its decision on campaign financing. "During the discussions in [Rahm] Emanuel's office, as well as the president's own prep sessions, the propriety of challenging the Supreme Court had never come up." The Obama administration, angered by *Citizens United*, considered the conservative Supreme Court majority "as another group of Republicans, deserving no greater deference than GOP senators or congressmen."[99]

No matter what his motivation, Roberts let Obama win the healthcare battle.[100] By making its decision hinge on the federal government's right to taxation, the court carries on the war against the reach of federal power and authority. It warns the Obama administration—and all those thereafter, since chances are Roberts will lead the court for up to another generation—that few federal laws are welcome. Having the federal government meddle in state affairs—even if it involves giving the states something, like increased monies for health care, as opposed to preventing something, like discrimination—remains diminished. "So long as conservatives hold sway on the Court," writes historian Jill Lepore, "the definition of 'commerce' will get narrower and narrower." Rendering laws unconstitutional in toto may prove difficult, as she attests.[101] After all, a less conservative Supreme Court violated its own states' rights principles for a Republican president.[102]

Unsafe at Any Speed: Nader and Warren Collide and Collude—Wall Street Reform and the Consumer Protection Act. Obama had difficulty including provisions in his historic financial regulation legislation that would increase the power of a state that facilitated a stakeholder society. But he did it. Following Arendt's ideas in regulating an all-pervasive *oikos*, Obama proclaimed that we must thwart a "culture of irresponsibility among *both* banks and borrowers." The Obama administration advocated constructing a consumer financial regulatory agency to "give consumer protection an independent seat at the table."[103]

Representatives of the financial industry, such as the American Bankers Association, opposed the plan to create a new oversight agency. On July 21, 2010, despite their objections, President Obama signed into law the Dodd-Frank Wall Street Reform and Consumer Protection Act. The law included leverage restrictions and capital requirements, restrictions on proprietary trading, and regulation of derivatives, swaps, and credit rating agencies as well as a consumer financial protection agency.[104]

More so than had been true with the ARRA, which attempted to mount a structural attack on the financial crisis, critical proposals of the Consumer Protection Act were watered down through lobbying, and the Obama administration by no means succeeded in getting everything through. Still, the Spinozan stakeholder-state-and-society perspective was clear and arguably constituted the largest transformation brought about by the act.

The Consumer Protection Act manifested a transformation in American capitalism. Earlier, Theodore Roosevelt had softened capitalism with the creation of the Bureau of Labor Statistics, the Workers' Compensation Program, and other progressive reforms that curbed some of the excesses of monopoly capitalism during the robber-baron age. Franklin D. Roosevelt regulated capitalism with the founding of the Securities and Exchange Commission, the National Labor Relations Board, the Fair Labor Standards Act, the Glass-Steagall Act (which transformed banking practices), and the establishment of the Federal Deposit Insurance Corporation.[105]

Obama's financial reform altered some basic principles underlying capitalism by tackling the consumer side of the equation. He created a whole new dimension—a consumer dimension—of capitalism that Warren had advanced or advocated applying specifically to the financial sector. She associated the excesses and abuses on Wall Street with the crisis of the struggling and shrinking American middle class.

Warren did not conceive of this in a vacuum. Instead, she imported her ideas from Canada. In a pivotal piece that outlined her philosophy, titled "Unsafe at Any Rate," Warren argued that an administrative agency was imperative to ensure the country's financial safety. Nothing less than the health and well-being of capitalism and democracy, Warren said, depended on it, given that the American middle class was in peril.

Originally conceived of as part of the Tobin Project, founded by Harvard Business School professor David Moss, the idea of regulating capitalism from the consumer side attracted Obama, since he is a behavioral tweaker, or at most a mild middle-class economic reformer, not a progressive, as so many traditional big-state liberals, radicals, and progressives active in Washington politics observe. Like the EPA's federalist framework, the ARRA, and the Affordable Care Act, the Consumer Protection Act reforms the structure and authority of federal financial regulators.[106]

Horizontal Structures. The Consumer Protection Act erects a Financial Stability Oversight Council (FSOC), charged with identifying and responding to any risks that endanger the financial system's stability. It also gives federal regulators resolution authority for "systemically important firms in danger of defaulting." The secretary of the Treasury chairs the FSOC; other members are the chairs or leaders of the main federal financial agencies, along with three officials from the states, who are nonvoting members.

The Consumer Protection Act is an example of horizontal federalism, since it builds its regulatory capacity on two existing substantive areas overseen by the states: consumer financial protection and insurance regulation. States regulate mortgage abuses, and they have clashed repeatedly with the Office of the Comptroller of the Currency (OCC) over enforcement of state consumer protection laws against national banks and their subsidiaries. That is no longer a problem. The act takes a restrictive approach toward preemption, providing that only inconsistent state law is preempted. As with the Clean Air Act, state laws offering greater protection to consumers are permitted. Only if state laws discriminate against, or interfere with the operations of, national banks does the federal board practice preemption. Here again, the Obama administration embraces a states' rights movement that a liberal could love.[107]

Finally, this legislation created the Consumer Financial Protection Bureau (CFPB), located in the Federal Reserve (Fed). This new agency, which Warren and later Cordray labeled "the bureau" to underscore its police powers or enforcement capacity, is led by one director appointed by the president. This insulates the director and the bureau from the day-to-day politics that govern the rest of the Fed. The Fed cannot reduce the bureau's budget, oversee its proceedings, or review its rules and orders. Instead, the bureau's regulations can only be stayed, or set aside, by the FSOC on a two-thirds vote. All of these measures will prevent the Republicans from practicing the politics of putting foxes in henhouses, as, for instance, George W. Bush did with Eugene Scalia, Antonin's son, who served as Bush's chief legal officer in the Department of Labor.[108]

Again, the states gain involvement in federal regulatory rulemaking. They are granted some authority to force the CFPB to act: "The Bureau shall issue a notice of proposed rulemaking whenever a majority of the States has enacted a resolution in support of the establishment or modification of a consumer protection regulation by the Bureau." Although the states are not allowed to enforce the consumer protection provisions of the Consumer Protection Act directly against national banks and federal savings associations, they are expressly granted power to enforce regulations issued by the CFPB and to enforce the act against state-chartered entities.[109]

The states have long been involved in insurance regulation. In 1945 Congress delegated the primary responsibility for regulating insurance to the states when it passed the McCarran-Ferguson Act. During debate over the Consumer Protection Act, insurance giant AIG and several financial guarantee insurers like Ambac raised the question of whether insurance regulation should be federalized. But the states lobbied, largely successfully, for preservation of their traditional oversight of insurance.

The Consumer Protection Act, writes political scientist Daniel Carpenter, constitutes the largest threat to capitalism "in the last 40 years." What he calls the "gilded network" has been "pried open by democracy itself." Appointments represent the key to this type of approach. The people Obama appoints, in other words, will make the difference between success and failure, but the states' involvement will entrench consumer protection in a way that will be difficult for subsequent presidents to undo.[110]

Progressive Rage. As of June 2012, the CFPB remains all progressive potential and no action. Indeed, the bureau's first actions on credit card reform, as mentioned in chapter 3, turned out to be a minor tweak. Cordray, whom Warren hired as the bureau's "enforcer" and subsequently endorsed when Obama passed her over, issued this timid reform that promises to help few consumers. Cordray is purported to pick his battles, given opposition from inside the Fed and outside in an election year. The bureau's first director chose not to launch an offensive against Wall Street or the financial sector.

Mocking Wall Street's continued penchant for hyperbolic language denouncing Obama's supposed "regulatory Jihad" or "regulatory tsunami of unprecedented force," the *New York Times* labeled Obama's record in curbing "dangerous practices by industry" "mediocre" in an editorial titled "The Phony Regulation Debate." Meanwhile the moderate academic left, as well as the moderate-to-left spectrum from progressives to traditional big-state liberals and radicals, condemned Obama almost as vociferously as Wall Street, blaming him for economic malaise that could go global as the EU falters.[111]

Obama's pro-growth, anti-austerity rhetoric could gain a second wind, given the leadership role European heads of state have been awarding him as the EU's economic crisis gets worse. Political journalists given access to the White House reported that Obama values *New York Times* columnist Paul Krugman's opinion. But Obama never supported old-fashioned state-centered reforms proposed by the likes of those liberals who felt Clinton betrayed them, such as Robert Reich. Nor did he opt for large Keynesian reforms in 2009. Like Clinton, Obama campaigned in 2008 on vague rhetoric about redistribution and the middle class. But even this got watered down with his first appointments of Robert

Rubin's disciples Timothy Geithner, who Obama has kept in place as
secretary of the Treasury, and Lawrence Summers. Like Clinton, Obama
denounces Wall Street in rhetoric and supports the financial sector in
practice.[112]

What's Left? Fighting Robots. Simply by virtue of building the bureau,
Obama, or a more liberal economic reformer in 2016, could turn middle-
class consumerism into economic reform, given the "deliberative" aspect of the federal regulatory process. Notice-and-comment periods give
activists the chance to go public or get the court of public opinion involved, influencing the president. Labor unions, public-interest groups,
and identity advocacy groups could turn consumer issues into employment and workplace rights issues.

The bureau created a new venue for activists and active citizens, were
they to unite and bridge the long-standing divisions that began emerging
in the mid-1970s and became debilitating for the Democrats in the 1980s.
With only 7 percent of the private workforce protected by unions, and
public unions under separate attack by Republicans and Democratic big
city mayors and governors across the United States, there are few venues
left for the Left. Occupy Wall Street, filled with students enmeshed and
ensconced in a global, horizontal movement, occupied fewer sound bites
in spring and fall 2011 than even *Time* predicted. Meanwhile the "dog-
eat-dog political competition over diminishing resources" could trigger
full-scale economic conflict and reform in a Hobbesian war of all against
all. Yet political declinists' dire economic predictions rarely come true.

Over the last quarter of a millennium, financial panics and adjust-
ments like those of the late nineteenth century, not full-bodied economic
and political meltdowns, were more the norm than national depressions,
worldwide recessions, and new deals. After all, the American middle
class has been declining since John F. Kennedy declared the War on Poverty. To be sure, economic erosion will continue as the poor and the
middle class continue to lose ground. And this loss will not be restricted
to the United States. Over the last ten years, technological advancements
in robotics, rather than Left or Right economic and industrial policies
in nation-states or in international or regional trade agreements, have
been responsible for unrecoverable job losses. Robots and high land and
water prices, not wages and salary costs, account for the last decade of
middle-class economic decline in the United States and Europe. The one
high-growth sector in wealthy nations—high tech—itself is starting to
face the perils associated with routinization. The fledgling middle classes
in high-growth nation-states like China, Korea, and India will face ero-

sion or, potentially, collapse. New recipes for new dishes are required in this new millennium, not twentieth-century solutions such as industrialization, postindustrialization, and globalization. This, however, does not beg the question: What does it take to trigger political reform? How can a president motivate people to participate or earn egalitarianism? Will those nations with more avenues for political participation better divide resources?[113]

The *Oikos* or the Social Sphere: Obama and Arendt. The social sphere is as important as the public and private spheres. Mourning the end of modernity in *The Human Condition*, Arendt maintains that it happened as the social sphere became increasingly important. On the one hand, the private sphere contained the household and the family. Privacy is the domain of necessity and repetition, in contrast to public life, which rises above physical necessity, creating a selfhood achieved by escaping the homogeneity of the life-world and appearing before others in the public common world. The individual trades the "what" of privacy for the "who" of political identity. Entering public life makes an individual visible and distinct. She becomes part of a plurality and begins engaging and interacting with others. One enunciates one's unique position in the world.

Arendt suggests that there is a fundamental and hierarchical difference between the public and private realms. In serving nature, labor, located in the private sphere, must be portrayed as "un-freedom." Its never-ending quality—basic human needs must always be met—makes it akin to slavery. Humans consume all fruits produced by labor, she argued. They must be perpetually replenished to sustain life.

Arendt equates labor with Aristotle's *oikos*, or the private realm of the household. She maintains that modernity ends as labor—driven by the ever-increasing priority given to the economy—which displaces the public. The social arena—society—intrudes with its private realm, and it thereby invades and conquers the public realm. Private needs and concerns destroy the boundary separating the public and private arenas. When the social realm gains a monopoly, the distinction between labor, work, and action is lost.

Meanwhile work is in the public sphere—the *polis*. Arendt argues that the individual can master nature by transcending it through work. To her, work creates a world distinct from anything given in nature. It is durable, not quickly consumed; it is semi-permanent; and it offers us relative independence from the actors and the acts that call it into being.

Work shapes and transforms nature, which makes it a distinctly non-animal or human activity. Because it is governed by human ends and intentions and is under our sovereignty and control, it contains within it a certain quality of freedom. Finally, it is inherently public—work cultivates an objective and common world. Work therefore stands between humans and can simultaneously unite them.

Whereas labor cannot furnish a common world within which humans can pursue their higher ends, given the absence of human freedom, work can. Work cannot be fully free—it is not an end in itself—but it is close enough. Work anticipates causes and articulates goals or ends. In Arendt's words, the quality of freedom is found in *vita activa*—the activity of action proper or doing work.

Freedom, for Arendt, is not an inner, contemplative, or private phenomenon. Instead, it is worldly and public. We become aware of freedom or its opposite in our intercourse with others, not in intercourse with ourselves. Like Augustine, Arendt perceives human action as something similar to taking initiative. It embodies a beginning.

Action as power and agency—the very stuff of politics—sets something into motion. Humans have the capacity to begin, to start something new, to do the unexpected—all of which we are endowed with by virtue of being born. Similarly, Obama believes that freedom results from action, although, as in the philosophy of Deleuze, Spinoza, Du Bois, and Dewey, it results from an ontology of doing, not being.

Necessity and freedom characterize the difference between the private and the public realms, and they create the all-encompassing social sphere that this book terms Spinozan. Action must be taken in public; one must make oneself known through words and deeds, earned egalitarianism, and eliciting the consent of others. We can exist only in a context defined by a plurality, or as behavioral economists call it, a "social context."

Network of Actions. Arendt creates an existentialist theory of action. She seeks the greatest possible autonomy for action, laying great stress on individual will and on decision as an "act of existential choice unconstrained by principles or norms." The person's timing, perspective, and standing all count. This is the plurality. She distinguishes genuine or authentic action from mere behavior—that is, habituated, regulated, automated human acts—in its capacity to initiate wholly new, unanticipated, unexpected, unconditioned results by the laws of cause and effect.[114]

But actions are justified only in light of their public recognition—and the shared rules of the community. It is the idea of active citizenship, of the value of civic engagement and collective deliberation about everything, that affects the political community. Any gathering of citizens in a public space is an authentic expression of this idea.

Arendt advocates that the enlightened individual transcend the narrow realm of the household and rise into the realm of politics. She champions political action over social concerns. Action constitutes the third part of the "human condition," and this is the political activity—power—of creating solidarity in pluralities with other political actors. A citizen participates, or acts, whereas the lesser forms of existence or parts of the human condition are labor and work. Labor means fulfilling nothing beyond the basics, such as finding food and shelter, while work, for Arendt, means that the person does more than providing for the absolute necessities yet nothing of lasting value. Only in action does a citizen have the capacity for completing great deeds.[115]

Action is the sine qua non of politics. Action in concert is identified as constructive or positive power. Arendt finds fault with the Platonic subordination of politics to philosophy: all thought—no action. Western philosophy devalued the world of human action, subordinating it to the life of contemplation, which concerns itself with essences and the eternal. Plato's metaphysics subordinates action and appearances to the realm of ideas.

Action also undermines the idea of identity politics. One's power stems from action—the agency of the political, not the private, subject. Action itself is akin to birth in that it is a beginning anew; it spurns the notion that a predetermined identity exists. Like Gilles Deleuze, as described in chapter 2, Arendt does not believe that there is an essence of our identity. No predetermined identity can exist. It is the difference between individualism and articulated individuality. They resist binary oppositions between sameness and difference. And this produces heterogeneous pluralities, or Madison's disinterested factions—fueled with power, but a power that leads to ever-shifting and only temporary consensuses. There is no public good—no unity—but rather an arena where we distinguish ourselves from one another. It is our differences that drive us together.

Arendt made this discursive practice more graphic by calling it "interest." It rejects the idea of the private realm pushing its way into and invading the political realm. We are not one happy family with "unmediated, unchanging expression of life-world impulses that blots out individuality and difference as though all of humankind were members of one enormous family which has only one opinion and one interest."[116] Rather than having the private realm instill a mass interest that "functions as a monolithic, monological expression of the people, Arendt promotes a form of interest that is diverse and agonal." This interest is produced from and productive of a plurality—a plurality of political subjects articulating their interests in speeches and deeds.[117]

For Arendt, inter-est is not solely a reaction to the material "in-between." It responds to the common world as a whole, which comprises not only the artificial world of things but also a discursive web of rela-tions. The actor engages in both the world of things and the inter-est of other subjects with whom she finds herself in a state of togetherness.[118]

Inter-est, Arendt claims, constitutes something that lies between peo-ple and can relate them and bind them together. It does not just promote, but is a connection among, subjects. This connection, however, is not sameness, but rather a commonality like the commons on which Obama concentrates—common goods and common solutions. Arendt argues that the fantasy of common identity or belief isolates us and removes us from the reality of one another. In a mode of articulating self, posi-tion, and desire, we continue reconsidering truths. This is tantamount to an "adversarial democracy," though one that does not reify interests or point backward.

This type of adversarial democracy places materiality and political discourse within the same space—deliberation—in relation, collectively, contextually, and transiently. Inter-ests are not tedious expressions of prior positionality but rather performances of difference that are deter-mined intersubjectively and embedded in materiality—contingent artic-ulations of differing positions, conditioned by the presence of others. As political scientist Jane Mansbridge puts it, the most important part of politics is "clarifying" one's interests—knowing what you want, not how to get it.[119]

We can never settle down into what Katherine Adams calls "that home away from home in *a priori* unity." Pluralistically including oth-ers' perspectives in our inquiry process gives us a way of adjusting for our own limitations, correcting our standards, improving warrants for our assertions, and recognizing the role of power and privilege in episte-mological theories. In seeking to involve consumers in their own literacy as a means of regulating capitalism, this is what Obama does.[120]

Consumerism and the *Oikos*—Reform, Not Radicalism, Let Alone Revolution. Consumerism constitutes a full-information critique of capitalism. It ac-cepts the basic principles of private property and profits that underlie capitalism, but argues that certain parts of the market do not work. It enhances the social sphere. This type of economic reform assumes that suppliers of credit products have an unfair advantage over consumers, who lack access to full information about products that are potentially dangerous to their financial health.

In his most anti–Wall Street speech, delivered in Osawatomie, Kansas, in December 2011, Obama made direct references to Theodore Roosevelt and the rules of capitalism. Given Obama's campaign literature and the near-collapse of capitalism at the end of 2008, many progressives thought that the president-elect would tackle income inequality directly through redistribution by means of the tax structure, or that he would seize his historic opportunity to nationalize the banks. But by November 24, 2008, when Obama selected his team of economic advisors—Geithner as secretary of the Treasury and Larry Summers as the head of the National Economic Council—it was clear that Wall Street capitalism would, at most, be reformed, not revolutionized.[121]

The last hurdle was the debate over the automobile industry—specifically, the fate of General Motors and Chrysler. The administration's most significant interference in the economy, aside from rescuing the banks, was restructuring these automakers. The United States bailed out both, and at one point it owned 10 percent of Chrysler and 61 percent of General Motors. "I would have guessed that bailing out big banks was going to be unpopular, and bailing out real companies where people work was going to be popular," said Summers. "But I was wrong. They were both unpopular. There's a lot of suspicion around. Why this business but not that business? Is this industrial policy? Is this socialism? Why is the government moving in?"[122]

As Ryan Lizza notes, the most Obama could say for his economic policies was that without them, "things would be worse." What was clear about Obama's economic policy was that he was at best a reformer, but more likely could be categorized as a regulatory tweaker. He believed at most in consumer protection. Creating consumer economic interest is more in line with Teddy Roosevelt's trust busting than with his cousin's penchant for Keynesian economics.[123]

Reformers had long identified consumerism as a way out of class conflict. In 1914 the progressive Walter Lippman called consumerism a "great characteristically American movement" and predicted that it was "destined to be stronger than the interest either of labor or of capital." Similarly, Walter Weyl, a proponent of New Democracy, wrote in 1912 that "to think of Americans as 'consumers' was thus to think of them as members of a kind of universal class, with a single common interest—an interest in buying things that were both 'cheap' and 'good.' The key to creating justice and social peace in democratic America lay in making consumers understand that they all shared this common interest."[124]

Elizabeth Warren argues that the state should regulate credit products for the same reasons it regulates other consumer products: they, too,
are dangerous if those who purchase them are not fully informed and the
state creates no guidelines and standards. What is more, Warren notes,
the credit market has changed. "Aggressive marketing, almost nonexis-
tent in the 1970s, compounds the difficulty, shaping consumer demand
in unexpected and costly directions." But Obama stopped listening. To
the great ire and consternation of progressive Democrats outside the
Beltway, Obama is not interested in economic reform.[125]

Part 5: Listening Power: The Collaborators—Taxing Norms

Why empower the executive branch? Why give state and local governments the power to influence the executive branch? As explained earlier,
Spinoza suggests that there are no real checks on state power. The state
has the right to rule in any manner it sees fit. This right, however, is only
theoretical. Practically, a state cannot, and will not, do this. A capricious state is a short-lived state. State apparatuses resolve the "inevitable
disagreements" among groups within civil society. But groups that are
more convincing, or that deliberate more, will be heard the best, and
therefore will receive the most protection. These groups build consensus
through reason and passion, concocting what makes sense to the largest
number of people.[126]

Collaboration is another fundamental principle undergirding a Spinozan stakeholder nation-state and society. This is the principle on
which the CFPB will succeed or fail. It flows from the participatory commitment and inclusive structure that facilitate multiparty cooperative exchanges.

Under the traditional regulatory model, industry and private individuals represent the object of regulation. The EPA targets companies
that pollute; the National Labor Relations Board seeks out employers
who violate laws governing minimum wages or maximum hours. In each
case, the company or the employer decides whether they will comply
with a fixed set of regulations.

By contrast, the stakeholder model does not have fixed subjects. All
individuals are "norm-generating subjects." That is, they are in constant
flux, creating norms and then changing them. These norm generators
constitute a partnership of equals. No privileges exist for either side of
this horizontal equation. Parity or equality characterizes this conversation between the company doing the polluting and the citizen ingesting

the pollution, and even citizens who do not reside in the polluted area but believe in clean air or water.

The goal of these norm-generating subjects is openness—being open to new ideas, or finding ingenious solutions in solving their collective problems. It is the very imagining, not just the managing and the maintaining, of public policy that accounts for these movable norms.

For this reason, feminist, critical race, and gay legal theorists who earlier practiced critical legal theory but rejected "the legal system as an engine for social change" have come aboard the stakeholder regulatory ideal. With its openness creating a space, and the very idea that there is no homogeneity of norms, they see how existing laws can promote change.[127]

What Stakes? Negotiated rulemaking, along with horizontal and diagonal federalism, launched the Spinozan stakeholder state and society concept in governance. The concept itself, however, goes back to the 1980s, when administrative lawyer Philip Harter described how stakeholders could, and should, have more of a voice in the regulatory process. By creating an open space for collaboration, a state that facilitated the negotiation of federal rules and fostered a stakeholder society could create an ever-evolving environment that promoted accountability on both sides.

Negotiated rulemaking underscores how intertwined and interdependent each player or actor is with all the others. When it works, a win-win language, rather than a zero-sum one, can be heard around the table. It matches means to ends by involving all stakeholders, yet still offers choices or policy options on the basis of competition rooted in difference.[128]

The players' participation also gives the government great legitimacy. The state must safeguard the process, ensuring that no group or party receives partial treatment. "For procedural legitimacy to be meaningful," writes Orly Lobel, "there must be a commitment to public values, such as political equality, which is endangered when power and wealth are deeply imbalanced." Obama captures the role of administrative law in creating a situation "in which the little politics of daily life offer citizens the opportunity to reflect in partial steps on the means and ends of their lives, and through this on the larger choices of the republic."[129]

Competition in Diversity. Diversity creates competition. In a Spinozan stakeholder society, norm-generating actors are essential. Difference is key, just like diversifying one's financial portfolio. Not only does it create balance and stability, but this type of thinking also constitutes the backbone of Obama's belief system. Competition creates pluralities— pluralities of beliefs, values, and ideas, which in turn generate more agendas, norms, and solutions. Values, beliefs, and therefore norms perpetually evolve or change. It's the journey, not the destination, that counts.

The state, in facilitating all this, transfers its legitimacy. Private economic interests help instill public values, but this means that no one can have a monopoly. No institution has the ability to regulate all aspects of contemporary public life. Inclusion and the proliferation of normative authorities encourage such an open community to adopt many different behaviors, approaches, methodologies, and practices.

The New Deal created bureaucracies, like the Social Security Administration, that many beneficiaries "experienced as faceless and inaccessible." By contrast, the "Renew Deal" administrative state "replace[s] remote impersonal relations . . . with face-to-face relations."[130] It converts impersonal duties into personal ones, and it makes participation key. Creating a small-scale focus offers people a sense of connectedness. Small units, even within a large administration, can generate more successful engagements, helping all parties involved reach solutions that can be sustained for a long time.

And by linking in different individuals and groups, these connections can help build deliberative and collaborative capacities, cultivating a context ripe for democratic engagement. Exponentially increasing the roles, capacities, and contexts in which people interact in a community helps neighbors to see their relationships as sellers and consumers, employers and employees, property owners and tenants, planners and citizens, and administrators and service recipients. It follows the golden rule—to rule and be ruled. Synergy results from this type of reciprocity. Engaging and encountering one another gives people the opportunity to develop their collaborative capacities.

It is this value of generating synergy that creates empathy and mutual trust, which in turn create what Orly Lobel describes as "social density." Social density offers more people control, even collective control. It produces more layers of social control and mutual surveillance. A term for this phenomenon in economics is "internalizing externalities." The benefit of a society with this degree of interconnection is that many individuals can and will follow norms that are against their immediate self-interest. Even without the threat of formal regulatory sanction, they do so because of the level of social density.[131]

Social density is not a substitute for hegemony or false consciousness. It is the norm that is internalized, not the state's externalities, as in
a Foucauldian state. Yet in a Spinozan state and society, all solutions are
temporary, not permanent. Each compromise constitutes a solution, not
an overall strategy. Different problems will raise different solutions, giving each party a chance to impart its values. No one side dominates.

Obama's "Race to the Top" grant competition represents this type
of thinking. He allotted $4.35 billion of the stimulus package for com-
petitive grants to schools that took specified steps to improve standards
and assessments, upgraded data systems, and strengthened the recruit-
ment and training of teachers. While only twelve states received grants,
the race inspired more than forty to adopt a common set of public school
(kindergarten through twelfth grade, or K–12) standards.[132]

This "race" also led dozens of states to lift their caps on charter
schools and institute rigorous teacher evaluation programs, though almost every teachers' union took issue with these measures. The money
and the competition proved effective at breaking the political logjams
that had frustrated reformers, giving them the momentum to move their
packages through state legislatures. And even when a state failed to secure funding, the Obama administration succeeded in getting it to reexamine its policies.

It came as no surprise that Obama's Race to the Top idea began in education. First, to achieve reform, particularly along the lines of middle-
class populism, Obama needs results in an area that means a lot to the
middle class. Second, the politics of education are notorious in that the
strongest interest groups—teachers' unions and school management—
both oppose change. The presidencies of Lyndon B. Johnson and George
W. Bush showed Obama that education could change only with a national initiative. So if Obama could get results in education, he could
surely apply the same technique in other areas. In 2011 Obama applied
Race to the Top logic to his whole budget. The aim is to wean federal
programs off so-called "formula" funding from the New Deal and the
Great Society. The administration hopes to give little money out in accordance with preset rules; instead, all funding will be competitive and
based on the extent to which a program is achieving its goals. The great
thing about the Race to the Top money, administration officials will tell
you, is that it proved so highly "leveraged."

At the center of Race to the Top lie performance-centered norms.
Obama insists that the programs seeking funding share their expectations—that is, that they create what is called a "shared expectation" of

comparable outcomes. The state then acts as a facilitator, promoting and standardizing innovations that start out small, local, and private. Scaling up, facilitating innovation, standardizing good practices, and researching and replicating success stories from local or private levels are central goals of government.[133]

The federal government's role is less one of direct action than one of providing financial support, strategic direction, and leadership for other governmental actors. This way of thinking embodies Spinoza's idea that government facilitates action. It is less involved in championing particular institutions and practices than in mobilizing resources, encouraging experimentation, facilitating comparison and evaluation of alternative approaches, and diffusing the best practices. Orchestration of the best practices found in different contexts has the potential to result in a "virtuous cycle of innovation and improvement."

Obama's Race to the Top, like the Renew Deal, "creates incentives and procedures to cultivate internal reflection about behavior." Instead of creating a legal system based on a set of rigid rules, the state facilitates certain practices. It "expands the center of legal thought beyond jurisprudence to include legis-prudence and process-prudence" as parts of "a more holistic legal regime."[134]

A Big-Box Betrayal? Most of Obama's detractors from his own political party, particularly the progressive, traditional liberal big-state Left, miss this point about the enlarged social sphere. Just as big-box stores started springing up all over rural highways in suburbia and then in the new "ruraburbia," decimating Main Street shopping across the country, they assumed Obama would produce big-state solutions that would return them to Main Street in their resegregated suburbs. But they forgot the 1970s and the 1980s in their own romantic pictures of resegregated suburbia, which spatially divided the growing economic inequality. The Democratic Party's response to Reagan's 1986 State of the Union address, wrote Jeff Faux, was a "paean to an entrepreneurial affluent American moving happily up the economic ladder, with only a mild and perfunctory reminder that the poor are still with us." Malls from the 1970s—the heyday of Democratic power in Congress, and then with Jimmy Carter as president—made it possible for Wal-Mart to achieve success in the 1980s and 1990s. Political geographers and scholars in public administration show that the trajectory from Main Street to malls to big-box stores, and then back again to quaint Main Street stores that sell organic produce and free-trade jewelry, has the Democrats putting more distance between themselves and issues of poverty.[135]

It's okay to go private—to create charter schools, for example—as long as one can be assured that not too many African American children will attend them. But then, when African Americans start battling for charter schools in urban areas, there is a cry against destroying all that is public. The Democrats and the Republicans join hands. Obama is now trying to untangle the decline of unions from that of the civil rights movement. But he cannot tackle issues as such as resegregation, or urban poverty, through the judiciary. Making all attempts through federalism, Obama can keep public schools in small segregated areas from stacking the deck and receiving the lion's share of public monies through local tax bases by re-creating standards in public schools and by loosening restrictions on who receives charter schools. Obama has eschewed the strong social welfare state and chosen instead to rely on his powers as the executor and implementer of all the national laws that states depend on, so he can have his secretaries of health and human services and education, as well as his attorney general, cherry-pick which states are implementing the many federalist public policies for progressive purposes. In Obama's view, the one-size-fits-all, large-state solutions from the Great Society benefited white nuclear families, not those of mixed race and ethnicity in urban areas.[136]

Neither Normal nor Moral. How can a deliberative democracy start naming interests and questioning norms? This is best exemplified in very practical terms in what Dryzek calls "post-positivist policy analytics." Post-positivist policymaking advances an "authentic democratization of policy process." It searches for subtle influences—such as material forces, discourses, and ideologies—that shape a public policy. The norm here is universal and hierarchical. Values of immorality and morality are absolute, and the idea of what constitutes morality is hierarchical.

Another, more insidious norm is rationality. Dryzek begins post-positivist policy analytics by critiquing the role of technocratic analysis. While few see technocratic analysis as pervasive and overwhelming, most see it as contingent and therefore believe it is acceptable to explore escapes from this type of analysis. Public policymakers are interested in conceptions of rationality in society and policy that are more expansive and subtle than the instrumental, means/ends rationality that defines the alternative. Technocratic policy analysis proceeds in the image of an omniscient, benevolent decision maker—a situation in which there is no politics. In a complex political system, rationalistic policymaking is possible only at rare moments of consensus and crisis, or in occasional areas insulated from pluralistic control, such as diplomacy and national security.[137]

Charles Lindblom's famous statement about the "science of muddling through" cannot be applied universally. This type of disjointed incrementalism reflects policymaking in the United States, but nowhere else. Muddling through is an American idea. It dresses up a technocratic, rationalist norm as universal when in fact it is particular. When norms change, policies change. Rational cost-benefit analysis is a perspective premised on a set of norms. Equating a corporation and an individual is a perspective, again reflecting norms. Counting a corporation and an individual each as one unit of analysis helps determine a specific outcome in American capitalism.[138]

Exposing Privileges. Most importantly, keeping expectations in flux makes unfair privileges known and can also name unknown privileges. American norms cultivate both known unfair and unknown privileges. A diverse society like the United States need not help its citizens become more independent. Rather, recognition of everyone's interdependence is required: Children depend on parents, middle-class parents depend on mortgage interest tax deductions, and the wealthy depend on favorable investment tax policies. Few people depend on nothing, or no one. Little is for free, or, better put, without strings attached.[139]

A quick tug on these strings reveals many knots and tangles, showing how interdependent the American individual, state, market, and society have become. Trying to untangle these strings helps us name privileges bestowed on some groups and individuals without much political reflection. Why does the middle class receive the largest subsidy from the state: the mortgage interest tax write-off, a benefit that costs more than welfare for the poor? Why do the state and society give little scrutiny to the morality of this expenditure, particularly in comparison to welfare? The primary question in American politics, as stated earlier, remains as Harold D. Lasswell stated it: Who gets what, when, and how? The answer changes, but the question stays the same.[140]

Not only managing expectations, but also destabilizing them and spurning universal social rights and entitlements, gives a Spinozan state the chance to bolster civil society by helping its citizens' "ever-becoming." Ever-becoming means existing without (or with few) limitations. It involves living in a state and society that promotes an individual's potential, though with the knowledge that it is not important to reach it. Ever-becoming means taking a journey without a destination. "Barack Obama will require you to work," explained Michelle Obama. "That you push yourselves to be better." There is no end, no pot of gold or Shangri-la on the other side of any rainbow. It is not teleological.[141]

For Spinoza and Obama it's all about the relationship. One person will help another depending on how they relate to each other. What do they share in their relationship? Some radical feminists follow the same logic. "Self-interest coexists with group interest," writes Katherine Adams, "each conditioning the other." The individual and society become successful in reciprocal and relational terms. To Spinoza, "there is nothing more useful to a man than a man." What this means for radical feminism is that "self-interest can promote a practice of coalition discourse that accommodates diverse truths," and is "centered . . . in material culture."[142]

A challenge for Spinoza and Obama is discovering what mutually benefits the individual and society. Another challenge is convincing the people to participate. These are practical problems, however, not philosophical ones. How can Obama solve these problems? The first ingredient is imagination. There must be a vision. Progressive Democrats should encourage voters not to imagine sharing, particularly not sharing with identifiable groups, but rather to envision "what they could all get" for their hard-earned tax dollars, knowing that they will be providing for more than themselves.

To put it differently, Spinoza is outlining a social sphere that pools its resources in a way that simultaneously benefits the individual and society at large. Two heads are better and stronger than one; two sets of taxes accomplish more than one. Spinoza proposes pulling together a potluck dinner rather than baking a pie. The test for Spinoza and Obama is figuring out what everyone should bring to the table and then deciding what, and how, to eat. How can the mutually inclusive power that each of us has be transformed into mutually inclusive public goods that benefit most, if not all, of us? How do we get the butcher, the barber, and the baker to agree? Obama has discovered the best way, which involves what he calls "universal appeals." He sees these appeals as "strategies that help all Americans (schools that teach, jobs that pay, healthcare for everyone who needs it, a government that helps out after a flood)." But then, Obama has discovered that not everyone comes to the table.[143]

Traditionally, though, a political theory based on self-interest is not considered transformative. In the United States, self-interest is usually associated with James Madison's notion of factionalism, republicanism, and partisanship. In *Federalist #10* Madison describes mutual animosity and competition among legislators. Whether it is factions, political parties, or contemporary interest groups, self-interest manifests itself as behavior that is "vexing." It shows how people oppress "each other rather than cooperate for common good."[144]

But Arendt argues that if interactions are to work, everyone must get something, and that something cannot be abstract. The interaction must be on a material level; it must be practical. As Arendt describes, it is the "table" between them—the materiality or physicality of it—that creates "an intimate reliance on others' recognition of others." Or, as Obama puts it, universal appeals and strategies can work "along with measures that ensure our laws apply equally to everyone and hence uphold broadly held American ideals (like better enforcement of existing civil rights laws)." And as they all become concrete, they "can serve as the basis for such coalitions even if such strategies disproportionately help minorities."[145]

Just like Spinoza before her and Obama after, Arendt rejects the Cartesian duality and suggests that self-interest can satisfy the mind and the body simultaneously on an individual and collective basis. What is necessary, however, is to satisfy needs—material, physical, intellectual, and emotional or psychological ones. The mind and the body, reason and passion, must be satisfied rather than compartmentalized, as Obama so concretely exemplifies with his universal appeals, strategies, and measures or social technologies.

The Trilemmas as Collaborators: Capture Capture Theory. Second-generation law-and-economics scholars, who are largely conservative, have recognized that governmental interventions can enhance both liberty and welfare. The very concept of linear maximization of individual welfare has been challenged. New institutional economics has also challenged conventional assumptions about economic actors as isolated individuals engaged in didactic exchanges. The new understanding is one of social beings whose actions and knowledge are at least partly constructed by their institutional settings.

Drawing on psychological analysis, behavioral law and economics has introduced the understanding that individual preferences are endogenous, a function of experience and existing collective norms. As a result, law-and-economics scholarship recognizes that freedom is not identical to unlimited choice and that governmental intervention is inevitable in a functioning market.[146]

To be most effective, the governance model must continue to explore such "inter-modal synergy and hybrid . . . governance modes," including the coexistence, complementarities, and mutual reinforcement of traditional regulation and new governance approaches.[147]

But did Obama do enough? With political scientists long criticizing him for not creating a jobs bill, only in 2011 did he begin asking for a

$447 billion American Jobs Act. It stalled in Congress, and prospects for
its passage faded as his first term neared its end. The HIRE Act of 2010,
giving tax breaks to businesses that created new jobs, transformed little,
since it received 90 percent less funding than Obama had requested. Republicans in the House and Senate made it plain: they refused to compromise. A poorly performing economy, after all, represented their primary
means of gaining congressional seats in 2012 and having a Republican
take back the White House.[148]

Gearing up for reelection, Obama, in his 2012 State of the Union
address, went further than in any other post–economic crisis proposal,
offering what economists called an "industrial policy." Many economists agree that the United States has experienced over three decades
of decline as manufacturing jobs have disappeared. Over 7 million jobs
disappeared in this time span, most being shipped overseas. But as former governor Jennifer Granholm of Michigan points out, "big trends—
like rising wages in developing countries, falling wages in America, and
a weaker dollar—have made moving work to or keeping work in the
United States a much more viable option." Having collaborated with
Governor Granholm when he saved Chrysler, the president adopted her
emphasis on "insourcing." "We have a huge opportunity at this moment, to bring manufacturing back," Obama said. "Tonight, my message to business leaders is simple: Ask yourselves what you can do to
bring jobs back to your country and your country will do everything we
can to help you succeed."[149]

The next day White House economist Gene Sperling said, "It's not
fighting against the trends. It's actually working with them." What the
Obama administration does is nudge small and large employers alike by
providing incentives such as cutting taxes for corporations that bring
back manufacturing jobs, doubling tax deductions for companies that
produce high-tech goods, and even creating job training programs in specific industries and sectors. At the same time, Obama plans on stripping
many corporations of their tax shelters and loopholes if they continue
shipping jobs offshore. "It all adds up to what an economist might call
an industrial policy," said another economist after Obama's speech.[150]

If he is reelected in 2012, will Obama succeed in creating an industrial
policy? It is highly doubtful. "Triangulations," "third ways," and "third
waves" receive less popular and scholarly respect than their forerunners.
Rather than cutting a swath or causing a splash, these so-called thirds
instead often carve out a tiny path or cause ripples. For instance, an increasing number of journalists and historians portray President Clinton's
"third way" as a continuation of the Reagan revolution. Third-wave

feminism began as a backlash against the second wave, but it has been channeled into so many directions that it now lacks coherence.[151]

Still, Obama's third way reflects a third American political tradition that creates an institutional *tri*lemma that could last when he leaves office. That is, the public policy implementation process now involves three or more players. It is inclusive and dynamic. Deliberation brings in a third party that is not usually welcomed into the process: outside community groups. Obama's third way asks Americans to recognize their interdependence and their interconnectedness by enlarging their involvement in an enlarged social sphere. And he implores the public to participate, and reach beyond themselves, though without sacrificing their individual self-interest.[152]

Deliberating Publics. In Obama's notion of progressive federalism, the overall goal of participation in the regulatory process is more important than even "ensuring the achievement of policy" goals. Participation enhances the ability of citizens to engage in political and civic life. At the stage of implementation, stakeholder participation has been referred to as a "revolution in the technology of public action."

The new participatory model involves what law professors call "transgovernmental regulatory networks." This type of regulatory regime is "fast, flexible, and decentralized." Transgovernmental groups help the federal government operate well, particularly in a "rapidly changing information environment." Not only Orly Lobel and a few law professors, but many experts in administrative law, consider this new system of regulatory reform revolutionary and herald its efficiency in fostering deliberative democracy, all of which gives the federal government more legitimacy as it solicits state and local interaction as well.[153]

None of this is to deny that both sides of the congressional aisle, in both the House and the Senate, know how to sabotage regulatory agencies. Republicans well understand the politics of sabotage (better known as the primacy of the status quo) within an administrative state, utilizing the executive branch for contrary purposes and making majorities and minority tools (the threat of filibuster) essential for different reasons. The question is whether Obama's constructions will be of any use to the next executive.[154]

5 Foreign Stakeholders: Just War and Just Peace in a New World Order of Universal Anti-Universalism

We are shaped by every culture, drawn from every end of the Earth, and dedicated to a simple concept: E pluribus unum—"Out of many, one."—**Barack Obama, Cairo, Egypt, June 4, 2009**

Obama's foreign policy embodies the final features of the Spinozan stakeholder state and society, concentrating on what is common and creating a cosmopolitan global commons. Obama promotes foreign policy on a *subsidiarity* basis. This means that the United States, instead of being *the* world's power, has decided to join a global chain or franchise and be one of many powers, pursuing multilateralism instead. Even for the toughest calls on "deciding whom to kill," including American citizen Anwar al-Awlaki, Obama, as commander in chief, took sole responsibility for his unilateral acts, all while seeking and cementing a multilateral alliance with NATO (starting off not in Camp David, but in Chicago, of all places). When he made it public that the United States had lost patience with Pakistan for hiding al-Qaeda and Taliban militants, Obama let the depth and intensity of the solidarity behind his leadership be known.[1]

Obama paired this show of power with his success in taking the stage as a global economic leader at the 2012 G8 and G20 meetings. At the G8, he used French president François Hollande's election to claim center stage as a pro-growth Eurozone promoter rather than an advocate of austerity economics, which was increasingly advanced by German chancellor Angela Merkel alone, and to unveil a "coordinated Los Cabos Growth and Jobs Action Plan."[2]

It is a truism in political science to say that in their second terms, American presidents turn from domestic policy to foreign policy—where they can wield their power with great effect and have possibly long-standing and even historic influence as global leaders—and Obama will be no exception. Where this book departs from journalists' accounts of Obama's foreign policy is that none of this should come as a surprise if one understands how Spinozan thought shapes his worldview. Obama's "confront and conceal" policies—including pulling out of Afghanistan, the extensive use of drones, and secret cyberattacks—provide evidence of this perspective. And whether one supports or opposes these policies, they pushed Obama onto the stage as a gallant global leader in search of common humanity, not a leader in need of an "education."[3]

Shared Burden Doctrine

Although he studied international relations at Columbia University, Obama has not stayed one foreign policy course. Foreign policy unfolds in reaction to world events, and, to be sure, Obama's policies have changed as a consequence of different events and different-sized international crises. But the character of Obama's vision, or his tough-love Spinozan worldview, has remained remarkably consistent. Obama's 2007 *Foreign Affairs* article "Renewing American Leadership" echoed this Spinozan theme. Then, speaking before the UN General Assembly in September 2009, Commander in Chief Obama reversed *E pluribus unum* to read "Out of One, Many," echoing the cooperative and collaborative theme as he announced that the United States would *reengage* with the world.

And finally, three years later, as Obama declared that the United States was pulling out of Afghanistan, out of a war he had escalated, he said, "We are building a global consensus." Revealing that he had secured NATO support before this meeting even convened showed just how supportive of an American president this alliance had become. "Our goal is not to build a country in America's image," Obama said, "or to eradicate every vestige of the Taliban." It is a policy, as a journalist reported, that the White House referred to as "Afghan good enough." Like every Democratic president since 1968, Obama does not want a

"Vietnam" dividing his domestic constituencies or harming the United States' reputation in the international community.[4]

Translating this complex theme into a doctrine that interweaves and layers unilateralism and multilateralism, this book refers to Obama's foreign policy as the shared burden doctrine. As such, this doctrine pulled the United States out of its "spiteful unilateralism," making it one nation among many—adopting multilateralism, albeit while ensuring its status as one of the most powerful nations, with Obama himself becoming the global leader. Even before NATO met in Chicago, the summer before the 2012 election, Obama offered a glimpse into what was about to happen. NATO passed him the global-leader baton, but not in the way they usually treated American presidents, as deep pockets or as the world's only superpower they loved to hate.[5]

This time an American president had earned it—and not because Obama had been given the 2009 Nobel Peace Prize, an award his domestic and foreign expert detractors enjoyed mocking. It became evident that Obama had started earning the international community's respect after the award ceremony, and after diplomacy. At the award ceremony itself, Obama stunned his supporters by outlining his commitment to power and force when diplomacy fails. "War is justified only when it meets certain preconditions," he said, "if it is waged as a last resort or in self-defense; if the force used is proportional, and if, whenever possible, civilians are spared from violence."

Obama relayed Augustine's, Aquinas's, and Spinoza's notions of "just war" *and* "just peace." The president lectured his audience. Obama gave them "the hard truth," going so far as to equate al-Qaeda with Hitler. It was a call to arms, not a peace speech, in which Obama argued that the United States' allies should dispel any wishful theoretical thinking that "violent conflict" could be eradicated, or that violence would end in "our lifetimes." Obama signaled to the whole world that he would use force when "justified."[6]

More Mammal than Bird

What Obama did with his Nobel lecture was to show that he was not another Jimmy Carter, who put human rights first. He also made it clear that he could not be portrayed as another Bill Clinton, a president who would hesitate if genocide occurred and give voice to regrets while in retirement. Obama accepts "just war" and, even more importantly, embraces "just peace" on a cosmopolitan basis, or one not indebted to

Eurocentric ideology. In 2009 he faced a new world order, and the president would do what it took as a unilateral and multilateral leader.

"As a head of [the American] state," he said, he had sworn "to protect and defend my nation . . . [and] face the world *as it is*." Then Obama proclaimed, "Make no mistake: evil does exist in the world." He added that "a non-violent movement could not have halted Hitler's armies. Negotiations cannot convince al-Qaeda's leaders to lay down their arms." He then implored the United States' allies to understand "that force may sometimes be necessary [and saying so] is not a call to cynicism—[but] it is a *recognition of history*; the imperfections of man and the limits of reason."[7]

All this was code for what journalists put front and center to the voting American public's imagination in 2012: Obama was a ruthless enemy. Only in 2011 and 2012 did the extent of his ruthlessness as a unilateral leader of a sovereign nation exercising executive action become known. In contrast to Carter and Clinton, the GOP would have difficulty characterizing Obama as a dove, a human rights softie, a weak failure in foreign policy, or finally as a hawk, given his invasion of Libya during the Arab Spring. As commander in chief, Obama is more mammal than bird, more wolf than dove or hawk, as he seeks to rebalance American foreign policy by looking at the Far East, not just the Middle East.[8]

Obama advanced the shared burden doctrine without compromising American sovereignty or the nation-state's self-interest. He threw the United States into a puzzle of foreign nations that are interlayered, interdependent, and interconnected, sharing power, authority, control, *and* legitimacy in *proper* proportions or measure. "It is my deeply held belief that in the year 2009," Obama explained, "—more than at any point in human history—the interests of nations and peoples are *shared*."[9]

After invading Libya in 2011, Obama said, "American leadership is not simply a matter of going it alone and bearing all of the burden ourselves. Real leadership creates the conditions and coalitions for others to step up as well; to work with allies and partners so that they bear their share of the burden and pay their share of the costs; and to see that the principles of justice and human dignity are upheld by all." In Kabul in 2012, he reiterated this. As American troops pull out, he said, they are sending "a clear message to the Afghan people: as you stand up, you will not stand alone." The agreement he negotiated "establishes the basis for our cooperation over the next decade, including shared commitments to combat terrorism." Obama pulled out despite a decade of military advisors briefing presidents about the powder keg that exists in the form of Shi'a-Sunni/Israeli relations in the Pakistan/Afghanistan/Iran/Israel balance-of-power equation. He pulled out in spite of Pakistan's reputedly most important general Ashfaq Kayani's concern that the region could ignite, a concern this general and others shared with Obama's predecessors.[10]

Two Pillars Behind "Just War and Just Peace": From Sinners to Fools; and the Limits of Tolerance and Reason

Obama's foreign policy has been described as an unlikely marriage of Woodrow Wilson's liberal internationalism and Richard M. Nixon's political realism. "America has shown arrogance and been dismissive, even derisive. . . . So I've come to Europe," said Obama, "to renew our partnership, one in which America listens and learns from our friends and allies, but where our friends and allies bear their *share of the burden.*" In joining an alliance, friendly foreign nations gain equal voice to express their respective nations' interests and engage in a diplomatic deliberative process. But this does not mean that all nations have equal power. Power is relational. It is proportional, and it is constantly and continually balanced and measured as nation-states join together in different, albeit perpetually shifting, power alliances.[11]

Two pillars support the Spinozan thought upholding Obama's foreign policy of "just war" and "just peace." First, Spinoza is no different from Christians from Paul to Augustine in his belief in a *redemptive* state. This belief is totally different from contemporary conservative Catholic or evangelical Christian thought. Embodying a third way between Hobbes's "war of all against all" and Rousseau's civil society, Spinoza does not believe either that a "state of discord is natural" or that diverse nation-states could achieve a "general will." As explained in chapter 3, Obama believes in civic religion and the Hebraic Bible, and that while heaven does not exist on earth, hell does.[12]

Evil exists. No persons or peoples are angels. Therefore, Obama insists that the necessity of the state stems from sinfulness in human nature. But in contrast to contemporary Christian thought, the kind of sin Obama, like Spinoza, addresses is not based on God, or on revealed truth, nor does it accept any type of love of humanity that comes with exclusions. Nor is it based on the gender binary that accepts rape as a crime of war but not a crime against humanity. Obama is against what this book describes as neotribalism, as described in chapter 3. When the president changed course by invading Libya, "we knew," he said, "that if we waited one more day, Benghazi . . . could suffer a massacre that would have reverberated across the region and stained the conscience of the world."[13]

Yet sin cannot be measured by any theoretical precept, or by faith. There are no absolutes, no juridical principles of right and wrong. What necessitates a state, as the theologian Spinoza sees it, are what he calls "fools," rather than sinners. Fools (*stulti*) must be stopped from destroying the freedom of those "wise" individuals who, through reason (*intelligens*), seek self-preservation and pursue their right to aspire toward perfectibility. The fool/wise person distinction, for Obama, is an elementary divide. An international community, in which individual nation-states suspend their sovereignty to find factual or empirical wisdom (*scientia*) to discover common solutions to common problems, necessitates a similar redemptive state.[14]

Second, Spinoza's theology—unlike Christianity, especially the theology of the United States as a Christian nation—is tolerant and all-inclusive. It is better described as politics and ethics than as truths, like natural laws in Christianity, or as universal human rights, a secular incarnation of Western Christianity in modern-day Europe. Obama's foreign policy is all about using power to find, use, and enforce common solutions that afford all people human dignity.

Like Aristotle and Machiavelli, Spinoza saw power as relational and reciprocal. Similarly, after Spinoza, it was Montesquieu, Tocqueville, and Max Weber who became Spinoza's heirs in terms of recognizing power as derived from a theory of praxis, not a theory of rights. As illustrated in chapters 3 and 4, this explains why Obama turns to the politics of elected office and rejects the judiciary. Like Spinoza, Obama supports political science, or what can be described as an empirical science of politics, in that he is fascinated with causal analysis and with understanding norms as motives for behavior, not as dictating standards for a polity, society, or culture. Obama rejects any abstractions such as a legal philosophy of the state and relies less on rigid principles, such as those established by UN resolutions and conventions, than on diplomacy.[15]

This rejection of universal truths becomes even more pronounced in foreign policy, where power in diplomacy is tantamount to leadership. Obama forges a foreign policy that unites nation-states that seek common goods, but these common goods are temporary, not permanent, and establish ethics, not universal truths. As Obama repeatedly uttered to the Iranian Republic, "nothing is off the table." Obama suspends value judgments even of rogue nations. There are no evil empires, no democratization, but also no absolute standards when it comes to establishing human rights. Obama concentrates on facts. He looks for a time-bound empirical basis for changing or redefining American self-interest and assessing whether or not to support an invasion or lend a humanitarian hand.

The Obama administration employs causal analysis, not ideology, and then finds logical conclusions to common problems that do not correlate with a Left/Right, idealist/realist, or Western/Eastern civilization binary. In Spinoza's imagination, peace, like a puzzle, must be solvable. In the pre-reelection news revelations, what caught the international community by surprise was how unerring or relentless Obama is once his mind is made up about a course of action. As Aaron David Miller, a conservative critic, observed, Obama is "George W. Bush on steroids."[16]

"Together, We Must Forge Common Solutions to Our Common Problems"

When Obama unveils a policy program, he follows a certain Spinozan pattern or cuts a discernible swath, a modus operandi, if you will. He does not necessarily follow this policy presentation path sequentially, but often simultaneously—or with a triangulating twist, throwing in three or more variables at once. The presentation of his foreign policy has been no different.

First, Obama lowers his audience's expectations by explaining why a Spinozan ethic is imperative. In his UN General Assembly speech, he noted that the "religious convictions that we hold in our hearts can forge new bonds among people, or they can tear us apart."[17]

Then, Obama proclaims hope: the world, he believes, can be pulled back from the brink of global environmental destruction. "The technology we harness can light the path to peace, or forever darken it. The energy we use can sustain our planet, or destroy it."[18]

Next, Obama offers a concrete vision or future, rather than relying on hope, which could after all be dashed. This future, Obama finally explains, stems from his own personal history. "The hope of a single child—anywhere—," Obama said, "can enrich our world, or impoverish it." By insisting that a child embodies hope, Obama presents us with a future. There are no rights, no wrongs, and no rigid principles dictating what "ought" to be.

Obama gained center stage as a global leader first by his actions—taken in good faith—and second, by the way he underscored Spinoza's idea about humankind's capacity for imagination. Thinking is what makes us human, so for Obama and Spinoza, imagination is what makes us strive toward self-preservation and perfectibility. As will be shown, this view explains how Obama could reverse course and support the Arab Spring.[19]

What distinguishes Obama's vision from the traditional conception of children as the future—a seemingly trite analogy—and makes it Spinozan is that to Obama, the child also offers us the extended family perspective of his childhood, and that of his children. That is, we—not the individual, the nation, or the world—must regard ourselves as *inter*dependent. The United States does not impose its unilateral will. "Let me be clear: No system of government can or should be imposed [upon] one nation by any other." But in forming an alliance, each nation-state must agree to be willing to reexamine its self-interests and suspend or bracket all judgment. Unlike a national government, however, an alliance, by definition, is temporary. It is only as good as its utility. It is only good as long as it lasts, since the different member states all have the right to act unilaterally and retain their sovereignty, but suspend that right and that sovereignty while seeking global solutions: "Together, we must forge common solutions to our common problems."[20]

Penultimately, Obama cements the three steps described above by taking into account human motives, applying empirical causal analysis, and then adding a simple zero-sum power play. He co-opts the players—or as many participants as he can—by inviting them to join him in achieving his grand design. "I am well aware of the expectations that accompany my presidency around the world," he told the UN. "These expectations are not about me. Rather, they are rooted, I believe, in a discontent with a status quo that has allowed us to be increasingly defined by our differences, and outpaced by our problems." But in inviting those players to the table, he reiterates the value of nonjudgment, tolerance, and inclusivity. In his 2012 State of the Union address, he said: "America is determined to prevent Iran from getting a nuclear weapon, and I will take *no options off the table* to achieve that goal." But he then assured Iran, "a peaceful resolution of this issue is still possible." "And far better," Obama added, "if Iran changes course and meets its obligations, it can rejoin the community of nations."[21]

Just as Obama invites all the players to the domestic policymaking table, he does the same with foreign policymaking, which includes both covert operations and diplomacy. He not only invites rogue nation-states like Iran to the table, but also works with rogue individual players through both covert operations and diplomatic channels. Obama or his emissaries warn them, as Spinoza describes, not to act like "fools." And, he says, "as Iran's leaders continue to ignore their obligations, there should be no doubt: They, too, will face growing consequences. That is a promise."

Obama believes that he alone must shoulder "responsibility" for all these decisions. And in doing so, he lets it be known that he relies on the "just-war theories of Augustine and Thomas Aquinas." What is missing from this medieval theology is Spinoza, who has a similar notion of just war and just peace. For Obama to be a Spinozan world leader means he is a leader that reflects the embodiment of the "united power of all." To live harmoniously, and be of assistance to one another, in a single nation, but even more importantly in an international community, each nation-state must understand the balance of power. Each nation coming to the table determines if it "is necessary for them to give up their natural right." Giving up the natural right in international relations is akin to an individual nation-state's decision to temporarily suspend its sovereignty in order to benefit from an alliance.[22]

But in Spinoza's and Obama's view, this temporary suspension is neither permanent nor universal. The relationship between the state and its subjects, and even more so between an international community and cooperative and collaborative nation-states, replicates a "balance of power." When power shifts and changes, so does the balance, and so does the community's leader. Obama's gaining NATO's full support in 2012 does not guarantee the same support in 2013.[23]

Further, if either the leader or the leading nation-state moves from good faith to bad—or, even worse, is corrupted, goes rogue, and no longer allows the compliant nation-states the right to self-preservation of their peoples—then either the individual leader or the nation-state has become what Spinoza calls a "fool," or what Augustine and Aquinas would call a "sinner." It is being a fool, being a sinner, being a rogue nation that leads the international community to gang up on that nation, and, in Spinoza's words, the leader or the state "causes its own downfall."[24]

As Obama said in his 2010 State of the Union address, this explains "why North Korea now faces increased isolation, and stronger sanctions." It also explains why Obama has no hesitation about ordering the assassination of someone born in New Mexico. And finally, it explains why in 2012, speaking before the pro-Israel lobby AIPAC, he said, "I have made clear time and again during the course of my presidency, I will not hesitate to use force when it is necessary to defend the United States and its interests." The tough-love, just-war theories of Augustine, Aquinas, and Spinoza, as the philosopher Georg Geismann demonstrates, underscore how even the "very possibility of guilt"—on a theoretical, let alone an empirical, level—does not exist.[25]

It is consonant with the just-war and just-leadership perspectives that Obama would act as the informal leader of an international alliance that depends on multilateral decision making, and that when the president conducts war as a democratically elected leader endowed with the right to act unilaterally as commander in chief, he would harbor no regrets about his decisions. When the nation is threatened by a citizen such as al-Awlaki, it is not surprising that Obama gives himself the right to smite even an American citizen fighting on foreign soil to save the nation's entire citizenry. Obama reacts to the same logic as Abraham Lincoln did when he suspended habeas corpus for American citizens during the Civil War.

As a global leader, Obama must act in good faith, but his leadership is contingent on the way he wields his power. A frequent misunderstanding about Spinoza is the idea that his notion of power and leadership recognizes "the right of the strongest." Might-equals-right is wrong. Any nation-state absent a "respective benefit" resulting from an agreement no longer recognizes the agreement. It is null and void. A nation-state's right to self-preservation *precedes* the agreement. "A compact is only made valid by its utility, without which it becomes null and void." If a nation-state, like a person, "judges that his pledge is causing him more loss than gain," then Spinoza recognizes his right to break it as a "right of nature."

Spinoza recognizes the absolutism of state authority by reserving it to a natural right—but this means that people act within their nature, not that there are human rights or any types of rights based in universalism. Put simply, there is no contradiction between "absolutism" and "reservation." The leaders' capacity to act with full authority or absolute power stems, in other words, from one's right to renounce it on the basis of empirical evidence. As Obama assured Israel, "We may not agree on every single issue—no two nations do, and our democracies contain a vibrant diversity of views. But we agree on the big things—the things that matter. And together, we are working to build a better world—one where our people can live free from fear; one where peace is founded upon justice; one where our children can know a future that is more hopeful than the present." A nation-state retains its citizens' right to self-preservation.[26]

Finally, Obama presents his perspective, or his "reality," for comparison to offset the complaint or accusation that he is not inclusive or does not listen. As he told the UN General Assembly: "Now, like all of you, my responsibility is to act in the interest of my nation and my people, and *I will never apologize for defending those interests.*" The president is telling world leaders not to be unreasonable with their expectations now that he has accepted responsibility for the failings of nearly all the presidents in office before him. Obama is providing world leaders with the Spinozan perspective that "reality is . . . 'with respect to our imagination.'"[27]

For Obama, the power play reflects Spinoza's idea that a collection of actors—people within a society, or nations within the global community—can choose to unite or choose to fight. Either way, it is a choice. As explained in chapter 1, Spinoza writes that "man is a wolf to man" or "man is a god to man." It works both ways. Although some individuals, or in this case nation-states, can behave like wolves, attacking others to advance their own gain, Spinoza emphasizes that other individuals, or nation-states, can act like gods or saviors, helping their peers for the sake of their own self-preservation and perfectibility. A collective of nation-states can coalesce and work together to ensure their own survivability.[28]

More Wolf than Hawk or Dove: How to Translate Spinoza from Administrative Law to Foreign Policy?

As Obama exerted leadership in getting NATO to coalesce as a community or a collective, he acted as a commander in chief who could be equated with neither traditional hawks nor traditional doves. From the perspective of the enemy, be it al-Qaeda, the Haqqani network, or other Taliban-linked groups, Obama could be better associated with a wolf, as Spinoza describes. When he perceives a zero-sum conflict in which the United States' interests are at stake, Obama is relentless.

Unlike that of former president George W. Bush, Obama's foreign policy does not push for the democratization of any country. He casts aside the idea that American political beliefs and values should be exported and emphasizes accepting countries with different values.[29]

To Obama, the Vietnam War provided an invaluable lesson that the generals invading Iraq should have heeded: the United States cannot and should not try to democratize the world, particularly the Middle East. Even when the Iranian regime was almost toppled by the so-called Twitter revolution in 2009, Obama wavered little.

In line with Spinozan thought, Obama's foreign policy is multilateral. His approach can be captured by an awkward administrative word, "subsidiarity"—so awkward, in fact, that the image might stick. Being a subsidiary means being part of a collective of nation-states. The term conveys the autonomy and freedom from universality, or what diplomats call sovereignty, that Obama advanced before the UN General Assembly. Within the regulatory world, subsidiarity deputizes parties to promote participation.

A foreign policy based on subsidiarity and participation advances diversity, competition, and experimentation. Indeed, this participatory design is akin to Justice Louis Brandeis's metaphor of the American states as "laboratories of democracy." Brandeis was speaking of states within the United States; Obama takes a similar approach with sovereign nations.

This type of political participation not only underscores diversity and encourages experimentation, but is premised on a decentralized power structure. Each nation-state has its own power, authority, and legitimacy. No common knowledge exists; no notion of impartiality or neutrality permeates the thinking behind decentralization. Rather, the challenge underlying this type of system is how to translate the separate units of power, authority, and legitimacy into a collective response or collective action.

Obama's foreign policy recognizes that all knowledge is partial and local. "Think globally, act locally" is the bumper sticker underlying this critical-theory notion. It is not for one nation to tell another nation what to do. This said, there is a presumption that the nation-state closest to a particular problem probably has the best grasp of the situation and can best help in devising a solution. No one nation-state should give the other nation-states less local discretion. They are all equals.

Synergy is another term for the global governance that stems from such a decentralized power structure. A free flow of synergy is contained within the Deweyan/Spinozan notion of interaction and interconnectedness that defines the Obama doctrine. Synergy collapses, or tension results, when foreign nations rely on beliefs and values that diverge from those of the United States. This occurs often, and no better example exists than the issue of human rights. But before examining the "betwixt and between" or threshold position that Obama maintains on human rights and democratization, the events surrounding Osama bin Laden's death will be mapped as evidence of Obama's preference for middle ground, or what some of his supporters could call "no-man's-land."

"Failure Is Never an Option—Not in America"

The cautious way Obama handled Osama bin Laden's capture and killing shows how he strives for this middle, anti-universalist ground. The successful mission gave Obama a bump in the polls: over 70 percent of respondents agreed with his decision to invade Pakistan and shoot bin Laden, though they also recognized how this al-Qaeda leader's death escalated the already looming threat of terrorism on United States soil. "Even while plotting a high-risk operation against Osama bin Laden Obama was the 'cool cat,'" British-American journalist Andrew Sullivan explained.[30]

Obama had previously exhibited no qualms about executing social movement leaders or assassinating Americans in a foreign country. Regarding bin Laden, as president-elect, Obama gave newscaster Katie Couric an exclusive: he told her that whether bin Laden "is technically alive or not" did not matter, since the United States had "pinned [him] down [so far] he cannot function." Then Obama added, "My preference *obviously* would be to capture or kill him." When that actually happened more than two years later, Obama received great kudos from the international press. One British journalist titled his piece "Obama Purrs Softly,—Then Flash—His Claws Kill."[31]

Obama's satisfaction with the United States' shooting of bin Laden came through during his press conference informing the nation of the news. "Justice has been done," said Obama. Where Clinton and Bush had failed, Obama's military had captured and killed the world's most wanted terrorist.[32]

Then, just as he did before the UN General Assembly meeting, Obama warned Pakistan's leaders, who had defied international norms by hiding bin Laden. Obama put Pakistan on red alert, telling its leaders that he suspected they were still hiding other terrorist trainers in plain sight, such as "possibly . . . Mullah Mohammed Omar, the one-eyed Taliban leader."[33]

Obama knew that the flow of money into Pakistan in the war against al-Qaeda was so great that Pakistan's defiance of America's interests became tantamount to violating a formal contract. All bets were off. Sovereignty need not be respected when Pakistan was helping al-Qaeda train terrorists to kill American civilians or military personnel in the United States or abroad. No more "safe havens," the Obama administration told Pakistan's leaders. The United States "now expects it to stop dithering and hunt down other fugitive terrorists."[34]

Robert Gates, who served as secretary of defense under Bush and Obama, and Admiral Michael Mullen, who chaired the Joint Chiefs of Staff under both presidents, "voiced some sympathy for their Pakistani counterparts." "If I were in Pakistani shoes, I would say I've already paid a price. I've been humiliated," Mr. Gates said. "I've been shown that the

Americans can come in here and do this with *impunity*." Speaking on behalf of Obama, Gates and Mullen practiced the president's character-istic tough love. No "real" sympathy was offered; rather, Obama sent Pakistan the message that they had one final chance to show the world whether they are staying "rogue."[35]

More importantly, the impunity with which bin Laden had operated meant to Obama that Pakistan had lost its sovereignty. According to J. Samuel Barkin, as human rights have become increasingly important in international relations, so has the need to understand the unspoken norms of the many different peoples and cultures around the world. The question of when intervention works depends on the strategic facts of sovereignty, but also on the legitimacy behind it. Sovereignty is defined as *"the right of the state to do as it sees fit within its jurisdictional do-main."* The legitimacy depends on the nation—how "criminal" was it for Obama to assassinate bin Laden in the court of domestic and world public opinion, or among his party's elite, and finally, in the elite public opinion of the UN and EU?[36]

Helping Vulnerable Populations

Moving from what requires the most discipline of a president to what requires the least, our second example of Obama's anti-universalism is substantiated in what his detractors would call his feeble backing of in-ternational human rights. Obama sought to distinguish himself and his foreign policy from Bush and his ideas on democratization immediately. Just two days after Obama's inauguration, the president sent a pair of special envoys, former senator George Mitchell and former ambassador Richard Holbrooke, to the Middle East for a "listening tour."[37]

Obama also sent Secretary of State Hillary Clinton trotting around the globe on a listening tour for the first few months of 2009. She took early trips to the Far East and the Middle East, went to Mexico in March, and in April visited Iraq and Lebanon, all to show that Obama was pre-pared to listen to and respect other sovereign nations. Before his inaugu-ration, Obama had explained: "Hillary Clinton, in her testimony during her confirmation hearing, expressed my views and the views of the ad-ministration that we can't delay. We can't kick the can down the road. We're gonna have to take a regional approach. We're gonna have to in-volve Syria in discussions. We're gonna have to engage Iran in ways that we have not before. We've gotta have a clear bottom line that Israel's security is paramount."[38]

Upon entering office, Obama met with military leaders, discussing how to remove troops from Iraq. "In Iraq, we are responsibly ending a war," Obama said. By late 2009 he had increased American forces in Afghanistan by 17,000 troops. In February of the following year, Obama announced a removal *and* escalation plan that angered both sides of the aisle.[39]

Before he took office, Obama had told those in the national and international arena, "We took our eye off the ball when we invaded Iraq. And now it's done." Then the president-elect told a newscaster why he disagreed with President Bush: "Our real focus has to be on Afghanistan" and the border regions, with "as much pressure as possible. . . . I am confident we can keep them on the run and ensure that they cannot train terrorists to attack our homeland. That's my number one priority as President of the United States." Before killing Osama bin Laden, Obama told the UN that he knew they were all working together "to disrupt, dismantle, and defeat al-Qaeda and its extremist allies."[40]

Obama's anti-universalism, his belief in ethics rather than morality based on universal truths, explains why he takes a position against human rights. This is not to say that Obama believes in treating prisoners, war criminals, or enemy nationals poorly. "On my first day in office, I prohibited—without exception or equivocation—the use of torture by the United States of America." To Obama, there is no sense in treating any vulnerable persons or peoples poorly.[41]

Poor treatment of war criminals makes the United States appear mean-spirited, causing damage to its reputation. "I ordered the prison at Guantanamo Bay closed," said Obama. "And we are doing the hard work of forging a framework to combat extremism within the rule of law. Every nation must know: America will live its values, and we will lead by example."[42]

But Obama surprised and angered many foreign policy experts coming from the Right, the middle, and the Left with his perspective on democratization and human rights, as well as with his decision to increase the American presence in Afghanistan, Pakistan, and the border regions where Taliban and al-Qaeda terrorists, responsible for the 9/11 attacks and posing a risk of future attacks on the United States and American military and civilian targets, reside. Considering all of these perspectives captures the breadth of Obama's anti-universalism, his belief in ethics rather than morality, and the way he advances difference and individuality rather than universalism, standardization, uniformity, and truth.[43]

"The Future Will Be Forged by Deeds and Not Simply Words"

Obama spurns Bush's foreign policy of American superiority and democratization. "Many around the world had come to view America
with skepticism and distrust," Obama proclaimed. "America has acted
unilaterally, without regard for the *interests* of others. And this has fed
an almost reflexive anti-Americanism, which too often has served as an
excuse for collective inaction."[44]

Without delivering any sermons on ships, as on the *Mayflower*, or
any other ship sailing foreign seas or headed home, Obama devised an
exceptional type of American exceptionalism in response to what an anthropologist called Bush's "evangelical *realpolitik.*" Like Woodrow Wilson before him, Obama carved out a multilateral foreign policy that rejects democratization.[45]

Samuel Huntington popularized the term "democratization" in
1991. This political scientist gave three operational parameters: first,
how fast democracy "rises"; second, the period of "positive" "net transitions" to democracy; and finally, "linked sets" of transitions to democracy in similarly situated nations. Huntington popularized an image of
Islam standing in polar opposition to John Winthrop's "city on a hill."
As the "chosen people," this story goes, Americans play missionaries
more than they police the world. The brand of tough love associated
with these missionaries comes from the Pilgrims or is associated with the
American Puritan tradition. Huntington's "clash of civilizations" thesis,
denounced by most academics, put Americans back on "top," at least in
the eyes of the neoconservatives vying for national control after the 9/11
attacks gave them emergency powers to reassert their ideological Cold
War propaganda.[46]

Around the World in 90 Days

Obama gave a series of foreign policy speeches from June through September 2009, for which he traveled "from London to Ankara; from Port
of Spain to Moscow; from Accra to Cairo," to send one single message.
Practicing multilateralism, Obama sought to reengage international
elites and world opinion on an array of issues, ranging from global economic crises and corruption to democracy and human rights. Obama
delivered his most notable speech in Cairo in June. This talk was an international bookend to complement his domestic bookend, "A More
Perfect Union," heard in Philadelphia in March 2008. In both speeches,

Obama underscored his commitment to religious tolerance *and* the rights of women and children.[47]

One month later Obama landed on Russian soil, where he refrained from issuing "any direct criticism of Russia's restrictions on political freedoms." He sought and got a commitment from Russian leaders that they "would pursue substantial reductions in our strategic warheads and launchers." Several days later Obama flew to Ghana, where he called the world's attention to post-colonial Africa and its corruption and absence of "good governance."[48]

Obama ended this international speaking tour in September before the UN General Assembly. In one tightly phrased and well-spoken paragraph, he explained that he knew that the world perceived Americans, and particularly their presidents, as practicing hypocrisy. He said the United States "has too often been selective in its promotion of democracy."[49]

Chinese Copyright?

With his aggressive promotion of multilateralism, the new president departed from both the Republican and the Democratic chief executives before him. In 1998 Bill Clinton took a trip to China that was aptly summed up as a "splashy, 10-day display of America's power and prestige." Clinton fashioned a policy of "constructive engagement," calling for close bilateral economic and political cooperation while at the same time urging democratization and human rights. But Clinton's overall record on human rights was riddled with inconsistencies and failures.[50]

President Obama's November 2009 visit to China shared little in spirit with Clinton's extravagant 1998 visit. Obama knows that China is second in the world in terms of economic strength, behind only the United States. He also fully understands the trade advantages that China enjoys, in addition to the United States' $900 billion debt to China in Treasury securities.

Obama sought a subdued entrance, agreeing to see the Forbidden City emptied of tourists and not to be heard over any airwaves or broadcast. One journalist called it "a low-key, four-day affair, part of a swing through Southeast Asia." Obama stuck to his promise to make no public statement about human rights. There was no grandstanding.[51]

Obama criticized China's censorship of the Internet. It isolates the Chinese, the president suggested, preventing them from sharing ideas with other sovereign nations. Obama did "tiptoe—ever so lightly—into that controversial topic," a journalist reported, telling "students in Shanghai that a free and unfettered Internet is a source of strength, not weakness."[52]

China rejected Obama's pitch for "a positive, constructive and comprehensive relationship that opens the door to partnership on the big global issues of our time." Obama had a comprehensive list of concrete issues to tackle with the Chinese, including "economic recovery, development of clean air energy, stopping the spread of nuclear weapons and the surge of climate change." These were "the big global issues of our time," and Obama sought a "partnership," promising to treat the Chinese as equals. But the Chinese diplomats rebuffed him.[53]

Obama appeared particularly irked when the Chinese failed to help the United States "defuse the situation surrounding Iran's nuclear weapon capacity." Obama thought he had found a realistic solution. Chinese leaders, however, had little respect for Obama's decision to sell weapons to Taiwan. In Xinhua, they scolded Obama, stating that this issue "concern[ed] China's sovereignty and territorial integrity and its interests." They warned the United States to "handle with caution."[54]

Here Obama was not changing the course of American foreign policy. He echoed Clinton's 1997 statement that Communist China stood "on the wrong side of history." According to conventional wisdom, China should have started honoring human rights earlier, given the democratizing effect of global trade and investment market forces. Yet this failed to occur. Trying to pressure Obama, some neoconservative human rights activists argue that "so far, his administration has been characterized by a marked turning away from interest in human rights and democracy." Even before he received the Nobel Peace Prize, many human rights activists grumbled about President Obama's human rights record.[55]

China never took what Robert Kaplan, from the Center for a New American Security, describes as "a *missionary* approach to world affairs, seeking to spread an ideology or a system of government." As Kaplan succinctly puts it, "moral progress in international affairs is an American goal, not a Chinese one." Instead, the Obama administration tried to persuade the Chinese government to create "a more market-oriented exchange rate" for the renminbi, their currency. Like his effort to get China's support in pressuring Iran, this effort failed.[56]

Even so, Obama boldly broke with almost a hundred years of U.S. foreign policy history, first by recognizing China as a global power, and second by ending Woodrow Wilson's era of "making the world safe for democracy." Obama does not support imposing human rights, in China or elsewhere. "We do not seek to impose any system of government on any other nation," Obama said, "but we also don't believe that the principles that we stand for are unique to our nation." Obama received international recognition for these words. As one editorial explained, it was "a welcome change from the mindset characterized by the 'American 21st century'" concept of the Bush administration that "called for the wholesale export of 'Americanism' to the world, no doubt, if necessary, by force."[57]

China is by no means the only country that resents the arrogance underlying the missionary approach. It was not that these countries disliked or rejected American values or a democratic belief structure; what they resented was having the United States dictate *its* values. Democratization was patronizing. No matter how good the values, it undermined the very idea of national sovereignty.[58]

This is not to say that Obama opposes human rights. The Norwegian Nobel Committee selected Obama because of his "extraordinary efforts to strengthen international diplomacy and cooperation between peoples" *and* for reinstating human rights at home.[59] As mentioned earlier, Obama reversed Bush's policies on interrogating and detaining terrorism suspects with one of his first executive orders. "You can't overstate the importance of that in terms of sending a signal to our own people and to the rest of the world that the United States is going to return to taking those commitments to fundamental human rights seriously," said Human Rights First director Elisa Massamino.

By contrast, George W. Bush continued to voice support for human rights and used his second inaugural address, in 2005, to put promoting democracy at the center of his foreign policy goals. The results of Bush's policies—in Iraq, the Middle East, and the rest of the world—are disputed. Whatever Bush's final legacy may be, many experts and advocates say Obama has shaped his approach to the issues in conscious contrast to Bush's more aggressive approach. "They are almost afraid to speak out against human rights abuses in any country because it's going to be like Bush," said Freedom House's Jennifer Windsor. As Human Rights Watch's Tom Malinowski put it, "The administration understandably wanted to distinguish itself from what it saw as the [Bush administration's] overly messianic and at times aggressive and hectoring approach toward these issues."[60]

Repairing Middle Eastern Bridges

Obama's lack of support for democratization (read Americanization) and human rights is best explained in his June 2009 Cairo speech, the first of his major foreign policy addresses that renounce universalism. Addressing the whole Muslim world, not just Egyptians, Obama spoke at length about the United States' support for promoting democracy. But democratic principles such as freedom, equality, and rule of law "are not just American ideas," Obama insisted. "They are human rights. And that is why we will support them everywhere." In what one commentator characterized as "his most King-like speech," Obama tried to bridge "one of the great divides of our age—between the United States and the Muslim world" by decrying American ideological supremacy.[61]

Obama not only deprived the United States of credit for these principles, but also expressed his admiration of Muslim culture and its role in "nurturing learning and progress, peace and pluralism." He praised Muslim civilization, saying, "These are the same values that America has sought to advance." And finally, Obama denounced "the stereotypes that Islam is only violent or that America seeks only empire."[62]

To democratization expert Thomas Carothers, vice president for studies at the Carnegie Endowment for International Peace, Obama's speech represents a recasting of the Bush administration's approach to promoting democracy. "He set out an alternative rhetorical framework that emphasizes that we will not impose democracy on others, that we recognize that different kinds of democracy exist and that we will be sure not to equate elections with democracy," Carothers says.[63]

Many pundits were puzzled by the Obama administration's decision to join the still-new UN Human Rights Council. The Bush administration had refused to join the council after it was created in 2006 to replace the UN Commission on Human Rights, which was widely criticized as weak and ideologically polarized. In its 2009 World Report, Human Rights Watch cites American opposition to the Human Rights Council as representative of the Bush administration's "arrogant approach to multilateral institutions." Indeed, the Bush administration had shown little interest in joining international human rights treaties.

Most notably, the Bush administration strongly opposed ratification of the UN treaty creating the International Criminal Court (ICC). President Clinton had signed the treaty in 2000 but deferred asking the Senate to ratify it until the ICC began operation, leaving the next president to deal with the sensitive issue of American sovereignty.

Once the ICC opened its dockets in 2002, Bush asked for the impossible. The president insisted that he would not ask the Senate to ratify the ICC treaty unless the court exempted American troops from prosecution. The UN could not make this concession without losing credibility. And Bush dropped all other action on international human rights covenants, including the Convention on the Rights of the Child and the Convention on the Elimination of All Forms of Discrimination against Women.[64]

During his campaign, Obama strongly criticized Bush's foreign policy record and argued that his administration's antiterrorism policies had caused the United States to lose respect around the world. Accepting the Democratic nomination on August 27, 2008, Obama promised to "restore our moral standing" if elected. He vowed to "build new partnerships to defeat the threats of the twenty-first century: terrorism and nuclear proliferation, poverty and genocide, climate change and disease."[65]

In office, Obama followed through on this vow by seeking the Senate's ratification of two "long-pending United Nations–sponsored treaties on women's rights and children's rights." In 2010, Obama knew that Senate action would be "in doubt because of continued opposition from social conservatives and others." A treaty without ratification by the Senate means that the United States refuses the force of law. "The United States signed both treaties during Democratic administrations, but Republican opposition in Congress—fueled by opposition from social conservatives—has prevented the Senate ratification needed to give the treaties force of law."[66]

Prissy Program Values

Obama assured nongovernmental organizations (NGOs) and their leaders that the United States would no longer proselytize. In funding problematic or divisive social programs, such as those that provide abortion or birth control, he pledged not to promote American beliefs and values. Knowing that deeds (read money) count more than speeches, Obama reallocated funding. He increased United States financial help for fighting AIDS and HIV as well as tropical diseases. The Obama administration decided in favor of aid for other treatable and preventable illnesses that kill millions, many of them children, each year.[67]

To Obama, middle-class identity is best characterized as an anti-identity of tolerance and an anti-identity that accepts difference. No assimilation is required. Obama's melting pot resembles a salad, as reviewed in the next two chapters, rather than a stew. Each person, each people, each nation should retain what makes it different, special, unique.

Nothing illustrates this better than Obama's perspective as reflected in his opposition to the American invasion of Iraq. The Iraq War "was American innocence at its most destructive, freedom at its most deceptive, universalism at its most naïve." Obama believes that it is not

American imperialism, but American idealism, that "endangers us." "There was a dangerous innocence to thinking that we would be greeted as liberators, or that with a little bit of economic assistance and democratic training you'd have a Jeffersonian democracy blooming in the desert."[68]

In Obama's view, foreign policy must be based on reciprocity, or what he calls "mutual reliance." The United States succeeded with the Marshall Plan after World War II because "we recognized that our security and prosperity depend on the security and prosperity of others." American idealism turns into a problem when we think "we can remake the world any way we want by flipping a switch, because we're technologically superior or we're wealthier or we're morally superior." This becomes dangerous because "our idealism spills into that kind of naïveté and an unwillingness to acknowledge history and the weight of other cultures, then we get ourselves into trouble, as we did in Vietnam."[69]

Bush's Arrogance

Obama's ideas about the dangers associated with America's idealism and arrogance, and its lack of reciprocity with other nations, stem from Reinhold Niebuhr's thoughts. It was Niebuhr—a pastor, teacher, activist, moral theologian, and writer—who argued that the twin values of American idealism and American arrogance were dangerous.[70]

Ever since the Pilgrims settled in Massachusetts, Niebuhr argues, American idealism and arrogance have been problematic because of their incongruity. The ideals conflict with political reality, presenting an "indictment of American moral complacency and a warning against an arrogance of virtue."[71]

American diplomats should not believe that they can "manage history." "The illusions about the possibility of managing historical destiny from any particular standpoint in history," Niebuhr argues, "always involve, as already noted, miscalculations about both the power and the wisdom of the managers and of the weakness and the manageability of the historical 'stuff' which is to be managed."[72]

To Niebuhr, reciprocity, or the idea that each nation has something to give and something to receive, is the most important aspect of international relations. Using unilateral power to gain "ideal ends" will backfire. Extending unilateral gifts will backfire as well. One nation cannot manage another nation's history, no matter how well-intentioned it may be. "In the liberal versions of the dream of managing history, the problem of power is never fully elaborated." The United States "is expected to gain its ends by moral attraction and imitation. Only occasionally does an hysterical statesman suggest that we must increase our power and use it in order to gain the ideal ends, of which providence has made us the trustees."[73]

Niebuhr observes the irony of the position the United States found itself in after World War II. First, it was ironic "that our nation has, without particularly seeking it, acquired a greater degree of power than any other nation of history" and that it had "created a 'global' political situation in which the responsible use of this power has become a condition of survival of the free world." And second, it was ironic that "a strong America is less completely master of its own destiny than was a comparatively weak America, rocking in the cradle of its continental security and serene in its infant innocence. The same strength which has extended our power beyond a continent has also interwoven our destiny with the destiny of many peoples and brought us into a vast web of history in which other wills, running in oblique or contrasting directions to our own, inevitably hinder or contradict what we most fervently desire."[74]

"The Enemy Is Us"

Concerned that the Cold War might become a "hot war," as early as 1952, Niebuhr foresaw the increasing globalization of the world. The United States did not have the capacity to bring the world freedom and happiness, especially through military means. Niebuhr insisted that, in the words of a commentator, the "failure to understand the limits of our power of our exceptionalism and of the illusion that we can manage all this history to accomplish our supposedly moral and 'good' ends for other nations" would harm the United States.[75]

Obama agrees with Niebuhr. According to him, 9/11 constituted one of those "occasional moments" when "hysterical statesmen" Bush and Cheney "argued for a profound increase in the nation's power to gain the 'ideal ends'" of bringing "freedom" to Iraq and the Middle East. But these statesmen could not manage Iraqi history. They had no control. The problem was not that they failed, but that they had even tried.[76]

Obama believes that American foreign policy should abandon any attempt to democratize nations other than its own. It is not for the United States to determine another sovereign nation's culture. "In his view of history, in his respect for tradition, in his skepticism that the world can be changed any way but very, very slowly," said *New Yorker* journalist Larissa MacFarquhar, "Obama is deeply conservative" about international relations.[77]

Arab Spring

The Arab Spring arrived early in the White House. It started on a hot
day in August 2010, when Obama instructed three National Security
Council (NSC) staffers—Samantha Power, a pro-humanitarian idealist;
Gayle Smith, who had worked on development issues for the Center for
American Progress before joining the Obama administration; and Dennis Ross, a Middle East expert with an extensive background in the region, including Israel—to reevaluate the costs and benefits of supporting
autocrats and authoritarian regimes. The report, a presidential directive,
was to be "tailored," "country by country."[78]

Following the same principles that underlie horizontal and diagonal federalism, and using the procedures for negotiated rulemaking outlined in chapter 4 to question prevailing norms, Power, Smith, and Ross
took on the task of deconstructing and reconstructing decades-old assumptions undergirding American foreign policy. Obama asked them to
"challenge the traditional idea that stability in the Middle East always
served U.S. interests." "The *taboos*, all the questions you're not supposed to ask," Obama insisted that Power, Smith, and Ross now ask.
Tipping his hand, Obama expressed his own "doubts that the Middle
East status quo was sustainable."[79]

Obama further suggested that Power, Smith, and Ross analyze what
would happen if a "strong push by the United States for reform" occurred. "The advent of political succession in a number of countries,"
Obama wrote, "offers a potential opening for political reform in the region." If the United States managed the coming transitions "poorly,"
Obama feared, it "could have negative implications for U.S. interests,
including for our standing among Arab publics."[80]

Power, Smith, and Ross unraveled American and Israeli security from
the United States' support of an Egyptian autocrat by testing "the assumption that the President could not publicly criticize President Hosni
Mubarak because it would jeopardize Egypt's coöperation on issues related to Israel or its assistance in tracking terrorists." These high-level
staffers reassessed, reevaluated, and reconsidered Egypt's underlying
motives for maintaining peace with Israel and joining the United States
in its fight against terrorism, concluding that "the Egyptians pursued
peace with Israel and crushed terrorists because it was in their interest to do so, not because the U.S. asked them to." By so doing, they
helped Obama undermine what he called a "crude stereotype" when
he spoke in Cairo in 2009. Obama wanted international public opinion

to change, and not to assume that the United States was solely "a self-interested empire."[81]

The Middle East Ignites

"Believe it or not, we finished our report the week that Tunisia exploded," one of the NSC troika told *Time*'s political journalist Joe Klein. On December 17, 2010, when a vegetable vendor, Mohamed Bouazizi, set himself ablaze in protest against his country's corruption, the Arab Spring began. Just after Obama had asked for the presidential directive, this one act of protest acted as a catalyst, igniting the whole region. And Obama's eighteen-page presidential directive became the blueprint for reversing course in American foreign policy: "Democracy in the Middle East, one of the most fraught issues of the Bush years, was suddenly the signature conflict of Obama's foreign policy." "All roads led to political reform," explained one senior official in the White House.[82]

Obama had anticipated conflict, having called for this directive after witnessing "evidence of growing citizen discontent with the region's regimes." But in supporting what he labeled the peaceful demonstrators' "*aspirations*," Obama did not adopt the language of idealists. Instead, he redefined American interests. Reform and democracy no longer belonged in the idealist column, since political reform was now in America's interest.

According to *New Yorker* political journalist Ryan Lizza, "Obama's analysis showed a desire to balance interests and ideals." Lizza's explanation, however, does not fully elucidate this binary. Given Obama's emphasis on inductive reasoning, and his belief in American interconnectedness and interdependence, the president's position reflects the logic of consilience and congruence rather than a balance between idealism and realism. Obama does not recognize values and interests as different in category, or in kind; he denies any inherent difference between the two, reflecting once again how his ideas embody a Spinozan perspective on governance.[83]

To Obama, benevolence—supporting the values of the demonstrators—stems from survivability. "Increased repression could threaten the political and economic stability of some of our allies, leave us with fewer capable, credible partners who can support our regional priorities, and further alienate citizens in the region," Obama wrote. Secretary of State Hillary Clinton elaborated: "Now, we were very clear in saying, 'We are supporting those who are protesting peacefully,' and we put our social media gurus at work in trying to keep connections going, so that we helped to provide that base for communicating that was necessary for the demonstrations."[84]

Obama rewrote American foreign policy interests, placing human security alongside national security, thereby transforming a value into an interest. After all, the president had asked Power, Smith, and Ross to test "the idea that countries with impoverished populations needed to develop economically before they were prepared for open political systems—a common argument that democracy promoters often run up against." All three discovered that this "conventional wisdom was wrong."[85] But this should have come as no surprise to Obama, since Smith's reputation in international affairs came from her belief that "human security"—a citizen's social, economic, and political rights—was no less vital than "national security." Like Obama, Smith advanced Spinoza's idea that benevolence stems from survivability, not universal or Enlightenment values. She premised humanitarian assistance on the argument that the United States could not afford to promote corrupt autocracies that trampled on their citizens' rights and left them in squalor.

Smith had long ago redefined values as interests, dismissing the realist/idealist binary in an attempt to redefine humanitarian aid and what the United States could do for the developing world. In a 2007 piece for *Democracy*, Smith advocated that a "new, stand-alone development agency should be established, headed by a Cabinet-level secretary and mandated to direct policy and coordinate all economic assistance." The United States, Smith believed, should engage in another Marshall Plan with its allies.[86]

Not surprisingly, the presidential directive authored by Smith, Power, and Ross concluded that instead of bankrolling autocrats, the United States and its allies could facilitate democracy and capitalism in the Middle East. "There is talk of free-trade zones and seed money for small businesses. A better idea, bubbling up from the Gulf, would be to establish a Middle East Infrastructure Bank—pushed hard by the United States and funded by the lush sovereign wealth funds run by oil-rich countries in the region, as well as China and Europe—to move quickly toward paving roads and building housing, followed by larger projects like power plants."[87]

None of this was foreign to Obama. He advanced his support for human security during his Nobel lecture in 2009, saying that "a just peace includes not only civil and political rights—it must encompass economic security and opportunity. For true peace is not just freedom from fear, but freedom from want."[88]

Hence Smith and Obama saw eye-to-eye, since the president himself discounted the idea that there was an inherent tension between realists and idealists. In his Nobel lecture he announced unequivocally, "I believe that peace is unstable where citizens are denied the right to speak freely or worship as they please; choose their own leaders or assemble without fear. Pent-up grievances fester, and the suppression of tribal and religious identity can lead to violence. . . . No matter how callously defined, neither America's interests—nor the world's—are served by the denial of human aspirations."[89]

To be sure, Obama had taken foreign policy advice from Samantha Power before. Just before entering the Senate following the 2004 election, Obama solicited her views. As president he appointed Power to become a senior director of multilateral affairs at the NSC, but she wielded little influence until he called for her help in drafting the presidential directive. A darling of the pro-democracy humanitarian left, Power believed that, in Lizza's words, "America and its allies rarely have perfect information about when a regime is about to commit genocide." In *A Problem from Hell*, published in 2003, Power argued that a president and America's allies must maintain "a bias toward belief" to prevent imminent massacres from occurring. Unlike Smith, Power took a strong idealist position.[90]

Obama had called for a "new beginning," siding more with Smith than with Power, on his first tour to the Middle East in the spring of 2009. Speaking in Cairo, Obama reconciled American values and interests by referring to our "mutual interest and mutual respect." What Obama resisted, as mentioned above, or what hit a nerve was what he called a "crude stereotype" that he heard leveled against the United States. In Obama's view, the United States should no longer be characterized as "a self-interested empire," though as president of a sovereign nation-state, he had a duty and a right to defend the United States' national interests, as observed in the opening of this chapter.[91]

Obama denounced this American imperialist stereotype, then proceeded to differentiate his notion of democracy from Bush's conception of democratization. Obama insisted that democracy means a government "that reflect[s] the will of the people," but that this does not mean that Obama determines *how* people should express that will. Obama offered no substantive rights—but he did emphasize procedural rights, while stopping short of advocating monitoring elections. "All people yearn for certain things: the ability to speak your mind and have a say in how you are governed; confidence in the rule of law and the equal administration of justice; government that is transparent and doesn't steal from the people; the freedom to live as you choose. These are not just American ideas," Obama added; "they are human rights."[92]

Overall, the presidential directive articulated the same logic Obama had laid out in his speech in Cairo in the spring of 2009, and again in Oslo during his Nobel lecture. Instead of supporting autocrats or authoritarian leaders who promise to repress religious fundamentalism, Obama redefined American interests as supporting the aspirations of Middle Eastern people for real democratic self-rule. And as events would unfold in both Egypt and Libya, Obama shored up these words with foreign policy action.[93]

Mubarak's Disposal

On January 25, 2011, eleven days after the Tunisian protesters peacefully pushed out president Zine el-Abidine Ben Ali, Obama gave his State of the Union address. Obama applauded the Tunisian demonstrators, who showed the world that "the will of the people proved more powerful than the writ of a dictator." Without mentioning the uprising in Egypt's Tahrir Square by name, Obama nonetheless expressed his support for "democratic aspirations of all people."[94]

That same day, while visiting the Middle East, Secretary Clinton announced her support for "free assembly." She did make reference to Tahrir Square, adding, "Our assessment is that the Egyptian government is stable and is looking for ways to respond to the legitimate needs and interests of the Egyptian people." Clinton supported Mubarak, though she too reflected the basic assumptions underlying the presidential directive. Speaking in Qatar as early as January 14, Clinton condemned Arab leaders for "resisting change."[95]

Clinton had appointed more idealists to key offices in the State Department than Obama brought to the White House. "Walking around the mazelike building in Foggy Bottom, you get the sense that if you duck into any office you will find earnest young women and men discussing globalization, the possibility that Facebook can topple tyrannies, and what is called 'soft power,' the ability to bend the world toward your view through attraction, not coercion." Most notably, Clinton made Anne-Marie Slaughter her director of policy planning. Slaughter was a Princeton professor whose reputation stemmed from her scholarly work as an idealist. But Slaughter did not stay for the Arab Spring. She left the Obama administration before the protest unfolded because of her frustration with the realists, whom she saw as being overly influential in foreign affairs.

Despite these appointments of idealists, Clinton "aligned herself with the most consistent realist in the Obama Administration: Secretary of Defense Robert Gates." Clinton had followed the realists, who had had more sway with Obama until the Arab Spring. Obama had stepped away from idealism in almost every major crisis, abandoning Slaughter's and the other idealists' position.[96]

Obama leaned toward realism for most of 2009, most notably when he decided to increase troops in Afghanistan. Obama had originally hoped to avoid the idealist/realist Middle East debate, appointing neither an idealist nor a realist to his inner foreign policy circle. Thomas Donilon, a longtime Washington lawyer, lobbyist, and Democratic Party strategist best known for being a nonideological fixer, became his national security advisor. Donilon and his deputy, Denis McDonough, hoped they could turn American foreign policy away from its preoccupation with the Middle East and create a new focus on Asia. They took office with the understanding that the NSC would dictate "the sole process through which policy would be developed."[97]

But in his Nobel lecture in 2009, Obama abandoned the spirit of nonjudgmental outreach and reform and surprised the "largely left-leaning audience by talking about the martial imperatives of a Commander-in-Chief overseeing two wars." Obama had done this type of about-face before. In 2002, in Chicago's Federal Plaza, Obama, then a state senator, "confounded his leftist audience by emphasizing the need to fight some wars, but not 'dumb' ones, like the one [approaching] in Iraq." Once again, Obama surprised the Right and the Left, the realists and the idealists.

Obama's aides rationalized this switch to journalists by explaining that the president prefers studying foreign policy consequences. As one explained, his anti-ideological idealist/realist position means that Obama prefers concentrating on achieving certain outcomes. "Obama's lengthy bumper-sticker credo," one White House official said, "did not include a call to promote democracy or protect human rights." Now, in 2011, faced with a real crisis of the aspirations of people of Egypt, Obama came flush up against the same dilemma.

At first, as demonstrators flooded Tahrir Square, Obama did not call for Mubarak to step down. Instead, he encouraged Mubarak to let Omar Suleiman, the new vice president, lead the transition. In this way, the Obama administration hoped, the Egyptians could avoid the cumbersome constitutional process. Members of the State Department, however, feared that such a transition would take too long to play out, and they feared that further chaos could result if religious fundamentalism took root.

But then, just four days after the uprising began, Obama decided the United States should support an immediate transition in Egypt. To ensure that it went smoothly, Obama sent an emissary, Frank Wisner, to speak with Mubarak. Face-to-face, Wisner would tell Mubarak that Obama no longer had faith that he could survive the protests. While Wisner flew to Cairo, Clinton spoke on five Sunday morning talk shows, announcing Obama's new call for an immediate "orderly transition."

A debate in the White House among Obama's senior advisors ensued. Should the president make a public statement? Before they could decide what to advise, "Obama joined the meeting unexpectedly," as one official remarked. Then, during the meeting, Mubarak himself appeared on television. Everyone in the room, including Obama, watched. "I am now careful to conclude my work for Egypt by presenting Egypt to the next government in a constitutional way which will protect Egypt," Mubarak said. "I want to say, in clear terms, that in the next few months that are remaining of my current reign I will work very hard to carry out all the necessary measures to transfer power." He was not stepping down. The demonstrators in Tahrir Square "erupted in rage" after what one journalist described as Mubarak's "meandering and confusing speech." Obama now "seemed to be uncomfortable," one White House official described, "taking an attitude of cool detachment from the people in the street."[98]

Obama telephoned Mubarak, and the longtime ruler of Egypt uttered the usual refrain about any power vacuum in the Middle East. This vacuum would be filled, he said, by the Muslim Brotherhood. Obama did not waver. Once he got off the telephone, he delivered a second public statement, more confrontational than his first. "An orderly transition must be meaningful, it must be peaceful," Obama said, "and it must begin *now*."[99]

In lending his support to the Egyptian protesters, Obama changed the entire course of American foreign policy. Worried by this historic departure, Israel and Saudi Arabia sounded alarms, and it "startled some people in the State Department." Secretary Clinton, they explained, "walked a very narrow line and managed to do it without making the Egyptians too angry on either side." Expressing the awkward position Clinton faced, these officials underscored the "inherent contradictions of an Administration trying to simultaneously encourage and contain the forces of revolution in Egypt."[100]

Taking the same position as Clinton once he landed in Cairo, Wisner expressed his belief that "President Mubarak's continued leadership is critical." The White House immediately retracted Wisner's comments, saying he "was not speaking for the U.S. government or the Obama Administration. He was speaking as a private citizen." In Wisner's view, the Obama administration "threw me under the bus." It was clear Obama now took "the side of the protesters." "Obama didn't give the Tahrir Square crowds every last thing they sought from him at the precise moment they sought it. But he went well beyond what many of America's allies in the region wished to see."[101]

The sequel shows the limits of the United States' attempts to influence events in other nations, as the demonstrations gave way to disappointments. Parliamentary elections gave the Muslim Brotherhood and other Islamist parties a majority, and a presidential primary led to a runoff between Mohammed Morsi, the Brotherhood candidate, and Ahmed Shafiq, a former Mubarak prime minister backed by the army. But the Egyptian supreme court dissolved parliament on dubious grounds and declined to disqualify Shafiq, even though Mubarak officials were barred by law from running. Although they had "toppled a pharaoh," reported the *New York Times*, "the small circle of liberals, leftists and Islamists who orchestrated Egypt's revolution say they realize they failed to uproot the networks of power that Hosni Mubarak nurtured for nearly three decades." Morsi subsequently fired a number of generals and high officials from the Mubarak era.[102]

Flying above Libya

Obama pulled another foreign policy about-face with Libya. Here again he redefined American values as interests, taking the side of the resistance. On February 26, 2011, the UN passed a resolution that placed an arms embargo and economic sanctions on the Libyan regime and referred Moammar Qaddafi to the International Criminal Court. Two days later the United States, through lobbying led by Clinton and Power, helped remove Libya from its seat on the UN Human Rights Council. By tightening an economic noose around Qaddafi and isolating him diplomatically, Obama, along with his allies, began wielding the tools that Power had outlined in *A Problem from Hell*. The debate then focused on whether the United States and others should intervene militarily in

Libya. UN officials proposed to set up a no-fly zone to prevent Libyan planes from attacking the forces of the protest movement, which had escalated into a full-scale rebellion in the eastern half of Libya.

To most experts in the American foreign policy community, the decision about intervention represented a "clear choice between interests and values." As former national security advisor Brent Scowcroft said, "Of all the countries in the region there our real interests in Libya are minimal." Secretary of Defense Gates's position also came as no surprise. Being the most committed realist in the Obama administration, he rendered the most resistance to the idea of a no-fly zone. No military action could be justified; like Scowcroft, Gates believed the United States had no "vital interest" to protect. "American Presidents usually lead the response to world crises," wrote Ryan Lizza, "but Obama seemed to stay hidden that week." When Clinton arrived in Paris on March 14, she told French president Nicolas Sarkozy that she had nothing to relay. Jumping to the wrong conclusion, Sarkozy interpreted Obama's silence as indicative of "American reluctance to do anything." Obama, he thought, had adopted the realists' position.[103]

But at UN headquarters in New York, as the French, the British, and the Lebanese drafted a resolution implementing a no-fly zone, Obama began talking with his advisors, asking them if this would stop what could become a gruesome scenario. With both his military and intelligence advisors concluding no, since Qaddafi would use tanks, not war planes, Obama made a startling decision. He agreed with the UN envoy that the United States should support full-scale military intervention, not a no-fly zone.

From the White House's East Room, Obama announced that the United States would command the military to intervene. So sudden and surprising was Obama's turnaround that some foreign dignitaries and officials, Lizza reports, thought perhaps "it was a trick." For the first time in its history, the UN authorized military action to stop an "imminent massacre," as Power's book had appealed for it to do in 2003. Human Rights Watch director Tom Malinowski said, "It was, by any objective standard, the most rapid multinational military response to an impending human rights crisis in history."[104]

By playing both sides of the foreign policy ideological binary with his actions in Egypt and Libya, Obama ended up alienating both realists and idealists in his administration. "On issues like whether to intervene in Libya there's really not a compromise and consensus," Slaughter said. "You can't be a little bit realist and a little bit democratic when deciding whether or not to stop a massacre." Zbigniew Brzezinski, "President

Carter's national-security adviser and the reigning realist of the Democratic foreign-policy establishment," whom Obama had consulted with several times during the campaign, had also become "disillusioned" with Obama's foreign policy.[105]

But both Slaughter's and Brzezinski's positions reflect the so-called Washington consensus that foreign policy can be categorized as realist or idealist. Obama has consistently rejected this binary since 2002. Obama's foreign policy ideas voice three themes. First, as described earlier, Obama adopted Niebuhr's position that the United States must, in Lizza's words, "act humbly in the world." He took it to heart that the United States was reviled by many of the world's peoples and leaders. In a 2007 speech at the Wilson Center in Washington, DC, Obama said, "America must show—through deeds as well as words—that we stand with those who seek a better life. That child looking up at the helicopter must see America and feel hope." Second, to act humbly, the United States must listen to its allies, not as a superpower, but as one power in an interconnected and interrelated whole. Finally, Obama believed that human security supported national security. He supported the demonstrators' "aspirations." This is a post-Niebuhrian position.[106]

Neoconservatives, as well as Republican and Democratic realists, roundly condemned Obama's foreign policy. With most of his decisions following these three themes, which they correctly noted represented the greatest shift in American foreign policy in forty years, Obama's critics scorned the actions characterized by one of his advisors as "leading from behind." The United States, they said, must lead from the front—not from behind. Obama was surrendering America's position as a superpower.[107]

"Leading from behind" also sent the message that Obama was encouraging "the local players" to realize that they "have a stake in the outcome—like the Europeans and the Arabs in Iraq—to protect their own direct strategic interests in a way that does not require direct U.S. military intervention." It also meant the United States would no longer try to "control events as they unfold." But other foreign dignitaries noted that "leading from behind" could be associated with leading from the shadows. In the shadows, the United States could retain the power to do "many things in private" while "saying little in public."[108]

No matter where he led from, from the shadows or from behind, Obama recognized that "whatever happens in the months ahead, Tunisia, Egypt, Libya, Yemen and even Syria will not be the same. Neither will other countries that have been able to contain or co-opt protest movements." Obama took a bold multilateral position. And many of Obama's supporters in Europe encouraged him to do more. Having declared in March that "Moammar Qaddafi has lost the legitimacy to lead," it was time for him to say the same about Syria's Bashar al-Assad. Foreign policy experts began analyzing the difference between the two leaders. "America supports the movements for democratic change in the autocratic republics, such as Tunisia, Egypt, Yemen and Syria. It respects the more conservative traditions of the pro-Western monarchies and sheikdoms, such as Jordan, Saudi Arabia, the United Arab Emirates, Bahrain, Morocco and Kuwait. This distinction isn't complicated, it just needs to be explained."[109]

For years, the United States took the side of autocrats who ensured secularism and promised to prevent theocracies from emerging in the Middle East. "In Egypt, they warn, the Muslim Brotherhood will overtake the young secular activists who bravely brought down dictator Hosni Mubarak. In Syria, they have claimed, Bashar al-Assad's dictatorship may be brutal, but it is a lesser evil than a Sunni majority that will oppress Christians, Shiites, and women." The Obama administration, however, came to see this position as preying on America's "fear" and presenting it with "false choices." As three academics trying to influence foreign policy proclaimed, "The choice facing Arab Spring nations at this point isn't one between religion and secular government. It's a choice between democracy that includes all parties—religious and secular—and a regime that imposes a rigid and exclusive secularism."[110]

Obama maintains that repressive secular regimes foster religious extremism. "For human history has often been a record of nations and tribes—and, yes, religions—subjugating one another in pursuit of their own interests. Yet in this new age, such attitudes are self-defeating. Given our interdependence, any world order that elevates one nation or group of people over another will inevitably fail. So whatever we think of the past, we must not be prisoners to it. Our problems must be dealt with through partnership; our progress must be shared." Obama has never rejected religion; rather, he rejects a "warped view of religion."[111]

The People's Aspirations

The Obama administration moved to protect people's aspirations in the Middle East. When people rise up against a ruler that lacks legitimacy, "it is the responsibility of all free people and free nations to make clear to these movements that hope and history are on their side." Religious groups, as this story goes, become radicalized and turn to violence when the state denies their autonomy and they cannot participate in politics.

"The leaders of [repressive] governments fear the aspirations of their own people," said Obama, "more than the power of any other nation." Obama committed American policy to what one article called "negative secularism."[112]

By April 2011 Clinton had outlined the administration's new commitment to furthering these aspirations. "Uprisings across the region have exposed myths that for too long were used to justify a stagnant status quo. You know the myth that governments can hold on to power without responding to their people's aspirations or respecting their rights." Then she outlined the "false narratives" the youth in these countries would no longer accept. "Despite the best efforts of the censors, they are connecting to the wider world in ways their parents and grandparents could never imagine. They now see alternatives."

Like Smith and Power, Clinton supported the idea of human security as a subset of national security. "The material conditions of people's lives have greater impact on national stability and security than ever before. . . . The balance of power is no longer measured by counting tanks or missiles alone. Now strategists must factor in the growing influence of citizens themselves—connected, organized and often frustrated." Clinton dismissed the argument that economic development should precede political rights by stating that "overall, Arab countries were less industrialized in 2007 than they were in 1970." The United States, as a result, would no longer wait for economic development to happen. "Reversing this dynamic means grappling with . . . how to match economic reform with political and social change? According to the 2009 Global Integrity Report, Arab countries, almost without exception, have some of the weakest anti-corruption systems in the world." Finally, she asked, when will "the door to full citizenship and participation finally open to women and minorities?"[113]

For these reasons, American foreign policy changed direction. As Clinton stated, "We put partnerships with people, not just governments, at the center of our efforts." Where the United States would make an impact would be in development. The Obama administration pledged $150 million to Egypt alone. Another $2 billion would go to small and medium private-sector investments in the Middle East and North Africa.[114]

Little Sticks: Humbly and without Arrogance

Mitt Romney, Obama's Republican opponent in the 2012 elections, tried tainting Obama's intervention in Libya as un-American, noting that we were "following the French into Libya." Former vice presidential candidate Sarah Palin described the president's actions as "dithering." In their view, Obama's position of "leading from behind" made the United States fall into some sort of coordinated or multilateral step with its allies, particularly its European allies.[115]

Obama tailors the American foreign policy response to the circumstances of each crisis, rather than grandstanding or creating a broad, expansive, unilateral doctrine as Bush did. The United States joined the Europeans when they saw "Qaddafi was on the brink of slaughtering thousands of rebels in Benghazi and other eastern cities"; only then did Obama push "for an even broader mandate for NATO forces." What some critics called Obama's "anti-doctrinal doctrine" recognized "differences in a way that Bush's fixed ideas did not." But in their view, this policy put the United States in a position of "no glory," and "no results could ever vindicate such a strategy." Similarly, in Syria, Obama encourages the protesters and reprimands Assad, expressing his "dismay" at the violence directed against the protestors by the regime, but he will not intervene unless or until there is consensus in the UN, and among American allies, that it is necessary.[116]

Europeans view Obama's new foreign policy differently. As one European characterized it, "a calculated modesty" can give a nation great influence. "Obama would not be the first statesman to realize that it can be easier to win if you don't need to trumpet your victory." On the domestic front, while some attacked Obama's "no glory" foreign policy, suggesting it diminishes "America's stature in the world," others noticed the similarity between this type of foreign policy and Obama's domestic politics, calling it technocratic. To them, "Obama's technocratic approach to governing has served him far better in foreign policy, where facts, expert appraisal and intelligence often trump ideology, than it has in domestic politics." Obama himself heralded the results of his new policy. "Without putting a single U.S. service member on the ground," he said in a Rose Garden press conference, "we achieved our objectives."[117]

Obama created a two-step process for supporting the aspirations of all peoples in the Middle East. From the beginning, Obama told autocrats that the "status quo" could not hold. But then Obama did not lead, but rather worked in conjunction with other, largely European nations. In Obama's view, the United States should be perceived as supporting not only the demonstrators' domestic agendas, but also legitimate Palestinian aspirations. Unlike most presidents who raise their public opinion ratings when they take popular actions abroad, like finding and kill-

ing Osama bin Laden or bombing Libya, Obama takes refuge. He is
quiet.[118]

Foreign journalists have described the Obama doctrine as "essentially defensive in nature." It emphasizes "disengagement from Afghanistan and Iraq" but does not call for "robust military intervention to prevent grave abuses of human rights." Libya proved an exception, or, as
one journalist described it, was "strategically convenient," since world
opinion was unanimously aligned against Qaddafi. Obama is more cautious with Iran and with Syria, recognizing them as sovereign nations
and subjecting them only to economic sanctions.[119]

According to one Israeli journalist, Obama's doctrine of "defensive
liberalism" "correctly diagnoses one of the main causes of instability
and anti-Americanism in the Middle East: namely the stagnant, dysfunc-
tional economic, social and political situation in the Muslim-Arab Middle East." To this commentator, the problem is that it is a "grossly over-
optimistic assessment of regional realities, which could have dangerous
unintended consequences." Obama compared the Arab Spring to the
Boston Tea Party and the American Revolution and to Rosa Parks's
struggle for civil rights, as well as the fall of the Berlin Wall in 1989 and
the Eastern European transition to democracy.[120]

For Obama, the central question in foreign policy is the legitimacy
of a state and society. Middle Eastern autocrats have lost power within
their countries because they lacked legitimacy with their own people,
and, as Obama pledged from the beginning of his presidency, at a certain
point the U.S. will follow international public opinion condemning these
societies. There is a tipping point. Before announcing that he would run
for president, Lizza explains, Obama tried out this middle position, arguing that "proselytizing about democracy and the haste to bomb other
countries in the name of humanitarian aid had 'stretched our military to
the breaking point and distracted us from the growing threats of a dangerous world.'" In his view, if an autocrat lost his legitimacy, such a loss
meant that American interests—stability in the region—would be compromised.[121]

No More Torture, Please

Obama's anti-universalism also explains why this executive stops short
of reprimanding China for its poor record on human rights, despite the
negative press he receives from the international and domestic human
rights community, all of whom stand to the left of the progressive wing
of the Democratic Party and therefore cannot join the GOP. This said,

Obama does not accept egregious human rights violations, but just as he does not advocate democratization, neither does he push his concern for human rights on other sovereign nations as part of his foreign policy. Other than by example, Obama does not propagate the American value and belief structure. "We know the future will be forged by deeds," Obama proclaimed, "and not simply words," so he tries to contain human rights violations, such as extraordinary rendition, within his own military policy.[122]

In his first week in office, Obama swiftly moved to redeem one of his promises by reversing some of Bush's antiterrorism policies. "He scrapped legal opinions that had questioned the applicability of the Geneva Conventions to suspected terrorists," stated one report. And he "shuttered the Central Intelligence Agency's secret prisons and set a one-year deadline for closing the Guantánamo prison camp."[123]

Obama's announcement came on the heels of a decision by Susan Crawford, the head of military commissions at Guantanamo Bay during the Bush administration, to dismiss charges against Mohammed al-Qahtani, the so-called twentieth hijacker. "We tortured Qahtani," she said, and "his treatment met the legal definition of torture." Philip Zelikow, another Bush official from the State Department, told Congress that "the U.S. government adopted an unprecedented program of coolly calculated dehumanizing abuse and physical torment to extract information. This was a mistake, perhaps a disastrous one. It was a collective failure, in which a number of officials and members of Congress of both parties played a part, endorsing a CIA program of physical coercion."[124]

Obama concurred with these initial actions and assessments by those in the Bush administration who regretted the president's position on torture. In the wake of 9/11, Obama said, the American government made some decisions "based upon fear rather than foresight," and the nation "went off course . . . using brutal methods like waterboarding." These tactics did not "keep this country safe," the president declared, but rather "undermine[d] the rule of law" and "alienate[d] us in the world." "The United States cannot stand up for justice and the rule of law when it sits idly on its own record of torture. It diminishes the weight of its moral authority to influence others around the world." Obama's final blow against torture, during his first heady months in office, came when he sought a seat on the UN Human Rights Council, "ostensibly to reform it from the inside."[125]

But Obama faced a dilemma. Whom should he please? Should he look ahead? Or should he look behind, holding members of the Bush administration accountable before the national and international human rights community and the ICC? Obama had no answer that would fully satisfy the progressive human rights wing of the Democratic Party. But this part of the Obama coalition could not turn to the GOP for relief in 2012. Nonetheless, the decision not to close the Guantanamo Bay facility constituted his biggest foreign policy failure in 2010, at home and abroad.

Senator Patrick Leahy, who represented Vermont and had worked closely with Obama during his days in the Senate, proposed that the United States conduct its own "truth and reconciliation" process, bringing all out in the open.[126] Obama, however, rejected Leahy's idea, stating in April 2009, "I'm a strong believer that it's important to look forward and not backward, and to remind ourselves that we do have very real security threats out there." He did not convene a truth and reconciliation process, as Leahy suggested.[127]

Members of the international human rights community hoped Bush officials could be held liable for violating the Geneva Conventions. They consider accountability to be the most important symbol of Obama's commitment to the UN's Convention against Torture and Other Cruel, Inhuman or Degrading Treatment or Punishment (CAT). Yet Obama did not comply with that treaty. The Obama administration still relies on the state secrets doctrine to frustrate tort claims, and Manfred Nowak, Moritz Birk, and Tiphanie Crittin argue that "President Obama has clearly indicated that he is not willing to fulfill his legal obligation under the CAT to bring any perpetrators of torture—whether those who directly committed torture or those who ordered, authorized, or condoned such practices—to justice."[128]

Nowhere was Obama's dilemma demonstrated better than when he tried to bring the detainees at Guantanamo Bay to trial, giving them access to the American court system instead of military tribunals. The Senate, still under Democratic control, sent him a strong, definitive vote of 90 to 6 against using any federal funding for the incarceration or transfer of these detainees. No state in the United States was prepared to accept or try any of the detainees. What is more, polls indicated that the American public strongly disapproved of bringing detainees stateside for trial. This constituted Obama's first significant defeat in Congress and in public opinion.[129]

But Obama's defeat in the Senate did little to quiet international public opinion. Foreign policy experts abroad as well as American human rights activists continued condemning Obama for not holding key members of the Bush administration accountable. Some hinted that records will also show that Obama condoned torture, suggesting that his stance is more rhetorical than real. "Once upon a time," a former military member wrote, "Americans across the political spectrum were united behind efforts to prevent torture and punish torturers."[130]

And to be sure, the United States had been solidly behind the Geneva Conventions. In 1988, under Ronald Reagan, the United States signed the Convention against Torture as well. A critic of Obama wrote that the convention clearly states that "no exceptional circumstance whatsoever . . . may be invoked as justification of torture." Like all other signatories of the CAT, the United States had to enact domestic laws criminalizing torture. And indeed, after a Democrat-controlled Senate ratified this treaty, Congress added a torture statute to the U.S. criminal code. In 1996 a Republican member of Congress sponsored the War Crimes Act. This legislation made "grave breaches" of the Geneva Conventions— like torture—federal crimes.

After 9/11, this solid bipartisan stand against torture disappeared. Worse, the Bush administration's practice of torture, as a critic explained it, "eliminated the possibility of rendering justice." As one scholar writes, "Prisoners who have been tortured without charges . . . will be denied the right even to question evidence obtained by torture, evidence that is being used to justify their continued imprisonment! And in a further Catch-22, many of these prisoners are being held under the notion that they can't [be] prosecuted successfully because the evidence proving that they are dangerous was obtained through the use of torture."[131]

What Obama did to avoid some of the most egregious torture charges leveled at the Bush administration was to suspend calling detainees "illegal enemy combatants." Dropping this title put the United States in formal compliance with the Geneva Conventions, though it still denied these detainees access to the American judiciary. Nor would recategorizing them end torture or extraordinary rendition. Yet it would mean that the United States would start offering information about all the people it detains. And presumably those detainees could be released when the United States and forty-two other nations end their "war on terror" by pulling out of Afghanistan and stopping the use of drones in Pakistan.[132]

By way of explanation, Obama spoke of the need to make sure the rule of law applies to Gitmo prisoners with "a process that adheres to rule of law, habeas corpus, basic principles of Anglo-American legal system . . . in a way that doesn't result in releasing people who are intent on blowing us up." In a controversial book, John Mearsheimer and Stephen Walt noted before Obama won the Democratic nomination that although "the United States was widely condemned for the abuses that

occurred at Abu Ghraib prison and also for the way it has treated detainees at Guantanamo," it is "not being held to a double standard." In support of Obama's multilateralism, they claimed that the United States is
"merely being expected to live up to its own stated values and to widely
accept human rights principles."[133]

But Obama's executive action on March 7, 2011, must have disappointed these two noted foreign policy experts, along with all the progressive and civil liberties activists in the civil rights and human rights
community. Obama issued an executive order that formalized the Bush
administration policy of indefinite detention without charges for the 172
prisoners remaining at Guantanamo Bay, as well as those in other loca-
tions, such as U.S. bases in Bagram, Afghanistan, and on the *Diego Gar-
cia*, located in the Indian Ocean.[134]

Having taken into account the criticisms of Human Rights Watch
and the ACLU, among many other watchdog organizations, Obama did
create a Periodic Review Board (PRB) process to review the detainees'
cases. But this board fully satisfied no political constituency. Obama's
order created the independent PRB process to determine the fate of the
detainees, but it did not include a new detention authority. Instead, it
established an alternative avenue of release for detainees who, in the administration's view, may be lawfully held under the 2001 Authorization
for Use of Military Force, as informed by the law of war.

"It's a significant improvement," wrote one critic, "over the Combatant Status Review Tribunal (CSRT), created by the Bush administration
in 2004 to rubber-stamp its determination that the detainees were 'enemy combatants' and avoid the habeas corpus review the Supreme Court
had just mandated in *Rasul v. Bush*. This time, detainees are assigned
personal representatives who, well, actually represent them." And, as
this foreign policy expert elaborated, the executive order bore "several
hallmarks of Obama's Guantanamo policy: a desire to strike a balance
between liberty and security (albeit one heavily weighted towards security); a professed respect for the separation of powers (while seeking
to enhance executive control at the expense of the judiciary); and a recognition that providing a better process will ultimately strengthen the
government's hand in defending its detentions in court." Overall, the
highest praise these critics gave Obama was that he was not Bush. The
new procedures and mechanisms failed to impress human rights or civil
rights activists at home and abroad, who know that extraordinary rendition has not stopped.[135]

Working with the UN in hopes of heading off this criticism back in
2009, Obama administration officials had stated, "We intend to seek,

as soon as practicable, Senate advice and consent to ratification of the Additional Protocol II to the 1949 Geneva Conventions, which elaborates upon safeguards provided in Common Article 3 and includes more detailed standards regarding fair treatment and fair trial." But human rights legal scholars studying the first two years of the Obama administration concluded that his "policy of change has had only a limited effect on the current U.S. antiterrorism practices." While the Bush administration's "worst" practices have been discontinued, "there are clear indications that the Obama Administration continues to detain suspects incommunicado (at least for short periods), use military commissions to try the main suspects of the September 11 attacks, return detainees to their countries of origin on the basis of diplomatic assurances in violation of the non-refoulement principle, and restrict habeas corpus rights of detainees."[136]

To domestic and international human rights activists, Obama's position on torture underscores his failures as commander in chief. The president, however, understands that neither domestic nor international human rights activists constitute the official diplomatic corps or the core of his Democratic base. Obama's Nobel lecture was a nod not to those at home, but rather to the leaders of the 120 nations that signed and ratified the Treaty of Rome in support of the ICC, including the large EU states such as the United Kingdom, Germany, and France, along with Japan. And for those attentive listeners, Obama offered a reason why he chose to increase troops in Afghanistan while pulling them out of Iraq. "I am the Commander-in-Chief of a nation in the midst of two wars. One of these wars is winding down," he said. "The other is a conflict that America did not seek; one in which we are joined by forty-three other countries—including Norway—in an effort to defend ourselves and all nations from further attacks."[137]

Obama's actions in office reveal a consistent concern with his historical legacy. His position against torture, such as waterboarding, indicates that he has chosen not to squander his presidency's capital by cleaning up Bush's position on torture, almost universally condemned in the international court of public opinion. Obama does not believe he is responsible for the United States' war in Iraq, given his position against it, and because he ended that war, as pledged and promised, by 2011. Obama remains one of forty-three commanders in chief from different nation-states involved in the war on terror fought in Afghanistan. The United States is no longer alone. To be sure, Obama leads this multilateral coalition. But his leadership gives him the capacity to take an interim position. If sovereign nation-states with universal jurisdiction decide to pick up former members of Bush's administration culpable for torture, such as Dick Cheney, Donald Rumsfeld, or John Yoo, Obama can decide whether or not it is in the United States' sovereign interest to intervene or to let them be tried for "crimes against all."[138]

Drones

While deploying new weapons in counterterrorism, such as drones and cyberworms, Obama let it be known that he has read the "just-war theories of St. Augustine and Thomas Aquinas." He made public how much he has wrestled with his decisions, inviting civilians and military advisors into the situation room and listening while they "battled and disagreed." He then revealed how "brutally difficult" the decisions are, but maintained that once he has made a decision, he has "no qualms." "On behalf of the United States," National Security Advisor Thomas Donilon said, Obama is "quite comfortable with the use of force."[139]

Obama embraces the "portrait" painted of him as "a steely commander who pursues the enemy without flinching." Nothing showed this better than the news of Obama's increasing deployment of drones. Until 2011, John Brennan, Obama's counterterrorism advisor, claimed that few to no civilian casualties occurred with drone attacks. Not surprisingly, Obama found this technology appealing, and he greatly expanded its use. Drones hit terrorism suspects in Pakistan as well as in Afghanistan, Yemen, and Somalia. Obama has issued orders for more than 307 strikes, whereas in the five years before Obama took office, Bush ordered only 44 strikes.[140]

Following the modus operandi described above, Obama expanded the use of these killer machines only after he "tighten[ed] up some procedures." As one source explained, Obama "didn't like the idea of 'kill 'em and sort it out later.'" Obama therefore shortened the chain of command, making each and every decision on the so-called "kill list" himself. Unlike Bush, he no longer allowed the CIA to "delegate down" the decision for a so-called "signature strike."[141]

Obama also insisted that every killing had to be "lawyered up," whether it involved CIA or military operations. He chose a liberal idealist and a pragmatic realist for the two different types of operations. Harold Hong Koh from the State Department spoke for the CIA, whereas Jeh C. Johnson spoke for those on the military's kill list. Koh, who had been the Clinton administration's top human rights official and a dean of Yale Law School, had a very different outlook than Johnson, a pragmatic former prosecutor who had a moderate record, but had pushed to expand the term "military combatants" to include "co-belligerents" so as to increase the number of drone strikes.

The Koh-Johnson rivalry gave Obama two warring perspectives. Obama also assembled a troika with four-star Marine General "Hoss" Cartwright, four-star Admiral Mike Mullen from the Joint Chiefs of Staff, and John Brennan, his top counterterrorism aide. No idealists, these three advisors met with the president and his national security advisors in what came to be called "terror Tuesday" briefings.[142]

In addition to expanding the United States' use of drones, Obama worked with Israel in an operation code-named Olympic Games that involved cyberattacking Iran. Obama established a cyberunit that "crossed the Rubicon," as a former official explained, when a worm named Stuxnet took out nearly a thousand of the five thousand centrifuges Iran had spinning at the time to purify uranium. Representing the "first attack . . . to effect physical destruction," rather than simply slow another computer or hack into it to steal data, Stuxnet was so successful that the Iranian government's only defense was to deny that the attack had happened.[143]

Obama's expansion of his executive power met resistance from all sides except his NATO allies. Human rights activists "expressed outrage" at the reported "counting method." "We have never before heard anything quite like the idea that if you have to be in a certain place and you happen to be of a certain age, that in and of itself can make you targetable," said Gabor Rona, international legal director at Human Rights First. Meanwhile neoconservatives taunted him, pointing out that this former "liberal law professor who campaigned against the Iraq war" now "personally oversees a 'kill list.'"[144]

Finally, Obama trampled on civil liberties. He used the Espionage Act of 1917—"an obscure first world war anti-spy law—six times" to punish breaches of security. Obama not only went after Private Bradley Manning for leaking classified information to WikiLeaks founder Julian Assange, but also went after "John Kiriakou, a CIA agent who leaked details of waterboarding, and Thomas Drake, who revealed the inflated costs of an NSA data collection project that had been contracted out." But is not so easy to prosecute under the Espionage Act unless people are in the military, the last case having been won in the mid-1980s. "Investigators will have to balance several competing interests—including punishment of leaks, preservation of remaining secrets, and freedom of the press," said Steve Aftergood, director of the Project on Government Secrecy with the Federation of American Scientists. This "explains why there have been relatively few prosecutions over the years."[145]

Obama, however, does not stand alone in his positions on either civil liberties or counterterrorism. In 2012 he led a "successful summit in Chicago of NATO," and he has made it no secret that "something changed in Chicago." The allies "charted the future course of the alliance in Afghanistan, bolstered NATO's partnerships with nations across the globe and made a commitment to ensure that the alliance will have the capabilities to meet the security challenges of today and tomorrow." Four countries—Poland, Romania, Spain, and Turkey—will host interceptors, ships, and radars, while a missile-defense ship under NATO operational control sits in the Mediterranean ready for a crisis. Obama gave operational control of U.S. radar in Turkey to NATO.[146]

Obama is attacked by foreign policy experts on the Left and the Right. He sparks outrage from the Left, more associated with idealists, who made a false assumption that Obama would promote international human rights and believes in universal truths. The president not only claims responsibility for each and every death he causes; he is relentless and ruthless. He has flipped on its head the idea that multilateral is code for soft and that unilateral means hawk. An agreement should be struck in the UN, and nothing less than a new Geneva Convention should be written to determine drone rules of engagement. Once out of office, Obama would not disagree. But as commander in chief asserting his powers as a world leader, Obama is neither traditional hawk nor dove, but rather a Spinozan wolf to his enemies and a saint to his allies.

Transnational Norms

Just as he rethought and transformed the norms underlying domestic policy with Race to the Top, the Affordable Care Act, the Consumer Protection Act, and his actions regarding climate control, Obama challenges existing foreign policy norms as well. He decenters a public policy by bringing together a variety of participants, with varying perspectives, who interact to generate new norms. Even when the participants do not have the formal capacity to make, implement, or execute law, they can still generate the norms that give rise to a domestic or foreign public policy. Yet changing, altering, assessing, or reassessing norms (and their underlying assumptions) is controversial, since norms dictate the rules of the game, or the rules of engagement. In foreign policy, Obama redefined American interests by supporting the protesters during the Arab Spring that blossomed in Tunisia, Egypt, Libya, and Syria, thereby altering the idealist/realist binary through experience or action—or, plainly put, history.[147]

This redefining of American interests by privileging demonstrators instead of dictators makes it clear that Obama consistently interjects two norms—accountability and responsibility—into his key domestic and foreign policy reforms. These twin norms are conceptually close, and they spawn equally similar behaviors and customs.

Not surprisingly, Obama injects these norms into his foreign policy by following a policy of multilateralism in the war on terror. Multilateralism is similar to Obama's notion of diversity through inclusivity, as seen in chapter 3. This said, the commander in chief understands that his preference for multilateralism captures little domestic support, either in the Democratic and Republican parties or in mainstream public opinion. Yet Obama realizes the truth of what one expert in global governance has written about a substantively different issue, global environmentalism: that "accountability and responsibility norms forged in domestic regulatory contexts cannot simply be transposed across borders." This author finds many "analytical challenges raised by the transnational (re)scaling of accountability and responsibility" that environmentalists have discussed in the context of a global commons. Not all of these issues can be replicated in critical thought about the multilateral war on terror. Can the war on terror conducted by forty-three nations be thought of as part of a commons? Or is this war qualitatively different from efforts at climate control? Will including more nations foster an international dialogue or incite a more deliberative public conversation at home?[148]

No matter what differentiates climate control from a multilateral war on terror, Obama's position is similar to the idea of "accountability deficits" in the literature on global environmentalism. Terrorism, too, is a transnational problem, even if counterterrorism efforts that are covert by definition cannot constitute the subject of a global commons.[149]

Obama began questioning the United States' largely unilateral position in the war on terror before taking office. In his Nobel lecture Obama outlined his rationale for increasing troops in Afghanistan in support of the forty-two other nations engaged there, while at the same time pulling troops out of Iraq along with the relatively few other nation-states still fighting there. Obama's multilateralism does partly explain his pattern of studying "consequences," as quoted earlier; but can counterterrorism, national and international intelligence gathering, and the way the United States treats detainees constitute the stuff of a commons? Counterterrorism, by its very nature, must be covert. Still, national intelligence gathering, particularly by a largely privatized military, and the treatment of detainees should be part of a public discussion. The United States' position on civil liberties and human rights affects each and every American citizen.[150]

Terrorism and counterterrorism, like pollution, can cause transnational harm. Privatizing military services such as intelligence gathering creates a significant role for public *and* private nongovernmental actors who act as contractors and subcontractors outsourcing the production of goods and personnel, all of which further complicates oversight or assigning accountability and responsibility. Other than the American use of drones, Obama has neither increased nor decreased Bush's reliance on governmental contracting and outsourcing of military functions. But Obama, more than Bush, faces oversight complications: first, because Bush's practices are now known, since journalists and watchdog organizations have begun making them public, and second, because Obama must answer to his base, which includes human rights activists and international elites, whereas Bush had, at most, to answer to civil libertarians, a very small constituency.[151]

Human rights violations, such as torture, create transnational harm by giving terrorists further justification for retaliation, making American troops and citizens, at home and abroad, vulnerable. They also violate the American citizenry's civil liberties. This helps explain why both war hawks and progressive human rights supporters rally in support of the Geneva Conventions. It also shows why and how Bush lost support from all partisan sides over his treatment of illegal enemy combatants from 2002 until he left office. A large separation-of-powers conflict emerged, for instance, over the passage of the Detainee Treatment Act of 2005, with Bush issuing a signing statement articulating his interpretation of the law and how narrowly he would execute it. Compounded by the Roberts court's 5–4 split ruling in *Boumediene v. Bush* (2008), which qualified and undermined both the legislative and the executive branches, the controversy shows how complex and multisided the detainee issue is for any president.[152]

Norms change standards, but for standards to be effective, they must be measurable, as in most of Obama's domestic policy reforms, such as Race to the Top (documented in chapter 4). The Obama administration, in other words, understands that for norms to change standards, the actors violating the standards, governmental or nongovernmental (public or private), must be sanctioned for breaking them if their legitimacy is to be ensured and if the state is to retain its power and authority. For these reasons, Obama's continuation of Bush's policies regarding treatment of detainees and the privatization of the military puts him in an

intractable position. Reducing accountability and responsibility to redress and answerability by using nongovernmental private agents clari-
fies how Obama's notion of multilateralism is more easily grasped in
principle than executed in practice.[153]

While it is not difficult to demonstrate harm in the war on terror,
such as violations of the Geneva Conventions, accountability becomes
more complex when the president, as commander in chief, is implementing a multilateral foreign policy to hold individuals, particularly from
a previous administration, as well as private contractors, responsible.
Lawsuits abound involving every variation conceivable under contract
law: former Blackwater employees have been tried for manslaughter,
and other employees have been punished for embezzling or misusing
public funds (such as hiring prostitutes or buying illicit substances).
There have been, and will be, employment lawsuits in which private contractors like Blackwater are sued for negligence and incompetence when
employees die.[154]

With both climate control and the war on terror, "governments seem
unable to prevent externally generated threats to the well-being of their
populations, while their diplomatic efforts to hold responsible actors to
account through international treaty negotiations clash with the geopo-
litical interests of other states." In both areas, "multilateral rule-making
processes give rise to inter-governmental institutions where chains of
public accountability are more remote and indirect than within domestic
political systems." And in both areas, Obama prefers "*delegated models
of accountability*, where international organizations are entrusted with
selected governance functions by participating states."[155]

Yet, as they continue, delegated models of accountability invite "criticism from those who view *accountability as intrinsically participatory*,
where those directly affected by holders of power are privileged as accountability claimants." It's a mess, in other words, that Obama alone
faces because of the different functional hats of the presidency. As commander in chief, diplomat in chief, executor in chief, and chief legislative
agenda setter, he must navigate the governmental contract and human
rights issues alone.[156]

Privileging Demonstrators over Dictators

To many in the human/civil rights and civil liberties communities—
Human Rights Watch and the ACLU, for instance—Obama has fallen
short. Although they uniformly concede that Obama is better than Bush,
the president's actions in support of treating detainees in accordance

with the Geneva Conventions have not been commensurate with his rhetoric in opposition to torture. In the view of both foreign policy realists *and* most idealists, Obama falls short despite his attempts from 2002 onward to redefine American interests along human and national security lines. With foreign policy experts aligned on both sides of this binary claim, Obama is categorically inconsistent.

One Obama administration idealist revised her opinion of the president after leaving office in 2011. Anne-Marie Slaughter, as described earlier, left her post in the winter before the Arab Spring. After serving as the State Department's director of policy planning from 2009 until February of 2011, she spent the remainder of 2011 explaining how Obama had been "misunderstood." Following foreign policy events from her academic post at Princeton, Slaughter now envisions a new frontier that revolves around a rethinking of the realist/idealist binary along horizontal lines, based on a relational or collaborative conception of power.

Unlike Obama, Slaughter does not practice the logic of congruence and consilience, but rather distinguishes between "power-with" and "power-over" in international relations theory. Idealists concentrate on soft power, "the power that a person, group, or institution exercises over other people, groups, or institutions, getting them to do something they would not have done on their own." By contrast, "power-with" is relational, horizontal, and collaborative. It is "the phenomenon we are witnessing in so many different places—the networked, horizontal surge and sustained application of collective will and resources."[157]

Slaughter's analysis also rearticulates Power, Smith, and Ross's presidential directive, completed just two months before she left office. "Collaborative power can take many forms," Slaughter writes. Describing events in Tahrir Square and Tripoli, she continues, "The first is *mobilization*; to exercise collaborative power through not a command but a call to action. The second form is *connection*. In contrast to the relational power method of narrowing and controlling a specific set of choices, collaborative power is exercised by broadening access to the circle of power and connecting as many people to one another and to a common purpose as possible. A third form (many more dimensions of collaborative power will likely emerge) is *adaptation*. Instead of seeking to structure the preferences of others, those who would exercise collaborative power must be demonstrably willing to shift their own views enough to enter into meaningful dialogue with others." What she elaborates is the fundamental difference: her kind of collaborative power is not only relational, but is also "not held by any one person or in any one place."[158]

Delivering a speech upon her departure, Slaughter criticized Obama for not being a rigorous idealist, and yet less than a year later, the president had converted her to the point at which she called his redefinition of American interests a "very smart debating move." Slaughter understands that by supporting the aspirations of protesters from Cairo to Tripoli to Damascus, the president successfully redefined American interests as the people's interests rather than those of the autocrats.[159]

Obama's multilateralism in foreign policy leads to what some have called "hybridization" in his domestic package of policy reforms relating to federalism, or "hybrids" in terms of moral agency and public accountability in international relations and foreign policy. Hybrids, considered inelegant by some and hip by others, help contemporary legal thought live with paradox, no matter what one's perspective.

For example, if one nation-state becomes too obsessive about the maintenance of its traditional boundaries—public and private sectors, profit and nonprofit, formal and informal, theory and practice, secular and religious, Left and Right—that is no longer a major concern with the shift to Renew Deal thinking. That paradigm moves beyond such pervasive dichotomies in search of sustainable structures. Its objective is not to police boundaries, but rather to seek out and open structures that will facilitate wider imaginative horizons.[160]

Inventing flexible, responsive administrative practices may be the only alternative to big, blunt bureaucracies, on the one hand, and private market mechanisms, on the other. This type of governance is democratic because it encourages the participation of more citizens and pays attention to more interests in legally reconciling the ongoing tension between the fear of big government and the need for a public response to social challenges.[161]

6

A Lose-Lose Leader, or a Script for a President?

"Out of Many, One People" Jamaican national motto similar to "E pluribus unum"

Obama's conception of a Spinozan stakeholder state and society engages people with, and from, different perspectives. It generates the norms underlying the American state, society, and economy, rather than developing a single, stagnant set of ideas, beliefs, and values. In effect, Obama embodies three forms of the Latin phrase *E pluribus unum* ("Out of Many, One").[1]

First, the vision behind Obama's policy platform, as one academic has noted, could reflect the Jamaican version of this Latin phrase: "Out of many, one people." The Caribbean *E pluribus unum* was sung by the unofficial ambassador of Jamaican culture, Bob Marley, who during one interview said, "People are people. Black, blue, pink, green—God make no rules about color, only society make rules where my people suffer and that [*sic*] why we must have redemption and redemption now." Marley's lyrics "One love, one heart / Let's get together and feel all right," no less, became part of the inauguration festivities for Obama in 2009.[2]

Second, *E pluribus unum* was part of the Founding Fathers' discussion about a national seal and its association with civic religion. Wealth and prosperity, as the story goes, is premised on the Protestant work ethic *and* a perpetual right to rebel. In 1782 Charles Thomson, a respected but less known Founding Father, suggested that the Great Seal of the United States should depict *annuit coeptis*, or the "eye above" image, seen today on the dollar bill. (*Annuit coeptis* is usually translated as "He [God] favors our undertakings.") But some sources maintain that *annuit coeptis* had another meaning: the all-seeing eye embodies Benjamin Franklin's notion that "rebellion to tyrants is obedience to God."

But it was Nicholas Philip Trist, a diplomat and Thomas Jefferson's grandson by marriage, who drew the correlation between *E pluribus unum*, *annuit coeptis*, and all men being "created equal" under the Declaration of Independence. When the Continental Congress abandoned the seal with "rebellion to tyrants is obedience to God," Trist said, Jefferson was so enamored with it that he turned it into one of his personal seals. It even garnishes one of the Monticello graveyard's metal gates.[3]

Some critics dismiss Trist, however, given the scandal over his involvement in the slave trade in Cuba.[4] They propose that Jefferson's supposed liking for this phrase was a product of either Trist's or Franklin's fertile imagination. To be sure, Jefferson used this seal, but those scholars remain in the minority who interpret him as first, perceiving Americans as "the chosen people"; second, making religion (even civic religion) tantamount to righteous rebellion; and finally, relying on Franklin's Protestant work ethic to rationalize prosperity and wealth.[5] Neither the U.S. Treasury nor the Jefferson Archives endorses the notion that "rebellion to tyrants is obedience to God" is a founding principle.[6]

By contrast, Obama's writings about Abraham Lincoln show that he concurs with the "four score and seven years ago" rhetorical flourish in the Gettysburg Address that made equality part of the American founding by including the Declaration of Independence. As one commentator put it, Lincoln did the heavy lifting that enabled Obama to claim equality as a founding principle, but this does not mean it is a religious one. Obama's conception of *E pluribus unum* as a statement about equality, premised on diversity or difference, gives John Winthrop's "City on a Hill" sermon a cosmopolitan civic religious twist, as discussed in chapter 3. Obama does not embrace a chosen people or endorse a *Protestant* work ethic. But the president does wholeheartedly support hardworking peoples and families motivated by any ethic or religion.

Obama leans toward the Jamaican version of *E pluribus unum*, a sentiment he embraces more than the neoconservative impulse to make the Declaration of Independence a document in support of civic religion or religious freedom. Most telling is that after Obama faced the contro-

versy over Pastor Jeremiah Wright and a minor flap with Rev. Rick Warren, the international evangelist and author of *The Purpose-Driven Life*,
the president selected Rev. Joseph Lowery for his inaugural benediction.
Lowery echoed Obama's sentiment about diversity and inclusivity of
peoples, not righteousness, prosperity, rebellion, and the Christian religion. In speaking of "the joy of a new beginning," the Reverend concluded, "we ask you to help us work for that day when black will not
be asked to get back, when brown can stick around, when yellow will
be mellow, when the red man can get ahead, man, and when white will
embrace what is right." Both Caribbean versions of the Latin phrase *E
pluribus unum and* Lowery's benediction convey cross-cultural solidarity, or positive energy and strength in difference and diversity.[7]

Golden, Shiny Babies in Three Spheres

It is this type of equality and solidarity in difference, inclusivity, and diversity that Obama has repeatedly, and consistently, proclaimed since
first taking office as a United States senator. Nowhere is the energizing
solidarity in diversity summarized better than in his speech "A More Perfect Union," from the 2008 campaign. In this speech Obama recounts his
own hybrid ancestry and relates his personal experience to the broader
diversity and complexity of the United States at large. Put simply, he renders his own translation of "out of many, one," making it "out of many,
we are one."

The act of becoming one, for Obama, mirrors his experience of being black in America, which he described as being "at once unique and
universal." Further, Obama himself embodies what the youth residing in
the former Confederate South call a "golden baby." With his mixed race
(read white/black), mixed ethnic (read midwestern American, African,
Indonesian), mixed continents (same as ethnic, only refocused through
a macro-spatial lens), mixed sectional (read urban and suburban with
a micro-spatial lens), and mixed class background intersected with his
spatial background (read urban/suburban in conjunction with the correlation between race, class, and education), the president has witnessed
a transformation.

Obama's multiracial heritage went from being considered all negative (miscegenation being effectively legalized in *Loving v. Virginia* when
he was five years old) to being considered golden. Privileged and un-
touched by poverty, a golden child is a rarity and supposedly better than
a white or black child. The baby glows. She shines. The embodiment of
luminescence and change, a golden baby is a rarity.

Another way to characterize mixed heritage is being liminal, or at a permanent threshold. "Betwixt and between" not only represents the turn of phrase cultural anthropologist Victor Turner coined to capture the vortex, but also conveys a permanent moment of historic flux or change—or a rare and fleeting momentary process in one of life's stages. It is heritage that helps explain Obama's penchant for a stakeholder society (read too interdependent to be dependent or independent) and accounts for the character of his political, economic, and social vision that undermines the *oikos-agora* described in chapters 2, 4, and 5. Consumer/citizens represent the deliberative democratic masses practicing consumer reform, extending the household to the economy across the private and public spheres or in an all-inclusive Spinozan social sphere.[8]

"Unique and Universal"

It would be incorrect, however, to interpret this Spinozan social sphere as either moderate or a compromise. It does not constitute a "watering down" of anybody or anything. Rather, Obama's twin notions of inclusivity and diversity contain some of the same essence as that encapsulated in "black power." One of Obama's pet phrases, arguably his greatest condemnation of someone's political behavior, is to say that they stand on "the wrong side of history." Tracking people on wrong/right sides is as close to a binary as the intersectional President Obama gets.[9]

This book argues that the postracial interpretation of Obama's presidency, which stems from Obama's universal understanding of racial and ethnic complexity, compounded by his intersectionality, is wrongheaded. Having been raised "betwixt and between" during his childhood, in addition to self-consciously placing himself at this intersection in early adulthood, in college, at university, and during law school, Obama understands (as Peter Halewood put it) the "central paradox of American life: that, despite having no biological/genetic basis, race nonetheless controls the American perception of reality, and whiteness is the lens through which all interpretation ultimately is refracted." Halewood updates W. E. B. Du Bois's double consciousness.[10]

Further, being a Harvard Law School graduate, and past president of *the* law review, means that Obama comprehends the immutable characteristics of civil rights categories and the significance of legal standing. He does not believe that the American judiciary promises the best way of resolving racial justice now that there are no more Bull Connors supporting de jure discrimination in combination with a very conservative federal bench. Remedies for de facto discrimination, such as affirmative action and integrating schools, moreover, have largely failed. Critics would argue they flopped. As a result, much of the discrimination practiced today has gone underground or, worse, encompasses social control hidden in plain sight.[11]

Often free of intent, today's discrimination is determined less by the law than by society, culture, and even the self, given the primary significance of unwritten and unspoken norms, values, and visceral beliefs. Absent intent, discrimination can go so far as to become socially controlling. Taking a Foucauldian twist, discrimination can become self-regulation by the very people who face it.

To comprehend whiteness is to be "nonracial." To say nothing, or to be silent—the absence of this adjective—in other words, means a person in the United States is white. Whiteness is invisible. But whiteness is ubiquitous. Whiteness strips norms, values, and beliefs—or informal and formal rules and standards—of all color.[12]

As a result, most white Americans regard racial problems as a "real and imagined" set of grievances that black Americans have with them— "the Negro problem." "It's personal," which is to say individual or specific to a group, visceral and emotional rather than rational, and quite possibly a "failure" issue instead of a societal or institutional problem. In 1909, characterizing Democratic and Republican progressive reformers' unwillingness or inability to go even this far, Du Bois said, "White reformers seemed to be unaware of the Negro problem or refused to admit its existence."[13]

Rights, Reversals, and (Re)Reversals

The 1960s civil rights legacy is filled with so many stops and starts that only the pivotal points can be addressed here. After *Brown v. Board of Education* (1954) and Dwight D. Eisenhower's perceived debacles with civil rights in Little Rock, Arkansas, came President John F. Kennedy's and Attorney General Robert F. Kennedy's efforts to pass antidiscrimination legislation as part of the New Frontier policy package in 1961. It was not until after President Kennedy's assassination, however, that the Civil Rights Act became part of Lyndon B. Johnson's legislative legacy, the Great Society, in 1964.[14]

The passage of the Civil Rights Act, and then the Voting Rights Act of 1965, occurred after what some describe as the Second Reconstruction, or as the culmination of a hundred years of activism and effort. Heating up from 1954 until 1965, Thurgood Marshall's and the NAACP's legal activism, Rev. Martin Luther King Jr.'s liberal nonviolent social movement against de jure discrimination, and Malcolm X's urban black power and nationalist radicalism addressing de facto discrimination all came to a head. Most notably, in 1965 an unpublished report named after its author, Daniel Patrick Moynihan, a staffer for the Labor Department, informally indicted, tried, and convicted the African American family in much of mainstream public opinion, causing a long-lasting controversy.[15]

Moynihan, an anti-Communist or Cold War, color-blind liberal, had tried to pull civil rights back into the personal realm by offering his expert opinion that "Negro social structure, in particular the Negro family, battered and harassed by discrimination, injustice, and uprooting, is in the deepest trouble." Moynihan's position created an intellectual firestorm. He reflected a perspective that had emanated from Cold War American Jews from large urban areas, who thought their ethnicity and religion should be differentiated from racial identity, particularly that of African Americans also living in urban areas.[16]

Despite this intellectual rift, four months after Kennedy's assassination in November of 1963, one of Johnson's crowning achievements—the Civil Rights Act—received its final legislative markup. As spring arrived, it was stalled in Virginian Howard W. Smith's Rules Committee in the House and stymied by northern Republicans in the Senate, all cooperating with Dixiecrats. But Johnson, a white liberal Texan from working-class roots and a former Senate majority leader, made sure the legislation would pass under his watch.

The compromise that triggered its passage was the Dirksen amendment. Republican senator Everett McKinley Dirksen of Illinois got enough Republicans to vote for the legislation with a provision ensuring that the Equal Employment Opportunity Commission (EEOC) would be the "only federal regulatory agency without its own enforcement mechanism." This amendment made Civil Rights Act enforcement feeble by assigning it to an administrative agency made intentionally weak, unlike any other federal quasi-judicial or quasi-legislative agency established in the twentieth century. Quite simply, this agency depended on the federal judiciary for its enforcement power. The amendment that broke the logjam, leading to passage of the Civil Rights Act, also set liberal boundaries, limiting antidiscrimination relief to the more elusive equality of opportunities, instead of concrete equality of outcomes.[17]

The Wrong Side of History

By June of 1965 everything had turned around again, this time thwarting relief from discrimination. "Events conjoined in the summer of 1965 to mark a watershed in the struggle for racial equality, and when the divide had been crossed each of these assumptions" about equality of results for the "black ghetto poor," as law professor Andrew Kull writes, "would quickly appear outdated." To be sure, the liberal Democrats made a ruckus in Congress, and President Johnson made a speech at Howard University in support of affirmative action and the principle of equality of result or outcome. "You do not take a person who, for years, has been hobbled by chains and liberate him, bring him up to the starting line of a race and then say, 'you are free to compete with all the others,' and still justly believe that you have been completely fair."[18]

Then, as Kull describes, the era of equality of outcomes ended just fifteen months after it had started:

> When the Moynihan controversy was at its height, the background of recent events included not only the enactment of the Voting Rights Act and the Howard University address, but also the start of the Vietnam buildup, the commitment of American ground troops to combat, and the riot in Watts . . . *the familiar liberal assumptions about the preconditions of racial equality were perceived as erroneous.*[19]

A toothless EEOC opened its doors soon after the events in Watts. Over the next four decades, while the EEOC effected some change in the workplace for women and people of color, it was overwhelmed by its workload and hobbled, as much as if not more than bolstered, by judicial enforcement. It has been an administrative agency in a permanent state of compromise until the Obama administration, as explained in earlier chapters.[20]

Segregation, Desegregation, and Resegregation

The Johnson administration changed course after the urban uprisings in Los Angeles, turning now against the institutional or structural explanation of American racism or any accounting for what Du Bois calls the "mechanization" of race, as described in chapter 2. President Johnson transformed the War on Poverty into the Great Society. As Kull writes,

"There was no time; there would be no money. From this pessimistic perspective, any explanation of unequal results in terms of unequal abilities became an apology for continued inequality and a contemptible exercise in 'blaming the victim.'" As politics professor Helene Slessarev explains, "President Johnson had given the drafters of the anti-poverty legislation two very specific guidelines." First, "rehabilitation, not income" was the new motto. And second, any rehabilitation program to help victims recover from the informal organizations of the community (read the ghetto) and the family (read single mother and absent father) should not "cost much money."[21]

In 1967 Mary Switzer received the power and authority to "socially" rehabilitate the poor in the Office of Economic Opportunity (OEO). A longtime high-level administrator, responsible for designing and then helping pass legislation creating institutions as diverse as the National Science Foundation, the Vocational Rehabilitation Administration, and community mental health centers, Switzer sought reforms that would materially and emotionally protect "maimed" children from their poor, ignorant mothers, all the while trying to fill the emotional gap left by the absence of their fathers. Not just Moynihan, but many other architects of the War on Poverty, had a deeply paternalistic and patronizing perspective, one that Switzer herself embraced, hoping to combat the "pathology of the ghetto" by rehabilitating the poor.

Opposed to community action and welfare rights, Switzer referred to the Johnson administration appointees responsible for the more participatory, political, or electoral aspects of the Great Society's War on Poverty as the "poverty boys." In her view, considering the situation in urban areas from "Harlem to Hough, Chicago to Cincinnati, Boston to Buffalo," the War on Poverty gave poor people false hope.[22] HEW secretary John Gardner, Switzer, and her longtime advisor Dr. Howard Rusk agreed with Lee Rainwater that African American mothers and children suffered from a "maiming" of their personalities that only social rehabilitation could help. The latter two, who were longtime disability advocates, distinguished social from physical or even mental rehabilitation.

In this view, no amount of money and no amount of participation by poor people or community activists seeking welfare rights could solve the "personal" problems of African Americans. The main economic program the Johnson administration devised under the War on Poverty was "a youth preemployment training program designed more to promote positive attitudes toward work than to provide specific job skills," since President Johnson sought "rehabilitation, not income."[23]

In hindsight, *Griggs v. Duke Power Co.* represents a high point in the civil rights era. "If an employment practice which operates to exclude Negroes cannot be shown to be related to job performance," wrote Chief Justice Warren Burger, "the practice is prohibited." The year 1971, in which a statute—the Civil Rights Act of 1964—received full federal judicial support that set future practices by statutory and common law precedents, constituted the peak of antidiscrimination protection. The nexus of national institutions lining up against discrimination in employment—Congress, the president, and the Supreme Court—was essential, since, as explained earlier, the EEOC had no enforcement power of its own.[24]

And then it stopped. Since 1971, and continuing to the present, piece by piece over forty years, every workplace protection except affirmative action in local, state, and federal governmental contracts has been undone. With the exception of voting rights, including the current debate about voter ID, an about-turn has happened in almost every civil rights venue: segregation, public education, higher education, and the workplace.[25]

In most communities, desegregation ended, and the nation revisited segregation. Or, as one consultant explained, the United States experienced "segregation, *de*segregation, and *re*-segregation" from the *Brown* decision in 1954 to the 1999 *Swann v. Charlotte-Mecklenburg Schools* decision. Meanwhile, universities turned to diversity as a value added, rather than as reparations for slavery.[26]

Obama himself witnessed the 1978 *Bakke* decision and the turn toward diversity. In 2003 University of Michigan president Lee Bollinger succeeded in maintaining the constitutionality of affirmative action on the basis of adding diversity, rather than repairing old wounds or acknowledging and compensating for slavery in the United States and the Caribbean—though only by a 5–4 decision that left affirmative action in higher education vulnerable to being decided again and defined even more narrowly. It did not take long. On the same docket, the Supreme Court endorsed the concept of diversity but restricted university admissions architects' room for maneuvering. The Rehnquist court ruled that this premier public university had violated the Fourteenth Amendment's Equal Protection Clause.[27]

The GOP launched a winning campaign in Michigan against socalled reverse discrimination, and the issue became electoral fodder. In 2006 the Michigan Civil Rights Initiative banned affirmative action by ballot. Voters in California and other western and southwestern states followed suit. In less than forty years, civil rights had done a complete somersault, landing close to where it started in the early 1960s. Malcolm X's speech—"the ballot or the bullet"—had resonance again.[28]

Two years later, in 2008, Obama's election threw public opinion and those active in the national electoral arena for another loop. Given the blame-the-victim mentality or rhetoric about the "personal" nature of discrimination, Obama's election gave some liberals evidence, and perhaps even hope, that racism had been conquered at last. But then, in the short space between the election and his inauguration, what some progressives in academia characterized as "white triumphalism" emerged as Americans, many of them white, patted themselves on the rhetorical back for finally achieving a "postracial" society.[29]

The Politics of Resentment: Cold War Ethnic Warriors with Glasses?

The postracial characterization, laden with white triumphalism and the accompanying fear of black power, was intentional. It is similar to the rhetoric that began in the late 1930s and continued until the passage of the Civil Rights Act and the Voting Rights Act, in which anti-Communist, antidiscrimination liberals and industrial union organizers, as well as pro–civil rights moderate Democrats and Republicans, insisted on portraying society as "color-blind." Ironically, under Richard M. Nixon, the GOP in 1969 set out to "recapture a portion of the black vote" by creating "black capitalism." This type of capitalism constituted a free-market attempt to cultivate more African American–owned small businesses as a means of revitalizing urban areas that had become increasingly isolated due to "white flight."[30]

But "black capitalism," which had initiated two-party competition for the black middle-class vote, did not last. The GOP discovered within a few years that despite "enticing the black middle class into its ranks," they had "greater electoral success in a political agenda that is openly *hostile* to black concerns." Bill Clinton decided not to "alienate" black constituents, though he too denounced affirmative action. While African American politicians and community leaders had emerged along with the black middle class, some scholars argue that these leaders "turned inward," especially after white flight in the 1970s and during the civil rights backlash from the 1980s onward.[31]

Obama experienced what Slessarev documents: the turn from law to politics. In the political arena, not only the concept *racism* but the social construct of race itself lacks the resonance of the issues of slavery, the Jim Crow years, and de facto discrimination. Since these concepts cannot be attributed to institutional, economic, or societal explanations, they get pushed back to explanations involving the individual or informal organizations, such as the family. These explanations separate, isolate, and ostracize African Americans, creating a so-called culture of poverty and social control and encouraging self-regulatory conduct. From this perspective the postracial language is similar to the rhetoric of the anti-Communist, pro-industrial Left that advanced racism and sexism while improving the economic conditions of the working class. It is similar to the culture of poverty that the Moynihan report triggered in 1962, leading to a political backlash against the few remedies effectively combating racism.[32]

Race lost its legitimacy. Like many other narratives in the twentieth and twenty-first centuries, the postracial narrative asserts that race can no longer be a source of black grievance underlying antidiscrimination laws and the socioeconomic data showing that the American dream still eludes most African Americans. The compound correlation between race, gender, ethnicity, and poverty was broken. The liberal intersectional interpretation expounded in the 1960s in support of welfare rights and civil rights, sometimes paraphrased as "equality of results," ended long before Obama was elected to national office.[33]

For Obama, who was left by an African father, grew up with a white single mother, and then was raised by white working-class grandparents, there was little relief or redress of the complexities caused by the intersectionalities of his race, ethnicity, gender, and socioeconomic class. Obama describes the compounded effect in *Dreams from My Father: A Story of Race and Inheritance*. Obama still recognizes that African American women today make less than white women or black men—67 cents, compared with 77 cents and 68 cents, respectively—for every dollar earned by white men in 2010. Is it not a coincidence, particularly to the woman (read autonomous person), that black women choose to earn less?[34]

The postracial argument propounded by journalists after the 2008 election, shaking all this off Obama and the United States, as best encapsulated by political journalist and essayist Matt Bai, provokes a strong response not from liberals, but from radical scholars who write on race as a social construct, racism, and theories of whiteness. During the election, Tom Wise, a political blogger, wrote:

> White privilege is when you can get pregnant at seventeen like Bristol Palin [Sarah Palin's daughter] and everyone is quick to insist that your life and that of your family is a personal matter,

and that no one has a right to judge you or your parents, because "every family has challenges," even as black and Latino families with similar "challenges" are regularly typified as irresponsible, pathological and arbiters of social decay.

To these critics in the school of theories of whiteness, "whiteness . . . continues to flourish." The absurdity of the postracial narrative about how the election of one mixed-race person to the presidency, even a man who became a leader of the wealthiest, most powerful country in the world, supposedly eradicated racism was not lost on them.[35]

Deracination, Nannies, and Therapies?

Further, the problem associated with triumphalism is not rhetorical, and not just the product of a fast-moving media that makes cultural fads go in and out of fashion faster than even ten years ago. This postracial rhetoric threatens to "deracinate" politics and, further, deracinate law, ensuring that race and all other identities return to the court of public opinion and the electoral arena.

The term *deracination*—arguably another noun coined by academics when a verb would do—means that a correlation between race and/or gender or socioeconomic class is denied, broken, or removed from rhetorical view entirely. It shows that white privilege is pervasive in public policy—not just civil rights policies, but all law and public policies, domestic and foreign. Deracination, as a goal of politics and public policy, rewards and solidifies whiteness because whiteness is seen and experienced by whites as a nonracial form of identity—it is merely a constellation of reified and "naturally occurring" privileges. It is an open question whether our law can be bent to the purpose of revealing these contradictions and the self-interest endemic in the deracination or postracial legal project.

Traditional cultural critics, like neocon sociologist Alan Woolfolk, echoed this critique of "the self," reconstructing or modernizing the 1960s social psychology theories that critiqued Sigmund Freud, and unpacked what paleoconservative historian Christopher Lasch called "the culture of narcissism." Woolfolk follows in the footsteps of psychologist Philip Rieff, who in 1966 penned *The Triumph of the Therapeutic*. This neocon insists on "the pervasiveness of deracination in a culture," quoting his mentor's statement that there is "nothing at stake beyond a manipulatable sense of well-being." Rieff, Lasch, and Thomas Szasz, a well-known psychologist, criticized Freudian-state (read nanny-state) solutions in the 1960s. Rieff, Lasch, and Woolfolk, among others sitting on academic perches in elite private universities, became public intellectuals, writing in right-wing magazines like *National Review* about the excesses of the New Frontier and the Great Society. When Nixon launched the politics of "resentment," the explanations offered by these "experts" stood ready for print.[36]

Perverse Postracial Rhetoric

The present postracial rhetorical debate drips with irony. It captures both the perversity and the irony embedded within theories of whiteness, as well as the struggles over individual versus societal blame and prevention and treatment versus rehabilitation. Obama, a mixed-race ethnic national leader, a liberal Democrat with one of the most progressive voting records in the Senate, in 2009–2010 led a dominant majority that did not recognize whiteness—either unaware of or refusing to claim the privilege of racial identity or lacking evidence that they had lost it or never had it. Obama's election assuaged liberal guilt, creating postracial triumphalism.

Obama's election also triggered conservative outrage, enough to spark the creation of the extremely conservative Tea Party social movement, then headed by Sarah Palin. Palin's leadership itself is also drenched in irony. She's a religious, though not particularly devoutly Christian, poorly educated, but charismatic and well-spoken woman in a country where heretofore only highly educated or very religious Christian women have led conservative movements.

Yet irony, like race, is problematic when it comes to making correlations with other factors, and even more difficult for a leader to manage. Given its many shades and nuances, a common definition of irony is necessary to offset conflict or to govern. Something ironic generates humor—either humor based in bitterness or its opposite, humor based in gloating. The Tea Party's perspective, or attitude, about the Obama administration, is the opposite of humorous.[37]

This book argues that the mixed-race lineage of the president is ironic, and that it is in this space—the space that is irony, within disjunctions, hypocrisy, and hatred, which can be witty, funny, and ugly—where race as a social construct can be seen. Yet irony can melt quickly, dissolving into sarcasm, and can therefore turn into gloating and slip into perversity. Intent—or its absence—is what separates a smart, sassy, or witty political barb uttered by a male or female, white or black political pundit from an ugly one.

A remark premised on sarcasm or gloating marred by intent (especially mal-intent, a characteristic not shared by irony) is one to which few voters react kindly any longer. Most American voters, in other words, no longer take pride in being racist. Even Republicans do not all agree with the Tea Party's perspective.

What is more, a black middle class does exist. Less than thirty years after passage of the Civil Rights Act, 30 percent of African Americans lived in suburban communities. Yet this does not mean race and racism are gone, or that the United States is in a postracial age. Instead, race and racism are more often lodged in the subtext, or taken out of the text entirely, consonant with Foucault's conception of normalization.

How Gold Turned White—An Environmental Context:
Race-Changes and Whiteness

Put differently, theories of whiteness involve "race-change," or the cross-pollination of racial stereotypes, such as blackface in early films like *The Jazz Singer* or *The Birth of a Nation*. Race-changes involve masquerades and impersonations, or even plain imitations, that help people in the United States cross color lines. Americans can comprehend how blackness has been devalued, and whiteness privileged, only by putting themselves in the other person's shoes or, in other words, experiencing discrimination.[38]

White suburban upper-middle-class Christian boys may want to act "black" to be cool, sporting low-hanging pants and no shoelaces. But being two steps removed or out of context, these boys do not know why the belts and the laces were removed. They do not understand the crisis of African American youth incarceration rates. To use fashion, rap, slang, or black rhythms, as rappers and modernist poets T. S. Eliot and e. e. cummings did, or to portray a "mixed-race child" in contemporary fiction, as Marilyn Hacker and Grace Paley did, "reinforces" boundaries and stereotypes. Out of context, these race-changes promote little social justice.[39]

The consistency in Obama's Spinozan vision has done just what white liberals and conservatives feared. Obama's policies give white Americans a racial identity by taking away or threatening their privilege, conscious or not. Liberal Democrats and Republicans do not support the argument, for example, that legal prescription drugs are more dangerous for American society than crack, an illegal drug.

This level of perception about racial justice rarely gets rewarded. Middle-aged or elderly, white prescription drug abusers vote, whereas crack addicts, as a rule, do not. Nor do users of these two types of drugs live in the same geographic areas. (The latter are more likely to be urban than suburban.) Nor do young unwed mothers and unwed fathers vote.

Liberal Democrats did not want to let abortions become scarce in certain states and not others, let alone certain rural areas. In 2005 former Secretary of Education William Bennett said, "If it were your sole purpose to reduce crime . . . you could abort every black baby in this country, and your crime rate would go down." Bennett's statement caused a media sensation. But then, the following year, in 2006, when two academic economists with no visible political agenda expressed the same idea in *Freakonomics*, it was a national bestseller. In their book Stephen Levitt and Stephen Dubner make a reverse correlation between race, abortion rates, and violent crime. It is both wrong and perverse.[40]

Unlike Bennett, Levitt and Dubner received little flak for their argument; instead, they were heralded largely as clever. *Freakonomics* even became a documentary. Levitt and Dubner made what social scientists have proved for decades to be a false claim about African American criminality in urban areas like New York and Chicago. Supposedly, crime rates plummeted in the late 1990s because black single moms prevented their criminally inclined fetuses from becoming black babies, and then becoming black adolescents and young adults. Fewer black babies were born. Stripped of mal-intent, the legalization of abortion meant precisely what Bennett said, but Levitt and Dubner tabled and graphed.[41]

Put in perverse or ironic terms, having liberated African American women practice their "right to choose" meant that they instituted social controls on themselves, and on their potential children, who did not have the "right to life." This second-wave feminist right pushed up against the conservative Christian religious Right, but few people protested the abortion of "unwanted black children." Supposedly, everyone feared the violent crime that young African American men allegedly committed.[42]

Why did so few liberal and progressive traditional welfare-state Democrats create a fuss about *Freakonomics*? On a national level, they did not want to focus on sectional socioeconomic differences between races and ethnicities. They preferred to ignore the fact that birth control is more commonly available for white minors in the suburban middle class than it is for African Americans and Latinas in urban areas, who lack health care and are affected more by the "just say no" abstinence policies of the GOP.

Despite the existence of a fledgling black middle class, the nexus between race, ethnicity, and class, correlated or undercut by the suburban/

urban spatial or geographic divide, is a difficult "truth" for liberal and progressive Democrats to tell their constituents. But do they want full inclusion? This newly emergent black middle class is trapped. By 2000 it had nowhere to go electorally. What Jesse Jackson called the *Rainbow Coalition* in 1992 never coalesced.

DWB

In the mid-1990s the situation for young African American men and women got worse. An important factor was "what certain practices do to blacks simply because they are *living black*." Analyzing the acronym "driving while black (DWB)," Laura J. Khoury argues that "the hidden purpose of racial profiling is to tame blacks to the point that they willingly feel discomfited when they are in the *wrong place*, or more clearly, *out of place*." This is social or spatial control.[43]

Not just with their African American constituents, liberal and progressive social-welfare Democrats have long been harmed by space, or sectionalism, when it comes to claiming legislative credit. Given the Electoral College and single-member plurality districts (space matters) the geographic self-interests of urban/suburban/rural/ruraburbian communities, reflected by their differing economic resources, present different challenges—challenges the two-party system cannot meet, given the absence of ideological breadth among the Democrats and the Republicans. Sectionalism affects national elections, influencing the presidency as well as Congress's midterm support for the executive.

Despite the splintering effect of the Tea Party and the Moral Majority, the GOP still remains the more homogeneous party of the two in the American two-party system, particularly now that all Republicans are "openly hostile" to African American community interests. They receive credit for practicing the politics of exclusion, or promoting intolerance under the guise of Christianity or what this book calls neotribalism with the war on women.

The Democrats benefit from disguising how much partisanship stems from sectionalism, limiting their ideological vision, or what Skocpol and Jacobs call the "narrative": President Obama has failed "to envelop his economic recovery efforts in a persuasive master narrative." They hide, or obscure, what this book calls sectional intersectionality, since it tugs and tears apart the Democratic coalition of African Americans, Jews, urban immigrants, the working class, white middle-class liberal and progressive men, and soccer moms.[44]

It is the urban poor, not the suburban working and middle classes or residents of ruraburbia, who deal with the most underage pregnancy and nonprescription drug abuse. But even when the Obama administration lost the battle over the health-care provision taking abortion out of the equation, it divided the Democrats, but not the Republicans. Most journalists insisted this was a result of Christian Right advancing its agenda, and in so doing, they ignored the theory of whiteness and the sectional complexities of the Democratic Party.

But many of Obama's policies, at least in their original form, challenge the epistemic and interpretive pillars of whiteness, chiefly their objectivity and neutrality—the very idea of normalcy or the normate. The Foucauldian sense of power makes it productive for the GOP to exclude African Americans. But it's the traditional liberal and progressive big-state social welfare Democrats' use of Foucault's notion of the race/power construction that clearly enrages and engages Obama and Attorney General Eric Holder, as shown in chapter 3.

Free from intent, these Democrats claim they have done enough for African Americans who, despite the failure of the Great Society, did it to themselves in the 1970s onward. It is these Democrats who ignore correlations between race and gender and imply that identity politics is to blame. It is these Democrats who claim that African Americans—particularly the men, who have been criminalized—opted out but were not excluded. Obama's interest in inclusion dressed up in the cosmopolitan language of diversity and difference disarms the Democrats by putting them on the defensive, making the president's public policies a threat to all the resources they reserve for their constituencies, as suburban and rural Democrats outnumber urban Democrats in the House of Representatives and the Senate.[45]

Obama's policies strip away the assumption of whiteness. Obama does not substitute blackness for whiteness, this book has argued, but rather difference for whiteness. Nor does he exchange nondenominational Protestantism for Catholicism. He is not merely reproducing a reversal, like reverse discrimination. But how do we produce knowledge about difference, and how do we know that what we claim to know is caught up with specific histories and relations of power? Race is socially constructed, socially produced, heterogeneous, and dynamic. Obama practices the politics of inclusion.[46]

Limits of Leadership?

Obama calls whiteness into question, not just in the policies covered in the previous chapters, but also on a structural level, in that he questions the 1960s legal paradigm that shaped liberal democratic assumptions about the political institutions that best serve liberalism—the informal ones like the family and the spatially bounded communities.

These assumptions were deeply embedded in institutional arrangements as well as intellectual ones, being shared by members of the civil rights community, who range in political perspectives from Jesse Jackson to Cornel West. That is, the judiciary, not the popular national branches of Congress and the presidency, was supposed to do what this book calls "save" the minority. It was the judicial branch, the Warren court, that ushered in what Hugh Graham labeled the "Civil Rights Era," and which best manifested the attitudes of Cold War, anti-Communist liberals, many of whom were of Jewish descent. African Americans—or for that matter, any type of identity politics, particularly intersectional ones, such as race, gender, sexuality, and class—suffer from dominant majorities who govern public opinion, electoral behavior, and politics.[47]

This institutional perspective on the origins of civil rights in the United States, however, neglects what I call the Foucauldian *Bakke* twist. This book has argued that the Burger court turned it all around, transforming the *negative* idea of affirmative action into the *positive* notion of diversity based on inclusion, even though voters undermined affirmative action. From the 1960s to the present, the United States went from miscegenation laws, to African American women practicing self-eugenics or choosing to abort potential troubled sons in urban areas, to golden babies. The *Bakke* decision, initially seen as a tremendous disappointment among liberal Democrats and civil rights movement leaders, erased the negativity of affirmative action. It broke the correlation between race and slavery.[48]

After *Bakke*, race was no longer considered an immutable category that denigrated or literally "blackened" a school. There was no compensatory element to race-conscious policies. Rather, this decision turned affirmative action into diversity, a positive term or condition describing the benefits of inclusion. *Bakke* turned being black into a positive, universal factor, or what I call a happy, self-help element. In other words, it turned "race" into difference. With the advent of diversity, or appreciating difference, African Americanism became a culture, celebrating Kwanzaa and the birth of golden babies.

And naturally, this "culture" was not restricted to African Americans, but became part of the multicultural version of American liberalism, a wide, all-encompassing, perpetually changing philosophy of inclusion. Diversity could be universalized and extended to all other cultures in the United States—Latinos and Latinas, Asians—all articulated by historian David Hollinger's notion of a "Postethnic America." Uncoupling African American and Jewish memories of atrocities in the United States meant that diverse racial and ethnic groups could challenge the *dominant* white culture. It separated intellectuals from the idea that the zero-sum legacy of slavery can be cured only by reparations. Neither African Americans nor American Jews should be blamed for slavery or the slave trade any longer.[49]

Foucauldian Twists

In *Discipline and Punish*, Foucault treats the history of penal law and the history of human sciences not as separate and overlapping, but as a common matrix. He shows how the two derive from a single process of "epistemologico-juridical formation," making each not the shining example of humanizing the penal system, but rather the reverse. By applying this type of Foucauldian language and regarding race as a social construct, one can see how affirmative action turned into diversity. It can also show how Obama is simultaneously "too black, and not black enough."[50]

Most of Obama's successful public policies, as shown in the previous chapter, contain these truth and reconciliation and diversity elements. So why does Obama receive so little credit for the passage of his public policy platform? The pundits' perspective on Obama's leadership shows that our first African American president cannot "transcend" race. Nor can he go "beyond" his multiracial, transnational identity. Obama is hounded by memory. With the elephant of his race in the room, Obama was heralded as a win-win candidate in 2008, but is regarded as a lose-lose leader.

Race explains the limits on Obama's success as a leader. "Nearly two years after Obama's inauguration," Skocpol and Jacobs argue, "we can highlight a series of happenstances and obdurate contextual realities that have profoundly limited and deflected Obama's reach for another New Deal, or obstructed change altogether." In addition to blaming Obama for not creating a narrative or delivering enough speeches rallying the public, they attribute the "fierce *political backlashes*" to a "constellation of institutional and semi-formal institutional reasons (the interplay between institutions, political parties, and social movements)."[51]

Skocpol and Jacobs rely on Skocpol's historical-institutional approach involving parties and social movements. First, Obama did not include a jobs program or a tax plan in the stimulus package or as a separate piece of legislation. "FDR came in when the patient was near death, whereas Obama wanted to keep the patient's raging fever from turning into pneumonia." "Starting at that misguided September 2008 session at the White House, Obama . . . [was] drawn into a save-Wall-Street-first approach to economic recovery policy that was highly unpopular and fabulously expensive."[52]

Second, Obama took too much advice from former chief of staff Rahm Emanuel and chief economic advisor Lawrence Summers, who tempered the 2008 stimulus package. "Obama hoped to use the stimulus to seed significant green energy projects, a move that would have injected more innovative industrial policy into the emergency recovery effort." Citing political journalist Jonathan Alter, Skocpol and Jacobs argue that "Obama backed off when it was pointed out that legal wrangling over environmental regulations could slow spending; he also retreated when Summers pushed back against the idea of featuring large infrastructure efforts as part of the recovery effort." Obama's White House tried "to hit the middle on the overall price-tag."[53]

Third, "perhaps naively, the newly installed Obama hoped to woo congressional Republicans with substantial up-front tax cuts of the sorts they had claimed to support in the past." Given American sectionalism, immigration reform and climate change are challenging for any president—the only holder of a national office—to bridge. To be sure, "Jimmy Carter had a stronger Senate majority than Obama. And FDR, John Kennedy, and Lyndon Johnson had *larger majorities* to work with when they pushed far-reaching social programs—although in those days, of course, many Democrats were southern conservatives."[54]

Finally, political journalists and academics writing largely sympathetic biographies and policy analyses, and some former Democratic domestic and foreign policymakers, argue that Obama needed more "education" to be an executive. Several books went so far as to highlight the president's lack of "education." Even Carter, the naïve human rights advocate, hardly ever had this charge applied to his governance while in office. Carter did not receive as many brickbats from members of his own party as Obama has, or see insulting articles published in newspapers Republicans claim have a "liberal bias" while running for reelection.[55]

Progress, Regress, (Re)Regress

Obama captures the complexity of racial progress and regress in the United States. His postracial narrative is considered a whitewashing by most of the African American community. Liberals and progressive Democrats remain disappointed with his record on building the big social welfare state that, like Roosevelt's, did not in the end serve African Americans. Roosevelt could not even pass anti-lynching legislation—national legislation that prosecuted people for the murder of African Americans killed for violating white supremacy or seeking redress or their rights. And after Johnson's Great Society, liberal Democrats did little to help African Americans left in decaying urban areas who faced eroding tax bases and white flight.[56]

A progressive Democrat, Obama had one of the most liberal voting records in the Senate, and as president he passed a historic public policy platform, including health care, financial regulation, and a stimulus package. He has altered forty-year trajectories with his changes in the war on drugs and other social policies on sexuality, as cited in chapter 3. Finally, in foreign policy, Obama has made historic changes in the United States' image abroad with his shared burden doctrine, portraying it as neither an arrogant democratizing nor Americanizing or righteous Christian nation. Yet Obama can still be accused simultaneously of whitewashing, being a neoliberal, and being a socialist.

Is Obama's identity prevailing because of his individuality? Or is he trapped by the different public perceptions of his identity, and all the textual and subtextual references therein? Had Obama campaigned on his identity—as a civil rights leader—few people believe he would have been elected. He would have been seen as an "us-against-them" politician, or simply as a partisan for African Americans. Had he gotten into office and done the big-state thing, he would have lost his individuality as a distinctive type of liberal who had long professed interdependency rather than a zero-sum state that promotes either the individual or society.

Obama's ideas represent a cultural rupture with the past. He accepts neither the umpire state nor the nanny state that sees the state as the solution. He rejects individualism, striving instead for public policies that enhance our individuality. Obama puts great faith in the individual, and yet he believes in individual and collective accountability. The president believes in redemption, though he "saves" the nation by relying on a cosmopolitan version of civic religion rather than one featuring good and evil, or heaven and hell, as discussed in earlier chapters. Envisioning the United States as an evolved postindustrial state and society, he suggests that a secular middle class both typifies and symbolizes the nation.

But it appears that rather than having his identity and his individuality represent a win-win, they have become a lose-lose. This predicament is similar to the one described by a set of psychologists: Obama's victory shows racial progress, but now support for Obama is being turned into a belief that racism is less of a problem in the United States today than it was in times past. The public has also expressed less support for policies designed to address racial inequality.[57]

When Obama calls attention to race or civil rights, however, he places himself in another predicament. Obama's approval rating dropped seven points among whites when he denounced the arrest of black Harvard professor Henry Louis Gates Jr. in his own home. This reaction prompted Obama to convene what he called a "beer summit" with Gates and the white arresting police officer, Sgt. James Crowley, meeting them at the White House.[58]

From a Crack House to the White House?

Few concepts have had as much influence since the 1980s as Foucault's notion of power/knowledge. In his view, power is wielded, exercised, but is neither good nor bad. It is hegemonic. Power/knowledge is contained within an institutional apparatus and its technologies, which, as Stuart Hall puts it, are inscribed in a power play. Prisons, armies, and hospitals are examples of such apparatuses where power plays in *Discipline and Punish*.[59]

Each locale or location exercises power differently. It depends on the *episteme*, or coordinates of knowledge, whether they are determined by a culture of doctors or scientists—who determine the best course of action and, therefore, give body to the exercise and play of power. In nineteenth-century French prisons, for example, the government adopted more humane measures of incarceration, making power more insidious and repressive than it had ever been under monarchial rule, despite the latter's use of torture and corporal power.

Like power/knowledge, race is a social and political construct. As Hall explains, race is no longer considered a scientific category. Race, as a discursive organizing category for exploitation and exclusion, is racism. The one-drop rule, developed by colonial empires, demonstrates this best. This rule claims to ground social and cultural differences in biological and genetic difference, whereas the so-called naturalizing effect makes race a scientific fact unresponsive to social engineering.[60]

It was at historically African American universities, such as Howard University, that Toni Morrison, the Nobel laureate for literature, wrote her first poems and Charles R. Drew taught medicine. Drew, who pioneered the classification of blood into categories and its collection and storage in blood banks, saved millions of lives with this discovery. Ethnicity, by contrast, is categorically different. Blood can be mixed. Kinship and intermarriage displace it.[61]

Until 1967, marriage between African Americans and any other ethnicity, white or Latina and Latino, was illegal in some states. The United States recognized the one-drop rule. But genetic difference became moot after the first two racial regimes ended. The first racial regime of slavery and chattel lasted until 1865, and then the second regime, the Jim Crow era, ended in 1967. In the third and fourth racial regimes, this social construction transformed regimes of social control. From the late 1960s onward, blackness became a "signifier of criminality." Racial profiling and "driving while black (DWB)" became a manifestation of this racial regime. Today, mass incarceration represents the last regime.[62]

All regimes serve the same purpose. As Foucault writes, "the actual roots of racism" are bound up in the nation-state's need "to use race, the elimination of races, and the purification of the race, to exercise its sovereign power." He goes on to write that racism is used "to take control of life, to manage it, to compensate for its aleatory nature, to explore and reduce biological accidents and possibilities." It provides rationalizations for exclusion.[63]

Racial profiling, then, as a manifestation of racism, is used to effect "racial purity" and control members of the non-normal (read African) who wander out of their geographically contained areas—urban ghettos. Their only crime is "driving while black." A heterogeneous racial society is complex and unpredictable; a homogeneous one is unified, and therefore simple and easy to survey and control.[64]

In addition to profiling, there is stereotyping, or what black feminist Patricia Hill Collins calls "controlling images." Stereotypes are crude generalizations and distortions that "so permeate the society that they are not noticed as contestable." The racist stereotypes about the Obamas during the 2008 election were manifold. They represented Obama as a "thug," the shiftless watermelon-loving, rib-eating wastrel, the "pimp," the "gangster," the "snob" or "uppity" one who does not keep to his assigned "place," the coon, the raging ranter who plays "the race card" as an excuse or diversion, and the violator of racist taboo who associates with white women.

Meanwhile Michelle Obama was typed as the "angry harridan" who cuts down her man. Fox News called her—a Princeton- and Harvard-educated lawyer who has been married to Barack Obama since 1992— "Obama's baby mama." No matter how "respectable," any black woman can be smacked back down to stereotypic ignominy. The "baby mama" label disgraces not only Obama's wife and the mother of his daughters, but all poor, single mothers deemed "illegitimate" by the sexual double or triple standard grounded in unjust systems of class, race, sex, and gender.[65]

Another common theme for stereotypes during Obama's campaign had to do with his mixed-race lineage. He was stereotyped as an "untrustworthy" and "unstable" mulatto, in a state and society that had derived the word "mulatto" from Latin, in which the word *mulus* means mule, "an animal produced from 'unnatural mating.'" In the nineteenth century, science classified "mulattos" as unnatural, describing them as "psychologically unstable and inferior to 'pure' Whites, although superior to 'pure' Blacks." They were also considered "immoral, criminal, sneaky, deceitful, and untrustworthy." One campaign button read, "Psychobama needs a shrink's office, not the oval office. Don't let this hater of his own whiteness set race relations back 100 years!"[66]

As a social construct, race is always changing. By giving constructionism a post-structural twist, however, one can emphasize social and interactional contacts. This social construct is based on contingency. To avoid essentialism, race as a social construct may reflect "the ambivalent complexity of lived experience," as one theorist explained.[67]

Obama himself understands that experience is partial, fragmented, and contradictory. Identification is always double-sided, involving one's relation to the "other." Social constructs result from this self/other double-sidedness rather than external differentiation. Who sees this more than Obama, who, as quoted earlier, sees being black as "unique and universal"? Obama believes there should be no a priori assumptions dictated by identity or ideology. To him, the term "unique and universal" means that race is neither natural nor neutral.[68]

Three Power/Knowledge Rules

Three rules help define power/knowledge and explain how race can be considered a similar construct. First, the repressive effects alone—racism—cannot be concentrated on. Race is a complex social function—a self/othering device that is practiced or exercised, is intersectional or crosscutting, and is not necessarily negative or repressive. Given that "the ascription of black hypermasculinity may have allowed Barack Obama to speak out against the Iraq war without being dismissed as being weak—at least in contrast to Hillary Clinton," Obama's race served a positive purpose.[69]

Second, race as a social construct is exercised within an institution. Understanding Obama ensconced within the presidency as an institution as well as within the executive branch helps us comprehend the irony of his success and the paradox of his failure. This institution depends on public opinion for legislative momentum.

Leadership, or what Paul Light called "going public," is how the executive branch wins people over.[70] It is standard wisdom that the White House leverages its power to persuade members of Congress to pass legislation. Given the two-year and six-year election cycles in the House of Representatives and the Senate, the president must wield public opinion to his advantage for successful legislative action. Elections are arguably less important than public opinion. Put differently, public opinion affects elections, and elections are a two-way street, reflecting presidential momentum in the midterm elections and presidential coattails during the presidential election.[71]

The Democrats suffered significant losses during the 2010 midterm elections, and the Tea Party was largely to blame for these losses. The Tea Party's attempts to shape the Republican Party show that the lens of race has become even more important. That lens also helps to explain how Obama fails to claim credit for his successful public policy program. The Tea Party sees Obama for the threat he poses—against white privilege and supremacy, or simply whiteness. The image of the black matriarch being displaced by omnipresent photos of the black nuclear family in the White House, complete with a new dog, helped spark the Tea Party. And contrary to all of the press's initial assumptions, the Tea Party were not poorly educated, unemployed Southern rednecks, but rather highly educated, gainfully employed, white middle-aged and older men.[72]

Nonetheless, mainstream academics and members of the press suggest that Obama lacks the power and capacity for self-sustaining leadership because he lacks "narrative," rather than because of the Tea Party. This statement is heard more from the Left than from the Right, more from the mainstream than from the fringe. "Why has the President never given major nationally televised speeches on the economy," Skocpol and Jacobs query, "and his overall recovery plan?"[73]

But Obama's presidency has been highly scripted. He used subtle symbols to celebrate the inauguration, like inviting the Tuskegee Airmen—the elite, segregated World War II corps—to join him. Obama has consistently brought a more diverse team and set of visitors to the White House than previous presidents. But most important is the consistency of Obama's thought, particularly in reaction to the different racial lens used to interpret his leadership.[74]

Third, power/knowledge gave Foucault the capacity to discover how the "soul" enters the scene of penal justice. The French inserted the soul by creating a legal practice premised on a corpus of scientific knowledge about punishment and incarceration. Experts delineated what was humane and inhumane treatment and showed how the body itself is invested in power relations. Similarly, using race as a social construct reveals how Obama threatens American society—not by passing more civil rights legislation or even by righting wrongs, but by stripping back the white veil covering the American state, economy, and society. And this book argues that both the Left and the Right—liberal Democrats and Republicans—judge his administration on the basis of race as a social construct, largely but not solely using a self/other distinction, "othering" Obama's leadership. It is scripting, the least offensive type of racial lens, and its self-regulating nature, which limits human capacity for deliberative thought and therefore deliberative democracy, that shows how race as a social construct enters the soul.

Scripting

The concept of scripts departs from profiling or stereotyping in that it requires those speaking to exercise self-discipline, and it lacks intent. Scripting means that a person, such as an employee, utters a dialogue constructed by someone else, such as her employer. Employers draft a dialogue to conform to a corporate vision, leaving space for the individual employee to give it her personal touch. Employees must buy into the corporate vision. The personal touch is secondary, requiring the employee to add a customer's name or providing for her age, or gender, to make the customer feel like she has been treated personally.

Scripting came into being with the standardization of the service sector in the late 1960s. It became a strategy for solving recurring service-oriented problems. Large companies began introducing speaking procedures (scripts) in response to liability fears. In places where formulaic interactions are routine, like McDonald's or other national fast-food chains staffed by low-skilled, low-waged workers with high turnover rates, scripting works well. Most employees, even those with little education, can memorize a script. McDonald's customers hoping to purchase the same food in Indiana as in California came to expect the comfort of scripting—standardized text with standardized food. By the 1970s other fast-food restaurants had adopted scripting, making it popular. In the

1990s Walmart carried scripting one step further in creating an entire position for it: the greeter.

Scripting not only keeps the employee from speaking with any intentionality or authenticity, but also contains an element of the idea that doing so is self-defeating; in Foucauldian terms, it is self-disciplinary. The person uttering the script lacks the power, the knowledge, the cultural socialization or sophistication, or the consciousness to understand that a script reflects corporate values. They do not have all the data produced by surveys and testing to know precisely how each text "scripts values." While most employees must realize that it deprives them of the freedom to interact with customers by restricting what they say, they do not usually understand the values underlying the text. But then, in accepting this corporate standard—the script—the employees normalize it. Performing the script is viewed simply as "part of their job." These employees do not ponder how this routinization, in "becoming normal," strips them, and the customers they serve, of the capacity for deliberation. Perhaps unconsciously or only tacitly, employees ingest and digest the corporate values underlying a script.

Scripting brought what others call a "production line" approach, or routinizing of customer interactions, into the service sector. Efficiency experts used technology to study patterns of interaction, which helped them to draft scripts and then determine their efficacy. To know what to expect is to anticipate the customers' needs and to avoid potential conflicts. National chains could collect large amounts of data, enlightening their employees about how most people will react to each part of the script. Knowing that customers might be persuasive and recolonize an employee, Bank of America, for instance, does not allow any one customer facing foreclosure or bankruptcy to deal with the same employee twice.

More often, however, scripting helps employees retain control of service. For example, most people will want to supersize a meal if the employee offers a bigger size of french fries at a specific point in the ordering script. The employee's very act of offering relieves the customer purchasing the meal from guilt about eating those extra calories. Indeed, consumer groups criticized the supersizing part of the McDonald's script on public health grounds. Rather than looking at the supersize decision on an individual-by-individual level—or, in other words, as an individual decision—these consumer groups turned the data against McDonald's to show the collective response. Most people do answer with "yes, supersize it" at this point in the script. The very fact of offering creates a public health hazard by contributing to obesity within society. Characterizing the offer this way—as corporate scripting—turned out to be a great consumer protection strategy. McDonald's agreed to take supersizing out of its script.

Scripting has also been described in management literature as a corporate "empowerment" approach. That is, management confers control over the work process by transforming the worker into one whose personal characteristics, appearance, and values match the image that the company is seeking to project and market. The employee undergoes a transformation. Once this transformation takes place, the company can allow the worker to make her own judgments in interactions with customers. Empowerment is a two-step process.[75]

Self-Scripting

What this two-step process does is create "self-regulation." Once the transformation has been made, and employees buy into corporate values, the data show that they start claiming the values as their own. But by claiming the corporate values as their own, workers are acting like managers. They are managers, however, who neither share managerial control nor receive managerial pay. Hence they have become self-regulated. Management control over self-regulated, empowered workers is inevitably more invasive of workers' private lives than any traditional form of supervision. Self-regulation alters employees' psychology as well as their souls.

One of the most vivid examples of scripting is contained in the recorded statement often played before a customer service representative answers a call, stating that "this phone call will be recorded to monitor for quality purposes." The recording of the employee giving her script serves three purposes. First, it collects data that can be used to monitor the employee for future disciplinary actions. Second, it provides data that will help the company to be more effective in selling customers merchandise or in serving them. Third, the recording creates evidence in case an employer would like to find a reason to terminate an employee. The salesperson must say everything in the script without a mistake. All the calls have been recorded, and the employer can sift through this mountain of evidence if it wants to terminate an employee for "good" cause.

Scripting creates a routine or procedure for how to speak. The scripted text remains flexible in that the employee plugs in the name, gender, and approximate age of a customer to add that personal touch, which makes it appealing to that customer. Scripting constitutes an oxymoron—it proceduralizes flexibility.

Scripting, Intersectionality, and Triple Consciousness?

Third-wave feminist Judith Butler cites Catharine MacKinnon's ideas about the "will of a masculine authority, and compelling a compliance with its command" as something similar to scripting. Scripting contains "performative" power. Through data-driven research, experts find ways to understand what part of the text can be routinized and what must remain flexible, knowing that the former 90 percent reflects corporate beliefs and values, whereas the last 10 percent is vital, yet superficial in terms of gaining customer support. It represents a scheme in which routine procedures can be modified to adapt to difficult or unusual problems.[76]

Legal education serves as an example. On the one hand, if law students are taught that every case should be approached as a unique problem or involves "open-ended lawyering," then these students will lack the efficient problem-solving skills necessary to engage in forward reasoning or backward reasoning to shore up their arguments with legal precedents. On the other hand, if a student approaches every case by following a routine script, she cannot learn how to solve difficult and ill-structured problems. Scripting, in other words, represents a balance between a performance that is entirely scripted—a routine performance—and one created for an individual purpose. Put differently, scripting creates a template that varies or is slightly altered for each person.[77]

Employment law takes this concept to a different and more cynical level. Since most civil rights law in the United States involves proving intent, scripts can be excised of intent. Researchers in corporate offices devise ways in which a script can still ensure an exclusionary goal without exposing intent, or intent at least on the part of those employees doing the performing. This strategy of disconnecting employee intent from corporate intent can be very effective in a society in which overt discrimination is no longer necessarily accepted. An employee free of personal animus can be more effective.

Given its capacity for crosscutting, scripting is similar to the theory of intersectionality first introduced by critical race theorist and third-wave feminist Kimberlé Crenshaw. Intersectionality accepts that racial discrimination, for instance, does not occur independently of the histories of gender or sexuality. In her classic piece on intersectionality, Crenshaw argues that a black woman is more than just the separate layerings of gender plus race. "An effort to develop an ideological explanation of gender domination in the Black community," she argues, "should proceed from an understanding of how crosscutting forces establish gender norms and how the conditions of Black subordination wholly frustrate access to these norms."[78]

Crenshaw scrutinizes what concepts of gender are dominant: How are race, class, and gender situated? Only after doing so can one study how gender and sex operate in tandem with histories of racial subordination. Gender, race, and class constitute crosscutting forces—norms—or unspoken values that then get embodied in a script.

Similarly, scripting is subtle. It is a notion akin to Du Bois's concept of the mechanization of race, and it takes into account double and even triple consciousness. Unlike other forms of discrimination, mechanization lacks intent. Similarly, identity scripts have stymied the communicative output of journalists and ordinary citizens. National Public Radio (NPR), for instance, featured two segments produced by "journalists of color" discussing how those journalists were "being held to a higher standard, where any hint of their positive reaction to the Obama campaign—even clapping when Obama enters the room—would be derided as black bias inherent in black identity."[79]

The harm is not the so-called higher standard, but rather that scripting creates "incentives for black journalists to excessively self-censor." They must overcompensate. "Identity scripts not only cause individuals to self-censor; they also warp conversations by distorting the way messages are received. These two dynamics are, of course, closely related."[80]

During the campaign Obama faced not just one, but a multitude of overlapping, sometimes crosscutting, and sometimes contradictory scripts. Besides "A More Perfect Union," a speech prompted by criticism of Rev. Jeremiah Wright, the pastor of Obama's predominantly black church, he rarely spoke about race. A desire to develop the broader public's interest in the issues may have been the primary motivation for his choice of issue framing. However, some commentators fear that there are issues disproportionately affecting communities of color that cannot be framed in ways that avoid explicit discussions of race—for example, the issue of race-based disparities in prison sentencing.[81]

If President Obama chooses not to engage with these issues for fear of being stereotyped—as opposed to some greater public policy rationale—deliberation is certainly stymied.[82] Note that it is not only pressures to conform to majoritarian norms that taint deliberation. Within minority groups, pressure to perform in-group identity scripts also stifles deliberation.[83] Cornel West's and Tavis Smiley's accusations, reviewed in an earlier chapter, about Obama not being black enough are applicable in this context. Civil rights critic Jacquelyn Bridgeman argues that in-group scripts often label those who fail to comply with their identity as "traitors" or "sell-outs."[84]

Scripting represents the most subtle, yet also the most invidious, form of discrimination. Unlike at McDonald's, there is no management; there is only "the American culture." It reflects the cultural aspects of race as a social construct for good and bad purposes. And most importantly, it offers great potential for self-regulation. Scripting shows how Foucault's power/knowledge notion can be applied to race. The dearth of caricatures of Joe Biden is further evidence of scripting whiteness.[85]

Five separate scripts have been applied to Obama:

Script 1: Blackness and Foreignness and Class

First, Obama's blackness casts doubt on his being "United States-ian." Born in Hawaii, the fiftieth and last state to enter the Union, in 1959, is Obama truly American? Being foreign-born would knock Obama out of eligibility for the presidency. No matter how many times experts fact-check this information, Obama's purported ineligibility, given his foreignness, keeps popping up.

This script stems from the larger script of African Americans being considered foreign by virtue of being African. It assumes that one's racial identity comes from one's local, national, and geographic ties to one's country. In this script, where one's birth takes place, to parents of what citizenship, as well as intergenerational continuity and the influences that face a child, all count. Here Obama fulfills each count as a foreigner, being, as he describes, "a black man with a funny name, born in Hawaii of a father from Kenya and a mother from Kansas."[86]

But Obama's own characterization of his grandmother's restlessness and discomfort with his blackness revealed how he went off in search of color. First, he immersed himself in the literature of W. E. B. Du Bois, Booker T. Washington, and Malcolm X. Second, Obama became a community organizer on the South Side of Chicago right after college, working not with prominent members of the civil rights movement, but rather with Saul Alinsky's organization. He sought to apply Alinsky's *Rules for Radicals* when he began organizing. Third, he married an African American woman, born of working-class parents who, as part of the Great Migration, had themselves been descendants of slaves. Finally, Obama sought "traditions associated with a local Black community," going so far as to become a regular member of Rev. Wright's largely black, evangelical church. This script includes the First Lady, Michelle Obama, and questions the "broader legacy of the historical, cultural, political, and economic status of Blacks."[87]

Meanwhile conservatives like Palin turn the blackness script into one of patriotism. For Palin, the United States, as a country, exists as an ideal. By focusing on it solely as an ideal, she demonstrates her patriotism, whereas Obama, she claims, does not. Obama's very reference to a "more perfect" union, Palin suggests, calls for improvement, and this very call shows that the United States is less than ideal. To Obama, this hope for improvement, itself reminiscent of Lincoln's second inaugural address, is evidence of his patriotism. "This union may never be perfect," Obama says, "but generation after generation has shown that it can always be perfected." It is the quest, the process, the journey, not the fiction that the United States embodies Palin's ideal, that Obama seeks.

The liberal progressive script of blackness as foreignness is expressed by Harvard professors Lani Guinier and Skip Gates as they compare a native-born black person from one of the Confederate states, who can trace her lineage to slavery, with an immigrant from Africa or the Caribbean. These two liberal law professors question affirmative action by exploring the intersection of race, class, and migration. Given that a disproportionate percentage of the blacks admitted to "elite" colleges are immigrants, those colleges' affirmative action policies might be "misdirected." American commentators rarely inquire more deeply into the racial experiences of black immigrants (beyond the observation that once they arrive in the United States they "learn" that they will be discriminated against by racists based on skin color).[88]

A final script about Obama's blackness and foreignness is emergent in the civil rights community's suggestion that Obama is not "black enough." During the campaign, some liberals were upset because of "the travesty that was the Obama campaign's response: that Obama was not now and had never been a Muslim." To be sure, Obama had muted his support for Muslims. The *New York Times* chronicled this phenomenon with an article headlined "Muslim Voters Detect a Snub from Obama." After Obama was elected, he changed his approach by publicly acknowledging his Muslim family members for the first time since the presidential campaign. Obama now offers a strong, resolute voice, arguing that "Muslims need not be feared." To Eddie Glaude, a Princeton professor of African American studies, "the question is then: How do African American communities engage issues in light of their particular experiences without being accused of pushing a racial agenda?"[89]

In April 2008 Tavis Smiley, a leading black commentator, abruptly left a popular morning show on Black Entertainment Television after criticizing Obama. At the time, host Tom Joyner told listeners that Mr. Smiley couldn't take "the hate" coming from listeners, who objected to his criticism. Further, prominent African American scholar Cornel West, asked if he would accept a White House post, responded with, "You find me in a crackhouse before you find me in the White House." West and other well-known African American public intellectuals repeatedly accused Obama of "playing" black people.[90]

There is a question as to whether Obama can represent the majority interests of African Americans—his people—given his blackness compounded by his duty to serve the entire nation. This criticism, one journalist claimed, plagues each and every person of color contemplating running for office. For instance, it plagued Secretary of State Colin Powell when he contemplated running for president in 2000.[91]

The theme in this blackness script is that as a non-Southern, multinational, multiracial person, Obama, like black immigrants, is supposed to be in "racial denial, with little or no understanding or empathy for the dynamics of U.S. racism." Alternatively, he is cast as one of the " 'racial traitors' (or 'sellouts') who affirmatively deny their Blackness and aspire to economic or social uplift through the assertion of group superiority to native-born Blacks."[92]

The nativist Right then embodies its hatred of Obama with its anti-immigrant rhetoric by making Arabs the face of its nativism. Its criticism of Obama for not being American suggests he is not just black, but also "brown." Obama was one of the "discursively brown people for whom citizenship is presumed to be an honor rather than a right, no matter what their legal status." The president's blackness—his African father and his self-identification as African American—made him vulnerable to being "crypto-Muslim."[93]

The discursive link between "black" and "Muslim" has multiple roots, including the religious identities of some enslaved Africans. With Malcolm X as its most famous and infamous member, Islam became a religious and political resource for many African Americans in the mid-twentieth century. Twenty percent of the Muslim population in the United States is African American. Aside from Arabs and Iranians, this makes African Americans, more than members of any other religion, more likely to "be kept in place by their 'Muslimization.' " Similarly, the traditional Muslim clothing in which one artist placed Barack Obama (who most often wore western suits on the campaign trail) was to be read as "potential Islamic terrorist." A photograph of Obama in a Kenyan ethnic group's traditional clothing was also deployed to support this physical appearance as racial/ethnic marker construct.[94]

Indeed, the Tennessee Republican Party put out a press release during the campaign with the headline "Anti-Semites for Obama." (A chain email in late 2007 had claimed that during Obama's Senate swearing-in ceremony, Obama supposedly "DID NOT use the Holy Bible. Instead, Obama used 'the Koran.'" The email then argued that after all, "the Muslims have said they want to destroy America from the inside out, what better way to start than at the highest level.")[95]

While this press release came out only in Tennessee, a Pew Research Center poll in September 2008 indicated that just 46 percent of Americans knew of Obama's Christian faith. While over 50 percent did not know his religion, 13 percent thought he was Muslim, whereas by November, 30 percent thought he was. Both Democrats and Republicans shared equally in this misperception.[96]

What is more, Hillary Clinton's campaign invoked Obama's Muslim identity during the primary numerous times. According to Lewis, "'Muslim' had become a separate, racialized category in post-9/11 America and there was a clear racist intersection for some between Obama's Blackness and his falsely perceived religious beliefs."[97] As Grant Farred, a Cornell Africanist, elaborated, Obama's middle name "'Hussein' so nicely evoked Saddam, the mad, evil Arab dictator repetition became a hope-against-hope inference that perhaps Obama *was* influenced by the fact that he has Muslim family members." Obama's name gave his opponents not just one, but two potential slurs, that "part of his family history lies in modern Africa, [and] that his first two names are Arab names as well—'Barack' (blessed) and 'Hussein' (the diminutive for one who is suitable, good, handsome). This repetition also intended to claim linkage." Only after former Secretary of State Colin Powell deconstructed the "Islamic beliefs equals terrorist beliefs" lie did this aspect of the "physical-image dirty-tricks game" become compromised in public opinion.[98]

Over the past forty years, there has been a significant decline in the proportion of Christians in the U.S. population, which dropped from 89 percent to 76 percent between 1969 and 2008. In part, the number of Muslims, Hindus, and Buddhists entering the United States accounts for this decline. Secularization accounts for another reason. The fastest growing group of people in these surveys is those who declare "no religion."[99]

And yet atheists—whom Obama identified with in his address in Cairo, claiming the United States is not a Christian nation, and has included in his Faith-Based Initiative—receive less support than any other group. Further, the seventh most common Obama-related search on the Internet, according to one critic, was Obama as "The Antichrist." Some critics argued that a McCain campaign advertisement, "The One," used coded words and images to send this frightening message to the faithful.[100]

Script 2: Blackness and Education

Second, Obama's blackness accounts for another script, though not about his foreignness as much as his education and how it transformed him, helping him rise to the upper class. Elitism was one of the biggest "charges" leveled against Obama after his "guns or religion" gaffe. His stellar educational record became a drawback—something one critic noted he had "to be careful to tone down or keep in check. He could not appear to be too 'uppity' after all." The mainstream liberal media portrayed this as a "class war"; supposedly Obama could not be in touch with the poor and the working-class people. But of course, a racial layer lurked underneath this "class war" allegation. Would Obama, "the newly-anointed, 'successful' Black, 'sell out' his (rarely her) less fortunate Black brothers and sisters?"[101]

At one point during the campaign, Obama tried to turn this correlation about education and African Americans around. "Why, he asked, had it suddenly become a bad thing for an African American man running for the Presidency to have attended and performed well at top-ranked schools? Didn't Americans want an educated and highly-skilled president?" Perhaps they did not. As a critic observed, Obama, with his Ivy League education, threatened "the sometimes overt, sometimes subconscious sense that class hierarchies are also supposed to be constrained by race."[102]

What white public opinion missed here is that many African Americans see education as a "pathway to power or resistance to racism." Parents sacrifice their own self-interest, working very hard to ensure that their children can attain educational distinctions they did not receive. Obama described his mother's determination that he succeed in school in *Dreams from My Father*. Michelle Obama's brother, Craig Robinson, described the same spirit. American capitalism complicates this aspiration. As Lewis underscores, "How is it possible to be proud of high educational achievement at elite mainstream or historically-Black schools and the economic class mobility gained thereby, while at the same time remaining true to the interests and needs of the majority of Blacks?"

Given segregation, your success leads to your alienation, since you join the all-white elite.[103]

Script 3: One-Drop Rule

A third script involves Obama's blackness as appearance or "biology." A study in early 2008 found that imagery depicting African Americans as apelike had largely disappeared in the United States. Obama's run for the presidency revived it. For instance, Mike Norman, a white Georgian, produced and sold a T-shirt with Obama as the children's-book character Curious George peeling a banana. Another company created an Obama monkey plush toy. When the toy met with public outcry, the toymakers initially yanked it, but then they reinstated it. They defended the "toy," arguing that it was "affectionate," like a teddy bear. Their intent, they insisted, had been to "transcend still existing racial biases," not provoke them.[104]

Equating African Americans with monkeys had the capacity to backfire in public opinion. At the end of the nineteenth century, social scientists concocted pseudo-biological categories that classified anyone with identifiable African ancestry as "Black" or "Negro." In the early 1920s this became legally and socially consolidated into a rule—the one-drop rule. This rule was initially intended to police intended white racial "purity."[105]

Obama's mixed ancestry did not provoke overt discrimination about his being black as much as it generated a "new uncertainty about blackness." Unlike children with two African American parents, who if "light-skinned" reminded African Americans that white slaveholders and other white men had sexually exploited African American women, Obama's mother's being white made his ancestry visible. Public accounts of Obama's life, in addition to his own memoir, accounted for his whiteness. As one academic described, "No public figure, not even Tiger Woods, has done as much as Obama to make Americans of every education level and social surrounding aware of color-mixing in general and that most of the 'black' population of the United States, in particular, are partially white."[106]

What gave even more literal meaning to blackness was Obama's wife, Michelle, whose parents were descended from slaves. The *New York Times* turned Michelle Robinson Obama's lineage into a front-page feature story tracing her ancestors. The publication of the article itself caused controversy. Some questioned whether Michelle Obama's physical blackness would be interpreted as making her appear "too an-gry." They celebrated perceived "makeovers" in her physical or social style that offset her blackness.[107]

A completely different reason why the blackness story became so im-portant was that "over one-third of African Americans doubt that the black population of the United States is any longer a single people." A 2007 Pew Research Center story indicated that black immigrants and their children are "overrepresented by several hundred percent among the black freshmen at Ivy League colleges." This population and their offspring do better in terms of education and socioeconomic status than the descendants of American slavery and Jim Crow.[108]

Blackness, these studies demonstrate, is not monolithic, and their re-sults "question the credibility of blackness as our default standard for identifying the worst cases of inequality, and for serving as the focal point of remedies." Indeed, in *The Minority Rights Revolution*, sociolo-gist John Skrentny argues that there was (in David Hollinger's words) a "largely unconscious step driven by the unexamined assumption" that conflated Asian Americans, Latinos, and American Indians, making them disadvantaged "like blacks." Were these non-descendants of slaves as deserving as blacks? Were Caribbean Americans or African immi-grants as deserving as African Americans?[109]

The twist is that Obama himself, like many light-skinned or bira-cial blacks, could and did choose blackness. Obama could have cho-sen "whiteness." Then, the question became, having chosen blackness, could a black president represent "all" people? Some within and out-side the campaign insisted Obama "transcend[ed] race." Others posed the more challenging question: "Could Blackness ever 'represent' all the people?"[110]

Americans have come to see white male status as a background norm against which candidates for the presidency are to be measured. But blackness as a social, political, and cultural concept raised widespread fears that it could represent only "special interests" that were threat-ening to the interests of the mainstream. The authenticity of Obama's stance on blackness, however, preoccupied only the white majority. Al-most all black voters dismissed the discussion about Obama's choices.

Script 4: The Culture of Blackness

A fourth script makes blackness a "cultural essence." One must belong to the "right Black church," listen to the right music of "New Orleans jazz, West Coast and French hip-hop, and South African reggae," watch "the right sport (basketball)," and utter "the right phrases and pop culture references." To be sure, both the Obamas received intense scrutiny for the "right" cultural signifiers.[111]

Turning black into a cultural essence creates a positive script. It redefines blackness as a cultural and a political commitment that involves fighting racism and achieving social justice in a rainbow coalition. It shows appreciation for African and Diaspora cultures and a willingness to learn about them and engage in cross-cultural dialogues. The concept of diversity began with the idea of blackness as cultural essence. From a strategic perspective, blackness or race cannot include everything, but it must be inclusive and flexible in order to remain viable and politically, culturally, and economically useful.[112]

But blackness as cultural essence had a dark side. Spatially, the choice of the ghetto turned it into a "product" and a "source of violence." Nowhere was this better expressed than in the controversy over a poster in which someone turned Shepard Fairey's iconic image of Obama into Heath Ledger's 2008 characterization of the Joker in *The Dark Knight*. Ledger's carnival-like mask, with its smeared war paint, signaled a change in the Joker's inner mechanism. "What had been a caricature became more real and threatening. An urbane mocker of civilized values became simply a deformed product of urban violence." By superimposing President Obama's face over the word "socialism," this anonymous Los Angeles poster "delights and distresses people roughly on the lines of the usual political cleavage." The poster had "two basic thrusts": Obama is "a crypto-socialist"; and he is "unpredictable and dangerous . . . like the Joker." Along spatial lines, this poster identified Obama "with the inner city, a source of political instability in the 1960s and 1970s," all the while making him "a lingering bogeyman in political consciousness despite falling crime rates." As a human rights organization reported, none of this showed how to "engage racial complexity without being threatened by it."[113]

Script 5: Scripting Gender

Finally, misogyny scripts blackness. Not all black male gender stereotypes disserved Obama. On the gender front, "Obama's presidential bid likely would not have succeeded had he not rejected that ascribed script [of hypermasculinity] by adopting a campaign tone that was unusually soft and reconciliatory for male politicians. Unlike white male politicians, Obama faced incentives to mute masculine traits." Obama could look tough on foreign policy, even with his opposition to the American war in Iraq, because of his blackness.[114]

During the campaign, T-shirts and buttons conveyed multiple incendiary meanings in one-liners. For instance, "I wish Hillary had married O. J." suggests she be battered and murdered, while "implicitly sideswiping" Obama, since the same image invokes the stereotype that equates "Black men (now including previously liked and trusted Black men) with brutes who menace White womanhood and Whites in general."[115]

Some conservative critics attempted to "other" both Democratic candidates simultaneously. One T-shirt succeeded with the phrase "Welcome to the Freak Show." One side showed what a commentator described as "a grimacing, shifty-eyed and shadowy Barack Obama," while the other side pictured "a crazed-looking and wildly laughing Hillary Clinton." Those who study the historical freak show suggest that its purpose was to make entertainment out of constructing, propagating, and reinforcing the "norm"—powerful white heterosexual Christian men of European lineage, who are well educated and financially flush. The norm is "stamped with an essence." By definition it must be taken for granted, invisible. As either other or deviant, freaks are "inferior, irrational, unintelligent, uncivilized, frightening or deficient."[116]

Pundit Paradox and Disappointed Liberals

Pundits and the public alike kept remarking that Obama's election showed tremendous racial progress. Who discovered this first? Obama, of course. Tackling racism poses a Catch-22 for the president. He has been boxed in by a less visible sort of racial stereotype, that of "the good one"—the black person white people love to love because loving him proves that there is "no hatred in our hearts." This status depends on the anointed black person remaining "above" race at all costs.[117]

Yet even if he wanted to, the president cannot remain apart from racialized frays; they are too much part of our domestic life. If Obama attempts to address real racial disparities, he risks being perceived as having broken the covenant of the "post-race" ideal. He will be accused of "playing the race card" or "reverse racism." Not only is he a "racist" by this measure; he is constantly compared with Hitler, Stalin, and Osama bin Laden. Patricia Williams, a Columbia law professor, wrote: "It's a truly perplexing development: fear of 'the black man' has been seamlessly flipped from nightmares about the rebellious dispossessed thug, to those of the too-powerful, much-too-smart-for-his-own-good, oppressively dispossessing autocrat. Indeed, in the alternative universe of Fox

News, President Obama is the new face of racism itself, a man who supposedly hates white people and is out to take away their guns, indoctrinate their children, and kill old people."[118]

From the beginning, the *New Republic* stated that white people's support for Barack Obama stems from a sense of misplaced guilt. But after his major speech on race during the primaries, when he disavowed the inflammatory rhetoric of his minister, he avoided overt discussion of the issue. His rare references to his background were usually subtle and framed as a message about America as a place of opportunity. Since becoming president, he has not talked much about discrimination or disparities.[119]

To some critics, Obama's focus on themes of racial harmony, postpartisan conciliatory politics, and accommodationist strategies seems relatively ineffectual compared with more radical and systematic transformations to reduce structural inequities, yet the configurations for change are constrained by the need to work within administrative parameters based on a market-dominated political economy.

The fear among activists and advocates was that Obama's historic election would undermine their efforts, such as the struggle for affirmative action programs and antiracism campaigns, since racial equality and balance had supposedly been achieved. "Closer to home, taken to its extreme in university settings, the postracial paradigm makes ethnic studies and Asian American studies obsolete, since racial differentiation becomes passé. In a time of racial unity and a black family in the White House, those who believe we only teach about racial victimization or racial separatism will argue this becomes meaningless and counterproductive to creating 'one America.' In these trying budgetary times when universities are facing severe cutbacks, ethnic studies programs on various campuses are vulnerable to dismantling, consolidation, reduction, or elimination."[120]

In this postracial narrative, we can acknowledge race or multiraciality and consider it a discernible asset, in this case symbolizing how a nation moves beyond its racist past. This postracial script is reminiscent of and reaffirms the palatable and celebratory brand of multiculturalism, which is devoid of historical context and ignores the complex ways in which racism is embedded in our society. It reflects, in some respects, the way a color-blind society would supposedly operate, by flattening out racial difference. Thus, in this scenario, race is no longer "a central axis of social relations," as articulated by Michael Omi and Howard Winant, but neither does it decline in significance. It becomes neutralized, developing basically into a nonentity, symbolically represented by traditionally red states that supported a "black" man for president.[121]

In contrast, critical race theorist and *Nation* columnist Patricia Williams reminds us of the everyday "quiet racism" that continues to permeate our society, underscoring the elusiveness of a color-blind fantasy. The pervasive racial subtext that reflects residual racial tensions persists; for example, as the national health-care reform debate unfolded, resolute critics conjured up the specter of "illegal" immigrants, presumably from south of the border, becoming freeloaders at the cost of deserving legal beneficiaries.[122]

In short, in 2012, some Americans feel that because some people of color have "made it," racial barriers to opportunity have been eliminated. In the view of this group, any remaining inequality is due largely to a lack of personal responsibility. This argument is flawed because while there has been racial progress, it is not as broad or as deep as postracialists assert. In addition, postracialists view the data separately from the historical and contemporary contexts in which they exist, thereby masking the need to examine the larger structural forces fueling disadvantage.

Obama moves back and forth between images of "more black than we thought" and "not as black as we thought." "When, prior to Wright's having persisted in outrageous public behavior, Obama defended Wright's ministry, there was some buzz that he was farther to the black side of the color spectrum than his previous image had been. Once he renounced Wright, exited from Wright's congregation, and increased the frequency with which photographs of his white grandparents were displayed, there was some buzz that he was farther on the white side of that spectrum than some had supposed. These oscillations do not mean that Obama is lacking in authenticity; they mean that once his blackness is destabilized, it can intensify or diminish in a variety of contexts, including trivial ones."[123]

7

The Prius Presidency: A "Paramount Empire of Reason"?

Obama's failures in leadership can be accounted for in terms of the productivity of race, or racial scripts. Another contributing factor, difficult to disentangle from how Obama's identity influenced his leadership, is the content of his public policy program. But how we perceive Obama depends on *who* we *are*, or our own identity, as discussed in chapter 6. We project our identities onto this president, since the multiplicity of his identity gives us so many ways to relate to him, as well as to reject him.

This final chapter looks through a deliberative democratic lens at how Obama has succeeded as a leader by promoting public reason in health care, immigration, and education. It shows how he has applied his own inductive logic of congruence and consilience, and how he tipped the balance toward passage of the Affordable Care Act. It also explores how both Race to the Top and Obama's implementation of the No Child Left Behind Act have helped foster productive forms of diversity and inclusion as they try to close the education gap correlated with race, ethnicity, place, and income. Finally, this chapter reviews how two very different social movements—the Tea Party and Occupy Wall Street—reacted to some of Obama's public policy reforms.

This chapter will argue that Obama achieved his greatest leadership success by using conservative *means* for progressive *ends*. Obama is only the second Democratic president since World War II to succeed in applying conservative tactics and strategies. While Republican leaders have profited from developments since the 1970s—manifested in a myriad of electoral blowbacks, reversals, and turnarounds associated with multiculturalism, multilateralism, and identity politics—Democratic leaders have had more difficulty gaining public opinion traction. Affirmative action for the rich, corporate welfare, or even the legacy admissions practices largely associated with elite private universities never gained much status as electoral issues in the 1980s, the 1990s, or after the millennium. And when Clinton tried to use the Bible for progressive purposes with his "new covenant," first introduced in his 1993 inaugural address, the attempt fell flat.

What differentiates Obama's conservatism from Clinton's "third way" or "New Democratic" conservatism is his emphasis on process and procedure. This emphasis is progressive, reflecting his politics of difference, universal anti-universalism, civic religion, multilateralism, cosmopolitanism, deliberative democracy, and increased political participation. Yet Obama's conservatism rings true, given his belief in righteousness and responsibility, which stems from the Hebraic Bible's Old Testament.

As many scholars and journalists have observed, Obama identifies with Joshua's exodus, rather than that of Moses. As the story goes, Joshua's exodus symbolizes Obama's success in taking one step out of the ring so he can duck direct punches. Obama avoids direct conflicts, or even rhetorical confrontation, with white people. For this reason, Obama is not seen as promoting identity politics, since he's not associated with directly combating racism.

Obama also uses inductive reasoning so that he does not have to "name names." He takes one step beyond consilience and congruence, as defined and discussed throughout this book, by seeking the common good, common ground, and common solutions. Yet do all of Obama's "commons" create *a* commons? He does not seek anything common, as a technocrat would. Nor does he equate the common good with a universal truth, or with the Enlightenment. What defines Obama is his hybrid, multiracial, multiethnic identity, an identity so complex, as articulated throughout the book, that it makes him identity-less.

What determined Obama most was his chosen profession as a grassroots organizer and his experience as a professor of civil rights law. Ironically, the United States' first black president is identified by what he *does*, not *who* he is. Obama, as a critical thinker and an optimistic realist, has a rare worldview. He is not an idealist. Because of his work at the local community level in grassroots organizing, Obama understands how to use real-world power; he appreciates and works within political and economic institutional limits and constraints; and he navigates American social and cultural norms, customs, and practices well.

Americans, Obama maintains, can strive toward perfection while understanding that perfection is beyond their grasp, on earth or in heaven. "We do not have to think that human nature is perfect," he said, "for us to still believe that the human condition can be perfected." Obama's worldview underscores his visceral or emotional understanding of existentialist Jean-Paul Sartre's definition of hell in the 1944 play *No Exit* ("Hell is other people!"). Unlike most Americans, Obama expresses little faith that heaven is much more than what is described in Paul Bowles's 1949 book *The Sheltering Sky*. We can have heaven on earth as long as we are protected from foreign peoples and their environs. We cannot afford to be unprepared or naïve as we progress through the wilderness as pioneers like Crèvecoeur, who must be prepared to carry *enough* provisions to cross through deserts and mountain passes.[1]

Reasoner in Chief

To analyze Obama's leadership, one must first ask: Did Obama "do the right thing" in privileging the Affordable Care Act over economic recovery? Did he do the right thing in prioritizing health care over a jobs bill or a historic chance to nationalize the banks, which would have forever changed the face of capitalism and neoliberalism? Will the healthcare plan last? Will it be a legislative achievement akin to Medicaid and Medicare, with collective memory fading about the fuss made by hospitals that refused to desegregate in order to receive funds? Was it temporarily stalled and stymied? Does the individual mandate clause in the Affordable Care Act, ground in the federal government's taxation powers, undermine his pivotal public-policy achievement?[2]

According to one view, when Obama tried following Rahm Emanuel's advice to compromise, negotiate deals, and "sweat the small stuff," premised on Arthur Schlesinger's honeymoon argument that no "serious crisis" should "go to waste," he squandered his resources on health care in a fight that almost failed, all while a recession was raging. The title of liberal political journalist Ron Suskind's book *Confidence Men: Wall Street, Washington, and the Education of a President* says it all: The first African American president lacked experience—he is the performer, but not the audience, let alone the writer or the director behind this experimental theater. Illustrative of Aristotle's notion of "dramatic irony," this view is patronizing.[3]

Or, relying on Richard Wolffe's less racially imbued images, the president is neither a "survivalist" nor a "revivalist," but rather is both. Health care, being Obama's signature issue, constituted the "heart of the American Dream." After noting that presidents had been working on health-care reform for "nearly a century," Obama labeled the American health-care system "our collective failure," claiming it "has led us to the breaking point." Obama inspires strong reactions as either a saint or a traitor, when he is neither. Obama is true to himself, or authentic.[4]

Jonathan Alter's *The Promise: President Obama, Year One* is the book Obama authorized to describe his first 100 days. As Alter wrote, Obama recognized hope, and he needed to deliver on his "promise." "A large portion of the citizenry had lost faith in the capacity of government to solve problems. . . . Obama's ability to tap into feelings of both hopelessness with the present state of affairs and hope for the future" was complicated. Obama argued that "no reasonable person" would support "the continuation of a health-care system that covers so few at such high cost with such bad outcomes." Economist Jeff Madrick phrased it succinctly in making the case *for* government: not big government, *a* government.[5]

Speaking before Congress on September 9, 2009, Obama said, "When any government measure, no matter how carefully crafted or beneficial, is subject to scorn; when any efforts to help people in need are attacked as un-American; when facts and reason are thrown overboard and only timidity passes for wisdom, and we can no longer even engage in a civil conversation with each other over the things that truly matter . . . at that point we don't merely lose our capacity to solve big challenges. We lose something essential about ourselves." One of Obama's early biographers said it was "the biggest speech of Obama's presidency."[6]

But what constituted the tipping point? Was it this speech in September, the health-care summit a year later, or the bipartisan meeting six months in between? During the health-care summit, Secretary of Health and Human Services Kathleen Sebelius put health-care providers, such as the AMA, "big pharma," and insurance companies, in an awkward position. She did it in part because Emanuel had encouraged the president to make sidebar deals with so many members of Congress that a number of commentators have pointed out that "health-care reform" is a misnomer, since the result was really health insurance reform.[7]

And it was at that summit that Obama reframed the terms of the debate on the Affordable Care Act, making it the outcome of deliberation that could be both congruent and consilient. Rather than jumping in again and again—being resilient—Obama believes we can reject false choices. As one rhetorician puts it, Obama's capacity to cultivate "public reason" contributed to the act's passage. He juxtaposed his health-care plan with the Christian fundamentalist, antigovernment Republican absence of a plan. He finally convinced Congress and the public that the spending of 17 percent of American GDP on private health care could be made public. As Geithner put it in a similar situation, "Plan beats no plan."[8]

In Obama's view, the Republicans in Congress and members of the health-care industry—physicians, nurses, executives in "big pharma" and health insurance companies—were *dis*honest. They colluded, engineering an *in*authentic debate that instilled fear. They knew that Americans feared higher costs and a loss of control over their physical and mental well-being and that of their loved ones. These special interests and antigovernment advocates manufactured a line of argument in an attempt to foster the emotion of fear about the Affordable Care Act. They concentrated on "achieving a short-term political goal" that could overwhelm rational deliberation or reason. They "counterfeited" public opinion. But Obama, in the words of James Madison, had faith that "over the long run . . . cool and calculated, rational argument would win out over passion and hyperbole," and that through ongoing public debate, the nation could "erect over the whole, one paramount Empire of reason."[9]

Obama's approach was grounded not in the belief that public policy could be based on positivistic scientific truth, but rather in a faith in the process of authentic debate, in which all sides would strongly argue for positions based on their best rational understanding of the issues. This is Madison's faith, translated by Hannah Arendt's inter-est, as explained in earlier chapters. Not everybody knows what they need or what self-interest they should maximize.[10]

Scholars will dispute for many years to come whether the Affordable Care Act is a glass half full or a glass half empty. What we do know is that the ideas in Obama's September 2010 speech at the health-care summit show a slightly seasoned president expressing his ideas better than he did in September 2009.[11]

The State of the State

Obama's leadership during his first term—as scrutinized by the Christian Right, the big-money Right, tennis-shoe Republicans, liberals, progressives, and those Democrats to the left of progressives or social activists—will generate scholarship for decades to come. What's clear is that much of the discourse about health care, the stimulus package, climate control, and financial regulation fell short of the kind of deliberative democracy outlined by political theorists.

All of Obama's legislative achievements—not just health care—depend on the same porous, progressive state scaffolding that involves a multitude of players. The charges of leadership failure to which Obama is most vulnerable are that he disappointed voters by being "professorial," distant, and technocratic. Emanuel's hard-nosed Chicago style supposedly saved Obama from being the "next Jimmy Carter," meaning a technocratic micromanager who does not fit in well with the Washington establishment because of how naïve, inexperienced, and idealistic he is, but there were some features of old-style politics that Obama could not overcome. "The Republicans had decided even before Obama was sworn in that they would use the rules to deny him success on every major issue," political journalist Elizabeth Drew observed. "Such obduracy was without precedent in modern times."[12]

The Affordable Care Act passed, and by being inclusive rather than exclusive, it served more than a procedural or strategic purpose, as observed in chapter 4. Obama operates on the basis of full inclusion with respect for reasoned argument, and like a grassroots organizer, he relies on the realism of working with available resources, knowing that neither Congress, the federal courts, nor K Street have engaged in an "authentic" or "reasonable" or "fair" dialogue, but instead preach fear and prey on voter apathy, indifference, and ignorance. He opened up the legislative process not merely to win passage of the Affordable Care Act, but because of his own logic. To Obama, that "last 10 percent of the way" logic—what reason gives people—is all that is needed to find common solutions.

Obama has embodied the Joshua exodus myth since getting into state politics, arguably even since law school. Obama has delivered the same message almost without fail since 2004: that inclusivity or diversity brings new people with fresh ideas into the deliberative decision-making process. If two sides agree on a common good, then we will discover that two sides (or three or more) make this common good double (or triple) fudge. Obama offers inductive logic—killing two birds with one stone is efficient. The deliberative process is a win-win-win. That is, it achieves the desired outcome, it is efficient, *and* it co-opts or shames the players, ensuring future cooperation.

Obama may be "professorial," but he does a few things that are unusual for professors: he listens before, during, and after his own lectures, and he does not mind taking political risks or failing. As Remnick notes, Obama is not an ideologue. He is not a technocrat. Rather, Obama practices pragmatism by defining ideas through action. He is a functionalist—someone who learns by doing, not by being or experiencing something. He stands above shame, not above ideas. Obama understands the random ripple effects that are caused by this type of action, or by doing, failing, and doing again. He embraces the logic of not deducing one's ideas from one origin or static pool of ideas.

But what Remnick gets wrong is his claim that Obama is a consensus seeker. In fact, he seeks *resolution*, not conflict or consensus. As with his justification for diversity with civil rights—Obama believes that inclusivity alone frees a debate—it is the participants who bring fresh ideas to the deliberative process. But there is emancipatory potential only *if* decisions are the "object of free and reasoned agreement among equals."[13]

Obama believes in deliberative democracy as a practice and as an ideal—he endorses process, proceduralism, and a progressive product, as a goal and as a method. Obama is mischaracterized as an Aristotelian technocrat who privileges process over content. Similarly, he has been miscast as a Platonic naïve idealist who promotes enlightenment as the antidote to ignorance, discrimination, prejudice, and parochialism. In fact, Obama has a Spinozan worldview that accepts and understands evil, but embraces the perfectibility of humankind.

Obama envisions a state that facilitates freedom and mediates equality of opportunity and earned egalitarianism rather than acting as a supreme authority or benign sovereign. He believes in survivability on the basis of aspiration, not achievement. Achievements are completed. Being finished deprives them of movement, whereas aspirations constitute continual movement or perpetual motion. Aspirations represent our potential. The United States is committed to its people's aspirations, but not because of paternalism, maternalism, or any form of benevolence that will undermine individual autonomy.

Obama embodies the third American political tradition not simply because he harks back to Thomas Jefferson's ideal of a small state filled with gentlemen farmers. Rather, he is a proponent of "buy local and think global"—of being a cosmopolitan with no Rawlsian liberal private/public distinctions, embracing an interdependent, complex whole.[14]

Obama believes that local participants represent action on the ground by virtue of their experience. Obama applies an experiential epistemology in advancing his Spinoza-Hegel-Du Bois-Arendt-Dewey-Alinsky-Niebuhr lineage. At the same time, he supports global ideas, based on his faith that only the best beliefs, values, and ideas will resonate across world cultures. In his view, neoliberalism, or American proprietary capitalism or imperialism, cannot be held accountable for Africans, South and Central Americans, Asians, or Middle Easterners drinking the political, economic, and social culture of Coca-Cola. This soda is not about American dominance, or its economic or cultural imperialism. Coca-Cola-ization tastes good to peoples from all five continents.

Obama is a cosmopolitan deliberative democrat who has progressive ideals and advances concentric circles of governance—the view that government should be involved in promoting citizen diplomacy found on the twin-towns and sister-cities level.[15] Not surprisingly, the Obama state is a federalist state that facilitates public policies derived from the common, though not necessarily the public, good. And Obama's foreign policy emanates humility. He no longer privileges the United States among other nation-states, let alone Western or Christian nation-states.[16]

Americans are the chosen people because we chose a sound and stable style of governance that promotes inclusivity, uniqueness, innovation, and ingenuity. The strength of our identity is the absence of an identity. There is no supremacy. The humility within Obama's foreign policy of multilateralism demonstrates this, as does his belief in civic religion or cultural pluralism. To Obama, the whole world should *aspire* to democratization and Americanization, not because we are a superior people, a wealthy people, but because we are a staid, stable, secure people who understand aspiration.

What happens when China, Brazil, or India becomes as wealthy as the United States? What happens when they reduce their income inequality and a more healthy polity emerges? If the middle class represents the state of aspiration for all people—democracy is middle class—then what happens to U.S. economic and military superiority? Obama hopes to change the machinery—to open up the process enough so that the international *demos* reflects difference, but not so much that American dominance declines. Obama thinks China and Southeast Asia threaten long-term U.S. interests more than the Middle East, Africa, or South America. He fears the success of Asia, not the failure of the suppression of religious fundamentalism. Obama is not a global economic declinist.

Obama is a reformer—a reformer who uses the political and economic institutional resources before him. The United States may never adopt climate change remedies or financial regulations that end pollution, promote universal well-being, or eliminate the excesses of capitalism. Nonetheless, Obama's type of Spinozan governance, or progressive federalism, represents our aspiration toward progress and our desire for perfectibility. Before delivering his inaugural address in 2009, Obama met with a number of journalists with conservative outlooks at George Will's house. Michael Barone, David Brooks, Charles Krauthammer, William Kristol, Lawrence Kudlow, Rich Lowry, and Peggy Noonan all came out to greet him on a chilly night. Obama hoped he could persuade them that he wanted "an end to the petty grievances and false promises, the recriminations and worn-out dogmas that for far too long have strangled our politics" (as he said in his 2009 inaugural address). It was Obama's nod to Jeffersonian statesmanship.[17]

As the 2012 election approached, Obama hoped to set a similar tone for the campaign, being presidential and again a statesman, above politics. When he took the Republicans to task, it was for being partisan, putting their electoral fortunes ahead of the country's needs. The GOP's response indicated their understanding that the race card would be a wild card. Ironically, this card morphed, getting transformed into an identity politics Obama could handle. A "war on women" went viral that spring. Obama has no problem defending women, who are more likely to vote for him and any Democrat than for any Republican, given the GOP's conservatism on this issue. And, as explained in chapter 3, Obama's positions on gender and sexuality help him cement a winning cultural coalition, one that challenges neotribalism as he stands up to those seeking relief from a conservative Supreme Court that seats no Protestants for the first time in its history. Will these justices identify with the expansive role religious institutions have played as a secondary social welfare state or charity state? Or will Obama limit the role of religion or convince those advocating for Christianity to relax its official position on abortion by restricting the churches' state action in schools and hospitals?

The Roberts court granted a broad ministerial exception to equal employment practices to those in charge of religious schools, as explained in chapter 3, preventing teachers from finding relief under civil rights law. In granting this exception, the court maintained that religious organizations did not have to follow federal laws. The unexpected battle over the constitutionality of health care put Obama in a similar position. But here, instead of battling for employment rights for a few, Obama is defending the reproductive rights of women and children, a divisive issue that concerns many. No matter which institution prevails with the policy, the Supreme Court or the executive branch, Obama is now the embodiment of a cultural transformation in the United States. Over the last twenty years, the United States has become a secular nation, and it has become less oppressive in terms of gender and sexuality rights.

Obama extends civic religion, contesting the idea of the United States as a Christian nation, all the while chastising the conservative Right. Even the moderate third-way Clinton Democrat E. J. Dionne insists that a Catholic Spring is under way, as "the vast majority of the nation's 195 dioceses did not go to court" over the mandate for employers to cover contraception in their health plans. If the United States breaks out into a full-fledged cultural cleavage, then the Democrats have finally found a foothold in the culture wars. But, in contrast to the 1980s, the Democrats are winning. The United States is not only less religious, but it is also less homophobic and more accepting of all peoples and all rights, including the rights of the transgendered. The former "moral majority" is now a minority.[18]

W(h)ither Deliberative Democracy?

The Tea Party was one of the earliest and angriest movements to spring up in response to Obama's new style of governance, as his progressive agenda understandably struck fear in defenders of the old white, male, Christian, heterosexual order. Yet it's not just the Right that has found Obama unsatisfactory. Ironically, Obama's worldview, a philosophy dedicated to inclusion, has found critics on all parts of the political spectrum, with leftists disappointed at the slow pace and less-than-sweeping changes that are inevitable features of a consultative system as well as angry over Obama's not being an economic reformer, while those in the middle who have grown comfortable with the Beltway consensus are alarmed at having their world shaken up.

Just as Ronald Reagan, the former Screen Actors Guild president, inspired fierce opposition from unions, Barack Obama, the former community organizer, has seen two grassroots organizations, the Tea Party and Occupy Wall Street, become serious social movement forces. The Tea Party sought exclusion of immigrants through strong state action. It also sought and gained sixty-six seats in Congress. Obama met this challenge by trying, and failing, to seize control of immigration as an issue for the Democrats to own.

Meanwhile the image propagated by Occupy Wall Street of "the 99 percent"—who are excluded from the vast wealth of the super-rich 1 percent—captured the public imagination. Staging demonstrations and setting up encampments across the nation, Occupiers relied on "open mike" assemblies to call for a new process and public participation. Yet by consciously deciding against making specific concessions and demands, the Occupiers lost their focus. Public officials in Oakland, Davis, and New York, among other localities, cleared the encampments and contained the demonstrations. Without the pressure of demands or disruptions, national, state, and local officials remained free from the need to make any political choices. Occupy Wall Street all but disappeared, becoming a rallying cry or a distraction for anarchists, the long-term unemployed, and the homeless. "As the widely anticipated May Day demonstrations and NATO protests came and went, general interest in Occupy has remained at a low simmer," one reporter noted, and "activists are looking beyond the 'Occupy' label that some feel has boxed in the movement—if it was ever a 'movement.' "[19]

This chapter argues, first, that the Tea Partiers, being seated in government, are bogged down by the rules of governing in the face of national elections and are no longer as free as they were in terms of social movement mobilization. Second, with Occupy Wall Street posing only a vague threat to the 1 percent, it asks why Obama could not use the 99 percent to reinvigorate and renew political participation and democratic deliberation. And third, it asks whether many of the new policies and procedures Obama has put in place—including the turn away from the courts and toward negotiated rulemaking to make regulatory policy, Race to the Top funding mechanisms that inspire the progressive imagination and solicit public participation, and the inclusion of previously marginalized groups—would be hard to undo if people, such as the 99 percent, started deliberating about common goods and solutions by coming to Obama's newly set sublocal, state, national, and global tables. If the youth behind Occupy Wall Street left the streets and parks and starting knocking on doors to get out the vote, could they make a difference?

While Obama's legislative accomplishments have been historic, this chapter will show that he may have succeeded in something even bigger, something every presidential candidate promises but few before Obama could accomplish: changing the way Washington works. Policy wonks talk about Keynes vs. Hayek or FDR vs. Reagan, but the real action is Locke and Rousseau vs. Spinoza, and thanks to Obama, Spinoza could win.

Yet Obama's reforms could also fall victim to their own success, since changing the federal government while simultaneously increasing its complexity may end up having little net effect on people's lives unless voters participate. Running the Washington policy machine on Spinozan principles of good governance is a very important change, but the final step will be to fulfill Spinoza's ideal in depth by getting all Americans involved in ongoing national conversations—not just activists and experts and leaders, but the people themselves. It's one thing—a very important thing—to get a group of representatives of different interests (or different nations, for that matter) around a physical or virtual table to talk. Getting individuals to participate directly and deliberate authentically in governance is much harder.

If the United States could raise its pitiful voter turnout to European levels, that would shift most policies in a progressive direction all by itself; but if those newly energized citizens would not just vote once every other year, but also make a habit of discussing proposals, negotiating rules, and exchanging information and views, something like true deliberative democracy might finally be established without the need for the open-mike romance. The success of Spinozan good governance stems from the participation of its peoples; conversely, the failure of this type of good governance results from public apathy. Public apathy—expressed both by lack of voter participation and by silence about the everyday implementation of public policies and their concrete consequences—opens space for inauthentic debate and deliberation. For an illustration of the difference between arguing and deliberation, one need look no further than the Tea Party.

Three Cups of Tea

On February 19, 2009, Rick Santelli, a CNBC commentator, went on a rant against "freeloaders" who he claimed were exploiting federal home mortgage reduction programs. At that moment, Santelli called for a "new American," though not one similar to the "new race" that French immigrant J. Hector St. John de Crèvecoeur envisioned in 1782. Santelli's new American drank English tea, not French coffee, on the frontier. Calling for the umpteenth incarnation of the little party that went down to Boston Harbor in 1773, Santelli and the Tea Party transformed protests about "overweening" federal government programs that fund "foolish borrowers and banks" into something tantamount to the revolutionary cry "no taxation without representation." At least that is what some disgruntled social conservatives heard.[20]

Given the Tea Party's odd lineage, in combination with its effectiveness, academics and pundits who considered it a chimera or a joke in early 2009 eventually began writing about it. If it had not succeeded in sending sixty-two members to the House of Representatives and four to the Senate in the 2010 midterm elections, it might still be nothing more than fodder for stand-up comedians, not pundits, academics, and political operatives. As the social movement story goes, political scientists Theda Skocpol and Lawrence Jacobs suggest, Santelli and commentator Glenn Beck incited unrest, and then "the rest of the media flocked to cover the events and follow up with grassroots networks holding meetings across the country." The heavy involvement of large media companies suggests that the Tea Party did not match the traditional definition of a grassroots movement, springing up spontaneously among an alarmed citizenry.[21]

The question, however, is less whether the Tea Party is a social movement than why it had such success in the 2010 midterm elections. Will this movement continue to succeed, or will it or its issues be co-opted by the GOP? Its participants saw themselves, and often dressed themselves, as heirs to the American revolutionaries of the 1770s, but in the words of American studies professor Jill Lepore, "what was curious about the Tea Party's revolution, though, was that it wasn't just kooky history; it was *anti*history." To what extent is the Tea Party a shadow movement for racism, like many conservative social movements before it? And to what extent is this movement reactionary, or triggered by what Barack Obama has done or pledged to do? How much of their success can Tea Partiers attribute to their nemesis, Obama, who, the previous chapter argued, is both a source and a product of the social construction of race? How is Obama perceived as a political leader by the two political parties, voters, and the public at large? What part of the debate involves Obama's essence, or the social construct that contains his identity?[22]

As Eugene Robinson writes, "It's not racist to join the tea party," but as explained in the previous chapter and aptly summarized by this columnist, Obama's identity "makes some people unsettled, anxious, even suspicious." Indeed, the GOP well understands the power and muscle of conservative social movements, such as the Moral Majority, which helped it obtain great success beginning in the 1980s. It comprehends a social movement's capacity to bolster or bring down its political prospects. Similarly, the Democrats running Obama's reelection campaign hoped the Tea Partiers would overplay their political hands.[23]

Bad Guards: Coercive Americanization

Flaring up again with the Arizona immigration debate, the Tea Party has sparked a new form of "coercive Americanization" resembling the policies of many nations in the European Union (EU). Although the first round of Americanization in the early twentieth century had a progressive impulse, as explained in chapter 1, with experts determining their needs, immigrants and "others" began experiencing xenophobia and oppression on local, state, and national levels that was intended "to strip them of their native cultures and loyalties"—to institute a "common culture," as neoconservatives like Norman Podhoretz would put it in the 1970s.[24] Yet "the stance of many coercive assimilation proponents smacks of racist overtones and is based on apprehension of 'others' and exclusionary thinking more than it is based on preservation of core values."[25]

It all culminated in 1919 with the Red Scare, the prohibition against alcohol, and the revival of the Ku Klux Klan (KKK). Five years later, in 1924, both the Republicans and the Democrats would refuse to condemn the KKK in their platforms. The leftover social strains and extreme patriotism from World War I had given rise to new obsessions, which resulted in the casting aside of civil liberties. African Americans and other ethnic groups "bore the brunt of this assault under the guise of becoming more 'American' and less 'foreign.' "[26]

In 1924 Congress passed, and Calvin Coolidge signed, the Immigration Act, establishing strict quotas for immigrants on the basis of race and ethnicity. Americanization itself ended when immigrants from northern and western European countries, such as Sweden, made clear that they "had no intention of 'melting' with certain 'other' races and cultures." The dominant ingredients did not relish being "polluted" by the wrong ethnicities and races.[27]

Immigration remained restricted for over forty years, until legislation lifting the quotas based on national origins passed in 1965. Two decades later, in 1986, Ronald Reagan signed legislation granting amnesty to undocumented workers. Since 9/11, however, with xenophobia barely below the surface, parts of the United States are moving toward the same sort of coercive assimilation that existed after passage of the 1924 Immigration Act, particularly now that George W. Bush, who kept a lid on its application to Latinas and Latinos, has left office. Obama is alone in seeking the immigration reform that both political parties have spurned.

At a rally for immigration reform that Obama addressed in the border city of El Paso, Texas, a reporter described a "billowing 162-foot-by-93-foot Mexican flag," which "was heavy with political overtones for 2012 and beyond, given the growing ranks of Latino voters in a number of swing states." Elected with 67 percent of the Latino vote, Obama sought in key states such as Arizona, Colorado, Florida, Nevada, New Mexico, and North Carolina "to reassure those increasingly frustrated voters of his commitment to liberalizing immigration laws as a moral and economic imperative, and to blame 'border security first' Republicans in Congress for his inability to deliver on that promise."[28]

In the wake of Obama's election in 2008, the Tea Party turned immigration into a polarizing issue, particularly in the West and Southwest, with the biggest battleground being Arizona. As LeAna B. Gloor writes: "In the modern-day discussion, coercive assimilation theories often take on a decidedly racist overtone . . . urging Americentric policies such as English-only education, strict immigration policies, stipulations of nationalistic criteria for citizenship, and eliminating programs aimed at helping minorities." They also seek "strict deportation and increasingly restrictive immigration policies in order to protect so-called American values."[29]

None of this was new to Obama. Cultural geographer Katharyne Mitchell says we are in a "multicultural backlash." Considering immigration reform potentially too explosive to be included in his initial legislative package of reforms, Obama waited until July 2010 before devoting an entire speech to it. In this speech, he pursued a three-pronged strategy for immigration reform.[30]

First, the Obama administration unveiled the DREAM Act, which would create a path to citizenship for approximately 11 million undocumented workers, giving them amnesty if they "come forward, pay taxes and a penalty, and learn English," as well as "legal status for foreigners who graduate from colleges here and want to remain and start businesses." Obama also hopes to give citizenship to foreign-born youth who get educated or join the military. This strategy could establish a long-term Democratic stronghold. The summer before the 2010 midterm elections, Obama used the DREAM Act to appeal to Latino and Latina voters as well as other middle-class voters turned off by anti-immigrant discourse, all while pointing a finger at GOP legislators who oppose a comprehensive overhaul. But Obama failed to turn the DREAM Act into law.[31]

Second, the Obama administration had the Justice Department "challenge a new state law intended to combat illegal immigration, arguing that it would undermine the federal government's pursuit of terrorists, gang members and other criminal immigrants." The Arizona law, signed by Governor Jan Brewer, criminalized undocumented workers by requiring local police officers to determine their status if the officers had a "reasonable suspicion" they might be in the country without legal papers. Governor Brewer argued that Obama, in opposing her state's anti-immigrant legislation, was pandering to the Latino and Latina vote. Tea Party supporters such as Senator Jon Kyl of Arizona, the Republican whip, claimed that the state's law responded to Obama's failure to cope with immigration. "All Americans would be better served," Kyl said, "if this administration focused on implementing proven border security solutions rather than engaging in demagoguery." In El Paso, lobbying for the DREAM Act, Obama mocked Republicans who said they would not support reform until the borders are secured. "Maybe they'll say we need a moat," Obama said.[32]

The Justice Department argued that the Arizona law diverted federal and local monies from law enforcement by having police officers focus on people who might not have committed crimes. This law, it claimed, creates a policy that provokes the "detention and harassment of authorized visitors, immigrants and citizens." "But diverting federal resources away from dangerous aliens such as terrorism suspects and aliens with criminal records," Attorney General Holder said, "will impact the entire country's safety." Targeting all states that pursue such measures, the Justice Department's suit says that "the Constitution and the federal immigration laws do not permit the development of a patchwork of state and local immigration policies throughout the country."

Using immigration and other issues, Tea Party groups became a major force in the 2010 midterm elections. Is it noteworthy that "conservative activists used money and grassroots campaigns to pull the Republican Party even further to the right, especially in congressional voting and public debates over social issues and taxes"? Perhaps the GOP has more political pull with the conglomerated national media than the Democrats did after Obama took office in 2009; yet with a whole body of political science literature weighted against this idea, tracking how the media switches sides on almost an election-by-election basis, it is doubtful. (To be sure, though, "Tea Partiers have [had] their greatest initial impact on Republican politicians." They have had success, as Skocpol and Jacobs note, "pressuring officeholders to oppose or repeal Obama initiatives such as health care reform," and helping to defeat in a series of key primaries any "Republicans who show any signs of dialogue or compromise with Democrats.")[33]

The Tea Party's success during Obama's first two years illustrates one problem with deliberative democracy: for it to be effective, all sides must have a chance to be heard, and all must engage in reasoned discourse in the spirit of give-and-take and solution seeking. If one side dominates the discussion by participating in disproportionate numbers, practices intolerance while seeking to perpetuate exclusion and entrench privilege, and is "full of passionate intensity" but uninterested in hearing others' views—is made up of wolves instead of gods, in other words— the process is unlikely to succeed. This is especially true when the chief opponents of the process, who should supply a counterweight, are full of ideas, but choose to present them outside channels where they might be able to make a difference.

The Occupation: A Neo-"Wobbly" Horizontal Movement or a Diaspora of Cosmopolitans?

The Occupy Wall Street movement first achieved widespread notice in late September 2011. Soon late-night pundits and comedians were making it the butt of many jokes about hygiene, New Age hippies, and its supposedly Canadian origins, most of them questioning the authenticity of the protesters encamped in Zuccotti Park in New York City's financial district (and at other Occupy sites around the country and the world). Yet whether or not it was instigated by the Canadian activist group Adbusters, Occupy Wall Street grabbed the imagination of progressive Democrats, leftists, radicals, and anarchists who felt frustrated, thwarted, and stymied by divided government.

A young person's movement, whose participants pride themselves on being global in location (demonstrating in virtual and physical squares and arenas), horizontal in organization (lacking an identifiable, let alone a charismatic, leader), and deliberatively democratic in process (egalitarian and consensus-oriented), Occupy Wall Street grew out of frustration with neoliberalism, the 2008 collapse of neoclassical capitalism that led to a prolonged American recession, chronic low participation rates in national elections, and a divided government resulting from the two-party system and increased partisanship incited by, among others, the Tea Party. Speaking on behalf of the "99 percent," the Occupiers voiced their disappointment with Obama's unrealized and unactualized campaign over the "change" and "hope" that they expected, but that hardly materialized.

This liberal or progressive social movement sprung up after it became apparent that Obama would not, or could not, lead the 99 percent into recovery. "It could be worse" does not play well, as pundits observed in the 2010 midterm elections—especially among those enduring long-term unemployment, or those first experiencing unemployment as newly minted college graduates burdened by student loans (along with the parents housing them, who harbored high expectations for them). Nor does an explanation based on the possibility of global economic and political decline fit on a bumper sticker or resonate, given American parochialism.[34]

In response, Obama could have played the separation-of-powers or divided-government blame game, since Congress already suffered from low public esteem, having hit a historic 82 percent negative rating during the 2011 budget negotiations. Yet having served in the Senate, Obama knew that such tactics could further stymie the possibility for a second-term legislative package of reforms. And while blaming Republicans works during presidential elections (but not midterm elections), there was always the possibility that public opinion could go negative, which would lead to electoral blowback for Democrats. Finally, blaming national political institutions in a country that prides itself on being patriotic could be downright self-defeating. Franklin D. Roosevelt never recovered as the New Deal coalition leader after the "switch in time that saved nine" stemming from his proposed "court-packing scheme."[35]

While the Tea Party emerged in 2009 in opposition to mainstream Republicans' attempts to recover their factional balance after George W. Bush left office, Occupy Wall Street grew out of liberals' and progressives' frustration with the Democratic Party in 2011 after it was captured by Wall Street and the global financial sector in the 1990s. As Princeton historian Sean Wilentz wrote, Bill Clinton, sandwiched between the two presidents Bush, should be categorized as part of the Reagan revolution, despite being a Democrat, and the Occupiers did not want a repeat of his presidency.

Obama may foster cultural change, but like Clinton, he has been a huge disappointment to traditional big-government liberals as well as progressives and anyone on the Left interested in economic reform that addresses income inequality. The one person in Obama's administration who shows little sign of even changing departments, let alone stepping down, is one of the first people Obama appointed, signaling his status quo orientation: Treasury Secretary Timothy Geithner.[36]

Occupy Wall Street could inspire much more discussion, both on specific measures like student loan forgiveness and on general topics like wealth redistribution and capitalism itself, but to do so, it would have to participate in regular politics instead of standing aloof from it. It would have to work around realistic constraints. While the Occupiers endorse Obama's message about the importance of fairness, inclusion, and equality, they have not as yet absorbed his point that the process of politics, particularly the part about hashing things out with those you disagree with, is as important as the outcome.

A "Silly" Administration?

As the 2012 election approached, Occupy Wall Street and the Tea Party both faced uncertain futures. Occupy Wall Street all but disappeared after the May Day demonstrations did not provide the movement with the momentum it hoped. Finally, the Tea Party bumped up against the normal constraints when it was left with a GOP candidate, Mitt Romney, whom it could hardly rally behind. Tea Partiers can only be described as less than enthusiastic about this "moderate" big-state Republican, who after all passed successful health-care reform when he governed Massachusetts.

All these hopes dashed by defeats are to be expected: social movement ideas, like third-party ideas, tend to get incorporated or digested into the stable American two-party system. Yet a new set of movements will come along, with different names, motivated by different issues, and perhaps in technological forms we do not yet know. Looking ahead, the question remains: Will the adherents of these movements, or any new ones, whether supporting Obama's progressive views or opposing them, buy into his concept of deliberative democracy and participate in it, instead of either standing outside the process or trying to dominate it through sheer volume? And looking back, why did a new and initially very popular president inspire many Americans to spend their summer vacations yelling at town hall meetings, and why have those who should be Obama's biggest fans found him surprisingly hard to like?

The frontier motif has been a powerful one throughout American history, and it is particularly appropriate for Obama, since a frontier is a border, and his multifarious identity straddles many borders. This book echoes a frontier theme articulated by the media the moment Obama announced his candidacy for president: that Obama is Lincoln, who went from a log cabin to the White House. As Garry Wills notes, one of Obama's most renowned speeches, "A More Perfect Union," resembles Lincoln's Cooper Union address in rhetorical sound and structure. Few of the details surrounding Lincoln's presidential campaign or election have been lost on Obama. Invoking Lincoln's memory, Obama launched his candidacy on the steps of the Old State Capitol in Springfield, Illinois. He introduced his running mate, Joseph Biden, on the same steps. At the same time, Obama underscored Senator Biden's service to Delaware, a slaveholding state throughout the Civil War.[37]

Indeed, in 2005, upon entering the Senate, Obama likened himself to Lincoln. Peggy Noonan, Ronald Reagan's former speechwriter and a conservative pundit, found this comparison arrogant, or perhaps even "uppity," though she stopped shy of the latter word and sentiment. Obama thought he was "Lincoln," Noonan said, "only sort of better."[38]

What eluded Noonan was that Obama focused on Lincoln as a political leader, rather than as a statesman or steward saving the nation.

Senator Obama took note of President Lincoln's "serial political failures." "Lincoln's determination . . . emerged from an awareness of his limitations," Obama explained in a 2005 *Time* essay (as summarized by the historian Susan Schulten), and he was driven by a "desire to transform his humble and rude background, and to remake not just himself but also the world around him." In *The Audacity of Hope*, Obama articulated this point about leadership and altruism better: "Like no man before or since," Lincoln "understood both the deliberative function of our democracy and the limits of such deliberation."[39]

Not all Obama supporters find this message convincing. It rings hollow to those who were expecting a quick economic recovery or, worse, hoping Obama would alter the course of global capitalism and reduce income inequality in the United States. It also fails to resonate with many progressives seeking significant changes who want more than rhetoric about ending the wars on poverty, terrorism, and drugs. "The Obama Administration's efforts on behalf of homeowners—known unfortunately as HAMP, HARP, and HASP—have all suffered" (according to *New Yorker* journalist George Packer) for lack of what Democratic liberal Senator Richard Durbin wanted to include: "a mechanism to force the banks to deal. Instead, the government has tried to give banks the incentive to modify loans, and that has hardly made a dent." Or, as Robert Kuttner explains in the *American Prospect*, Obama's liberal and progressive critics believe that his "government has lost credibility as a necessary force for economic recovery and fairness, undermining the Democrats' core appeal to voters."[40]

Melinda Henneberger, blogging for the *Washington Post*, writes, "If Alinsky were alive today, he'd surely be camped out in front of the White House, using every trick in his book, 'Rules for Radicals,' to point out the many ways in which the president is not an infiltrator of the dreaded establishment, but the personification of it." Radicals, liberals, and progressives in the media remain disappointed. In many cases this disappointment stems from "othering" or "scripting" of the president, particularly when he falls short of supporting big-government solutions, as when he dropped the so-called public option in health care or reauthorized the No Child Left Behind Act.[41]

These critics, however, ignore the one progressive area in which Obama has had the biggest impact, as this book shows: social policy surrounding identity issues affecting workers with disabilities, transgendered people, and gays and lesbians as well as the traditional groups associated with race and gender. Allowing class to trump identity, these liberals and progressives have downplayed Obama's resistance to foreign and domestic public policies that champion the "normate," or all forms of cultural supremacy, in identity politics—be it supremacy based on race, gender, heterosexuality, or physical, intellectual, or mental ableism. Obama has ignited a new type of culture war with his position on cosmopolitanism and civic religion. He is challenging the role of religion in the United States. Is this a Christian nation, as the conservative churches and the American judiciary believe? Or will there be a "Catholic Spring," as *Washington Post* columnist E. J. Dionne suggests? One bishop who compared Obama to Hitler and Stalin lost ground in the religious freedom argument as others charged him with issuing rhetoric that was "shrill and simplistic."[42]

Othering: The Democrats to Leave Behind No Child Left Behind?

A representative example of the progressive Democrats' "othering" was their response to Obama's acceptance of funding increases for charter schools as part of the No Child Left Behind Act reauthorization. Is this community-organizing chief executive threatening to them because he calls into question the underlying "whiteness" behind the big state, last seen in the Great Society? Obama's community-empowerment public education policy raised the hackles of progressive Democrats. Overseen by Secretary of Education Arne Duncan, the policy challenged the way the federal and state governments treated immigrant and African American children in urban areas.

As discussed earlier, African American leaders, particularly those in urban areas, thought the Democrats had abandoned them during the War on Poverty. In Obama's view, the judiciary betrayed the poor in 1973, when the Supreme Court reversed a Texas district court's decision by ruling that public education in the United States was not enough of a "fundamental right" to warrant strict scrutiny. In *San Antonio Independent School District v. Rodriguez*, it ruled that wide inequities among San Antonio–area public school districts did not violate the equal protection clause of the Fourteenth Amendment. Rendering another devastating blow, the Burger also court ruled that strict scrutiny did not apply to *how* states financed their public schools. Wealthy districts could spend what they liked, given the court's strong position on local control.[43]

According to this ruling, nothing in the text of the Constitution substantiated the idea that public education should be beyond local control, or based on equity under the Fourteenth Amendment. Of course, public education did not exist when the Founding Fathers drafted the original document in 1787. At that time, and for another eighty years, slaves could be beaten or jailed for literacy.

Then, in 1997, in *City of Boerne v. Flores*, the Rehnquist court, a Supreme Court associated with "new federalism," made a ruling on religious freedom that could be applied to education. It was a surprise, so much so that one author jokingly referred to it as "Boerne supremacy."[44]

In keeping with William Rehnquist's preference for states' rights, the court ruled that U.S. state constitutions prevented Congress—the national legislative branch—from defining by statute the *content* of a state's constitution. States could determine what their constitutions meant by a guarantee of religious freedom, or educational freedom, or any freedom. In making this decision, the justices wrote what could be called the "enough!" doctrine, or adequacy theory.

How much freedom is enough? Is it enough educational freedom for someone to get admitted into an institution of higher education (technical school, junior college, or university)? Is it enough to get a job at McDonald's, or at the *New York Times*? In this separation-of-powers decision, the Rehnquist court ruled that Congress (but not the executive branch) lacked the power to determine the substance or content of a right granted by a state constitution. The fact that forty states would later emulate or copy one another was irrelevant to the Rehnquist court, as we will see below. The case involved layers, more layers, and even more layers, and soon became not a marble cake, but a brownie, since enough is not easily quantifiable.[45] It is subjective or depends upon a perspective or an overlapping and intersecting set of perspectives—the perspective of the citizen, the informal unit or institution, such as a family, the political actor, the formal political and economic institution, and time—historical and political time.[46]

When Enough Is Enough

Rodriguez coupled and compounded race, ethnicity, income, and education during the Great Society. Initiated in 1968, before Johnson's presidency ended, the case serves as evidence that *Griggs v. Duke Power Co.* (1971) was the high-water mark for antidiscrimination cases. In addition to emphasizing the absence of equality of educational results between Edgewood and Alamo Heights, Texas, the plaintiffs showed that children of immigrants, and African Americans, experience higher high school dropout rates and are less likely to attend, let alone graduate from, universities or local junior colleges and technical training schools.

Rodriguez emphasized the dollar amounts that wealthy districts spent compared with poorer districts. Discrimination was documented in terms of numerous discrepancies: parents in the wealthy school district voted to give their children 20 more square feet of building space per student, along with more than twice as many library books, 40 percent more teachers, and three times as many guidance counselors as those in poorer school districts. It was all about money.

All of these statistics indicating a large inequity between the districts could be correlated, and they helped account for the greater success of the students in the wealthier Texas district in graduating from high school and then, in many cases, going on to public and private colleges and universities. Instead of allowing conservatives to attribute the difference to the "negro family," the civil rights leaders behind *Rodriguez* documented the differences between the students on all levels—space, books, teachers, and guidance counselors—not just when they exited the public school system. But all to no avail. In the almost five years before the Burger court handed down the *Rodriguez* ruling, the inequities only got worse. The former Confederate state of Texas called them a violation of equal protection, but the national Supreme Court rejected the intersectional correlation between education, race, ethnicity, and socioeconomic status, or the American version of class.

Conservative Methods in Service of Progressive Goals

For Obama, *Rodriguez* was a watershed moment, the point when he began searching for political, not judicial, relief: "The Supreme Court never ventured into the issues of redistribution of wealth and sort of more basic issues of political and economic justice in this society." Not even the Warren court, famed for its civil rights decisions, had ever been "radical," Obama explained. "It didn't break free from the essential constraints that were placed by the founding fathers in the Constitution . . . [that] the Constitution is a charter of negative liberties. It says what the states can't do to you, says what the federal government can't do to you, but it doesn't say what the federal government or the state government must *do* on your behalf." Then he added, "One of the, I think, tragedies of the civil-rights movement was because the civil-rights movement became so court-focused, I think that there was a tendency to lose track of the political and community-organizing activities on the ground that are able to put together the actual coalitions of power through which you bring about redistributive change, and in some ways we still suffer from that."[47]

The original plaintiffs in *Rodriguez* followed what scholars call "equity theory." Students from poor districts contested the dearth of resources, arguing that this inequity violates the equal protection clause under a substantive interpretation of the Fourteenth Amendment, not a procedural one. After what Obama called the "tragedy" of *Rodriguez*, reformers found a different approach to making public education more equitable, called "adequacy theory." Using the provisions of a state's own constitution, educational reformers argued that children from poorer districts had been denied their guarantee of an "adequate" education. They claimed that states could guarantee what they should *do*— which is to say, the state guarantees a positive liberty. Federal courts began to agree, circumventing the Rehnquist court. But how much education is "enough"? How do you determine what is "adequate"? The quality of a school's output must be measured in some way.[48]

Testing is one obvious method, but test results can be spun or misinterpreted, which is why they are so controversial. One report found that the United States ranked seventeenth of the sixty-five nation-states participating in a literacy test involving fifteen-year-olds. The Obama administration, and other advocates of educational reform, called this "a Sputnik moment." When this statistic is broken down by ethnicity, the gap gets even wider. When white American students take this test, they come in sixth, whereas Asians win second place overall. But, as one commentator observed, Latinos and African American students ranked forty-first and forty-sixth among the sixty-five nations, respectively. In his view, Latinos and African Americans "dragged the U.S. average down."[49]

Is the commentator lacking in racial and ethnic self-consciousness? Or is he writing that among sixty-five nations, boys and girls, males and females who are of Latin or Central American or African or Caribbean lineage and/or Catholic or Protestant faith descend, or "fall to," this ranking? Stating so subtly that parceling out students by race and ethnicity constitutes discrimination, this commentator brings a new twist to the "blame the victim" approach. Nothing in Duncan's educational reforms indicates that Obama is interested in having nationally standardized tests single out these two ethnic and racial groups, let alone causally correlate them with "dragging" the United States down.

What Obama has pledged is "to narrow the achievement gap between rich and poor students," not to equalize funding. To Duncan, a high school diploma is (to quote a 2004 report) a "broken promise," because it no longer "reflect[s] adequate preparation for the intellectual demands of adult life." To keep anyone from blaming the Obama administration for inaction, Duncan said, "Our first priority is to have Congress rewrite the law. If that doesn't get done, we have the obligation to provide relief in exchange for reform."[50]

Duncan exercised his regulatory discretion as secretary of education to liberate states from No Child Left Behind's primary provision. By 2014 the law requires that a state's students be deemed proficient in reading and math—they must hit a demonstrable standard for adequacy, or at least come close enough. Duncan will waive this requirement "in exchange for . . . flexibility"—by which he means that the states should promote Obama's progressive priorities. In granting these waivers, Duncan will rely on "a formula the administration used last year in its signature education initiative, the Race to the Top grant competition." Race to the Top, as described in chapters 3 and 4, gave money to school districts that, first, "opened new space for charter schools"; second, "toughened teacher evaluation systems"; and third, "remade their worst-performing schools, among other things." Many of these districts were in poor urban and rural areas.[51]

The greater issue is that Duncan hopes his executive discretionary power will equate increasing the value of a diploma with meeting a common set of rigorous standards, so that new measures or indices can be developed to create a meritocracy not correlated with income disparities in the United States. Generally called Common Core Standards, they originated in the American Diploma Project, which many states and state organizations sponsored.[52]

All but two (Alaska and Texas) of the fifty states joined this initiative, and then forty of those forty-eight adopted the Common Core Standards. With so many states buying in, money is not the issue. Nor is it the states' turn rightward or the GOP's dominance on the state level. Critics, initially liberal and progressive Democrats during the Bush administration as well as teachers' unions, condemn Duncan and Obama on the basis of the politics of self-interest rather than ideology.[53]

The Obama administration argues that standardized testing, or the "one-size-fits-all" approach, can be progressive. Opponents say that, given how expansive the United States is in terms of space, as well as how diverse it is terms of its peoples, culture(s), and religions, the one-size-fits-all approach erodes diversity and inclusivity. How can a large, multicultural nation-state adopt one set of criteria? During the Progressive

Era, the New Deal, and the Great Society, this used to be a conservative argument, not a liberal one.[54]

The Democratic Disconnect

The disconnect between Obama and progressive Democrats on national education reform, reflected in part in the animus expressed toward Secretary Duncan, is profound. What can parents of poor children do, other than put large amounts of time and effort into creating private schools within public schools—better known as charter schools? Charter schools are also under attack, largely by suburban liberals and suburban liberal states, such as Ohio, not states with large urban and rural populations, like New York. Why would Obama not seek to reform through reauthorization of a bipartisan piece of legislation signed by a conservative Republican president that could serve as a school reform vehicle? Why would Obama and members of his administration—namely, Duncan and Attorney General Eric Holder—not try to accomplish his public policy agenda, which puts public education front and center?

Progressive Democrats in Congress downplay how the government, on the federal, state, and local levels, was neither objective nor neutral when it left these children and their parents to fend for themselves. Why would the African American community—particularly the educated elite, not the black middle class that escaped to the suburbs—rely on the American nation-state, the federal government, the fifty states, or the thousands of municipalities for help? Why would the African American community not want a modicum of control over federal public funds to provide for their own children, knowing how the state(s) had failed, have failed, and continued to fail them? Finally, why would Obama support public sector unions when many of those unions' leaders have also abandoned urban areas in search of suburban solutions? Charter schools typify the Obama approach in the way they encourage experimentation, supplement existing public schools instead of replacing them, and help the poor without being explicitly designed to do so, since increasing choice and competition is good for every student.[55]

Duncan was the chief booster behind the Race to the Top competition, which is now a primary financial accounting equation for how federal funding is awarded for all domestic social programs, not just for public education. Obama and Duncan realize that current problems may escalate before solutions for entrenched, hundred-year-old social problems like public education can be found. Over 80 percent of public schools in the United States could "be failing by next year under the standards of the Bush-era No Child Left Behind law," said Duncan in March 2011. That could create a crisis. "This is why we have to fix the law now. Nobody can support inaction and maintain the status quo."[56]

What a Difference a Dollar Makes

Obama supported Secretary Duncan knowing that his record was divisive, particularly his support for charter schools. What the two reformers from Chicago share is their disappointment in urban liberals from the 1970s and 1980s, and now progressive Democrats in suburban districts, who have shirked their responsibility to help the poor improve their condition and to address the many intractable social issues stemming from poverty that the Johnson administration last attempted to "solve."

Obama, the community organizer, knows that the Great Society's War on Poverty did not originate within the Johnson administration. The Ford Foundation initiated the fundamental concept behind it. Originally titled the "Gray Areas program," the War on Poverty was an urban renewal plan. The history of this policy illustrates two sources of Spinozan state power—philanthropy and European cross-pollination—that have led to significant reform in the United States. It also informs Obama's openness to any source of ideas and money that can help make a difference—again, at the expense of big-government purists who shun private solutions to public problems.

Foundations brought public libraries to "every small town," and they created the Public Broadcasting System (PBS) and the national 911 emergency response telephone system. Democrats, particularly progressive ones, have good access to funding from private philanthropic foundations. From January 2007 through August 2008, Obama received twelve times as much in donations from these foundations as Republican Senator John McCain did. Philanthropists knew that under the Bush administration, "the federal government was not willing to work with them in the same way as previous presidencies had been willing to." As a result, many "progressive grant makers focused their efforts on changing the political climate until a more sympathetic president took office." What foundations do is "showcase solutions to social problems, such as poverty, housing, public education," all "with the help of the Obama administration, of course."[57]

Valerie Jarrett, a key White House staff member and a longtime Obama family friend and advisor, has a history of working for, and with, philanthropic organizations. Obama himself served on the boards of the Joyce Foundation and the Woods Fund in Chicago. He also chaired the

Annenberg Challenge in Chicago. And, as a journalist describes, "his mother at one time worked for the Ford Foundation in Indonesia." As predicted, the Obama administration is about "promoting partnerships with the private sector, partnerships with the faith community, and partnerships with philanthropy."[58]

During his rise up the political ladder, Obama noticed someone from his old Columbia University neighborhood, Morningside Heights: Geoffrey Canada, who founded and runs the Harlem Children's Zone, a program funded by governmental entities, foundations, corporate executives, and financial institutions. From 2000 onward, Canada introduced Baby College parenting workshops, the Harlem Gems preschool program, the Asthma Initiative (which teaches families to better manage this illness), the Promise Academy, and an anti-obesity program. As Canada describes it, this antipoverty program is "cradle to college," covering high-risk children and young adults, though only one in a hundred blocks in New York City.[59]

When Obama still sat in the Senate in 2007, he sought his own antipoverty initiative that would replicate Canada's program, establishing "promise neighborhoods" modeled after the Harlem project in twenty cities. Like Canada, Obama believed in "an all-encompassing, all-hands-on-deck anti-poverty effort that is literally saving a generation of children in a neighborhood where they were never supposed to have a chance."[60]

In Obama's, Duncan's, and Canada's view, why not try? "It's a new day for many because the people who are populating the government have strong philanthropic ties and nonprofit ties, so that's a different relationship. You can pick up the phone and talk to someone," says Gara LaMarche of Atlantic Philanthropies. "There is access that was unthinkable in the Bush administration."[61]

Guardians Armed with No Truth, but an Ethic of Fresh Salads on the Frontier?

No president, let alone Obama, has had an easy time passing immigration reform, especially during the second half of a presidential first term. The debate surrounding this issue, however, shows "the seriousness of Obama's intent" and how he uses federalism for progressive, not conservative, purposes, with the exception proving, or at least underscoring, the rule. The DREAM Act strengthens the idea that Obama subscribes to the tossed-salad immigrant-nation metaphor. Unlike the well-known assimilationist melting-pot metaphor, in which the different ingredients

blend into a big cauldron of stew with one dominant ingredient, like to-
mato paste, the salad metaphor views peoples as components that retain
their full and distinct flavors. The salad metaphor came out of the diversity debate, rooted in the Supreme Court's 1978 *Bakke* decision.[62]

The immigration reform debate cements Obama's national and international emphasis on difference without focusing on the divisiveness of
race. As mentioned in chapter 1, Obama's notion of American exceptionalism is embodied by Crèvecoeur. This French frontier farmer envisioned
the United States becoming a nation of individuals who would make up
a completely "*new race* that would eventually affect [*sic*] changes to the
world scene through its labour force and its subsequent posterity."[63]

This new race would promote civic virtue and combat corruption.
"Consequently, they emulate Crèvecoeur's American farmer and surrender their 'ancient prejudices and manners.' The French frontiersmen
and women purchased land, and tried creating Asylums, or 'Azilums' as
many colonists spelled their American wilderness in rural Pennsylvania,"
all in the hopes of practicing civic virtue. Ironically, Crèvecoeur himself
returned home to France. Enlightenment thinkers welcomed him as he
sat down and penned his utopian tracts about the brave new world in
North America housing French frontier farmers. Crèvecoeur and his fol-
lowers "wanted America to be the exception—the exception to the corruption and licentiousness of Versailles' court life, the exception to mo-
narchical despotism and feudal privileges, the exception to revolutionary
excesses and violence. They romanticized a simpler, rural and more virtuous way of life than could be found in decadent and corrupt city life."
They dreamed of the assimilation-by-salad metaphor—where everyone
retains their individuality, rather than coming to a consensus.[64]

Post-Ethnicity and Pots

In the Progressive Era another reformer, Israel Zangwill, believed in retaining the crisp individuality of different races and ethnicities in an immigrant nation. But motives are often forgotten. Zangwill's 1908 play
The Melting Pot is often used as evidence by the progressives who fa-
vored Americanization or the suppression of individual groups by a
dominant culture. Zangwill, however, intended just the opposite. He
argued that "the process of American amalgamation is not assimilation
or simple surrender to the dominant type, as is popularly supposed, but
an all-round give-and-take by which the final type may be enriched or
impoverished."[65]

The postethnic or tossed-salad metaphor preceded the culture wars of the late twentieth century. What Tea Partiers, neocons, and some progressive Democrats fail to mention is that "American immigration policies became restrictive based on race, [as] an example of state sponsored racism intended towards reducing the diversity of the melting pot." As Sarah Simons explained in 1901, "The function of assimilation is the establishment of homogeneity within the group; but this does not mean that all variation shall be crushed out. In vital matters, such as language, ideals of government, law, and education, uniformity shall prevail; in personal matters of religion and habits of life, however, individuality shall be allowed free play. Thus, the spread of 'consciousness of kind' must be accompanied by the spread of consciousness of individuality."[66]

As Gloor explains, a multiethnic, multiracial, mixed society can maintain "interdependent cohesion based on national solidarity while maintaining distinct cultural histories not dependent on like-minded homogeneity. . . . Right now, what America needs is a definitive social direction that leans away from coercive assimilation dogma and towards a truly inclusive national identity." She concludes, "True American dreamers should not settle for anything less." Indeed, the proposed DREAM Act tries to make immigration acceptable to more Americans by granting citizenship to immigrants who fulfill middle-class aspirations. Frustrated that Congress would not pass immigration reform, in June 2012 Obama took executive action. Obama will no longer deport any of the estimated 800,000 young immigrants without documentation if they were brought to the United States as children. Senior White House advisor David Plouffe explained that "the president's move wouldn't be a 'permanent fix,' but was adamant that 'the only way to do that is for Congress to pass the Dream Act.'" If Obama can add the middle class to immigration's traditional supporters among liberal activists and businesses seeking cheap labor, he could create another of his win-wins.[67]

The Prius President: The Running Contradiction of Obama vs. Obama

No matter what scripts exist, as described in chapter 6—black, white, cosmopolitan—Obama performs one script very well in terms of clarity and consistency: He speaks a universal anti-universalism about accountability and responsibility. He is a stern or tough-love father figure. While comparisons with other "great" presidents fall short, Obama can be evaluated in terms of his leadership, or success and failure, on his own terms—Obama versus Obama. Like the long-distance runner in track, it is his personal record (PR) that counts. And by the legislative success "standards" of the PR that Obama held up or gave himself, he succeeded. In terms of presidential character, or Obama following the consistency of his own character, he did very well. Things that Obama had less control over were his public and professional reputation, along with world events, natural disasters, and catastrophes.[68]

Obama crossed his legislative success finish line by signing the Patient Protection and Affordable Care Act. (Preferring either an acronym that would stick in voters' minds or a brief title containing the key words, the Obama administration settled on calling it the Affordable Care Act.) The health insurance issue had "eluded presidents for 100 years" before the Affordable Care Act. As Obama explained to those witnessing the act's signing, "History is not merely what is printed in textbooks. It doesn't begin or end with the stroke of a pen. History is *made*."[69]

The remarks about making history were uncharacteristic of his presidential style. "No Drama" Obama normally chooses subtle statements of success. He prefers to be characterized as having modesty, humility, and grace rather than being considered arrogant, aloof, disengaged, technocratic, a consensus seeker. Did Obama let his guard down? Did he take off his veil? Was this the real reason, the real motive that explains why Obama almost singlehandedly insisted that health care become his standard of presidential success?[70]

The predictability of unpredictable events—like the Gulf oil spill or the earthquake in Haiti, as well as ongoing foreign policy developments—has been documented. As argued by Richard Neustadt in 1960, and by Stephen Skowronek in the 1990s, the president, acting as chief executive and commander in chief, should try to turn unpredictable events into credit-claiming capital to demonstrate his leadership skills. And, as many presidential scholars suggest, the question is not *if* such events occur, but how well the president, the White House staff, and his administration are able to spin them.[71]

To be sure, as chapters 3, 4, and 5 show, Obama's package of public policy reforms all followed a similar institutional framework: room for executive action in terms of horizontal and diagonal federalism and regulatory reform that involves local, state, national, and global participants in and out of office. He passed legislation when he could muster support in Congress, and when he could not, as with education, immigration, and climate control, Obama wielded as much executive action as possible. Looking ahead, the question is, how strong is the scaffolding upholding Obama's state?

Put positively, Obama's notion of deliberative democracy stems from inclusivity, diversity, and faith in the uniqueness of humanity. He believes the preferred mode of leadership is not derived from the analytical abstract unit of one, but rather from "one-on-ones" (in community organizer–speak or grassroots politics). Put negatively, Obama represents the absence of exclusivity and difference. He is a universal anti-universalist who created a porous state through federalism and regulatory reform, and he rejects scientific experiments that are premised on old-fashioned positivism or Newtonian cause and effect, but endorses those based on logical argumentation.

Given that Obama sees no *telos*, he is a proceduralist and a consequentialist. Like the Deweyan pragmatists, he views process as tantamount to outcome, since there is no ending, no march toward progress. But this never-ending journey can be embodied by an existentialist rite of passage, as in the popular documentary *March of the Penguins*. The logic behind Obama's reasons is based on consilience and congruence, or inductive reasoning, as he takes life's journey.

Obama embraces the adage that we are all snowflakes, every one unique; but as each flake falls and lands on a sidewalk or in a drift, its motion and position indicate the snow's direction. While the snowdrifts alter traffic patterns among people walking, driving, skiing, sledding, or falling, there is no "good" or "bad" direction. It depends on the person's perspective. It is random. Obama withholds or brackets all judgment. There is no judging which shape is more or less beautiful, more fun or dangerous. There is no controlling or orchestrating or determining what happens when the snowdrift blows left, right, or sideways. And there is no point in anticipating whether, like a snowflake, we will drift ahead or blow backward. To be sure, there are better directions for the snow to fall for pedestrians, skiers, drivers, and children on sleds. It all depends on the collective purpose, compounded by the individual's perspective, all combining with the individual and collective intent of the snowdrift.

Obama is positive about his anti-positivism. He has faith in the absence of faith, but embraces the pursuit of perfectibility and the futility of looking for purity as the mainstay of his own spirituality or civic religion, as reviewed in chapter 3. Unlike most Americans, Obama believes in "hell on earth" but demonstrates little faith in heaven on earth. He is as culturally optimistic as the next American, but a disciplinarian on earth, relying on positive and negative "nudges." He created a minimal national state resting on behavioral economics, as described in chapter 4, but this state—like most of the fifty states accepting monies for progressive purposes—facilitates citizen action and involvement, and it facilitates the creation of political institutions as communities, each with a distinct culture. Obama's nudges turn political institutions on the local, state, national, or global level into communities at work.

The "Who and How" of Deliberating Democrats

Oft-quoted political theorist Joshua Cohen offers a concise definition of deliberative democracy, writing that this type of governance involves "outcomes" that are "legitimate to the extent they receive assent through participation in authentic deliberation by all those subject to the decision in question." For deliberation to be authentic, real, or legitimate, it must be, as theorist Seyla Benhabib describes, "free and unconstrained."[72]

The debate among deliberative democracy theorists revolves around how any specific institution or structure defined by rules and procedure can be unconstrained. The first question is *who* deliberates. What is the role of the person who deliberates, and what is her relationship with the government? And second, *how* do we deliberate—what *rules* help dictate this relationship when the individual begins deliberating in the institutional setting?

John Rawls, a liberal theorist, often paired in opposition with Benhabib and philosopher Jürgen Habermas, solves the problem simply by limiting the public square's space. No "background culture" disturbs the deliberative process because of the public/private distinction inherent in liberalism. Like coats, backgrounds can be checked at the deliberative door. Meanwhile Benhabib and Habermas extend the discussion, asking whether deliberators can truly be egalitarian or identityless. Does identity, culture, education, class, or personality account for irreconcilable differences in backgrounds?

The contest, then, over which differentials in power can be reconciled, or how to best deal with any inequity or discrepancy, whether it is an immutable characteristic like ethnicity or personality or something mutable such as education or class—is intellectually tackled in two ways.

Analytical political theorists and behavioral economists suggest that background differences can be erased, or rendered sufficiently insignificant, by random samples. The question is how to choose those samples. While most democratic theorists agree that a deliberative body must be small to engage in effective dialogue, like a Greek polis or city-state, methodological fights abound over what statistical methods work best to find this elect population of deliberators. John Dryzek and James Fishkin, for instance, maintain that citizen juries work well. Yet "New England town meetings have shown that such gatherings cease to be effective for large populations," says Fishkin. For example, during August of 2009, when Congress recessed and the members returned to their districts to discuss Obamacare, few constituents came out in support of it.

Such gatherings "may work in communities of a few hundred, but when the population reaches the many thousands, attendance drops and the connection to citizens atrophies."[73]

Town hall meetings rest on "an illusion," Fishkin elaborates, "that a district of 650,000 potential voters can be represented by the unscientifically self-selected who decide to show up." Instead, the meetings become "amorphous" and "unpredictable" and therefore function as "invitations for interest groups and grass roots campaigns to capture the public dialogue." "In the current town hall format," he wrote, like that of the meetings at which members of Congress reported to their constituents about Obama's health-care initiative, "shrill voices can easily silence the rest." While Fishkin presents a vivid critique of American town hall meetings, there is a library of literature on every possible configuration for carrying out deliberative democracy, each being differentiated or catalogued by scholars from a different analytical methodology. The general conclusion: Size matters.[74]

Power and Identity among Deliberators

The second means of distinguishing power differentials among deliberators concentrates on culture. So-called difference democratic theorists, who recognize the radical emancipatory potential of deliberative democracy, conduct a battle over autonomy, power, and individual perspective and subjectivity. Collective decisions made through reasoned debate hold great promise for hearing from "powerless or oppressed groups." These theorists concentrate on finding out how reasoning can be free from power or domination.

Dryzek, Iris Marion Young, and Philip Pettit, among others, question what type or types of power a deliberating democrat brings to the public square. Pettit offers his own dialogical deliberation process to level power differentials that, while not free from domination, acknowledges the role power plays.[75]

Pettit goes so far as to define freedom as non-domination. By contrast, Young and Dryzek recognize power, but they take the position that deliberative democracy has difficulty mixing with identity politics, since conflicts cannot be resolved by consensus. There is no consensus about nationalism, or Christian fundamentalism in opposition to liberalism. But there can be tolerance, reciprocity, and fairness.[76]

Young goes further, rejecting a "reasonable person standard" for fairness. Reason, being premised on a norm, should only motivate civil discourse; it cannot dictate the "content" of what constitutes *being* reasonable. No one can "erase" her identity, but the process of self-identification alone, Young argues, opens dialogue, making it more inclusive given its authenticity. Discourse can then address power differentials, address exclusivity, and find strategies for inclusivity.[77]

The question for Young in terms of social movements is if or when activists should enter dialogue. The emancipatory potential of deliberative democracy makes it appealing to difference theorists like Young, Dryzek, and Pettit. For Dryzek, deliberative institutions should be relatively autonomous, deliberating at a distance from the sovereign authority. Activists and social movements outside the government gain a great deal by participating in issue-specific networks. These networks are contained.[78]

A Reversal in Participatory Politics

What this book shows is not how shallow the public opinion pool is, but how difficult it is for the public to participate and deliberate in the American system of representative democracy, given its medieval currents and riptides of power. Had the United States been modeled more after a classical (Greek or Roman) republic, it might have more people participating or splashing around in social movements and, therefore, roiling the waters of the discussions necessary to conduct democracy—representative, deliberative, or participatory democracy.

The success of the Tea Party and Occupy Wall Street shows that the very act of choosing a representative in the American Republic, whether this representative governs on the state or federal level, constitutes what J. G. A. Pocock over thirty years ago called almost a "revers[al] of participation." To Pocock, the federalist structure underlying the American Republic lacks civic virtue, or what is described more expansively in contemporary political theory and, in this book, as a Spinozan ethic of reciprocal interdependence. Contrary to what Federalist James Madison contended in his argument in favor of a large and extended republic, the American system of representative democracy concentrates power instead of diffusing it.[79]

John Dewey, the pragmatist who authored *The Public and Its Problems* in 1927, might not be that surprised, given how difficult the media and public events are to orchestrate. Nor would Walter Lippman, who penned *The Phantom Public* in 1925 as a means of engaging Dewey, a public intellectual he revered, with the hope of igniting a discussion about the different types of democracy. While Skocpol and Jacobs, among many others, correctly characterize the Tea Party's "*over-the-top*

rhetoric" as *"laced with racial innuendo,"* is this surprising in a nation
that has an active public or one that practices little deliberative democracy? Meanwhile Occupy Wall Street became the media darling, with
Time naming "The Protester" its Person of the Year for 2011.[80]

Viewed from the summer of 2012, it seemed that if Obama could
win reelection, avoid the disappointment that usually characterizes presidents' second terms, and use his first-term accomplishments to motivate
people to get involved and stay involved, he could establish something
resembling a true deliberative democracy in the United States. If that
didn't happen, Obama will still have made great strides, both in passing
legislation and in improving the functioning and responsiveness of government, but he will have to await a Joshua of his own to get the people
fully involved and guide them across the last river that lies in front of
them.

Epilogue

Roberts's Rules Reign

Obama did it. He led a full-spectrum rainbow coalition of vulnerable peoples across the river with the wind of public opinion behind him. Joshua's exodus prevailed. Those last steps over a raging river required him to tuck crosscutting, shifting, and multiple identities and issues into symbolic and significant public policy reforms built via executive action (leaving them vulnerable if Obama had lost reelection and still susceptible to federal court rulings). While both the Right and the Left speak in the twentieth-century language of zero-sum single issues such as race, class, and/or gender, Obama knew that *multi-* is where it's at.

What Obama, the former grassroots organizer, learned during his first administration is how little legislative room he had to maneuver in the face of an assertive Congress and a conservative federal judiciary. Nonetheless, this book argues that Obama comprehended this by his first one hundred days and worked well within the political and institutional constraints before him. Obama achieved a great deal, even if not everyone knew about it, reflecting his politics of difference, universal anti-universalism, civic religion, multilateralism, cosmopolitanism, and deliberative democracy.[1]

Obama's achievements are exhibited in his style of

leadership or his *modus operandi*. What he accomplished during his first administration is potentially so long-lasting that his second administration plans to protect his achievements by customizing and institutionalizing them through implementation and enforcement, further cementing his rainbow constituency's support. Obama could also be recognized as an effective leader because of his strategic use of conservative means for liberal ends, all during his first term.

To be sure, Obama has progressive policy preferences. But what this book shows is that Obama is passionate about strategy and technique; and he is preoccupied with administrative process and procedures as a means of increasing presidential power and leadership. Only a former constitutional law professor could exhibit such a love of process, knowing that while it may be technical, it is not *a*political or technocratic.[2] Obama's reelection, then, casts him as a politician, but a rare one: not the preening, credit-claiming type, but one who takes the principled long view as a statesman or a unilateral executive—though it could take his own party and the public at large a while to catch up.

A Textbook Presidency

The paradox of Obama's presidency is that in order to be sustained, his achievements had to be buried—by his inner White House staff, senior members of his executive branch, and the fledgling constituencies of cultural change profiting from these reforms. Obama's reelection depended upon his knowing not to crow, brag, or *kvell* about his achievements. Mainstream political journalists pilloried him for this, but they got it wrong.[3] If Obama learned anything, it was what all post–World War II presidents have discovered: Congress cannot be counted on in these partisan times, so do not call attention to unilateral executive action until it gains a constituency, since the legislative branch could crush it through obstruction and delay.[4]

Presidential leadership involves public prestige *or* professional reputation, but in the end both prestige and reputation stem, directly or indirectly, from the pivotal role that national and international public opinion play.[5] Only the court of public opinion cuts across partisan polarization, given the constitutional constraints of bicameralism, separation of powers, and federalism. Obama learned early in 2009 that acquiring a stellar professional reputation would be difficult, if not impossible, since even moderate members of the GOP refused to cooperate with him or his administration, forcing him to focus on being a so-called unilateral executive.

To be sure, Obama made public displays in those first days, with the stimulus package and health care, but his inability to gain ground with even "reasonable" Republicans drove this lesson home and gave him the public opinion leverage to shame the key obstructers. Sometimes this power tactic, best associated with congruence and consilience—or the truth-and-reconciliation negotiation process (not to be confused with a compromise-and-consensus bargaining process)—succeeded, sometimes not. As discussed in chapter 4, it worked with health care but not with climate control. When Obama failed with Congress, he directed Cabinet members and agency heads to achieve as many executive-action victories as he deemed politically feasible.[6]

To be sure, when an issue ran out of political steam without overwhelming public opinion support, Obama dropped it, perhaps publicly disappointing the agency director, like the EPA's Lisa Jackson, or embarrassing a key advisor, as when he failed to appoint Elizabeth Warren to head the CFPB. Still, a remarkable number of Cabinet secretaries, assistant secretaries, and directors and commissioners of regulatory agencies stuck with him, weathering the public humiliation, taking one for the Obama team.[7]

And it was Obama alone who decided which public-policy reforms to press full court and which specific provisions to drop, like increasing the threshold for the millionaires' tax in the fiscal cliff negotiation process. And it was Obama who chose to pursue and implement executive action, as chapters 3 and 4 explain, in areas such as health care, climate control, education, and immigration reform, as well as cementing civil rights for all vulnerable populations.

What is more, Obama selected controversial political appointees to head his Cabinet-level departments and administrative agencies, with the prominent exception of economics. The regulatory agencies (the NLRB, the EPA, the FCC) and the quasi-independent agencies housed in Cabinet-level departments—such as the CFPB in Treasury, the FDA in Health and Human Services, the EEOC in Justice, and OSHA and FLSB in Labor—were largely led by political appointees who reflected his vision. Concentrating Obama's efforts in these departments and independent agencies meant that he could hide most of his significant and symbolic cultural reforms from the public view. His opponents rarely gained enough public-opinion traction to reverse them—to end transgender passports, for instance.

By contrast, Obama's choice in his economic team has been disappointingly mainstream, as he leaned toward Rubinesque pro–Wall Street economic reform from the very beginning (with the one caveat of his being for consumer reform, as seen in chapter 4). Obama's preference for the Clinton economic team reflected how little this topic—economic reform—captured his attention, being a reformer foremost for the *aspiring* middle class.[8]

While Obama chose the direction for public-policy reforms, he did so by building on public opinion—specifically, pivotal pockets of it determined twenty-first-century style by social technology, including social media and open-source journalism, which makes the public more fickle, erratic, and unpredictable. Obama sought reforms that promoted people and issues defined by the intersection or multitude of their identities. These crosscutting (or what this book calls transuniversal) issues—like sexuality, reproduction, and climate control—depend on many overlapping layers of governance or institutional support from a plethora of sources in foreign nation-states, NGOs, domestic NGOs, states, cities, and municipalities.

What Textbook?

The Obama administration's package of significant and symbolic public-policy reforms embodies the term "intercurrence," coined in APD to explain how public-policy reforms result from multiple overlapping and competing institutional forms, which the 2012 campaign buried. Institutions shape formal and informal political identities, altering the path of social movements, thereby shaping public opinion. The "inter-" in *intercurrence* is akin to Obama's view of interdependence and interconnectedness.

The "currence" in intercurrence, this book concludes, is similar to an electrical current or the energy that creates power. The sparks it gives off stem from the constitutional constraints caused by separation of powers, state sovereignty, and federalism. Sparks fly as the institutions that these powers exhibit shift, and energy overflows; they occur when there is no institutional conduit or outlet for public opinion. Obama, for instance, chose *not* to enforce the Defense of Marriage Act (DOMA). Of all the laws, Obama singled this one out. He chose "negative" power to see if sparks would fly when there was no outlet for LGBTers longing for recognition as families. As the sparks flew, it became apparent that social-conservative positions upholding heterosexuality had sufficiently diminished.

Obama greatest achievement was that he used the "currence" in intercurrence—the power or electricity that gave him traction—to renovate old agencies, relying on his unilateral powers as executive. Most significantly, Obama used conservative means—horizontal and diagonal federalism and the full extent of his unilateral executive powers, with negotiated federal rulemaking and recess appointments—to achieve progressive results. Obama knew that separate branches no longer share powers, or at least it has become increasingly difficult to do so on a national level, given the current polarized partisan climate. This explains why Obama put federalism in the unilateral executives' arsenal.

Obama's reelection is textbook. It's just that the textbook has changed. Failing united government, Obama took three steps. First, he pleased the constituencies in his rainbow coalition by using his unilateral executive powers to enact reforms. Second, the primary opposition advertising and opposing these reforms—the Tea Party, newly established with a foothold in Congress after its success in the 2010 midterm elections—tried and failed to capture the 2012 Republican nomination, and tried and failed to shift public opinion to their side. The more Mitt Romney responded to the Tea Party and social conservative pressure, the more Obama won national public opinion. But key players within Obama's rainbow coalition knew that the future of these reforms depended on his reelection. And finally, Obama and this coalition understood what going viral means and how it creates bubbles or pockets that carry great weight in public opinion, like the micromarketing practiced by social media. Indeed, the criticism of Obama that rang truest for this author was that his arrogance and overconfidence made the public believe he could not be bothered to debate Romney. Obama's body language betrayed this truth, and it was this that triggered public opinion against him, momentarily making it a competitive election.

But how could a president that few from the Right or the Left called "a leader" afford to air this hubris in public? Obama knew the narrative that he was considered a national leader or a win-win candidate in 2008 who became a lose-lose president in the first two years of his administration, achieving his own legislative benchmarks yet still losing enough support to cost his party dearly in the 2010 midterm elections, making 2012 no electoral stroll through the park.

Reason 1: Peggy Noonan Was Right

Obama believes he has few peers. The president he measures his performance against over and over again is Abraham Lincoln. Obama should not be likened to FDR but to Lincoln, the most unpopular president who is today cherished in the disjunctions of political time. It took almost a hundred years for Lincoln to become popular or to be held in high scholarly esteem.[9] Lincoln was one of the most polarizing presidents in American history, and few scholars attributed his success to his legislative leadership. More scholars credit his long-term vision or the importance of his politics in saving "the Nation."[10]

While no one can tell in such an early appraisal, it is possible that Obama's Old Testament sense of righteousness and responsibility has helped him avoid being pegged as an identity politics leader, and instead he might be considered a statesman-like leader rather than a politician, since he seeks the common good, common ground, and common solutions, all by conservative means. Like Lincoln, Obama understands how to wield real-world power and is criticized most for being a pragmatist (read opportunist).

Reason 2: It's Not the Story, but the Spectrum
or What Colors Are in a Rainbow

Obama recovered thanks to the quiet support of the rainbow coalition. This rainbow differs from Jesse Jackson's rainbow in that it accepts all colors; knowing that each single color alone is marginalized, it must go for the full spectrum or unity to have any real power. Exit polls gave Obama a three-to-one edge among the 5 percent of voters who identified themselves as LGBTers, giving him the "ultimate advantage," which pushed him over the edge.[11] LGBTers along with African Americans, Latinos, Asian Americans, and Jews may each, as a group, be individually small, a single color in the rainbow with a specific *cultural* hue, but together they made up one-third of the electorate.[12]

Yet it's easy to forget what a difference a month made. After the first debate in October 2012, the Romney Republicans thought they stood a chance of breaking this bridge. So how did Obama recover? He counted on the pockets within the national American constituency, like the *T* for transgendered in the LGBTers, to know their self-inter-est, in the Arendtian sense. That is, this constituency understood that in responding to the underlying complexities of most public-policy issues, they must fight hard against two-pronged forks or binary choices culturally constructed by social conservatives *and* old-fashioned big-state Leftists.

Reason 3: Crazy Cracked Teapots and Conservative Court Justices

Obama benefited from the Tea Partiers' move into governance after the 2010 midterm elections, polarizing the GOP's internal coalitional constituencies when unity was needed. The Republicans, like any political party in a two-party system, are vulnerable to divide and conquer, and while the Tea Party is considered fringe or an outlier within the GOP, it does not stand alone but sustains institutional strength from the Roberts court.

For the first time ever, the Supreme Court is filled exclusively with justices from the Ivy League and exclusively from the Jewish and Catholic faiths. The WASP hold over the Court, which lasted from its inception until the 1980s, is gone. The primary institution that Obama has battled—and will undoubtedly continue to battle, given the 2013 Supreme Court docket—was held in check the summer before the election when Chief Justice Roberts cast the deciding vote and wrote the opinion sustaining Obamacare.

Obama 2.0: A New Culture War?

Obama instigated a new culture war. Supporters and opponents realized what was at stake, though the Obama campaign downplayed most of the president's achievements, from toxic socially conservative issues like DOMA to his economic reforms like stimulus, financial regulation, and climate control. Yet Obama's legacy is *less* dependent on what he may do in a second term than on his rewriting the narrative about how profound a change in direction can be—not least, turning the United States' direction to the new global capitalist commons, positioned not toward petroleum and the Middle East but rather toward Asia: China, India, and Myanmar and the three spheres—public, private, and social.

As the first president ever to have direct control over the economy through appointment powers, Obama realizes that the United States can achieve much with the new consumer reform, but he has already done the state-building excavation on that. Had Obama not been reelected, all this potential—being based on executive action more than legislative action—would have been reversed. It was up to the next president to discover the power potential in the CFPB, as it was to fortify or tear down his achievements in many other areas—civil rights, global affairs, climate control, to name just a few. But, as it happens, the rainbow coalition won the latest skirmish in the culture war, which means Obama gets to implement Obama, as Obama 1.0 moves into version 2.0.

January 1, 2013

Notes

CHAPTER ONE

1. This book derives a functional conception of governance from three foundational bodies of work in political science, particularly American political development (APD). First, it is indebted to the historical institutionalism of Karen Orren and Stephen Skowronek, namely their definition of "multiple, overlapping, and competing institutional forms," including intercurrence, as outlined in *The Search for American Political Development* (New York: Cambridge University Press, 2004). Second, it builds on Anne Norton's post-colonial understanding of the meaning and consequences of political identities, well expressed in *On the Muslim Question* (Princeton, NJ: Princeton University Press, 2013) and *95 Theses on Politics, Culture and Method* (New Haven, CT: Yale University Press, 2004). Finally, it relies on Rogers Smith's recognition of supremacy, or what he calls ascriptive Americanism, in his multiple traditions approach, which captures racial, gender, and class inequalities that appear in *Civic Ideals: Conflicting Visions of Citizenship in U.S. History* (New Haven, CT: Yale University Press, 1999) and "Beyond Tocqueville, Myrdal, and Hartz: The Multiple Traditions in America," *American Political Science Review* 87 (1993): 549.

2. Suzanne Mettler, *The Submerged State: How Invisible Government Policies Undermine American Democracy* (Chicago: University of Chicago Press, 2011); Marie Gottshalk, *The Shadow Welfare State: Labor, Business, and the Politics of Health Care in the United States* (Ithaca, NY: Cornell University Press, 2000); Christopher Howard, *The Hidden Welfare State: Tax Expenditures and Social Policy in the United States* (Princeton, NJ: Princeton University Press, 1999); Jacob S. Hacker,

The Great Risk Shift: The Assault on American Jobs, Families, Health Care, and Retirement—And How You Can Fight Back (New York: Oxford University Press, 2006). For a comprehensive list, see Robert Lieberman and Desmond King, who catalog many of these states in comparative perspective in "Ironies of State Building: A Comparative Perspective on the American State," *World Politics* 61 (2009): 547.

3. Barbara Vobejda, "Clinton Signs Welfare Bill Amid Division," *Washington Post*, August 23, 1996.

4. For a classic political science account capturing tensions between rights and obligations or duties inherent in both liberalism and feudalism, see Karen Orren, *Belated Feudalism: Labor, the Law, and the Liberal Development of the United States* (New York: Cambridge University Press, 1991). Containing a similar strain of what this author calls a simultaneous strain of supremacy advancing regressive and progressive progressivism, see the civil liberties/civil rights work on the 1960s, characterized by the political thought of Daniel Patrick Moynihan's culture of poverty thesis, which was informed by the progressive era anthropologist Oscar Lewis. In APD, scholars who combine historical institutionalism, informal institutions, such as ethnicity, the family, marriage, epistemological communities, and political parties as machines describe this tension and how it is constructive and destructive or discriminatory depending on the person, the place, the event, the situation, and or the historical contingency and/or political time. See Priscilla Yamin, *American Marriage: A Political Institution* (Philadelphia, PA: University of Pennsylvania Press, 2012); Paul Frymer, *Black and Blue: African Americans, the Labor Movement, and the Decline of the Democratic Party* (Princeton, NJ: Princeton University Press, 2007); Victoria C. Hattam, *In the Shadow of Race: Jews, Latinos, and Immigrant Politics in the United States* (Chicago: University of Chicago Press. 2007); Ruth O'Brien, *Crippled Justice: The History of Modern Disability Policy in the Workplace* (Chicago: University of Chicago Press, 2001); and Helene Slessarev, *Betrayal of the Urban Poor* (Philadelphia, PA: Temple University Press, 1997).

5. For magazine article accounts, see Katherine Boo, "The Marriage Cure: Is Wedlock Really a Way Out of Poverty?," *New Yorker*, August 18, 2003; and Mark Lilla, "The Tea Party Jacobins," *New York Review of Books*, May 27, 2010.

6. Laura Laubeová, "Melting Pot vs. Ethnic Stew," *Encyclopedia of the World's Minorities* (Chicago: Fitzroy Dearborn Publishers, 2000); J. Hector St. John de Crèvecoeur, *Letters from an American Farmer*, ed. Susan Manning (Oxford: Oxford University Press, 1997); and J. Hector St. John de Crèvecoeur and Henri L. Bourdin, *Sketches of Eighteenth Century America: More Letters from an American Farmer* (Kessinger Publishing, LLC, 2007, originally published in the United States by Yale University Press, 1925). Quote from Catherine T. C. Spaeth, "America in the French Imagination: The French Settlers of Asylum, Pennsylvania, and Their Perceptions of 1790s America," *Canadian Review of American Studies* 38 (2008): 248, 258.

7. Olivier Zunz, *Why the American Century?* (Chicago: University of Chicago Press, 1998), tracks the large increase in the middle class to the New Deal

as a social ideal and rising incomes after World War II. See also Rich Morin, *America's Four Middle Classes*, Pew Research Center, July 29, 2008, http://www.pewsocialtrends.org/2008/07/29/americas-four-middle-classes/.

8. The Pew Research Center tracks changing demographics, from increasing support of gay marriage by Obama's constituency of the youth, to the historic low of Americans marrying. See D'Vera Cohn, Jeffrey Passel, Wendy Wang, and Gretchen Livingston, *Barely Half of U.S. Adults Are Married—A Record Low: New Marriages Down 5% from 2009 to 2010*, Pew Research Center, December 14, 2011, http://www.pewsocialtrends.org/2011/12/14/barely-half-of-u-s-adults-are-married-a-record-low/; and *The Generation Gap and the 2012 Election: Section 8: Domestic and Foreign Policy Views*, Pew Research Center, November 3, 2011, http://www.people-press.org/2011/11/03/section-8-domestic-and-foreign-policy-views/, for recent surveys on these and other family issues.

9. Stanley Crouch, *The Artificial White Man: Essays on Authenticity* (New York: Basic Books, 2004), 4.

10. Barack Obama, "A More Perfect Union" (speech, Philadelphia, March 18, 2008), https://my.barackobama.com/page/content/hisownwords/.

11. See Ruth O'Brien, *Bodies in Revolt: Gender, Disability, and a Workplace Ethic of Care* (New York: Routledge, 2005), 21–24 and 67–70.

12. Crouch, *Artificial White Man*, 4.

13. David Marquand, *The End of the West: The Once and Future Europe* (Princeton, NJ: Princeton University Press, 2011).

14. Alonzo L. Hamby, "Is There No Democratic Left in America? Reflections on the Transformation of an Ideology," *Journal of Policy History* 15 (2003): 3, gives a concise and critical overview.

15. T. H. Marshall, *Citizenship and Social Class* (London: Pluto Press, 1987, originally published 1950).

16. See Julie Nokov, "Rethinking Race in American Politics," *Political Research Quarterly* 61 (2008): 649–59; and Priscilla Yamin, "The Search for Marital Order: Civic Membership and the Politics of Marriage in the Progressive Era," *Polity* 41 (2009): 86–112.

17. Trevor Norris, "Hannah Arendt and Jean Baudrillard: Pedagogy in the Consumer Society," *The Encyclopedia of Informal Education*, http://www.infed.org/biblio/pedagogy_consumer_society.htm. Norris ties these two thinkers together in a clever critique of consumer society, referencing Hannah Arendt, *The Human Condition* (Chicago: University of Chicago Press, 1958), and Jean Baudrillard, *The Consumer Society: Myths and Structures* (London: Sage Publications, 2004, first published in France in 1970). For classic texts on cultural studies, see Stuart Hall, "Cultural Studies: Two Paradigms," *Media, Culture, and Society* 2 (1980): 57; Jacques Le Goff, *History and Memory* (New York: Columbia University Press, 1992); and Mari J. Matsuda, *The Memory of the Modern* (New York: Oxford University Press, 1992). For legal expressions of this intersected with feminism, see Alyson Cole, " 'There Are No Victims in this Class': On Female Suffering and Anti-Feminism," *NWSA Journal* 11 (1999); and Michael Kammen, *Mystic Chords of Memory: The Transformation of Tradition in American Culture* (New York: Alfred K. Knopf, 1991).

18. Francis Fukuyama, *The End of History and the Last Man* (New York: Basic Books, 1992); and Daniel Bell, *The End of Ideology*, 2nd ed. (Cambridge, MA: Harvard University Press, 2000).

19. Benjamin R. Barber, *Jihad vs. McWorld: How Globalism and Tribalism Are Reshaping the World* (New York: Ballantine Books, 1995); and Toby Miller, "Creepy Christianity and September 11," *SubStance* 37 (2008): 128.

20. Jacqueline L. Salmon, Kimberly Kindy, and Michelle Boorstein, "Obama's Faith-Based Office to Depart from Bush's Precedent," *Washington Post*, February 5, 2009.

21. Obama, "A More Perfect Union." Obama shored up this message with a $500 million Fatherhood, Marriage, and Family Innovation Fund in 2010, and in 2006 he sponsored the Responsible Fatherhood and Healthy Families Act. See also U.S. Department of the Treasury, *General Explanations of the Administration's Fiscal Year 2011 Revenue Proposals* (2010), 305, available from www.ustreas.gov.

22. Obama, "A More Perfect Union." See U.S. Department of the Treasury, *General Explanations of the Administration's Fiscal Year 2011 Revenue Proposals* (2010).

23. Fourth Part, Proposition 35, in Spinoza, *Ethics*, rev., trans., and ed. G. H. R. Parkinson (London: J. M. Dent & Sons, 1989), 163; and Barack Obama, "Iowa Caucus Victory Speech" (Des Moines, IA, January 3, 2008).

24. David Remnick, *The Bridge: The Life and Rise of Barack Obama* (New York: Alfred Knopf, 2010), 121, 229–30. Obama wrote a blurb for Reinhold Niebuhr's *The Irony of American History* (Chicago: University of Chicago Press, 2008), calling him "one of my favorite philosophers." Obama's writings and interviews shed little light on the philosophers who were most influential in developing his political thought. See James T. Kloppenberg, *Reading Obama: Dreams, Hope, and the American Political Tradition* (Princeton, NJ: Princeton University Press, 2010), who suggests, like Remnick, that Obama must have been heavily influenced by pragmatism. Where this book departs from Kloppenberg's analysis is in the search for causality as well as in the decisive role he ascribes to John Rawls and rationality, trying to establish his influence in terms of direct causality. Not finding this, Kloppenberg writes, "Rawls's arguments played a decisive role in debates about justice when Obama was studying political science, then law, and when he was teaching at the University of Chicago Law School," and "before, during, and after the years when Obama was studying law, references to Rawls's writings peppered the pages of the [*Harvard Law Review*]."

25. Obama, "Iowa Caucus Victory Speech."

26. Barack Obama, "Main Street Speech to Wall Street Crowd" (New York, NY, September 17, 2007).

27. On the Walter Lippmann and John Dewey debate, see John Dewey, *The Public and Its Problems* (New York: H. Holt, 1927); Walter Lippmann, "The Hope of Democracy," *New Republic*, November 12, 1916, 231; and Walter Lippmann, *Public Opinion* (New York: Harcourt, Brace, 1922).

28. Obama's idea of the frontier is in complete opposition to that of Frederick Jackson Turner, as expressed in "The Significance of the Frontier in American History," *Report of the American Historical Association* (1893): 199–227,

delivered at the World's Columbian Exposition in Chicago. Critics have long observed the racism underlying Turner's ideas. For an interpretation free from racism, see Patrick Griffin, *American Leviathan: Empire, Nation, and Revolutionary Frontier* (New York: Hill and Wang, 2007).

29. Margaret Talev, "Young Voters Vent Frustration to Obama in MTV Forum," McClatchy Washington Bureau, October 14, 2010; and Richard Wolffe, *Revival: The Struggle for Survival inside the Obama White House* (New York: Crown Books, 2011), 131. Obama has 50 employees and 100 volunteers answering correspondence, including 400,000 daily emails. According to Wolffe, *Revival*, 129–30, this is unprecedented for the White House Office of Presidential Correspondence. See Ashley Parker, "Picking Letters, 10 a Day, That Reach Obama," *New York Times*, April 19, 2009.

30. Beth Reinhard, "Bringing Obama's 2008 Voters Back in 2012," *National Journal*, February 3, 2011. Voters from the ages of 18 to 29 declined by 6 percent, and "the proportion of minority voters slipped 3 percentage points, the steepest decline recorded over those 20 years."

31. Dayo Olopade, "Charm Offensive," *American Prospect*, June 26, 2009; and Wolffe, *Revival*, 27.

32. Louis Hartz, *The Liberal Tradition in America* (New York: Harcourt Brace, 1955). Political scientists have been significantly more persuaded by the Hartzian approach than have historians. Political scientists Karen Orren and Stephen Skowronek write that it "is difficult to imagine how one might move further away from the developmental conception of American politics without calling into question the enduring significance of liberal ideals altogether." Orren and Skowronek, *Search for American Political Development*, 72. See *Studies in American Political Development*, created in 1986, as well as *Polity* and the *Journal of Policy History*. See Carol Nackenoff, "Groundhog Day Again?: Is the Liberal Tradition a Useful Construct for Studying Law, Courts, and American Political Development?," *Good Society* 16 (2007): 40–45; Joyce Appleby, *Capitalism and a New Social Order: The Republican Vision of the 1790s* (New York: New York University Press, 1984); and Jerome Huyler, *Locke in America: The Moral Philosophy of the Founding Era* (Lawrence: University Press of Kansas, 1995).

33. See James Kloppenberg, "In Retrospect: Louis Hartz's *The Liberal Tradition in America*," *Reviews in American History* 29 (2001): 474–75; and John Locke, *Two Treatises of Government*, chap. 19, "Of the Dissolution of Government," sec. 222 (New York: Barnes and Noble Library, 2004), 123–5. Kloppenberg, a professor of history, writes that "Hartz's vague and imprecise analysis did to American thinkers what Walt Disney had done to Davy Crockett." Given Hartz's dominance in political science, Kloppenberg concludes that "criticizing Hartz thus ruffles feathers across the contemporary political spectrum. Too many people, right and left, have too much invested in the idea of an American liberal tradition to surrender it without a fight." Historian Sean Wilentz writes that "the great weakness of Hartz's approach was that, as a unified field theory of American political thought, it turned politics in a modern liberal polity into fake battles fought with wooden swords." Wilentz, "Uses of The Liberal Tradition: Comments on 'Still Louis Hartz after All These Years,'" *Perspectives on Politics* 3 (March 2005): 118.

34. Locke, *Two Treatises*, chap. 2, "Of the State of Nature," sec. 6, 4. and Maurice Cranston, "Are There Any Human Rights?," *Daedalus* 112 (1983): 1.

35. Locke, *Two Treatises*, chap. 5, "Of Property," sec. 35, 20. See also Peter C. Myers, "Between Divine and Human Sovereignty: The State of Nature and the Basis of Locke's Political Thought," *Polity* 27 (1995): 629–49.

36. Bell, *The End of Ideology*; and Paul Roazen, "Introduction," in Louis Hartz, *The Necessity of Choice: Nineteenth-Century Political Thought* (New Brunswick, NJ: Transaction Publishers, 1990), 8.

37. Cranston, "Are There Any Human Rights?," 2.

38. Some fault political economist C. B. Macpherson's interpretation of Hobbes that emphasized "possessive individualism," the cornerstone of modern capitalism, which influenced a generation of students. Macpherson was trained by Harold Laski. See C. B. Macpherson, "Introduction to Thomas Hobbes, *Leviathan*" (London: Penguin, 1968), 9–63. See also C. B. Macpherson, *The Political Theory of Possessive Individualism* (Oxford: Oxford University Press, 1962). See also Peter Hayes, "Hobbes's Bourgeois Moderation," *Polity* 31 (1998): 53–74. Finally, see Locke, *Two Treatises*, chap. 8, "Of the Beginnings of Political Societies," secs. 95–98, 52–53; and Cranston, "Are There Any Human Rights?," 4.

39. Locke, *Two Treatises*, chap. 2, "Of the State of Nature," sec. 6, 4.

40. Ibid.

41. Alex Scott Tuckness, in "Discourses of Resistance in the American Revolution," *Journal of the History of Ideas* 64 (2003): 547–63, makes the argument that there is no need to debate whether the Lockean or liberal tradition is more dominant than the Humean or republican tradition since there are multiple traditions, as Rogers Smith in *Civic Ideals: Conflicting Visions of Citizenship in U.S. History* (New Haven, CT: Yale University Press, 1999) also argues.

42. Isaiah Berlin, *Liberty: Incorporating Four Essays on Liberty* (New York: Oxford University Press, 2002, originally published 1969).

43. See Daniel Rodgers, "Republicanism: Career of a Concept," *Journal of American History* 79 (1992): 11–38; and Mark M. Smith, "Making Sense of Social History," *Journal of Social History* 37 (2003): 165–86.

44. Garry Wills relies on David Hume in *Explaining America: The Federalists, with a New Introduction* (New York: Penguin Press, 2001). See also chap. 15, "The Americanization of Virtue," in J. G. A. Pocock, *The Machiavellian Moment: Florentine Political Thought and the Atlantic Republican Tradition* (Princeton, NJ: Princeton University Press, 1975).

45. Beginning in the late 1980s, political scientists have taken a more nuanced position neither in support of nor in opposition to Hartz, starting with David Greenstone, in "Political Culture and American Political Development: Liberty, Union and the Liberal Bipolarity," *Studies in American Political Development* 1 (1986): 1–49. Arguably the harshest criticism of Hartz's dominance in American political development is Rogers Smith's book *Civic Ideals*. Finally, with Hartz writing in the late 1950s, when religion played a marginal role in politics, the absence of religious thought in his work has only recently been addressed, given the rise of the Right. See James A. Morone, *Hellfire Nation: The Politics of Sin in American History* (New Haven, CT: Yale University Press, 2003). See also Sandra M. Gustafson, "Histories of Democracy and Empire," *American Quarterly*

59 (2007): 107–33, for an interesting distinction the early Americanists in American Studies now insist on making between themselves and those who study the period after 1835, whom they call the U.S.-Americanists; and Carol Nackenoff, *The Fictional Republic: Horatio Alger and American Political Discourse* (New York: Oxford University Press, 1994).

46. Burnham was a realignment theory scholar whose work predated American political development in political science. See Walter Dean Burnham, "Party Development and the American Mainstream," in *The American Party System: Stages of Political Development*, ed. William Nisbet Chambers and Walter Dean Burnham (New York: Oxford University Press, 1981), 3–32. See also Werner Sombart's 1906 book *Why Is There No Socialism in the United States* (New York: Sharpe, 1976), mentioned by many in American political development to show that the question of American exceptionalism predated Hartz. Kenneth Finegold and Theda Skocpol, *State and Party in America's New Deal* (Madison: University of Wisconsin Press, 1995), offered an early historiography of APD, particularly in juxtaposition with Marx and Weber.

47. See Skowronek and Orren, *The Search for American Political Development*, for a good overview of the field; as well as Romain Huret, "All in the Family Again? Political Historians and the Challenge of Social History," *Journal of Policy History* 21 (2009): 239–63. See also Theda Skocpol, *States and Social Revolutions: A Comparative Analysis of France, Russia and China* (New York: Cambridge University Press, 1979); Stephen Skowronek, *Building a New American State: The Expansion of National Administrative Capacities, 1877–1920* (New York: Cambridge University Press, 1982); and Karen Orren, *Belated Feudalism: Labor, the Law, and Liberal Development in the United States* (New York: Cambridge University Press, 1992) for standard works as the field began burgeoning. Historian Gordon S. Wood supplemented the Founding Fathers and other primary members of the revolutionary elite with political tracts written by secondary members of this elite in *The Creation of the American Republic* (New York: W. W. Norton, 1969, first ed. University of North Carolina Press, 1969). This text of social history relied upon discourse theory, itself influenced by E. P. Thompson's *The Making of the English Working Class* (New York: Pantheon Books, 1964). Wood's republican perspective spawned a whole series of articles in American political development around the Progressive Era and the New Deal from Gerald Berkowitz, Amy Bridges, Daniel Carpenter, Howard Gillman, Ira Katznelson, Victoria Hattam, Eileen McDonagh, Suzanne Mettler, and Anne Norton to Karen Orren, Theda Skocpol, Stephen Skowronek and Rogers Smith as well as its own journal, titled *Studies in American Political Development*.

48. For an overview of the assumption "that the social democratic welfare states of Scandinavia were the norm," see Peter Baldwin, "Beyond Weak and Strong: Rethinking the State in Comparative Policy History," *Journal of Policy History* 17 (2005): 14; and Marshall, *Citizenship and Social Class*. See also Martin Bulmer and Anthony T. Rees, *Citizenship Today: The Contemporary Relevance of T. H. Marshall* (Bristol, PA: UCL Press, 1996). In criticizing Hartz, historians found other interpretations of the founders' vision: see Bernard Bailyn, *The Origins of American Politics* (New York: Vintage Books, 1970); Wood, *The Creation of the American Republic*. The republican interpretation evoked a

strong reaction from scholars who advocated the primacy of Lockean liberalism, as Zoltan Vajda explains. See Vajda, "John C. Calhoun's Republicanism Revisited," *Rhetoric & Public Affairs* 4 (2001): 433–57; Robert E. Shalhope, "Toward a Republican Synthesis: The Emergence of an Understanding of Republicanism in American Historiography," *William and Mary Quarterly* 29 (1972): 49–80.

49. See chap. 15 of Pocock, *The Machiavellian Moment*; John P. McCormick, "Machiavelli against Republicanism," *Political Theory* 30 (2003): 615–44; and Jean-Jacques Rousseau, *The Social Contract*, translated and introduced by Maurice Cranston (London: Penguin Books, 1968). This is the mainstream interpretation of Rousseau reflected by the work of Arthur M. Melzer, *The Natural Goodness of Man: On the Systems of Rousseau's Thought* (Chicago: University of Chicago Press, 1990); and Roger D. Masters, *The Political Philosophy of Rousseau* (Princeton, NJ: Princeton University Press, 1968).

50. Paul Pierson, "Increasing Returns, Path Dependence, and the Study of Politics," *American Political Science Review* 94 (2000): 251–67.

51. Rousseau, *The Social Contract*, book I, chap. 6, "The Social Pact," 59–60.

52. Alexis de Tocqueville, *Democracy in America*, vol. 2, chap. 2, "Of Individualism in Democratic Countries," sec. 2 (New York: Barnes and Noble. 2003), 469. Joan Wallach Scott, *Gender and the Politics of History* (New York: Columbia University Press, 1999); and Kimberlé Crenshaw, "Demarginalizing the Intersection of Race and Sex: A Black Feminist Critique of Antidiscrimination Doctrine, Feminist Theory and Antiracist Politics," *University of Chicago Legal Forum* (1989): 139–67.

53. Nancy Hirschmann, "Toward a Feminist Theory of Freedom," *Political Theory* 24 (1996): 49; and O'Brien, *Bodies in Revolt*, 63; and Rousseau, *The Social Contract*, book 1, chap. 7, "The Sovereign," 64.

54. Gabriel Kolko, *Railroads and Regulation: 1877–1916* (W. W. Norton, 1970); and Skowronek, *Building a New American State*; *Muller v. Oregon*, 208 U.S. 412 (1908), http://www.oyez.org/cases/1901-1939/1907/1907_107; *Lochner v. New York*, 198 U.S. 45 (1905), http://www.oyez.org/cases/1901-1939/1904/1904_292; see also Carol Nackenoff, *Jane Addams and the Practice of Democracy* (Urbana: University of Illinois Press, 2009).

55. Peter Kivisto, "What Is the Canonical Theory of Assimilation?," *Journal of the History of the Behavioral Sciences* 40 (2004): 151.

56. Morone, *Hellfire Nation*.

57. See Ezra Klein, "The Lessons of '94, The Three Reasons the Clinton Administration's Health Care Reform Effort Failed, and How the Next Democratic President Can Get It Right," *American Prospect*, January 22, 2008; http://www.prospect.org/cs/articles?article=the_lessons_of_94; Paul Starr, *The Social Transformation of American Medicine* (New York: Basic Books, 1982): 280–86; and James Colgrove, "Reform and Its Discontents: Public Health in New York City during the Great Society," *Journal of Policy History* 19 (2007): 3–28. The 1993 conservative coalition against the Clinton health-care reform had a $15 million "Harry and Louise" television advertisement campaign orchestrated by the Health Insurance Association of America, turning public opinion against it just when the president needed to "go public" to counteract his own party's hostility to the plan. "It was a terrible error to have the President doing what Congress

was supposed to do." Robin Toner, "Harry and Louise and a Guy Named Ben," *New York Times*, September 20, 1994. See also Rousseau, *Social Contract*.

58. Jean-Jacques Rousseau, *The Basic Political Writings*, trans. Donald A. Cress (Indianapolis: Hackett, 1987), 49. While the standard view makes this contrast, with some going so far as to equate Rousseau's idea of Justice with Platonic forms, there are a few who do not. See Melzer, *Natural Goodness of Man*; and Masters, *Political Philosophy of Rousseau*. For a more recent overview of the debate, see David Lay Williams, "Justice and the General Will: Affirming Rousseau's Ancient Orientation," *Journal of the History of Ideas* (2005): 384–85, 388. Williams takes the positivist position and also refers to Plato, arguing that the General Will is transcendently constrained, which is to say that it "presuppose[s] the existence of universal and immutable standards."

59. Rousseau, *Social Contract*.

60. Hirschmann, "Toward a Feminist Theory of Freedom," 49.

61. Mark Pittenger, "A World of Difference: Constructing the 'Underclass' in Progressive America," *American Quarterly* 49 (1997): 26–65.

62. Margaret Sanger promoted abortion, but was after all a eugenicist. "More children from the fit," her grandson Alexander Sanger quoted Margaret Sanger, "less from the unfit—that is the chief issue of birth control." See Alexander Sanger, "Eugenics, Race, and Margaret Sanger Revisited: Reproductive Freedom for All?," *Hypatia* 22 (2007): 210–17; and Dorothy Ross, *The Origins of American Social Science* (New York: Cambridge University Press, 1991), 387.

63. The more subtle view taking into account economic and cultural aspects of the United States and social movements is seen in the works of Victoria Hattam, *Labor Visions and State Power: The Origins of Business Unionism in the United States* (Princeton, NJ: Princeton University Press, 1993); Gretchen Ritter, *Goldbugs and Greenbacks: The Antimonopoly Tradition and the Politics of Finance in American 1865–1896* (New York: Cambridge University Press, 1997); and Julie Nokov, *Racial Union: Law, Intimacy, and the White State in Alabama, 1865–1954* (Ann Arbor: University of Michigan Press, 2008).

64. Editorial, "Boomerang Diplomacy," *Washington Post*, December 12, 2003.

CHAPTER TWO

1. Trevor Norris, "Hannah Arendt and Jean Baudrillard: Pedagogy in the Consumer Society," *The Encyclopedia of Informal Education*, http://www.infed.org/biblio/pedagogy_consumer_society.htm.

2. Joan Wallach Scott, *The Politics of the Veil* (Princeton, NJ: Princeton University Press, 2007); and David Marquand, *The End of the West: The Once and Future Europe* (Princeton, NJ: Princeton University Press, 2011).

3. T. H. Marshall, *Citizenship and Social Class* (London: Pluto Press, 1987), originally published 1950).

4. For a collection that incorporates post-1989 views of citizenship, see *Democratization in America: A Comparative-Historical Analysis*, ed. Desmond King, Robert C. Lieberman, Gretchen Ritter, and Laurence Whitehead (Baltimore, MD: Johns Hopkins University Press, 2009).

NOTES TO PAGES 29-33

5. For the complexity of the analysis, and the intent or varying perspectives promoting different political, social, and cultural ends, see Anne Norton, *On the Muslim Question* (Princeton, NJ: Princeton University Press, 2013).

6. Norton, *On the Muslim Question*; Scott, *Politics of the Veil*; and Marquand, *End of the West*.

7. Hannah Arendt, *The Human Condition* (Chicago: University of Chicago Press, 1958); and Jean Baudrillard, *The Consumer Society: Myths and Structures* (London: Sage Publications, 2004, first published in France in 1970). See Michael Hardt, "Jefferson and Democracy," *American Quarterly* 59 (2007): 41.

8. William E. Connolly, *The Terms of Political Discourse* (Oxford: Basil Blackwell, 1974), introduced this into political theory in political science, and entered the political theory mainstream with *theory & event* in the 1990s.

9. Helene Cooper and Robert F. Worth, "In Arab Spring, Obama Finds a Sharp Test," *New York Times*, September 25, 2012.

10. See Rosemary Garland Thomson, *Extraordinary Bodies: Figuring Disability in American Culture and Literature* (New York: Columbia University Press, 1996). See also Jay Dolmage, "Disabled upon Arrival: The Rhetorical Construction of Disability and Race at Ellis Island," *Cultural Critique* 77 (2011): 24–69.

11. Elinor Ostrom, *Governing the Commons: The Evolution of Institutions for Collective Action* (Cambridge: Cambridge University Press, 1990); Charlotte Hess and Elinor Ostrom, eds., *Understanding Knowledge as a Commons: From Theory to Practice* (Cambridge, MA: MIT Press, 2006), 10–11; Elinor Ostrom, "Polycentricity, Complexity, and the Commons," *Good Society* 9, no. 2 (1999): 39, 40; and Noëlle McAfee, "Three Models of Democratic Deliberation," *Journal of Speculative Philosophy* 18 (2004): 52.

12. Harry C. Boyte, "Public Work and the Politics of the Commons," *Good Society* 20 (2011): 85.

13. Alinsky, quoted from Boyte, "Public Work," 95. See Carmen Sirianni, *Investing in Democracy: Engaging Citizens in Collaborative Governance* (Washington: Brookings Institution Press, 2009); Xavier de Souza Briggs, *Democracy as Problem Solving: Civic Capacities in Communities Across the Globe* (Cambridge, MA: MIT Press, 2008); and Albert W. Dzur, *Democratic Professionalism: Citizen Participation and the Reconstruction of Professional Ethics, Identity, and Practice* (University Park, PA: Pennsylvania State University Press, 2008).

14. Ira Katznelson, *Shaped by War and Trade: International Influences on American Political Development* (Princeton, NJ: Princeton University Press, 2002).

15. Stephen J. Levitt and Stephen J. Dubner, *Freakonomics: A Rogue Economist Explores the Hidden Side of Everything* (New York: Harper Perennial, 2006). In *Superfreakonomics: Global Cooling, Patriotic Prostitutes, and Why Suicide Bombers Should Buy Life Insurance* (New York: Harper: Perennial Press, 2011), 4–5, Levitt and Dubner pose the question of reproductive rights by referring to women in India, making themselves less vulnerable to criticism than in their first book.

16. Mark Lilla, "The Tea Party Jacobins," *New York Review of Books*, May 27, 2010.

17. Arendt, *Human Condition*, 1, 2, 4, 208; *Support for Same-Sex Marriage Edges Upward: Majority Continues to Favor Gays Serving Openly in Military*, Pew Research Center publication, October 6, 2010, http://people-press.org/2010/10/06/support-for-same-sex-marriage-edges-upward/; and Norris, "Hannah Arendt and Jean Baudrillard."

18. Paul Stob, "Kenneth Burke, John Dewey, and the Pursuit of the Public," *Philosophy and Rhetoric* 38 (2005): 226–38; Matthew Caleb Flamm, "The Demanding Community: Politicization of the Individual after Dewey," *Education and Culture* 22 (2006): 35–54; and Lawrence J. Engel, "Saul D. Alinsky and the Chicago School," *Speculative Philosophy* 16 (2002): 75–102.

19. The dominance of Hartz has enabled historians and political scientists to dismiss grassroots interpretations or radical interpretations of American history as "un-American." James Kloppenberg writes that Hartz "came to prominence just as John Dewey's ideas went into eclipse." This book concurs that "it is not the sober-minded Hartz but the democratic 'seer' [Walt] Whitman who appears the more reliable guide to and the shrewder analyst of American culture." Kloppenberg, "In Retrospect," 474.

20. Kloppenberg, "In Retrospect," 474.

21. My contemporary interpretation of Spinoza stems from the radical Australian feminist interpretations of Elizabeth Grosz, Genevieve Lloyd, and Claire Colebrook. See Claire Colebrook, "From Radical Representations to Corporeal Becomings: The Feminist Philosophy of Lloyd, Grosz, and Gatens," *Hypatia* 15 (2000): 89.

22. I take a similar position that an alternative notion of an "ethic of care" can be adopted by examining survivability rather than benevolence in *Bodies in Revolt: Gender, Disability, and a Workplace Ethic of Care* (New York: Routledge, 2005). For other interpretations that do not view care from the perspective of benevolence, see Martha Albertson Fineman's body of work, including *The Autonomy Myth: A Theory of Dependency* (New York: New Press, 2005); Louis Menand, "The Science of Human Nature and the Human Nature of Science," *Sign Language Studies* 5 (2005): 182–83; and Debra Kodish, "Envisioning Folklore Activism," *Journal of American Folklore* 124 (2011): 31–60.

23. Amy Allen, "Power, Subjectivity, and Agency: Between Arendt and Foucault," *International Journal of Philosophical Studies* 10 (2002): 131–49, 142–43.

24. Arendt, *Human Condition*, 200.

25. Allen, "Power, Subjectivity, and Agency," 142–43; and Arendt, *Human Condition*, 140.

26. Warren Montag, "Who's Afraid of the Multitude? Between the Individual and the State," *South Atlantic Quarterly* 104 (2005): 658; and Barack Obama, *The Audacity of Hope: Thoughts on Reclaiming the American Dream* (New York: Crown Publishing Group and Three Rivers Press, 2006), 193.

27. Barack Obama, "Reclaiming the American Dream" (speech, Bettendorf, IA, November 7, 2007).

28. Obama, *Audacity of Hope*, 49; and Duane R. Patterson, "Michelle Obama's Vision of America," *Townhall.com*, February 15, 2008, http://townhall.com/tipsheet/duanerpatterson/2008/02/15/michelle_obamas_vision_of_america.

29. Spinoza came into great currency in the 1990s. See Gilles Deleuze, *Expressionism in Philosophy: Spinoza*, trans. Martin Joughin (New York: Zone, 1990); Gilles Deleuze, *Spinoza: Practical Philosophy*, trans. R. Hurley (San Francisco: City Lights Books, 1988); Gilles Deleuze, *Difference and Repetition*, trans. Paul Patton (London: Athlone Press, 1994); Moira Gatens and Genevieve Lloyd, *Collective Imaginings: Spinoza Past and Present* (London: Routledge, 1999); Moira Gatens, *Imaginary Bodies: Ethics, Power and Corporeality* (London: Routledge, 1996); Moira Gatens, "Feminism as 'Password': Re-thinking the 'Possible' with Spinoza and Deleuze," *Hypatia* 15 (2000): 72; and Michael Hardt and Antonio Negri, *Multitudes: War and Democracy in the Age of Empire* (London: Penguin, 2004). Gatens coins a new term—Deleuzo-Spinozist—as a way of referring to Deleuze's interpretation of Spinoza.

30. See the explanation of perfectibility in Georg Geismann, "Spinoza—Beyond Hobbes and Rousseau," *Journal of the History of Ideas* 52 (1991): 51. Geismann derives this interpretation from Spinoza, *The Collected Works of Spinoza*, ed. Edwin Curley, *Ethics III-IV* (Princeton, NJ: Princeton University Press, 1985).

31. Jeffrey Ball, "Charting the Road of Inquiry: Deleuze's Humean Pragmatics and the Challenge of Badiou," *Southern Journal of Philosophy* 44 (2006): 399–400.

32. Paul C. Taylor, "What's the Use of Calling Du Bois a Pragmatist?," *Metaphilosophy* 35 (2004): 112–13.

33. W. E. B. Du Bois, *The Souls of Black Folk* (New York: Signet Classics, 1995, originally published 1903). Randall Kenan's introduction has robust existential reflections.

34. Taylor, "What's the Use of Calling Du Bois a Pragmatist?," 109.

35. Cynthia D. Schrager, "Both Sides of the Veil: Race, Science and Mysticism in W. E. B. Du Bois," *American Quarterly* 48 (1996): 557.

36. Taylor, "What's the Use of Calling Du Bois a Pragmatist?," 112.

37. Schrager, "Both Sides of the Veil," 554–55.

38. Du Bois, *Souls of Black Folk*, 45; and David A. Frank and Mark Lawrence McPhail, "Barack Obama's Address to the 2004 Democratic National Convention: Trauma, Compromise, Consilience, and the (Im)possibility of Racial Reconciliation," *Rhetoric & Public Affairs* 8 (2005): 572.

39. Sarah Donovan, review of *Collective Imaginings: Spinoza, Past, and Present*, by Moira Gatens and Genevieve Lloyd, *Hypatia* 19 (2004): 178.

40. Thomas J. Sugrue, *Not Even Past: Barack Obama and the Burden of Race* (Princeton, NJ: Princeton University Press, 2010), 3. Obama promoted this view and went to great lengths to cement in the American imagination a redemptive progress narrative from Lincoln through King.

41. Quoted from David Remnick, *The Bridge: The Life and Rise of Barack Obama* (New York: Alfred Knopf, 2010), 23.

42. Sugrue, *Not Even Past*, 15. Both Remnick and Sugrue emphasize the Joshua theme.

43. Ibid., 15.

44. Ibid., 2–3. I differ from Sugrue, who argues that Obama embraces William Julius Wilson's landmark study, *The Declining Significance of Race*, on the culture of poverty.

45. In an article edited by his mentor, Ernest Burgess, Alinsky explained that his greatest success was "an experimental demonstration of a community organizational procedure predicated upon a functional conception of a community." Saul D. Alinsky, "Community Analysis and Organization," *American Journal of Sociology* 46 (1941): 798.

46. Engel, "Saul D. Alinsky and the Chicago School," 51; and John Dewey, *Logic: The Theory of Inquiry* (New York: Henry Holt, 1938).

47. William James, "The Chicago School," *Psychological Bulletin* 1 (1904): 2; and Engel, "Saul D. Alinsky and the Chicago School," 52. Pragmatism embraced social constructionism.

48. Harry C. Boyte, "A Different Kind of Politics: John Dewey and the Meaning of Citizenship in the 21st Century," *Good Society* 12 (2003): 5.

49. Dewey, *Logic*.

50. David Remnick, *The Bridge: The Life and Rise of Barack Obama* (New York: Alfred Knopf, 2010), 163.

51. Ibid., 133–40. Kellman recommended a biography of John L. Lewis and Robert Caro's *The Power Broker*.

52. Remnick, *The Bridge*, 179–80. Obama does believe that leadership matters, particularly charismatic leadership.

53. Mike Miller, "Special Feature: Organizing Youth," *Social Policy* 34 (2003): 107.

54. Alinsky, quoted in "Special Feature: Organizing Youth," 108. Alinsky lost most of his financial support in the early 1950s, though he succeeded in 1963 with the Temporary Woodlawn Organization, which prevented the University of Chicago from expanding at the expense of local African Americans. Some African American leaders took credit away from Alinsky, who died a "forgotten man." See Sanford D. Horwitt, *Let Them Call Me Rebel: Saul Alinsky, His Life and Legacy* (New York: Alfred Knopf, 1989).

55. Robert E. Lindquist and James F. Essman, "Overcoming Addiction: A Twelve Step Program for Building Power and Revitalizing the Labor Movement," *Social Policy* 36 (2006): 20.

56. Obama, quoted in John R. Talbot, *Obamanomics: How Bottom-Up Economic Prosperity Will Replace Trickle-Down Economics* (New York: Seven Stories, 2008), 35.

57. Barack Obama, "Calls for Middle Class Tax Cut Speech" (July 9, 2008), ABC News Radio, https://historymusings.wordpress.com/2012/07/09/full-text-obama-presidency-july-9-2012-president-barack-obamas-speech-extending-bush-era-tax-cuts-for-middle-class-families/.

58. Engel, "Saul D. Alinsky and the Chicago School," 52; and Barack Obama, "A More Perfect Union" (speech, Philadelphia, March 18, 2008).

59. Larissa MacFarquhar, "The Conciliator: Where Is Barack Obama Coming From?," *New Yorker*, May 7, 2006, 48, http://www.newyorker.com/reporting/2007/05/07/070507fa_fact_macfarquhar; and John B. Judis, "Creation Myth," *New Republic*, September 10, 2008, http://www.tnr.com/article/creation-myth.

60. Frank and McPhail, "Barack Obama's Address to the 2004 Democratic National Convention," 579, 582. See also Matthew Frye Jacobson, *Roots Too:*

White Ethnic Revival in Post Civil Rights America (Cambridge, MA: Harvard University Press, 2006); and O'Brien, *Bodies in Revolt*, 63–65.

61. Barack Obama, "Iowa Caucus Victory Speech" (Des Moines, IA, January 3, 2008).

62. Cornel West criticizes Obama because "when you run from history, you run from memory," and says that "he should be able to acknowledge and affirm all of the sacrifice that has gone in for him to be where he is." Dr. Julianne Malveaux, president of Bennett College, said, "I agree with Cornel completely. The fact is that he basically perpetrated a whitewash of our history." http:// www.pbs.org/kcet/tavissmiley/archive/200808/20080828_drsjuliannemalvea .html; transcript on http://yourblackpower.blogspot.com/2008/08/your-black -politics-did-barack-obama.html (August 29, 2008). See also the debate between civil rights activists and Shelby Steele, a conservative who believes in racial transcendence, in Richard Fausset, "Obama's Race Is Seen as a 'Bonus,'" *New Republic*, November 3, 2008; Nathaniel X. Turner II, "Barack Hussein Obama: The Meteoric Rise of a Race-Neutered Presidential Candidate," *Black Agenda Report*, June 6, 2007, http://www.blackagendareport.com/node/10239; Obama, "A More Perfect Union"; John Dewey, *Individualism Old and New* (Amherst, NY: Prometheus Books, 1999), 33. Finally, see Larry A. Hickman, "Pragmatism, Postmodernism, and Global Citizenship," *Metaphilosophy* (2004): 65–81; and see Jacobson, *Roots Too*, 179, for his argument that the conservative pluralists reassert "white hierarchy, primacy, and exclusion" but dress it up as civic nationalism. Obama rejects both the New Left multiculturalism and the conservative pluralists.

63. See Katherine Adams, "At the Table with Arendt: Toward a Self-Interested Practice of Coalition Discourse," *Hypatia* 17 (2002): 15; and Judis, "Creation of a Myth."

64. Frank and McPhail, "Barack Obama's Address to the 2004 Democratic National Convention," 571–72.

65. Philip Goodchild, "Deleuzean Ethics," *Theory, Culture, & Society* 14 (1997): 39–50.

66. Gilles Deleuze, *Empiricism and Subjectivity: An Essay on Hume's Theory of Human Nature* (New York: Columbia University Press, 1991), 133; Goodchild, "Deleuzean Ethics," 39–41; and Deleuze, *Spinoza*, 23.

67. Zygmunt Bauman, *Postmodern Ethics* (London: Blackwell Publishers, 1993); and Zygmunt Bauman, *Wasted Lives: Modernity and Its Outcasts* (Cambridge: Polity Press, 2004).

68. Zygmunt Bauman, *Life in Fragments: Essays in Postmodern Morality* (Oxford: Wiley-Blackwell, 1995), 55.

69. Goodchild, "Deleuzean Ethics," 43.

70. James Livingston, "'Marxism' and the Politics of History: Reflections on the Work of Eugene D. Genovese," *Radical History Review* 88 (2004): 31.

71. Barbara Thayer-Bacon, "Pragmatism and Feminism as Qualified Relativism," *Studies in Philosophy and Education* 22 (2003): 424.

72. Ibid., 425–26.

73. Thayer-Bacon, "Pragmatism and Feminism"; and Hickman, "Pragmatism, Postmodernism, and Global Citizenship," 65–81, 71.

74. Nicholas O. Pagan, "Configuring the Moral Self: Aristotle and Dewey," *Foundational Science* 13 (2008): 240. Quoted in Daniel Savage, *John Dewey's Liberalism: Individual, Community, and Self-Development* (Carbondale, IL: Southern Illinois University, 2002), 2, from James Dewey, *Essays in Experimental Logic* (Chicago: University of Chicago Press, 1918), 181.

75. Shaun O'Dwyer, "The Classical Conservative Challenge to Dewey," *Transactions of the Charles S. Peirce Society* 37 (2001): 494.

76. Ibid., 500, 507.

77. Thayer-Bacon, "Pragmatism and Feminism," 417; and Philip E. Devine, *Relativism, Nihilism, and God* (Notre Dame, IN: University of Notre Dame Press, 1989), 43.

78. Thayer-Bacon, "Pragmatism and Feminism," 418.

79. Devine, *Relativism, Nihilism, and God*, 28.

80. Deleuze, Spinoza, 54, referring to Spinoza, *Ethics*, II, 37–39; Gilles Deleuze, *Spinoza: Practical Philosophy*, Robert Hurley, trans. (San Francisco: City Lights Books, 1988), 55–57, 114–21; and Gilles Deleuze, *Difference and Repetition*, trans. Paul Patton (London: Athlone Press, 1994). For the Euclidian history preceding Spinoza, see Leonard Mlodinow, *Euclid's Window: The Story of Geometry from Parallel Lines to Hyperspace* (New York: Simon and Schuster, 2002), 34–35. For practical applications, see Catherine Mary Dale, "A Queer Supplement: Reading Spinoza after Grosz," *Hypatia* 14 (1999); 8–9; and Jean L. Cohen and Andrew Arato, *Civil Society and Political Theory* (Cambridge, MA: MIT Press, 1992).

81. Second Part, Proposition 18, in Spinoza, *Ethics*, rev., trans., and ed. G. H. R. Parkinson (London: J. M. Dent & Sons, 1989), 66–67.

82. Third Part, Proposition 18, in Spinoza, *Ethics*, 62.

83. Geismann, "Spinoza," 48–51.

84. Adams, "At the Table with Arendt," 16–17.

85. Ibid.; Thayer-Bacon, "Pragmatism and Feminism"; and Devine, *Relativism, Nihilism, and God*, 39–40.

86. Adams, "At the Table with Arendt," 2.

87. Ibid., 3. See also Gloria Anzaldúa, *Borderlands: The New Mestiza = La Frontera*, 2nd ed. (San Francisco: Aunt Lute Books, 1999).

88. Susan Stanford Friedman, *Mappings* (Princeton, NJ: Princeton University Press, 1998), 22 and 47.

89. Diane L. Fowlkes, "Moving from Feminist Identity Politics to Coalition Politics through a Materialist Standpoint of Intersubjectivity in Gloria Anzaldúa's *Borderlands/La frontera: The New Mestiza*," *Hypatia* 12 (1997): 105–124.

90. Jane Mansbridge, "Self-Interest and Political Transformation," in *Reconsidering the Democratic Public*, ed. George E. Marcus and Russell L. Hanson (University Park: Pennsylvania State University Press, 1993), 96.

91. Adams, "At the Table with Arendt," 4–5.

92. Ibid., 8.

93. The American political values of freedom and equality are usually seen in balance, not one as a prerequisite of another. "Most of the time, equality means equality of opportunity or treatment, and perhaps the most frequent middle American conception of equality is equality of opportunity for people to work hard so as to achieve success, whether in escaping poverty or becoming rich,"

writes Herbert J. Gans in *Middle American Individualism: Political Participation and Liberal Democracy* (New York: Oxford University Press, 1988), 37.

94. Obama, *Audacity of Hope*, 68.

95. Obama, quoted in Talbot, *Obamanomics*, 175–86. Talbot titles a chapter "Cooperation Is the Key."

96. Amartya Sen, *Development as Freedom* (New York: Anchor Books, 1999), chap. 5. See Andrew Glyn, *Capitalism Unleashed: Finance Globalization and Welfare* (Oxford: Oxford University Press, 2006), 167 and 175. The United States and the United Kingdom have the greatest income inequality among the wealthy nations, with the Scandinavian countries on the other end of the spectrum with the least amount of it.

97. Gatens, "Feminism as 'Password,'" 62–63.

98. Norris, "Hannah Arendt and Jean Baudrillard"; and Benjamin R. Barber, *Jihad vs. McWorld: How Globalism and Tribalism Are Reshaping the World* (New York: Ballantine Books, 1995).

99. Obama, quoted in Talbot, *Obamanomics*, 181.

100. To expand the notion of internal rational and emotional constraints, see Kristen Renwick Monroe, Adam Martin, and Priyanka Ghosh, "Politics and an Innate Moral Sense: Scientific Evidence for an Old Theory?," *Political Research Quarterly* 62 (2009): 614–34, for an excellent overview. See also Rebecca Newberger Goldstein, *Betraying Spinoza: The Renegade Jew Who Gave Us Modernity* (New York: Schocken Books, 2009); 9–17; and Leonard Mlodinow, *Subliminal: How Your Unconscious Mind Rules Your Behavior* (New York: Pantheon Books, 2012); on the assumptions underlying rational actors.

101. Obama, *Audacity of Hope*, 63.

102. See Thomas J. Papadimos and Alan P. Marcho, "A Struggle with Obligation: Ethical Reflections on a Transplantation Program," *Hospital Topics* 80 (2002): 19–20; and Obama, "A More Perfect Union."

103. Judy Purdom, "Connections," *Hypatia* 15 (2000): 21–22. See Gatens, *Imaginary Bodies*, chaps. 7 and 8.

104. Geismann, "Spinoza," 40. See Genevieve Lloyd and Moira Gatens, "The Power of Spinoza: Feminist Conjunctions," interview by Susan James, *Hypatia* 15 (2000): 43–50.

105. Lloyd and Gatens, "Power of Spinoza," 43–50.

106. Ibid., 50–51.

107. Geismann, "Spinoza," 44–45, 48.

108. Moira Gatens and Genevieve Lloyd, *Collective Imaginings, Spinoza, Past and Present* (New York: Routledge, 1999), 105.

109. Geismann, "Spinoza," 37.

110. Ibid., 43; Purdom, "Connections," 21–22. See Gatens, *Imaginary Bodies*, chaps. 7 and 8.

111. Spinoza was committed to a diversity of faiths. See O'Brien, *Bodies in Revolt*, 67–69.

112. Geismann, "Spinoza," 41.

113. Ibid., 42–43.

114. Ibid., 52–53.

115. Christopher Norris, *Spinoza and the Origins of Modern Critical Theory* (London: Basil Blackwell, 1991); and Lloyd and Gatens, "Power of Spinoza," 43–50.

116. See Ernst Cassirer, *The Philosophy of the Enlightenment*, trans. Fritz C. A. Koelin and James P. Pettegrove (Princeton, NJ: Princeton University Press, 1951). Progress does not necessarily coincide with the perfectibility of humankind, as it does with the Enlightenment. Spinoza is associated with the moderate Enlightenment that advances skepticism. See Jonathan Israel, *Radical Enlightenment Philosophy and the Making of Modernity, 1650–1750* (New York: Oxford University Press, 2002) and Antonio Damasio, *Looking for Spinoza: Joy, Sorrow, and the Feeding Brain* (New York: Harcourt Press, 2003). For an excellent review of both books, see also Connolly, "Radical Enlightenment."

117. For comparative purposes, the term "wealthy nations" is preferred to either "first world" (vs. "third world") or "industrialized" (vs. "developing") because, as a result of globalism, many formerly third-world nations have a middle class equivalent to that in the United States, and the United States has some pockets of poverty that rival those in what were formerly called third-world or developing nations. See "N for Negri: Antonio Negri in Conversation with Carlos Guerra," ed. and trans. Jorge Mestre et al., *Grey Room* 11 (2003): 95, in which Negri says, "The First and Third are present inside every state." See also Michael J. Perry, *The Idea of Human Rights: Four Inquiries* (New York: Oxford University Press, 1998).

118. J. David Roessner's introduction in "Symposium on Innovation Policy," *Policy Studies Review* 3 (1984): 431, says that the United States has always had innovation policies: "Rooted in the Constitution itself, the Patent Act of 1790 acknowledged the value to the nation of stimulating the rate of invention by granting inventors temporary monopoly control over the sale of the physical embodiment of their ideas."

119. Frederick Jackson Turner, "The Significance of the Frontier in American History," *Report of the American Historical Association* (1893): 199–227. See also Patrick Griffin, *American Leviathan: Empire, Nation, and Revolutionary Frontier* (New York: Hill and Wang, 2007).

120. See Robert J. Lacey, *American Pragmatism and Democratic Faith* (DeKalb, IL: Northern Illinois University Press, 2007); Robert Westbrook, *Democratic Hope: Pragmatism and the Politics of Truth* (New York: Cornell University Press, 2005); and Morris Dickstein, ed., *The Revival of Pragmatism: New Essays on Social Thought, Law, and Culture* (Durham, NC: Duke University Press, 1998).

121. Obama, *Audacity of Hope*, 8. An immigrant nation long recognized more for tolerance, yet the question is: is slavery is the exception? Or do the vestiges of slavery remain, becoming manifest in white supremacy or ethnocentric supremacy of some kind? See Rogers Smith's view of supremacy in APD, well expressed in "Beyond Tocqueville, Myrdal, and Hartz: The Multiple Traditions in America," *American Political Science Review* 87 (1993): 549. See also Catherine A. Holland, "Giving Reasons: Rethinking Toleration for a Plural World," *theory & event* (2000): 4. For the more general question of liberalism, multiculturalism, and

tolerance, see Michael Walzer, *On Toleration* (New Haven, CT: Yale University Press, 1997); and Will Kymlicka, *Multicultural Citizenship* (Oxford: Clarendon, 1995).

122. Professor of religion Curtis J. Evans, in *The Burden of Black Religion* (New York: Oxford University Press, 2008), uses this phrase in deference to George Frederickson, *The Black Image in the White Mind, The Debate on Afro-American Character and Destiny, 1817–1914* (New York: Wesleyan University Press, 1971).

123. Ed Sherwood, "Obama and Black Liberation Theology: Questions Still Unanswered," *Washington Times*, May 2, 2008, is an example of an editorial from the Right. See also "The Silencing of Bill Ayers and Jeremiah Wright," *National Review Online*, November 1, 2008. In 2006 *National Review* came out in support of Obama's perspective on religion when he reprimanded Democrats for not understanding the value of religion as an expression of social justice; see Peter Wood, "Obama's Prayer: Wooing Evangelicals," *National Review*, July 6, 2006; E. J. Dionne, "Obama's Eloquent Faith," *Washington Post*, June 30, 2006. See Jonathon S. Kahn, review of *W. E. B. Du Bois: American Prophet*, by Edward Blum, *Callaloo* 31 (2008): 622.

124. Remnick, *The Bridge*, 174.

125. See Scott, *Politics of the Veil*, for an excellent overview of the resurgence of nationalism and racism in France. See also Robert Caplan and John Feffer, *Europe's New Nationalism: States and Minorities in Conflict* (New York; Oxford University Press, 1996); and Joel S. Fetzer and J. Christopher Soner, *Muslims and the State in Britain, France, and Germany* (Cambridge: Cambridge University Press, 2004).

126. See the Walter Lippmann and John Dewey debate in John Dewey, *The Public and Its Problems* (New York: H. Holt, 1927); Walter Lippmann, "The Hope of Democracy," *New Republic*, November 12, 1916, 231; Walter Lippmann, *Public Opinion* (New York: York; Harcourt, Brace. 1922); and Amartya Sen, *Development as Freedom* (New York: Anchor Books, 1999), 292–97, which connects this debate about freedom with pragmatism found in both Dewey's and Obama's notion of human capability.

127. Remnick, *The Bridge*, 163; and Barack Obama, "A Politics of Conscience" (speech delivered to United Church of Christ General Synod, Hartford, CT, June 23, 2007), http://www.asksam.com/ebooks/releases.asp?file=Obama-Speeches.ask&dsn=A%20Politics%20of%20Conscience. "Such a perspective," explains Harry Boyte, "recognizes each person as a unique, meaning-making, story-telling and immensely complex individual." Harry C. Boyte, "Public Work and the Politics of the Commons," *Good Society* 20 (2011): 95.

128. Boyte, "Public Work," 91. See Harry C. Boyte, "Reframing Democracy: Governance, Civic Agency, and Politics," *Public Administration Review* 65 (2005): 536–46.

CHAPTER THREE

1. John R. Talbot, *Obamanomics: How Bottom-Up Economic Prosperity Will Replace Trickle-Down Economics* (New York: Seven Stories, 2008), 175.

2. Republican bloggers claimed him, with "Right Speech, Wrong Convention," http://www.nationalreview.com/corner/83000/right-speech-wrong-convention /roger-clegg; and "Barack Obama: A Republican Soul Trapped inside a Democrat's Body," http://www.ashbrook.org/publicat/oped/morel/04/obama.html.

3. Barack Obama, "2004 Democratic National Convention Keynote Address" (July 27, 2004), http://www.americanrhetoric.com/speeches/convention 2004/barackobama2004dnc.htm. My italics.

4. See Kathy Weimers, "Birth Control Controversy—How Did We Get Here?," *The Fact Finders* (March 23, 2012), http://www.thefactfinders.org/1 /post/2012/03/birth-control-controversy-how-did-we-get-here.html.

5. Jon Swaine, "Obama Offers 'Amnesty' for Up to 800,000 Young Illegal Immigrants," *Daily Telegraph*, June 16, 2012; David Usborne, "Obama Lifts Deportation Threat for 800,000 Young Illegal Immigrants; President Builds on Support among Hispanic Voters in Swing States with Shock Announcement," *Independent*, June 16, 2012; and "Plouffe Defends Obama Immigration Change, Criticizes Romney," *Los Angeles Times*, June 17, 2012.

6. I am appropriating the term *neotribalism* mainly from the postmodern Left, which applied it to the Burning Man and Rainbow subcultures, among others. By contrast, this application, returning the term to its historical roots, equates neotribalism with the conservative patriarchal beliefs that are transnational in the fundamentalism of the three religions. It does so to highlight the global religious resurgence beginning in the 1970s and 1980s that tries to reassert patriarchal rule in the face of an ever-changing world that no longer supports violence against women and violence against children. For the rise of the conflict, see Nikki R. Keddie, "Secularism and Its Discontents," *Daedalus* 132 (2003): 14–30; and Gilles Kepel, *The Revenge of God: The Resurgence of Islam, Christianity, and Judaism in the Modern World* (University Park, PA: Penn State University Press, 1993), For the romantic Left, see Michel Maffesoli, *The Time of the Tribes: The Decline of Individualism in Mass Society* (London: Sage, 1996). For American participation in the UN's efforts to stem violence against women, see Luisa Blanchfield, *United Nations System Efforts to Address Violence Against Women*, Congressional Research Service, July 12, 2011, 11–13, which outlines UN Resolutions 1325, 1888, and 1889 [UN documents S/RES/1325 (2000); S/ RES/1888 (2009); S/RES/1889 (2009)]. Resolution 1325 "addresses the impact of war and conflict on women and highlights the need for protection of women and girls from human rights abuses." Resolution 1888 "demands that all parties to armed conflict 'take appropriate measures to protect civilians, including women and children, from all forms of sexual violence.'" . . . "The United States, which served as Security Council president for September, strongly supported the adoption of the resolution, with U.S. Secretary of State Hillary Clinton serving as Chair of the Council meeting when the resolution was adopted." Resolution 1889 addresses "obstacles to women's involvement," and it emphasizes "the responsibility of all States to end impunity and prosecute those responsible for all forms of violence committed against girls and women in armed conflict, including rape and other sexual violence." The UN Agency for Women merged several preexisting entities: the Office of the Special Adviser on Gender Issues and the Advancement of Women (OSAGI); the Division for the Advancement of

Women (DAW); the UN Development Fund for Women (UNIFEM); and the UN International Research and Training Institute for the Advancement of Women (INSTRAW). Blanchfield lists, for example, the issues of "raising awareness of VAW in local and national governments—particularly among law enforcement, parliamentarians, government ministries, and the judiciary."

7. See Mona Eltahawy, "Why Do They Hate Us? The Real War on Women Is in the Middle East," *Foreign Policy* (May/June 2012), http://www.foreignpolicy .com/articles/2012/04/23/why_do_they_hate_us; E. J. Dionne Jr., "A Catholic Spring?," *Washington Post*, May 24, 2012. The Eltahawy article went viral with 70,000 "likes." See "Visualizing the War on Women Debate," *Foreign Policy*, July/August 2012.

8. For divisions between Catholic nuns and priests, see Amy Davidson, "The War on Nuns: Two Women Go to Rome," *New Yorker*, June 1, 2012, http://www.newyorker.com/online/blogs/closeread/2012/06/the-war-on-nuns -two-women-go-to-rome.html#ixzz1yMQFvS7s. For the RFRA, see Marie A. Failinger, "Finding a Voice of Challenge: The State Responds to Religious Women and Their Communities," *University of Southern California Review of Law and Social Justice* 21 (2012): 137; Martha Minow, "Is Pluralism an Ideal or a Compromise?," *Connecticut Law Review* 40 (2008): 1287; and Martha Minow, "The Judge: Religion and the Burden of Proof: Posner's Economics and Pragmatism in *Metzl v. Leininger*," *Harvard Law Review* 120 (2007): 1175.

9. Eltahawy, "Why Do They Hate Us?"

10. The Supreme Court undermined the Violence against Women Act of 1994 in a 5–4 decision, *United States v. Morrison*, 529 U.S. 598 (2000), ruling that the federal government lacked the power to enforce it under the commerce clause of the U. S. Constitution and under Section 5 of the Fourteenth Amendment. See Laura Bassett, "White House Threatens to Veto House GOP's Violence Against Women Act," *Huffington Post*, May 15, 2012, http://www .huffingtonpost.com/2012/05/15/violence-against-women-act-white-house -veto-threat_n_1519402.html. For religious freedom and universalism, see Seyla Benhabib, "Claiming Rights across Borders: International Human Rights and Democratic Sovereignty," *American Political Science Review* 103 (2009): 691– 704; Joan Wallach Scott, *The Politics of the Veil* (Princeton, NJ: Princeton University Press, 2007); Joan Wallach Scott, *Parité! Sexual Equality and the Crisis of French Universalism* (Chicago: University of Chicago Press, 2005); Anne Norton, *On the Muslim Question* (Princeton, NJ: Princeton University Press, 2013); Ayelet Shachar, *Multicultural Jurisdictions, Cultural Differences and Women's Rights* (New York: Cambridge University Press, 2001); and Dag Ølstein Endsjø, *Sex and Religion: Teachings and Taboos in the History of World Faiths* (Chicago: University of Chicago Press, 2011).

11. Michael Gerson, "Obama's Crumbling Catholic Vote," *Washington Post*, May 22, 2012. The Catholic Church lawsuits against the Obama administration include the New York and Washington archdioceses, the Michigan Catholic Conference, Catholic Charities in Illinois, Mississippi, Missouri, and Indiana, health care agencies in New York, and two dioceses in Texas.

12. Susan Crabtree, "Catholics' Suit Draws Dividing Line for Obama," *Washington Times*, May 29, 2012; "A Religious Exception?," *Los Angeles*

Times, May 30, 2012; and Eric Schmidt, *Restless Souls: The Making of American Spirituality* (New York: Harper, 2005), 287. Obama said, "My mother saw religion as an impediment to broader values like tolerance and racial inclusivity. She remembered churchgoing folks who also called people nigger." Quoted in Leigh E. Schmidt, "Spirituality in America," *Wilson Quarterly*, Summer 2005, 43. Obama saw her as extremely spiritual, though she did not attend a weekly sermon at church. Obama expanded home visiting programs, hoping to please both sides. See Heather D. Boonstra, "Home Visiting for At-Risk Families: A Primer on a Major Obama Administration Initiative," *Guttmacher Policy Review* 12, no. 3 (2009), http://www.guttmacher.org/pubs/gpr/12/3/gpr120311 .html.

13. The speech was uncharacteristically Reaganesque or sunny. See http:// www.washingtonpost.com/wp-dyn/articles/A19751-2004Ju127.html.

14. Dewey's progressivism never became manifest in the New Deal. See Susan Schulten, "Barack Obama, Abraham Lincoln, and John Dewey," *Denver University Law Review* 86 (2009): 807–18.

15. David Leonhardt, "How Obama Reconciles Dueling Views on Economy," *New York Times*, August 24, 2008; and Richard Cohen, "Obama Loses Veneer of Deniability with Intelligence Leaks," *Washington Post*, June 11, 2012.

16. Obama prefers advice from academics, not lawyers or lobbyists. These academics include Austan Goolsbee, a progressive, market-oriented behavioral economist, and Cass Sunstein, director of the Office of Information and Regulatory Affairs within the Office of Management and Budget, both from the University of Chicago. See Ron Suskind, *Confidence Men: Wall Street, Washington, and the Education of a President* (New York: Harper, 2011), 15–17. Among the journalists, Suskind gives the most attention to behavioral economics and social science.

17. Barack Obama, "A More Perfect Union" (speech, Philadelphia, March 18, 2008), http://www.huffingtonpost.com/2008/03/18/obama-race-speech-read -th_n_92077.html.

18. Barack Obama, "Stimulus Speech" (George Mason University, Fairfax, VA, January 8, 2009), http://www.nytimes.com/2009/01/08/us/politics/08text -obama.html?pagewanted=all; Barack Obama, "Speech in Osawatomie, Kansas" (December 6, 2011): "we're not forgetting the poor. They are going to be front and center."

19. Talbot, *Obamanomics*, 56–58; and Ken Wheaton, "Debate Surrounding Obama's 'Julia' Is a Rare Thing—One that Matters," *Advertising Age*, May 14, 2012.

20. Kevin Leicht and Scott Fitzgerald, *Postindustrial Peasants: The Illusion of Middle Class Prosperity* (New York: Worth Publishers, 2006); "About the Middle Class Task Force," Office of the Vice President, http://www.white-house.gov/strongmiddleclass/about. No official definition of the middle class exists. See Thomas J. Billitteri, "Middle-Class Squeeze: Is More Government Aid Needed?," *CQ Researcher* 19, no. 9 (Washington, DC, Congressional Quarterly Press, 2009). Obama defined the middle class at a presidential candidates' forum at Reverend Rick Warren's Saddleback Church (Lake Forest, CA, August 15,

2008), CNN Live Events Transcript, http://transcripts.cnn.com/TRANSCRIPTS /0808/16/se.02.html.

21. Joel Kotkin, "The End of Upward Mobility?," *Newsweek*, January 16, 2009, http://www.thedailybeast.com/newsweek/2009/01/16/the-end-of-upward -mobility.htm.

22. See Billitteri, "Middle-Class Squeeze"; and Jennifer Goloboy, "The American Middle Class," *Journal of the Early Republic* 25 (2005): 537.

23. Sullivan and Wheary are quoted in Billitteri, "Middle-Class Squeeze," 2.

24. See Jacob S. Hacker, *The Great Risk Shift: The New Economic Insecurity* (New York: Oxford University Press, 2006); Obama, "Speech in Osawatomie, Kansas"; and "Inside the Middle Class: Bad Times Hit the Good Life," Pew Research Center Publications, April 9, 2008, http://pewresearch.org/pubs/793 /inside-the-middle-class.

25. Duane R. Patterson, "Michelle Obama's Vision of America," *Townhall .com*, February 15, 2008, http://townhall.com/tipsheet/duanerpatterson/2008 /02/15/michelle_obamas_vision_of_america; Obama, "Speech in Osawatomie, Kansas." See *Historical Effective Tax Rates, 1979 to 2005: Supplement with Additional Data on Sources of Income and High-Income Households*, Congressional Budget Office, December 3, 2008, http://www.cbo.gov/publication/20374.

26. Elizabeth Warren and Amelia Warren Tyagi, *The Two-Income Trap: Why Middle Class Mothers and Fathers Are Going Broke* (New York: Basic Books, 2003).

27. Elizabeth Warren, "Unsafe at Any Rate: If It's Good Enough for Microwaves, It's Good Enough for Mortgages: Why We Need a Financial Product Safety Commission," *Democracy*, December 2007; *Assessing Treasury's Strategy: Six Months of TARP*, Congressional Oversight Panel, April 7, 2009, http:// cybercemetery.unt.edu/archive/cop/20110401232137/http://cop.senate.gov /reports/library/report-040709-cop.cfm.

28. "Congressional Republicans have been howling," one journalist explained, "about the prospect of her [Warren] leading the agency." In support, 89 Democrats in the House of Representatives endorsed her, along with liberal interest groups and consumer advocacy groups. David Corn, "Elizabeth Warren: Passed Over for CFPB Post, But . . . " *Nation*, July 17, 2011.

29. Jim Puzzanghera, "A Battle over Consumer Agency; House Republicans Clash with Elizabeth Warren, Who's Helping Launch the Unit," *Los Angeles Times*, May 25, 2011; Helene Cooper and Jennifer Steinhauer, "Bucking Senate, Obama Appoints Consumer Chief," *New York Times*, January 5, 2012.

30. "Nominee Has Taken On Banks Before." Joining the 44 of 47 Republicans who protested Warren's appointment, Democratic Senator Max Baucus suggested that the bureau regulates "all financial products and services, so if it involves a dollar changing hands, they can regulate it, or she can, because she actually has total discretion" over consumer financial products. Together, they proposed a five-person bipartisan commission rather than a single director.

31. Ben Protess, "Director or Not, Wall Street's Newest Cop Is Ready for Duty," *New York Times*, June 21, 2011; and Michael Lyle, Heath Tarbert, and Sunny Thompson-Weil, "Dodd-Frank, One Year Later: A Primer on the Federal Rulemaking Process," *Metropolitan Corporate Counsel*, August 2011.

32. James Q. Wilson, *Bureaucracy: What Government Agencies Do and Why They Do It* (New York: Basic Books Classics, 1991); Daniel J. Gifford, "New Deal Regulatory Model: A History of Criticisms and Refinement," *Minnesota Law Review* 68 (1983–1984): 299; Ernesto Dal Bo, "Regulatory Capture: A Review," *Oxford Review of Economic Policy* 22 (2006): 203; and John Shepard Wiley Jr., "A Capture Theory of Antitrust Federalism," *Harvard Law Review* 99 (1985–86): 713.

33. Martha Joynt Kumar, "The 2008–2009 Presidential Transition through the Voices of Its Participants," *Presidential Studies Quarterly* 39 (2009): 823. Not since Nixon had a president made a faster transition. See also Michael Falcone, "Obama Camp Pulls Issue Pages from Transition Site," *New York Times*, November 11, 2008.

34. Joe Biden, "Middle Class Task Force," http://www.whitehouse.gov /strongmiddleclass; "President Obama: America 'Not Better Off' Today than Four Years Ago," *ABC News*, October 3, 2011; and Thomas Byrne Edsall, *The Age of Austerity: How Scarcity Will Remake American Politics* (New York: Doubleday, 2012).

35. Jesse Jackson, "Gingrich Plays Old South Race Card of a Bygone Era," *Chicago Sun Times*, January 23, 2012.

36. "Presidential Proclamation—Father's Day" (June 18, 2010), http://www .whitehouse.gov/the-press-office/presidential-proclamation-fathers-day.

37. "Obama on Gay Marriage Position: 'I'm Still Working on It,'" *Huffington Post*, January 18, 2012, http://www.huffingtonpost.com/2011/10/03 /obama_n_993393.html; Naomi Gerstel, "Rethinking Families and Community: The Color, Class, and Centrality of Extended Kin Ties," *Sociological Forum* 26 (2011): 1–20; and Robert Pear, "Gay Workers Will Get Time to Care for Partner's Sick Child," *New York Times*, June 22, 2010.

38. My italics. "No major party presidential candidate ever presented a more ambitiously aggressive gay rights platform than did Barack Obama," wrote Jane Schacter. Obama supported the Employment Non-Discrimination Act (ENDA), the Matthew Shepard Hate Crimes Act, and increased funding for HIV assistance while opposing the Defense of Marriage Act (DOMA) and the Don't Ask, Don't Tell policy. Jane S. Schacter, "The Early Obama Administration: Capacity and Context: LGBT Rights and the Obama Administration's First Year," *Stanford Journal of Civil Rights & Civil Liberties* 6 (2010): 147.

39. Sara E. Farber, "Presidential Promises and the Uniting American Families Act: Bringing Same-Sex Immigration Rights to the United States," *Boston College Third World Law Journal* 30 (2010): 333. Farber cites an "Open Letter From Barack Obama, Candidate for President of the United States" (February 28, 2008), on file with Organizing for America, http://www.gaylesbiantimes .com/?id=5331&issue=915.

40. Ed O'Keefe, "Change in Passport Language Is Boon to Gay Rights Activists," *Washington Post*, January 12, 2011; "Obama's War on the Traditional Family; Radical Groups Dictate Administration," *Washington Times*, July 1, 2010.

41. Obama, "A More Perfect Union."

42. Ibid.

43. Ibid.

44. Ibid.; and Rosemarie Garland Thomson, *Extraordinary Bodies: Figuring Physical Disability in American Literature and Culture* (New York: Columbia University Press, 1997).

45. Alexis Simendinger and Jeannette J. Lee, "Reaching for the Baton," *National Journal*, November 8, 2008, 71; Jonathan Alter, "America's New Shrink," *Newsweek*, March 2, 2009, 19–23; and Ceci Connolly and R. Jeffrey Smith, "Obama Positioned to Quickly Reverse Bush Actions," *Washington Post*, November 9, 2008.

46. Obama wrote to federal staffers describing an "intention to scale back on contracts to private firms doing government work, to remove censorship from scientific research, and to champion tougher industry regulation to protect workers and the environment." Carol D. Leonnig, "Obama Wrote Federal Staffers about His Goals," *Washington Post*, November 17, 2008.

47. See Vice President Joe Biden, "Middle Class Task Force," http://www.whitehouse.gov/strongmiddleclass. In 2009 Obama suspended executive orders that diminished the federal government's oversight of governmental projects affecting threatened and endangered species; eased policies restricting trade and travel to Cuba; and rescinded the Bush ban on federal funding of most types of stem cell research save those using existing stem cell lines. Obama also directed his science advisors to write recommendations that differentiated political advice from scientific appointments; Bush created the practice of not relying on scientific advisors. See Neil Munro, "No End to Cloning," *National Journal*, March 14, 2009.

48. "Obama Announces White House Office of Faith-based and Neighborhood Partnerships," White House, Office of the Press Secretary, press release, February 5, 2009, http://www.whitehouse.gov/the_press_office/ObamaAnnounces WhiteHouseOfficeofFaith-basedandNeighborhoodPartnerships//.

49. My italics. Jeffrey Toobin, "Bench Press: Are Obama's Judges Really Liberals?," *New Yorker*, September 21, 2009, 42.

50. Ibid.

51. Barack Obama, "What I See in Lincoln's Eyes," *Time*, June 26, 2005, http://www.time.com/time/magazine/article/0,9171,1077287-2,00.html#ixzz1 DgirS6wq; and Toobin, "Bench Press."

52. Toobin, "Bench Press."

53. Ibid.

54. See John R. Burke, "The Contemporary Presidency: The Obama Presidential Transition, An Early Assessment," *Presidential Studies Quarterly* 39 (2009): 574.

55. Carl Tobias, "Diversity and the Federal Bench," *Washington University Law Review* 87 (2010),1197–98, 1943. Women constitute 20 percent of federal judges, whereas African Americans constitute 8 percent. Florence Allen was the first female appellate judge, then in 1950, William Hastie became the first African American circuit judge and Burnita Shelton Matthews became the first woman on a U.S. district court. In 1967 Thurgood Marshall became the first African American Supreme Court justice.

56. Tobias, "Diversity and the Federal Bench," 1203.

57. Ibid., 1204–5.

58. Martha Fineman, *The Neutered Mother and the Sexual Family and Other Twentieth Century Tragedies* (New York: Routledge, 1995); Elizabeth Grosz, *Volatile Bodies: Toward a Corporeal Feminism* (London: Routledge, 1994); Rosemarie Garland-Thomson, "Integrating Disability, Transforming Feminist Theory," *NWSA Journal* 14 (2002); and Ruth O'Brien, "Other Voices at the Workplace: Gender, Disability and an Alternative Ethic of Care," *SIGNS: Journal of Women in Culture and Society* 30 (2005): 1529.

59. Nancy Scherer, "Diversifying The Federal Bench: Is Universal Legitimacy for the U.S. Justice System Possible?," *Northwestern University Law Review* 105 (2011): 590.

60. Scherer, "Diversifying The Federal Bench," 610 ff.

61. Quoted from Toobin, "Bench Press." George H. W. Bush appointed her to the United States District Court for the Southern District of New York on Senator Daniel Patrick Moynihan's recommendation, and Clinton appointed her to the United States Court of Appeals for the Second Circuit in 1998.

62. Pat Buchanan, "A Quota Queen for the Court," *Creators Syndicate*, June 1, 2009; and Peter Baker, "Court Choice Pushes Issue of 'Identity Politics' Back to Forefront," *New York Times*, May 31, 2009.

63. The Supreme Court reversed the opinion in the firefighters' favor. Buchanan, "A Quota Queen for the Court"; and Alexandra Marks, "For Blacks, a Hidden Cost of Obama's Win?," *Christian Science Monitor*, July 5, 2009.

64. Quoted from Toobin, "Bench Press."

65. Joan Biskupic, "Calls for Recusal Intensify in Health Care Case," *USA Today*, November 20, 2011, http://www.usatoday.com/news/washington/story/2011-11-20/supreme-court-obamacare-health/51324806/1.

66. See excerpt from David Remnick, "Portrait of the President as a Young Law Student," blog, March 31, 2010, Brennan Center for Justice, http://www.brennancenter.org/blog/archives/16481/, in which he quotes Obama as follows: "I would learn power's currency in all its intricacy and detail, knowledge that would have compromised me before coming to Chicago but that I could now bring back to where it was needed, back to Roseland, back to Altgeld; bring it back like Promethean fire." Harvard Law School was the "perfect place to examine how the power structure works."

67. Charlie Savage, "For an Obama Mentor, a Nebulous Legal Niche," *New York Times*, April 8, 2010.

68. "Chief Justice Roberts' Key Role in Health Care Ruling," *PBS Newshour*, July 2, 2012, http://www.pbs.org/newshour/bb/law/july-dec12/roberts_07-02.html; Joel Gehrke, "Tribe: John Roberts, 'Student of Mine,' Will Uphold Obamacare," *Washington Examiner*, June 26, 2012, http://washingtonexaminer.com/tribe-john-roberts-student-of-mine-will-uphold-obamacare/article/2500672#.UGXBz7SVjfY; and "What the Seers Saw," *Washington Post*, June 29, 2012.

69. Remnick refers to Tribe as a civil libertarian in *The Bridge*, 192. My italics.

70. Remnick, "Portrait."

71. For good explanations of the ethic of care, see Martha Albertson Fineman, *The Autonomy Myth: A Theory of Dependency* (New York: New Press, 2005); Joan Tronto, *Moral Boundaries: A Political Argument for an Ethic of*

Care (New York: Routledge, 1993); and Eva Feder Kittay, "Welfare, Dependency, and a Public Ethic of Care," *Social Justice* 25 (1998): 123.

72. Andrew Hurrell, "Brazil and the New Global Order," *Current History* 109 (2010): 60; Matt Bai, "Is Obama the End of Black Politics?," *New York Times Magazine*, August 6, 2008.

73. Michael Paulson, "What Lies Beneath, Why Fewer Americans Believe in Hell than in Heaven," *Boston Globe*, June 29, 2008, http://www.boston.com /bostonglobe/ideas/articles/2008/06/29/what_lies_beneath/.

74. Alan F. Segal, *Life After Death: A History of the Afterlife in Western Religion* (New York: Random House, 2004). See Kenneth D. Wald and Allison Calhoun-Brown, *Religion and Politics in the United States* (New York: Rowman and Littlefield, 2010).

75. Remnick, *The Bridge*, 192; Stephanie Vallejo, "Harvard Law School Dean Martha Minow Considered for Supreme Court Vacancy," *Boston.com*, April 13, 2010, http://www.boston.com/news/politics/politicalintelligence/2010/04 /harvard_law_sch.htm; and Peter Baker, "Obama Meets with Senators in Effort to Speed Court Choice," *New York Times*, April 22, 2010. Martha Minow's father, Newton K. Minow, a lawyer and a former Federal Communications Commission (FCC) chair, was known for giving a speech in 1961 referring to television as a "vast wasteland" given the dearth of public interest programming.

76. For an understanding of Minow, see *Making All the Difference: Inclusion, Exclusion and American Law* (New York: Cornell University Press, 1991); and "Public Values in an Era of Privatization: Public and Private Partnerships: Accounting for the New Religion," *Harvard Law Review* 116 (2003): 1229.

77. Hope Lewis, "Defining Race: Transnational Dimensions of Race in America," *Albany Law Review* 72 (2009): 1049–52.

78. Obama is attacked by the progressive Left and the civil libertarian Right, if one follows journalists such as Remnick, Ryan Lizza, and George Packard at the *New Yorker*, and Rich Lowry and Jonah Goldberg of *National Review* as well as Todd Gitlin of the *New Republic* and my esteemed colleagues Peter Beinart, who writes for the *Daily Beast* and the *New York Review of Books*, and Eric Alterman, who writes for *The Nation* and for the Center for American Progress among other publications. This is the weak link a multitude of reviewers found in James T. Kloppenberg's *Reading Obama: Dreams, Hope, and the American Political Tradition* (Princeton, NJ: Princeton University Press, 2010), given his ideational causal claims about Obama (correlations not causation). There is a gendered element also about Obama's ethic of reciprocity, which cannot be equated properly with Rawls's emphasis on due process in theory, but not in practice (which takes us full circle back to Spinoza). Rawls is no different than other dead political thinkers, such as Spinoza, Nietzsche, Marx, Heidegger, Arendt, Ayn Rand, or Leo Strauss, who get co-opted, and their ideas reinterpreted for political purpose. See David Gordon, "Going Off the Rawls," *The American Conservative* (July 28, 2008), http://www.theamericanconservative.com/articles /going-off-the-rawls/; and http://democracy.livingreviews.org/index.php/lrd /article/viewArticle/lrd-2009-5/15.

79. See Minow, *Making All the Difference*; Martha Fineman, *The Neutered Mother and the Sexual Family and Other Twentieth Century Tragedies* (New

York: Routledge, 1995); Martha Nussbaum, http://bordeure.files.wordpress .com/2008/09/human-rights-and-human-capabilities.pdf; Ruth O'Brien, *Bodies in Revolt: Gender, Disability, and a Workplace Ethic of Care* (New York: Routledge, 2005); Richard H. Thaler and Cass R. Sunstein, *Nudge: Improving Decisions about Health, Wealth, and Happiness* (New Haven, CT: Yale University Press, 2008); and Anne-Marie Slaughter, "Interests vs. Values: Misunderstanding Obama's Libya Strategy," *New York Review of Books Blog*, March 30, 2011, http://www.nybooks.com/blogs/nyrblog/2011/mar/30/interests-values-obamas -libya-strategy/, echoing the 1990s ethic of care debate. See also Carol Gilligan, *In a Different Voice* (Cambridge, MA: Harvard University Press, 1993).

80. See Marcia Clemmitt, "Teen Pregnancy: Does Comprehensive Sex-Education Reduce Pregnancies?," *CQ Researcher* 20, no. 12 (March 26, 2010), http://cqresearcherblog.blogspot.com/2010_03_01_archive.html.

81. Quoted from Clemmitt, "Teen Pregnancy"; Hannah Arendt, "Truth and Politics," in *Between Past and Future: Eight Exercises in Political Thought* (Baltimore: Penguin Books, 1977); Hannah Arendt, *On Revolution* (New York: Viking, 1963); and Linda Zerilli, "Truth and Politics," *theory & event* 9 (2006): 7.

82. Lori Watson, "Constituting Politics: Power, Reciprocity, and Identity," *Hypatia* 22 (2007): 107.

83. Catharine A. MacKinnon, *Feminism Unmodified* (Cambridge, MA: Harvard University Press, 1987), 87. Radical feminists appreciate Wollstonecraft's belief that equality and difference are not antagonistic aims. See Watson, "Constituting Politics," 109; Virginia Sapiro, *A Vindication of Political Virtue: The Political Theory of Mary Wollstonecraft* (Chicago: University of Chicago Press, 1992).

84. Wendy Brown, *States of Injury* (Princeton, NJ: Princeton University Press, 1995), 153.

85. See Iris Marion Young, *Inclusion and Democracy* (New York: Oxford University Press, 2000), 5–6; Darrin Hicks, "The Promise(s) of Deliberative Democracy," *Rhetoric & Public Affairs* 5 (2002): 224; and Kerry H. Whiteside, "Justice Uncertain: Judith Shklar on Liberalism, Skepticism, and Equality," *Polity* 31 (1999).

86. David G. Levasseur and Diana B. Carlin, "Egocentric Argument and the Public Sphere: Citizen Deliberations on Public Policy and Policymakers," *Rhetoric & Public Affairs* 4 (2001): 407–31; and John S. Dryzek, *Deliberative Democracy and Beyond: Liberals, Critics, Contestations* (New York: Oxford University Press, 2000), 228.

87. Dryzek, *Deliberative Democracy and Beyond*, 229; and Watson, "Constituting Politics," 103.

88. Noëlle McAfee, "Three Models of Democratic Deliberation," *Journal of Speculative Philosophy* 18 (2004): 44. McAfee relies on John Dewey.

89. Dryzek, *Deliberative Democracy and Beyond*, 229. See Jean L. Cohen and Andrew Arato, *Civil Society and Political Theory* (Cambridge, MA: MIT Press, 1992).

90. Gideon Rossouw, "Truth or Memory: After the South African TRC, or When the Politics of Forgiveness Gives Way to Politics of Power/Dominance," *Memory Politics: Education, Memorials, and Mass Media, Social Science Research*

Center, Berlin (October 21–23, 2009), http://www.irmgard-coninx-stiftung
.de/fileadmin/user_upload/pdf/Memory_Politics/Workshop_2/Rossouw
_Essay.pdf.

91. Tobias, "Diversity and the Federal Bench," 1206.

92. Nikolaos A. Stavrou, "The Obama Presidency in Philosophical and Historical Context," *Mediterranean Quarterly* 20 (2009).

93. Quoted in Nicholas O. Pagan, "Configuring the Moral Self: Aristotle
and Dewey," *Foundations of Science* 13 (2008): 246, from James Dewey, *Ethics*
(New York: Henry Holt, 1932), 14, 202–3.

94. Hicks, "Promise(s) of Deliberative Democracy," 240.

95. McAfee, "Three Models of Democratic Deliberation," 47–48.

96. David G. Levasseur and Diana B. Carlin, "Egocentric Argument and the
Public Sphere: Citizen Deliberations on Public Policy and Policymakers," *Rhetoric & Public Affairs* 4 (2001): 418–19.

97. James Livingston, "Marxism and the Politics of History: Reflections on
the Work of Eugene D. Genovese," *Radical History Review* 88 (2004): 31.

98. Barbara Thayer-Bacon, "Pragmatism and Feminism as Qualified Relativism," *Studies in Philosophy and Education* 22 (2003): 427, 431–32.

99. Hicks, "Promise(s) of Deliberative Democracy," 249.

100. James Dewey, *The Public and Its Problems* (Ohio University Press, Ath-
ens, 1954), 166, 154. My italics. See Matthew Caleb Flamm, "The Demanding
Community: Politicization of the Individual after Dewey," *Education and Culture* 22 (2006): 35, 46; Larry A. Hickman, "Pragmatism, Postmodernism, and
Global Citizenship," *Metaphilosophy* 35 (2004): 65.

101. Dewey, quoted in Cornel West and Eddie S. Glaude Jr., *African American Religious Thought: An Anthology* (New York: Westminster John Knox
Press, 2003).

102. William E. Connolly, "The Radical Enlightenment: Faith, Power, Theory," review of *Radical Enlightenment Philosophy and the Making of Modernity, 1650–1750*, by Jonathan Israel, and *Looking for Spinoza: Joy, Sorrow and
the Feeling Brain*, by Antonio Damasio, *theory & event* 7 (2004): 17; Lloyd and
Gatens, "Power of Spinoza," 50–51.

103. Eugene Robinson, "Racism and the Tea Party Movement," *Real
Clear Politics*, November 2, 2010, http://www.realclearpolitics.com/articles
/2010/11/02/race_and_the_tea_partys_ire_107805.html; and "NAACP President Ben Jealous: Tea Party Leaders Need to Take Responsibility," *ABC News*,
July 3, 2010.

104. Garry Wills, *Nixon Agonistes: The Crisis of the Self-Made Man* (Boston: Houghton-Mifflin 1969), chap. 3; "Success for Obama Hinges on Economic
Policies," *Daily Yomiuri*, August 31, 2008; and Larissa MacFarquhar, "The
Conciliator: Where Is Barack Obama Coming From?," *New Yorker*, May 7,
2006, http://www.newyorker.com/reporting/2007/05/07/070507fa_fact
_macfarquhar.

105. See Peter Clark, Kevin Capuzzi, and Cameron Fick, "Medical Marijuana: Medical Necessity versus Political Agenda," *Medical Science Monitor* 17
(2011): 249; and Laura J. Khoury, "Racial Profiling as Dressage: A Social Control Regime!," *African Identities* 7 (2009): 64.

106. Khoury, "Racial Profiling as Dressage." See also Amy Goldstein, "New Strategy to Fight Teen, Adult Drug Addiction; But to Make It Work, Some Say Administration Needs to Up the Funding," *Washington Post*, May 24, 2010; William J. Chambers, "Policing the Ghetto Underclass: The Politics of Law and Law Enforcement," *Social Problems* 41 (1994): 177; John V. Elmore and Yvonne Rose, *Fighting for Your Life: The African American Criminal Justice Survival Guide* (Phoenix, AZ: Amber Books, 2004); and Jeannine Marie Delombard, *Slavery on Trial: Law, Abolitionism and Print Culture* (Chapel Hill: University of North Carolina Press, 2007), 77.

107. Khoury, "Racial Profiling as Dressage," 63, 72; and David Garland, *The Culture of Control: Crime and Social Order in Contemporary Society* (Chicago: University of Chicago Press, 2001). Khoury refers to Kara Gotsch of the ACLU's National Prison Project in citing these statistics. Secretary of State Hillary Clinton rendered a "mea culpa," stating that the "war on drugs" had failed. Mary Beth Sheridan, "On Mexico Trip, Clinton Criticizes U.S. Drug Policy; She Says Her Country Shares Blame for Violence," *Washington Post*, March 26, 2009.

108. Michelle Alexander, *The New Jim Crow: Mass Incarceration in the Age of Colorblindness* (New York: New Press, 2010). 6. Alexander not only received media attention, but James Forman Jr. wrote "Racial Critiques of Mass Incarceration: Beyond the New Jim Crow," *Yale Law Journal* 87 (2012): 2, calling more attention to the issue. Ira Glasser also attended. See Ira Glasser, "American Drug Laws: The New Jim Crow," *Albany Law Review* 62 (2000): 703. A LexisNexis search produces 229 articles using the same name.

109. Prescription substance abuse treatment admissions for over-twelve-year-olds quadrupled between 1998 and 2008, according to "Officials Highlight New Approach to Drug Control Policy before Congress," White House, Office of National Drug Control Policy, press release, July 22, 2010, http://www.whitehouse.gov/ondcp/news-releases-remarks/obama-administration-officials-highlight-new-approach. The 117-page blueprint mentions African Americans only one time.

110. For the term "penal populist," see Albert W. Dzur, "The Myth of Penal Populism: Democracy, Citizen Participation, and American Hyperincarceration," *Journal of Speculative Philosophy* 24 (2010): 355; and A. Bottoms, "The Philosophy and Politics of Punishment and Sentencing," in *The Politics of Sentencing Reform*, ed. C. Clarkson and R. Morgan (Oxford: Clarendon Press, 1995), 40.

111. Dzur, "Myth of Penal Populism," 357; John Braithwaite and Philippe Pettit, *Not Just Desserts: A Republican Theory of Criminal Justice* (Oxford: Oxford University Press, 1990), 35; and Todd J. Gillman, "It's No Longer a 'War' on Drugs, So to Speak," *Dallas Morning News*, March 16, 2009.

112. Kimberly Atkins, "U.S. DOJ Backs Retroactive Reduction of Crack Sentences," *Lawyers Weekly USA*, June 7, 2011. The Roberts court did not permit the Obama administration to do this retroactively, and Holder therefore changed the policy so it applied only to those who had not been sentenced in *Dorsey v. United States* 11-5683 and *Hill v. United States* 11-5721 (2012); see http://www.scotusblog.com/case-files/hill-v-united-states/. See Robert Barnes,

"Justices Weigh Cocaine Sentencing Law," *Washington Post*, April 18, 2012; and "Abiding by the Fair Sentencing Act," *New York Times*, April 18, 2012.

113. For a full explanation of DWB, see David A. Harris, "The Stories, the Statistics, and the Law: Why 'Driving While Black' Matters," 84 *Minnesota Law Review* (1999): 265, http://academic.udayton.edu/race/03justice/dwb01.htm.

114. Peter Katel, "Legalizing Marijuana: Should Pot Be Treated Like Alcohol and Taxed?," *CQ Researcher* 19, no. 22 (June 12, 2009); Stephanie Nano, "Number of Prescription Drug Deaths Has Tripled," *Washington Post*, November 2, 2011.

115. Thomas J. Billitteri, "Government and Religion: Was the U.S. Founded as a 'Christian Nation?'" *CQ Researcher* 20, no. 2 (January 15, 2010).

116. Ibid.

117. The President's Interfaith and Community Service Campus Challenge Advancing Interfaith Cooperation and Community Service in Higher Education, http://www.whitehouse.gov/administration/eop/ofbnp/interfaithservice; in the Department of Education, see Initiatives, Faith-based and Neighborhood Partnerships (FBNP), http://www2.ed.gov/about/inits/list/fbci/index.html.

118. Ira Lupu, interview by Jesse Merriam, "Hiring Law for Groups Following a Higher Law: Faith-Based Hiring and the Obama Administration," Pew Forum on Religion and Public Life, January 30, 2009, http://www.pewforum .org/Church-State-Law/Hiring-Law-for-Groups-Following-a-Higher-Law-Faith -Based-Hiring-and-the-Obama-Administration.aspx; Michael Sean Winters, *Left at the Altar: How the Democrats Lost the Catholics and How the Catholics Can Save the Democrats* (New York: Basic Books, 2008).

119. "A Religious Exception?," *Los Angeles Times*, May 30, 2012.

120. See Roy Speckhardt, Executive Director of the American Humanist Society, "Take Action: Tell President Obama to Stop Faith-Based Employment Discrimination!," http://www.americanhumanist.org/news/details/2011-06 -take-action-tell-president-obama-to-stop-faith-based; Roy Speckhardt, "Breaking: President Obama Caves to Religious Pressure on Reproductive Access," http://www.americanhumanist.org/news/details/2012-02-breaking-president -obama-caves-to-religious-pressure; David Wylie, "Ads Use Obama as Atheist Role-Model," http://www.canada.com/life/Obama+atheist+role+model/11955 07/story.html#ixzz1I7QgtR8j.

121. Gerard V. Bradley, "The Audacity of Faith," *Public Discourse*, May 18, 2012, http://www.thepublicdiscourse.com/2012/05/5378.

122. *Hosanna-Tabor Evangelical Lutheran Church and School v. EEOC*, 10–53 (2011).

123. "Catholics Sue Obama over Birth Control Mandate," *New Zealand Herald*, May 22, 2012; "Obama and the Contraception Mandate," *Christian Science Monitor*, May 23, 2012; Crabtree, "Catholics' Suit Draws Dividing Line for Obama"; and "A Religious Exception?," *Los Angeles Times*, May 30, 2012.

124. Crabtree, "Catholics' Suit Draws Dividing Line for Obama."

125. Melinda Henneberger, "Is Catholic Church Taking on Obama?," *Washington Post*, June 8, 2012.

126. D. A. Frank, "Obama's Rhetorical Signature: Cosmopolitan Civil Reli-

gion in the Presidential Inaugural Address, January 20, 2009," *Rhetoric & Public Affairs* 14 (2011): 605.

127. Bruce Lincoln, "Bush's God Talk," *Christian Century*, October 5, 2004, 22–29 and http://www.religion-online.org/showarticle.asp?title=3135. See David S. Gutterman, "Presidential Testimony: Listening to the Heart of George W. Bush," *theory & event* 5 (2001): 10.1353/tae.2001.0013, for provocative analysis.

128. Philip S. Gorski, "Barack Obama and Civil Religion," in *Rethinking Obama*, ed. Julian Go, Political Power and Social Theory, no. 22 (Emerald Group, 2011), 179–214. Gorski's view is reminiscent of Robert N. Bellah, "Civil Religion in America," *Journal of the American Academy of Arts and Sciences* 96 (1967): 1.

129. Barack Obama, "A Politics of Conscience" (speech delivered at the United Church of Christ General Synod, Hartford, CT, June 23, 2007), http://www.ucc .org/news/significant-speeches/a-politics-of-conscience.html. See Michael Gerson, "The Gospel of Obama," *Washington Post*, June 29, 2007, http://www .washingtonpost.com/wp-dyn/content/article/2007/06/28/AR2007062801792 .html; Laurie Goodstein, "Faith Has Role in Politics, Obama Tells Church," *New York Times*, June 24, 2007, http://www.nytimes.com/2007/06/24/us/politics /24obama.html.

130. Albert R. Jonsen and Stephen Toulmin, *The Abuse of Casuistry: A History of Moral Reasoning* (Berkeley: University of California Press, 1988); Michael M. J. Fischer and Mehdi Abedi, *Debating Muslims: Cultural Dialogues in Postmodernity and Tradition* (Madison: University of Wisconsin Press, 1990); and Klaus K. Klostermaier, *A Survey of Hinduism*, 2nd ed. (Albany: State University of New York Press, 1994); Frank, "Obama's Rhetorical Signature," 602.

131. David Brooks, "Obama, Gospel and Verse," *New York Times*, April 26, 2007; "Obama's Favorite Theologian? A Short Course on Reinhold Niebuhr," Pew Forum on Religion and Public Life, June 26, 2009, http://pewresearch.org /pubs/1268/reinhold-neihbuhr-obama-favorite-theologian.

132. Edward W. Said, *Culture and Imperialism* (New York: Knopf, 1993), 336.

133. Stanley Fish, "Barack Obama's Prose Style," *New York Times Opinionator*, January 22, 2009, http://opinionator.blogs.nytimes.com/2009/01/22 /barack-obamas-prose-style/. Fish quotes the *Oxford English Dictionary* definition of *parataxis*, which means "the placing of propositions or clauses one after the other without indicating . . . the relation of co-ordination or subordination between them." "The opposite of parataxis," he explains, "is *hypotaxis*, the marking of relations between propositions and clauses by connectives that point backward or forward." "The power is in discrete moments," claims Fish, "rather than in a thesis proved by the marshaling of evidence." Kwame Anthony Appiah argues, in *Cosmopolitanism: Ethics in a World of Strangers* (New York: W. W. Norton, 2006), xv, that it is Obama's individual "obligations to others" that makes his theology cosmopolitan.

134. Frank, "Obama's Rhetorical Signature," 620. See Rebecca Newberger Goldstein, *Betraying Spinoza: The Renegade Jew Who Gave Us Modernity* (New

York: Schocken Books, 2006), 9–15, for a connection between identity, scientific method, and contemporary science.

135. Frank, "Obama's Rhetorical Signature," 609.

136. Barack Obama, "The Fiery Urgency of Now" (speech delivered at the Jefferson-Jackson Dinner, November 10, 2007, Des Moines, Iowa), http://www .discoverthenetworks.org/viewSubCategory.asp?id=1642.

137. Frank, "Obama's Rhetorical Signature," 602.

138. Ibid., 615.

139. Leonard Mlodinow, *Euclid's Window: The Story of Geometry from Parallel Lines to Hyperspace* (New York: Free Press, 2002), 34–35; and Gilles Deleuze, *Spinoza: Practical Philosophy*, Robert Hurley, trans. (San Francisco, City Lights Books, 1988), 55–57, 114–21.

140. Frank, "Obama's Rhetorical Signature," 620–21; Barack Obama, "Inaugural Address" (Washington, DC, January 21, 2009), http://www.lyc-perier .ac-aix-marseille.fr/spip/IMG/pdf/The_White_House_-_Blog_Post_-_President _Barack_Obama_s_Inaugural_Address.pdf.

141. Obama, "Inaugural Address."

142. Ibid.

143. "Gingrich's Version of American Exceptionalism Could Insult Our Allies," *Atlantic*, November 22, 2011.

144. D. A. Frank, "Arguing with God, Talmudic Discourse, and the Jewish Countermodel: Implications for the Study of Argumentation," *Argumentation and Advocacy* 41 (2004): 71–86.

145. In the late 1990s the federal government spent $2 billion annually on abstinence-only programs without scientific evidence of their effectiveness. See Frank F. Furstenberg, *Destinies of the Disadvantaged: The Politics of Teenage Childbearing* (New York: Russell Sage Publications, 2007); Heather D. Boonstra, "Advocates Call for a New Approach After the Era of 'Abstinence-Only' Sex Education," *Guttmacher Policy Review* 12 (2009); and Sharon Jayson, "Obama Budget Cuts Funds for Abstinence-Only Sex Education," *USA Today*, May 11, 2009, http://www.usatoday.com/news/health/2009-05-11-abstinence -only_N.htm.

146. Lynn D. Wardel, "*Loving v. Virginia* and the Constitutional Right to Marry, 1970–1990," *Howard Law Journal* 41 (1997–1998): 289.

147. Jerry Markon and Sandhya Somashekhar, "In Gay Rights Victory, Obama Administration Won't Defend Defense of Marriage Act," *Washington Post*, February 23, 2011. See *Massachusetts v. United States Department of Health and Human Services* 698 F.Supp.2d 234 (2012), which alleges that DOMA "violates the Tenth Amendment and the Spending Clause." Massachusetts was the first state to recognize same-sex marriage.

148. Sandhya Somashekhar and Peyton Craighill, "Slim Majority Back Gay Marriage, Post ABC Poll Says," *Washington Post*, March 18, 2011.

149. Mark Landler, "Obama Still Lets Surrogates Take the Lead as Gay Rights Momentum Builds," *New York Times*, December 31, 2011; Robert Barnes, "Same-Sex Marriage Headed to High Court," *Washington Post*, June 6, 2012; and David G. Savage, "Key Part of Marriage Act Ruled Invalid," *Los Angeles Times*, June 1, 2012. In addition to Massachusetts, gay marriage is rec-

ognized in the District of Columbia, Iowa, Connecticut, New Hampshire, New York, Vermont, Washington, Maryland, and California (pre-Proposition 8).

150. Alberto Alesina, Edward Glaeser, and Bruce Sacerdote, "Why Doesn't the United States Have a European-Style Welfare State?," *Brookings Papers on Economic Activity* 2001 (2001): 209.

151. "Americanization implied the unquestionable superiority," wrote Isaac Berkson in his classic 1920 study, "of the Anglo-Saxon race and culture." See Philip Davis, ed., *Immigration and Americanization: Selected Readings* (New York: Ginn, 1920), 655; Robert A. Carlson, *The Quest for Conformity: Americanization through Education* (New York: John Wiley, 1975), 79, 83; John Higham, *Strangers in the Land: Patterns of American Nativism, 1860–1925*, 2nd ed. (New York: Athenaeum, 1981), 235. The Bureau of Naturalization was established in 1906. See Desmond King, *Making Americans: Immigration, Race and the Origins of the Diverse Democracy* (Cambridge, MA: Harvard University Press, 2000), 55–68. In *What I Saw in America* (New York: Dodd, Mead, 1922), G. K. Chesterton wrote, "The American Constitution does resemble the Spanish Inquisition in this: that it is founded on a creed."

152. Barack Obama, "Iowa Caucus Victory Speech" (Des Moines, IA, January 3, 2008), http://www.asksam.com/ebooks/releases.asp?file=Obama -Speeches.ask&dn=Iowa%20Caucus%20Night. In math, the logic of necessary and sufficient creates a duality. That is, for any X and Y statements, X is necessary for Y is tantamount to the statement that Y is sufficient for X. Put differently, there is a material equivalence. Andrew Brennan, "Necessary and Sufficient," *Stanford Encyclopedia of Philosophy*, August 15, 2003; revised October 4, 2011, http://plato.stanford.edu/entries/necessary-sufficient/.

153. Barack Obama, "A Secure Energy Future" (speech, Dayton, Ohio, July 11, 2008), http://www.asksam.com/ebooks/releases.asp?file=Obama-Speeches.ask &dn=A%20Secure%20Energy%20Future.

154. Barack Obama, "On a New Beginning" (speech delivered at Cairo University in Cairo, Egypt, June 4, 2009), http://www.whitehouse.gov/the-press-office /remarks-president-cairo-university-6-04-09. See also Barack Obama, "Presidential Victory Speech" (Grant Park, Chicago, November 4, 2008), http://www .asksam.com/ebooks/releases.asp?file=Obama-Speeches.ask&dn=Election%20 Night%20Victory%20Speech.

155. Obama, "A More Perfect Union."

156. The post–World War II democratization movement in the United States and Europe extended some of these turn-of-the-century progressive ideas about Americanization, including first eugenics, and later the whole man theory, which contained a conception of normalcy similar to that underlying eugenics. The "whole man theory" of reform relied on normalcy as a means of restoring injured and diseased minds and bodies. See O'Brien, *Crippled Justice*, 27–29, 34–40; and for how genetics carries on normalcy theory given in reproduction, and how the mind and body informed normalizing of sexuality, primarily LGBTers, see O'Brien, *Bodies in Revolt*; 9–20; Kelly Dahlgren Childress, "Genetics, Disability, and Ethics: Could Applied Technology Lead to a New Eugenics?," *Journal of Women and Religion* 19/20 (2003): 1965. Since 2005 there has been an explosion of work intersecting the mind, body, neuroscience, and genetics with sexuality.

157. Progressivism often contained beliefs and values that were bipartisan or could not be equated with the left or the right, such as eugenics or different supremacist views about the mind, the body, and the intellect. Randall Hansen and Desmond S. King, "Eugenic Ideas, Political Interests, and Policy Variance: Immigration and Sterilization Policy in Britain and the U.S.," *World Politics* 53 (2001): 237–38. Theodore Roosevelt; Oliver Wendell Holmes Jr.; sociologist Edward A. Ross; political scientist Harold Laski; David Starr Jordan, the president of Stanford; Charles William Eliot, the president of Harvard; and Marxist revolutionary Emma Goldman were eugenicists. See Louis Menand, "The Science of Human Nature and the Human Nature of Science," *Sign Language Studies* 5 (2005): 181. See also Thomas C. Leonard, " 'More Merciful and Not Less Effective': Eugenics and American Economics in the Progressive Era," *History of Political Economy* 35 (2005): 687; Lawrence R. Goodheart, "Rethinking Mental Retardation: Education and Eugenics in Connecticut, 1818–1917," *Journal of the History of Medicine and Allied Sciences* 59 (2004): 90; and Dana Seitler, "Unnatural Selection: Mothers, Eugenic Feminism, and Charlotte Perkins Gilman's Regeneration Narratives," *American Quarterly* 55 (2003): 61.

158. Barack Obama, "Main Street Speech to Wall Street Crowd," (New York, NY, September 17, 2007); and Obama, "A More Perfect Union."

159. Lawrence J. Engel, "Saul D. Alinsky and the Chicago School," *Journal of Speculative Philosophy* 16 (2002): 52; and Obama, "A More Perfect Union."

160. Obama, quoted in Talbot, *Obamanomics*, 154.

161. Claire Colebrook, "From Radical Representations to Corporeal Becomings: The Feminist Philosophy of Lloyd, Grosz, and Gatens," *Hypatia* 15 (2000): 89.

162. Georg Geismann, "Spinoza—Beyond Hobbes and Rousseau," *Journal of the History of Ideas* 52 (1991): 43.

163. Obama, quoted in Talbot, *Obamanomics*, 47.

164. "Selfishness blights the germ of all virtue; . . . individualism is of democratic origin, and it threatens to spread in the same ratio as the equality of condition." Alexis de Tocqueville, *Democracy in America*, trans. Henry Reeve, part 1, book 1, chap. 2. (New York: Barnes and Noble, 2003), 469.

165. Minnie Bruce Pratt, "Identity: Skin, Blood, Heart," in *Yours in Struggle: Three Feminist Perspectives on Anti-Semitism and Racism* (Brooklyn: Long Haul Press, 1984), 39; and Obama, *Audacity of Hope*, 75–76.

166. Obama, *Audacity of Hope*, 291.

167. Moira Gatens, "Feminism as 'Password': Re-thinking the 'Possible' with Spinoza and Deleuze," *Hypatia* 15 (2000) 59–60; Seyla Benhabib, *Critique, Norm and Utopia: A Study of the Foundations of Critical Theory* (New York: Columbia University Press, 1986), 347; and Seyla Benhabib, *Situating the Self: Gender, Community and Postmodernism in Contemporary Ethics* (New York: Routledge, 1992), 5. Quotations from Adams, "At the Table with Arendt," 24; Pratt, "Identity," 39; and Obama, *Audacity of Hope*, 293.

168. Adams, "At the Table with Arendt," 3.

169. Tavis Smiley and Cornel West, *Charlie Rose*, October 30, 2007.

170. Genevieve Lloyd and Moira Gatens, "The Power of Spinoza: Feminist Conjunctions," interview by Susan James, *Hypatia* 15 (2000): 43; and Barack

Obama, *Dreams from My Father: A Story of Race and Inheritance* (New York: Three Rivers Press, 2004), 88.

171. Luciana Parisi, "Information Trading and Symbiotic Micropolitics," *Social Text* 22 (2004): 45.

172. Geismann, "Spinoza," 39.

173. Connolly, "Radical Enlightenment," 21–24.

174. Obama, *Dreams from My Father*, 293.

175. Obama, *Audacity of Hope*, 274, 275, 276.

176. Ibid., 287.

177. Ibid., 291.

178. Max Weber, *The Protestant Ethic and the Spirit of Capitalism*, trans. Talcott Parsons (Dover Publications, 2003). See Lutz Kaelber, "Weber's Lacuna: Medieval Religion and the Roots of Rationalization," *Journal of the History of Ideas* 57 (1996): 465–85.

179. Obama, quoted in Talbot, *Obamanomics*, 35.

CHAPTER FOUR

1. See Miriam Galsto, "Taking Aristotle Seriously: Republican-Oriented Legal Theory and the Moral Foundation of Deliberative Democracy," *California Law Review* 82 (1994): 331.

2. See Orly Lobel, "The Renew Deal: The Fall of Regulation and the Rise of Governance in Contemporary Legal Thought," *Minnesota Law Review* 89 (2004) 346–48.

3. Obama reverses the "trend since Reagan to use [a] growing variety of executive powers to influence states: from waivers to rulemaking, memoranda, demonstration projects, grant conditions." It moves away from devolution's "loose on means, tight on goals" mantra. Thomas L. Gais, "Federalism during the Obama Administration," Nelson A. Rockefeller Institute of Government, Annual Conference of the National Federation of Municipal Analysts, Santa Ana Pueblo, New Mexico, May 7, 2010, http://www.rockinst.org/pdf/federalism /2010-05-07-federalism_during_obama_administration.pdf; Hari M. Osofsky, "Diagonal Federalism and Climate Change: Implications for the Obama Administration," *Alabama Law Review* 62 (2011): 300–301; and Timothy J. Conlan and Paul L. Posner, "Inflection Point? Federalism and the Obama Administration," *Publius* 41 (2011): 421.

4. John Schwartz, "Obama Seems to Be Open to a Broader Role for States," *New York Times*, January 29, 2009; and Lobel, "Renew Deal," 571. See also Katherine Adams, "At the Table with Arendt: Toward a Self-Interested Practice of Coalition Discourse," *Hypatia* 17 (2002): 1–2.

5. Osofsky, "Diagonal Federalism."

6. Dayo Olopade, "Charm Offensive," *American Prospect*, July–August, 2009.

7. Lobel, "Renew Deal," 459.

8. Gais, "Federalism during the Obama Administration"; Richard H. Thaler and Cass R. Sunstein, *Nudge: Improving Decisions about Health, Wealth, and Happiness* (New Haven, CT: Yale University Press, 2008); Meredith Wilensky, "The Tailoring Rule: Exemplifying the Vital Role of Agencies in Environmental

Protection," *Ecology Law Quarterly* 38 (2011): 473; and Alexandra B. Klass, "Property Rights on the New Frontier: Climate Change, Natural Resource Development, and Renewable Energy," *Ecology Law Quarterly* 38 (2011): 63.

9. Gillian E. Metzger, "Constitutional Transformations: The State, the Citizen, and the Changing Role of Government: Symposium: Contractual Civil Procedure and the Current State of Federalism: Federalism under Obama," *William and Mary Law Review* 53 (2011): 569–70. See Sarah Kliff, "States Join to Create Tool for Implementing Affordable Care Act," *Washington Post*, June 8, 2012.

10. In 1999, William J. Clinton issued Exec. Order (E.O.) 13,132 for the Unfunded Mandates Reform Act: http://www.epa.gov/lawsregs/laws/e013132. html. See Catherine M. Sharkey, "Administrative Law under the George W. Bush Administration: Looking Back and Looking Forward: Federalism Accountability: 'Agency-Forcing' Measures," *Duke Law Journal* 58 (2009): 2125, which argues that the 1999 order created "robust interchanges during the notice-and -comment period." This gave Obama only an effective enforcement mechanism. See also Peter Harkness, "What Brand of Federalism Is Next?," *Potomac Chronicle*, January 2012, quoting Don Borut calling Bush's federalism "coercive," or even more bluntly "shift-and-shaft federalism."

11. Cass R. Sunstein mixes administrative law with civic republicanism, liberalism, and pragmatism in "Beyond the Republican Revival," *Yale Law Journal* 97 (1988): 1566; and "Administrative Substance," *Duke Law Journal* 607 (1991): 612–16. See also Bruce Ackerman, "Constitutional Politics/Constitutional Law," *Yale Law Journal* 99 (1989): 484–85.

12. John S. Applegate, "Beyond the Usual Suspects: The Use of Citizens Advisory Boards in Environmental Decisionmaking," *Indiana Law Journal* 73 (1998): 901.

13. Lobel, "Renew Deal," 363–64. See Kim Geiger, "Food: USDA May Ease Chicken Inspections: The Proposal Speeds Production Lines and Slashes the Number of Federal Checkers," *Los Angeles Times*, June 6, 2012.

14. Sean Wilentz, "The Worst President in History," *Rolling Stone*, April 19, 2006.

15. Lobel, "Renew Deal," 344.

16. Ibid., 345, 355.

17. In instituting deregulation, the Reagan administration relied heavily on the Office of Management and Budget. See Exec. Order 12,291, of which Sally Katzen, in her statement at a hearing before the House Judiciary Subcommittee on Commercial and Administrative Law on "Federal Rulemaking and the Regulatory Process" (Congressional Documents and Publications, U.S. House of Representatives, July 27, 2010), said, "Time and again, complaints were lodged with Members of Congress (and in the press) that the OIRA process was totally opaque, and there was considerable suspicion that OIRA staff were meeting with outsiders (presumably representatives of industry) and then acting as conduits to accomplish at OMB what could not be accomplished at the agencies." Clinton issued Exec. Order 12,866, spelling out the disclosure requirements that would govern OIRA review meetings. Then Bush used this mechanism defeating it by having the OIRA administrator's presence at such meetings "a rarity rather than the norm." Obama revoked the Bush executive orders modifying Exec. Order

12,866, restoring the Clinton order: http://regulation.huji.ac.il/papers/jp5.pdf; Robin Bravender and J. Lester Feder, "W. H. takes aim at federal rule book," *Politico*, May 27, 2011, http://www.politico.com/news/stories/0511/55796.html#ixzz102exJDF7.

18. Matt Madia, "The Obama Approach to Public Protection, Rulemaking," *OMB Watch* (September 2010), http://www.ombwatch.org/files/regs/obamamidtermrulemakingreport.pdf.

19. Katzen, hearing on "Federal Rulemaking and the Regulatory Process."

20. Ibid.

21. Martha Fineman, *The Autonomy Myth: A Theory of Dependency* (New York: New Press, 2005).

22. Ronald Mann, "Nudging from the Debt: The Role of Behavioral Economics in Regulation," *Lydian Blog* (January, 2011), http://www.pymnts.com/assets/Lydian_Journal/LydianJournalFebLawReg.pdf. See Daniel Kahneman and Amos Tversky, "Judgment under Uncertainty: Heuristics and Biases," *Science* 185 (1974): 1124.

23. Thaler and Sunstein, *Nudge*; and George Packer, "The New Liberalism: How the Economic Crisis Can Help Obama Redefine the Democrats," *New Yorker*, November 17, 2008.

24. Packer, "New Liberalism."

25. Ibid.

26. Albert W. Dzur, "The Myth of Penal Populism: Democracy, Citizen Participation, and American Hyper-Incarceration," *Journal of Speculative Philosophy* 24 (2010): 354. See also Dan Ariely, *The Honest Truth about Dishonesty: How We Lie to Everyone—Especially Ourselves* (New York: Harper, 2012); and Leonard Mlodinow, *Subliminal: How Your Unconscious Mind Rules Your Behavior* (New York: Pantheon, 2012) for popular explanations. Ariely relies on John Rawls's theory of justice, which, being indebted to rationality, creates an odd fit, though it is an assumption that most behavioral social scientists make.

27. Dzur, "Myth of Penal Populism." Ostrom works on "public choice theory," examining environmentalism, while also studying political and economic concepts of cooperation, trust, and collective action in a theory identified as "institutional analysis and development" (IAD).

28. Packer, "New Liberalism."

29. Ibid.

30. Barack Obama, *The Audacity of Hope: Thoughts on Reclaiming the American Dream* (New York: Crown/Three Rivers Press, 2006), 39–40.

31. "Fact Sheet: Reforms to Protect American Credit Card Holders: President Obama Signs Credit Card Accountability, Responsibility, and Disclosure Act" (May 22, 2009), www.Whitehouse.Gov/The_Press_Office/Fact-Sheet-Reforms-To-Protect-American-Credit-Card-Holder; F. Mussweiler and T. Strack, "Numeric Judgments under Uncertainty: The Role of Knowledge in Anchoring," *Journal of Experimental Social Psychology* 36 (2000): 495; N. Stewart, "The Cost of Anchoring on Credit-Card Minimum Repayments," *Psychological Science* 20 (2009): 39–41; and Thaler and Sunstein, *Nudge*, 3.

32. My italics. Robert Shull, former director of regulatory policy at OMB Watch, quoted in Frank O'Donnell, "How Anti-Regulation Is Obama's New

Regulatory Czar?," *Wonk Room*, January 10, 2009, http://thinkprogress.org /economy/2009/01/10/172541/cass-sunstein-anti-regulation/.

33. Mann, "Nudging from the Debt."

34. Mann, "Nudging from the Debt." See also Cass R. Sunstein, "Smarter Regulation," *White House Blog*, February 7, 2011, http://www.whitehouse.gov /blog/2011/02/07/smarter-regulation, arguing the "art of rule-writing is to maximize the benefits and minimize the costs to the public as a whole"; and Tim Fernholz, "Obama's Deregulatory Moves Unlikely to Sway Business Community," *National Journal*, January 20, 2011.

35. Fernholz, "Obama's Deregulatory Moves."

36. Exec. Order 13,563—Improving Regulation and Regulatory Review, January 18, 2011, http://www.whitehouse.gov/the-press-office/2011/01/18 /improving-regulation-and-regulatory-review-executive-order.

37. Max Fisher, "Conservative Hero in White House Faces Off With Beck," *Atlantic Wire*, September 9, 2009, http://www.theatlanticwire.com/politics /2009/09/conservative-hero-in-white-house-faces-off-with-beck/27035/.

38. Cass R. Sunstein, "A 21st Century Regulatory System," *White House Blog*, May 26, 2011, http://www.whitehouse.gov/blog/2011/05/26/21st-century -regulatory-system.

39. Fernholz, "Obama's Deregulatory Moves"; Alan Fram, "Obama Push to Revamp Regs," *Washington Post*, May 30, 2011; and O'Donnell, "How Anti-Regulation Is Obama's New Regulatory Czar?"

40. The Congressional Review Act (CRA) of 1996 gives a congressional majority the ability to disapprove final agency regulations. Speaker John Boehner demanded that Obama give a rundown of all planned federal regulations projected to cost $1 billion or more. Steve Cochran, "Power to the Polluters: Rand Paul Is Eroding States' Right to Clean Air," *Climate 411* (blog), Environmental Defense Fund, November 3, 2011, http://blogs.edf.org/climate411/2011/11/03 /power-to-the-polluters-rand-paul-is-eroding-states'-right-to-clean-air/.

41. Emily Long, "Opposition Builds against Obama on Disclosing Contractor Campaign Gifts," *National Journal*, May 13, 2011.

42. Kathleen Miller, "Hiring Violations by Contractors at New High," *Washington Post*, June 11, 2012.

43. Disability rights activists and the U.S. Chamber of Commerce supported the ADAAA, which "explicitly overruled" what one employer-side labor law blog called the "excellent decisions" of *Sutton v. United Air Lines*, 527 (1999) 471 and *Williams v. Toyota Manufacturing of Kentucky*, 534 (2002) 184: Robin A. Shea, "New ADAAA regs: the untold story!!!" *Employer and Labor Insider*, http://www.employmentandlaborinsider.com/discrimination/bah-humbug -what-nobody-else-will-tell-you-about-the-adaaa-regulations/. See Ruth O'Brien, *Crippled Justice: The History of Modern Disability Policy in the Workplace* (Chicago: University of Chicago Press, 2001), chap. 6 for how *Sutton* and *Williams v. Toyota* presented a perverse interpretation of the ADA that "crippled" justice, or did not prevent discrimination against people with disabilities, and that 18 years later led to the bipartisan passage of the ADAAA. See also Kim Koratsky, "President Obama Taps New Head of EEOC," *Wyatt Employment Law Report*, July 20, 2009.

44. "Obama Appoints Pro-Gay Business Terminator as EEOC Head," Public Advocate of the United States, March 31, 2010, http://www.publicadvocateusa .org/news/article.php?article=5699. Concerned Women of America reported that this "radical homosexual activist" also wrote the Employment Non-Discrimination Act.

45. "Obama Appoints Pro-Gay Business Terminator."

46. Sixty-one civil rights, disability rights, and health-care organizations and forty-eight employer and industry groups participated in the regulatory process. See O'Brien, *Crippled Justice*, 163. See also Elizabeth F. Emens, "Evolutions in Antidiscrimination Law in Europe and North America: Disabling Attitudes: U.S. Disability Law and the ADA Amendments Act," *American Journal of Comparative Law* 60 (2012): 205.

47. "EEOC, Regulations to Implement the Equal Employment Provisions of the ADA as Amended," *Federal Register* 76, no. 58 (March 25, 2011), http://www.gpo.gov/fdsys/pkg/FR-2011-03-25/pdf/2011-6056.pdf.

48. Ruth O'Brien, *Bodies in Revolt: Gender, Disability, and a Workplace Ethic of Care* (New York: Routledge, 2005), 2. See "The New ADAAA Regs—Get the Facts You Need to Stay in Compliance," webcast, Society for Human Resource Management, March 29, 2011, http://www.shrm.org/multimedia/webcasts /Pages/legislativewebcast.aspx?marquee=OH; http://www.ohioemployerlaw blog.com/2011_04_01_archive.html. The National Association of Evangelicals testified against the ADA's Title I (employment) provisions on grounds of religious liberty. "Statement on the ADA Amendments Act of 2008," *CQ Federal Department and Agency Documents Regulatory Intelligence Data*, September 17, 2008.

49. O'Brien, *Bodies in Revolt*, 2.

50. Luke Rosiak, "Discrimination Lawsuits Double as Definition of 'Disability' Expands," *Washington Times*, June 1, 2012; and Marjorie Censer, "Proposal on Hiring Disabled Raises Concerns," *Washington Post*, May 28, 2012. Obama also ruled that 7 percent of employees who work with federal contractors should be workers with disabilities.

51. Dzur, "Myth of Penal Populism," 358–60.

52. Ibid.

53. John R. Talbot, *Obamanomics: How Bottom-Up Economic Prosperity Will Replace Trickle-Down Economics* (New York: Seven Stories, 2008), 34.

54. Liz Cohen, *A Consumers' Republic: The Politics of Mass Consumption in Postwar America* (New York: Vintage Press, 2004).

55. Alexis de Tocqueville, *Democracy in America*, vol. 1, chap. 12, "Political Associations in the United States," sec. 2. (New York: Barnes and Nobles, 2004), 158–61.

56. Obama, quoted Talbot, *Obamanomics*, 175.

57. John S. Dryzek, "Pragmatism and Democracy: In Search of Deliberating Publics," *Journal of Speculative Philosophy* 18 (2004): 75. See also John S. Dryzek, "Deliberative Democracy in Divided Societies: Alternatives to Agonism and Analgesia," *Political Theory* 33 (2005): 218.

58. Aaron Smith, "Post-Election Voter Engagement," *PewInternet*, December 30, 2008, http://www.pewinternet.org/Reports/2008/PostElection

-Voter-Engagement/Part-1--Many-who-were-active-online-during-the-campaign
-expect-to-remain-involved.aspx?view=all; Aaron Smith, "The Internet's Role
in Campaign 2008," *PewInternet*, http://www.pewinternet.org/Reports/2009/6
-The-Internets-Role-in-Campaign-2008.aspx; and John Horrigan, "Obama's Online Opportunities," *PewInternet*, December 4, 2008, http://www.pewinternet
.org/Reports/2008/Obamas-Online-Opportunities.aspx. See Roy Mark, "Obama
Names Innovation Team," *eweek*, November 11, 2008, http://www.eweek
.com/c/a/Government-IT/Obama-Names-Innovation-Team/. Obama named
telecom analyst Blair Levin, Google's Sonal Shah, former IAC/InterActiveCorp
executive Julius Genachowski, former Cisco CTO Judy Estrin, Frontline Wire-
less co-founder John Leibovitz, and Google lawyer Andrew McLaughlin to join
the Innovation Team making "innovations" in four distinct categories called
government, national priorities, science, and civil society. All four teams ad-
vised about access, data and information, and outreach or facilitating civic
participation.

    59. Open Government at the Federal Election Commission, http://www.fec
.gov/open/index.shtml; and *Citizens United v. Federal Election Commission*
Report, Open Secrets, http://www.opensecrets.org/news/reports/citizens_united
.php, accessed September 30, 2012, no date posted. See also http://www.opensecrets
.org.

    60. Smith, "The Internet's Role in Campaign 2008." See Roy Mark, "Obama's
Internet Allies Plan Continued Engagement," *eweek*, January 2, 2009, http://
www.eweek.com/c/a/Government-IT/Obamas-Internet-Allies-Plan-Continued
-Engagement/. See also Patricia Moynagh, "A Politics of Enlarged Mentality: Hannah Arendt, Citizenship Responsibility, and Feminism," *Hypatia* 12
(1997): 27.

    61. Katelyn Sabochik, "Petition the White House with We the People,"
http://www.whitehouse.gov/blog/2011/09/22/petition-white-house-we-people;
Equal Futures App, http://equalfutures.challenge.gov.

    62. O'Brien, *Bodies in Revolt*, 67–69.

    63. D. A. Frank, "Obama's Rhetorical Signature: Cosmopolitan Civil Reli-
gion in the Presidential Inaugural Address, January 20, 2009," *Rhetoric & Public Affairs* (2011): 572.

    64. "White House Launches Campaign to Cut Waste: Vice President to Take
on Making Government More Accountable," White House, Office of the Vice
President, press release, June 13, 2011, http://www.whitehouse.gov/the-press
-office/2011/06/13/white-house-launches-campaign-cut-waste-vice-president
-take-making-gover, focuses "on rooting out misspent tax dollars and making
government spending more accessible and transparent for the American people."

    65. "Equal Futures App Challenge," http://equalfutures.challenge.gov.

    66. See Jane Mayer, "Schmooze Or Lose, Obama Doesn't Like Cozying
up to Billionaires. Could it Cost Him the Election?," *New Yorker*, August 27,
2012, http://www.newyorker.com/reporting/2012/08/27/120827fa_fact
_mayer#ixzz27xGEQUe5.

    67. Georg Geismann, "Spinoza—Beyond Hobbes and Rousseau," *Journal of
the History of Ideas* 52 (1991): 44–45, 48. See also Moynagh, "Politics of Enlarged Mentality."

68. Challenge.gov, http://challenge.gov. All the federally sponsored online platforms provide and will provide data that will outlast the Obama administration to determine the level of political participation that is beyond the scope of this book now.

69. Fernholz, "Obama's Deregulatory Moves." The horizontal push stems from the EPA's response to *Massachusetts v. EPA*, 549 U.S. 497 (2007) as well as its participation in the legislative process, including failed efforts to pass cap-and-trade legislation. In a 5 to 4 majority, the court upheld requests from twelve states and several cities that the EPA regulate carbon monoxide.

70. Krista Yee, " 'A Period of Consequences': Global Warming Legislation, Cooperative Federalism, and the Fight between the EPA and the State of California," *University of California, Davis Law Review* 32 (2008): 185–86; "National Climate Program Act," 15 U.S.C. §§ 2901-2908 (2002), http://www.oceancommission .gov/documents/gov_oceans/Act.PDF; and Jillian S. Hishaw, "Gone with the Wind: Coal, Fire and Brimstone—A Legal Analysis of the New Reality Facing the Coal Industry," *Environmental & Energy Law & Policy Journal* 5 (2010): 104 for an explanation of the intersection of local, state, federal, and global environmental laws an public policies.

71. Osofsky, "Diagonal Federalism," 248.

72. Ibid., 262.

73. Ibid., 243, 282.

74. Ibid., 250.

75. Ibid., 277.

76. Ibid., 251–52.

77. Ryan Lizza, "Money Talks: Can Peter Orszag Keep the President's Political Goals Economically Viable?," *New Yorker*, May 4, 2009. Orszag is not an academic behavioral scientist and economist like Sunstein, who had a joint appointment in the law school and the political science department at the University of Chicago. Orszag, whose father is a well-known mathematician who taught at Yale, chose Wall Street and national politics. He served in the Clinton administration and subscribed to Robert Rubin's economic ideas, even joining the Hamilton Project and working for Citibank after leaving the OMB. See also Ron Suskind, *Confidence Men: Wall Street, Washington, and the Education of a President* (New York: Harper, 2011), which explains Orszag's relationship with Larry Summers and behavioral economics.

78. Osofsky, "Diagonal Federalism," 252, 259–61.

79. Quoted from Osofsky, "Diagonal Federalism," 272.

80. Tseming Yang and Robert V. Percival, "The Emergence of Global Environmental Law," *Ecology Law Quarterly* 36 (2009): 615, 618.

81. Sayre, quoted in Osofsky, "Diagonal Federalism," 301–2.

82. Ibid., my italics. Putnam refers to the Biblical story of King Solomon. The logical equation of "necessary and sufficient" is: If *If a, then b* and its converse, *If b, then a*, are both true, we say "*a if and only if b*." This type of thinking is found in the Euclidean logic; the Hebraic Bible, and Spinoza's *Ethics*, chaps. 2 and 3.

83. Jonathan Alter, "The Theater of Big Change," *Newsweek*, February 18, 2008, 34; and "Success for Obama Hinges on Economic Policies," *Daily Yomiuri*, August 31, 2008, 8.

84. "Success for Obama," 8.

85. Ibid.

86. Richard Wolffe, *Revival: The Struggle for Survival inside the Obama White House* (New York: Crown Books, 2011), 132.

87. Lobel, "Renew Deal," 372–74.

88. Barack Obama, "Iowa Caucus Victory Speech" (Des Moines, IA, January 3, 2008).

89. "Rejuvenating US Healthcare System—President Obama Creates History," *eHealth*, April 1, 2010, http://ehealth.eletsonline.com/2010/04/11385/; and Peter Ferrara, "Repeal Health Care Fascism," *American Spectator*, February 25, 2009, http://spectator.org/archives/2009/02/25/repeal-health-care-fascism/. For a progressive view, see David Goldhill, "How American Health Care Killed My Father," *Atlantic*, September 2009, 38, 40.

90. David A. Hyman, "Follow the Money: Money Matters in Health Care, Just Like in Everything Else," *American Journal of Law and Medicine* 36 (2010): 370.

91. "Rejuvenating US Healthcare System."

92. Ibid. Obama's health care plan immediately banned insurance companies from denying "coverage for children with preexisting conditions"; allowed children to stay on their parents' insurance plan until they are 26 years old, and eliminated deductibles or copays for preventive services like mammograms. The "real tipping point" happens in 2014, when (1) mandated insurance exchanges, which are partially government-funded insurance carriers that individuals and small businesses can tap into, and (2) the mandate to buy insurance will begin. Michael Gorsegner, "Healthcare One Year Later: Leaders and People Still Debating Bill's Impact," WPMT-TV, York, PA, March 23, 2011.

93. Gais, "Federalism during the Obama Administration."

94. Liberal Democrats Charles Rangel, Henry Waxman, and George Miller proposed a Medicare-like public option, which would have been available to people under 65 years old as well as providing subsidies for people to purchase insurance if they made less than four times the federal poverty rate. Theodore R. Marmor and Jonathan Oberlander, "Health Reform: The Fateful Moment," August 13, 2009, http://www.nybooks.com/articles/22931.

95. Wolffe, *Revival*, 17.

96. N.C. Aizenman and Amy Goldstein, "Judge Strikes Down Entire New Health-Care Law," *Washington Post*, February 1, 2011.

97. Adam Liptak, "Supreme Court Upholds Health Care Law, 5–4, in Victory for Obama," *New York Times*, June 28, 2012.

98. *U.S. v. Lopez*, 514 U.S. 549 (1995); *U.S. v. Morrison*, 529 U.S. 598 (2000); and *Garrett v. University of Alabama* 531 U.S. 356 (2006). See Ruth O'Brien, *Voices from the Edge: Narratives about the Americans with Disabilities Act* (Oxford: Oxford University Press, 2004), chap. 15.

99. Ezra Klein, "Unpopular Mandate: Why Do Politicians Reverse their Positions?," *New Yorker*, June 25, 2012, http://www.newyorker.com/reporting /2012/06/25/120625fa_fact_klein#ixzz2839p0EEd. From the judiciary's perspective, the first judge to rule against the individual mandate was Judge Henry Hudson, of Virginia's Eastern District Court, who is elected, and who was invested in a Republican consulting firm called Campaign Solutions, which worked

NOTES TO PAGES 160–162

with McCain and Bush, Swift Boat Veterans for Truth, and Ken Cuccinelli—the Virginia state attorney general who is one of the plaintiffs in the lawsuits against the Affordable Care Act. But the more sweeping ruling came from the Northern District of Florida's Judge Roger Vinson. He deemed Obamacare unconstitutional.

100. Jeffrey Toobin, *The Oath: The Obama White House and the Supreme Court* (New York: Doubleday, 2012), 286, 196.

101. Toobin calls it "folly to pretend that Roberts had discovered his inner moderate" in *The Oath*, 298.

102. James Surowiecki, "Was the Health-Care Decision Good for Republicans?," *New Yorker*, June 28, 2012, http://www.newyorker.com/online /blogs/newsdesk/2012/06/was-the-health-care-decision-good-for-republicans .html#ixzz283FIquDp; Jill Lepore, "Benched: The Supreme Court and the Struggle for Judicial Independence," *New Yorker*, June 18, 2012, http://www.newyorker .com/arts/critics/atlarge/2012/06/18/120618crat_atlarge_lepore. "What people think about judicial review usually depends on what they think about the composition of the Court. When the Court is liberal, liberals think judicial review is good, and conservatives think it's bad." In *West Coast Hotel Co. v. Parrish*, 300 U.S. 379 (1937), the decision constituting "the switch in time that saved nine," the fifth vote was also cast by a chief justice, Charles Evans Hughes. It upheld the minimum-wage requirement in the Fair Labor Standards Act, representing a different substantive economic track. It was not simply the case opening the judicial door to the New Deal in terms of constitutionality. See Ruth O'Brien, "'A Sweatshop of the Whole Nation': The Fair Labor Standards Act and the Failure of Regulatory Unionism," *Studies in American Political Development* 15 (Spring 2001): 33.

103. *Gore vs. Bush* 538 U.S. 98 (2000).

104. "Financial Regulatory Reform: A New Foundation: Rebuilding Financial Supervision and Regulation," Department of Treasury, 56, http://www .treasury.gov/initiatives/Documents/FinalReport_web.pdf.

105. "Pew Financial Reform Project Reviews Dodd-Frank Act," June 29, 2011, http://www.freeusf.com/2011/06/pew-financial-reform-project-reviews .html.

106. Martin J. Sklar, *The Corporate Reconstruction of American Capitalism, 1890–1916: The Market, the Law, and Politics* (Cambridge: Cambridge University Press, 1988).

107. See Michael S. Barr, *Banking the Poor: Policies to Bring Low Income Families into the Financial Mainstream*, Brookings Institution Research Brief, September 2004, 1–21. For criticism from the Left, see Thomas Byrne Edsall, *The Age of Austerity: How Scarcity Will Remake American Politics* (New York: Doubleday, 2012); Jeff Madrick, *Age of Greed: The Triumph of Finance and the Decline of America* (New York: Doubleday, 2012). For progressive criticism trying to push Obama, see the publications and reports of the Center for American Progress, a think tank headed by Neera Tanden.

108. See Gretchen Morgenson, "Countrywide to Set Aside $8.4 Billion in Loan Aid," *New York Times*, October 5, 2008. *Watters v. Wachovia Bank, N.A.*, 127 U.S. 1559 (2007) and *Cuomo v. Clearing House Ass'n*, 129 U.S. 2710

(2009) conflict. See also Matthew J. Nance, "The OCC's Exclusive Visitorial Authority over National Banks after *Clearing House Ass'n v. Cuomo*," *Texas Law Review* 87 (2008–2009): 811; John Schwartz, "Obama Seems to Be Open to a Broader Role for States," *New York Times*, January 29, 2009; and Metzger, "Constitutional Transformations," 567, 584.

109. Scalia practices private litigation in defense of employers, not employees, yet he served Bush's Department of Labor. See Scalia's profile at http://www.gibsondunn.com/lawyers/escalia; and Catherine Ho, "Employment Lawyer Fights Regulations," *Washington Post*, May 13, 2012.

110. Metzger, "Constitutional Transformations," 586.

111. Lawrence R. Jacobs and Theda Skocpol, *Obama's Agenda and the Dynamics of U.S. Politics* (New York: Russell Sage Foundation, 2010), 40–41.

112. "The Phony Regulation Debate," *New York Times*, May 27, 2012. The many blogs about the economy in the *New York Times*, *Nation*, *New Republic*, *New York Review of Books*, *Atlantic*, and *Huffington Post* capture the moderate academic to traditional big-state Left to radical criticism of Obama. An angry consensus had emerged by 2010, long before Obama began running for reelection in 2012.

113. Tara Siegel Bernard, "Consumer Bureau Declines to Resist Upfront Credit Card Fees," *New York Times*, April 13, 2012; and E. Scott Reckard, "Watchdog Retreats on High-Cost Credit Cards," *Los Angeles Times*, April 13, 2012.

114. Edsall, *Age of Austerity*. See Adam Davidson, "Making It in America," *Atlantic*, January/February 2012, http://www.theatlantic.com/magazine/archive/2012/01/making-it-in-america/8844/.

115. Hannah Arendt, *The Human Condition* (Chicago: University of Chicago Press).

116. Jacobs and Skocpol, *Obama's Agenda*, 40–41; Adams, "At the Table with Arendt," 10–11.

117. Hanna Fenichel Pitkin's explanation about the human condition in "Justice: On Relating Private and Public," *Political Theory* 9 (1981): 3. See also Seyla Benhabib, "Feminist Theory and Hannah Arendt's Concept of Public Space," *History of the Human Sciences* 6 (1993): 97–114.

118. Adams, "At the Table with Arendt," 10–11.

119. Ibid., 13.

120. Ibid., 17–18. Or, as Seyla Benhabib argues about Jürgen Habermas's position, what reason is there to believe that communication leads to consensus? Arendt does not see consensus, but rather a type of relationality that perpetually transforms itself, or as Minnie Bruce Lou Pratt writes, it is not about "dismantling the home of unjust privilege—it is understanding and agreeing that there is middle class, white, heterosexual privilege."

121. Adams, "At the Table with Arendt," 27–28; Barbara Thayer-Bacon, "Pragmatism and Feminism as Qualified Relativism," *Studies in Philosophy and Education* 22 (2003): 418–19.

122. Geithner's plan was the "stress tests," in which nineteen banks were examined to see how much capital they would require if the economy worsened, so as to restore confidence in the banks and reassure investors.

123. Ryan Lizza, "Inside the Crisis; Larry Summers and the White House Economic Team," *New Yorker*, October 12, 2009. Lizza reports that Austan Goolsbee, a University of Chicago economist Obama appointed to direct the President's Economic Recovery Advisory Board (PERAB), who also served as a deputy for Christina Romer, the chief economic advisor, was the person in the room who "cast the strongest of the no votes" on bailing out Chrysler. Obama sided with Summers over Goolsbee, but Goolsbee thinks he persuaded Obama to make it provisional: if the Fiat deal fell through, no help would be offered by the federal government to Chrysler. Goolsbee succeeded Romer as the chief economist for the Council of Economic Advisors and served as a White House Cabinet member until summer 2011. See Stephen Amberg, "Reconfiguring Industry Structure: Obama and the Rescue of the Auto Companies," in Gerald Berk, Victoria Hattam, and Dennis Galvan, eds., *Unstructuring Politics* (Philadelphia: University of Pennsylvania Press, forthcoming).

124. Lizabeth Cohen, *A Consumers' Republic: The Politics of Mass Consumption in Postwar America* (New York: Vintage Press, 2003), 408; and James Q. Whitman, "Consumerism versus Producerism: A Study in Comparative Law," *Yale Law Journal* 117 (2007): 349 for explanations of consumerism in historical perspective.

125. Walter E. Weyl, *The New Democracy: An Essay on Certain Political and Economic Tendencies in The United States* (New York: Harper & Row 1964, originally published 1912), 250–51.

126. Elizabeth Warren, "Unsafe at Any Rate: If It's Good Enough for Microwaves, It's Good Enough for Mortgages: Why We Need a Financial Product Safety Commission," *Democracy*, December 2007, 9–10.

127. Geismann, "Spinoza," 46, 48.

128. Lobel, "Renew Deal," 449.

129. Matthew J. Parlow, "Civic Republicanism, Public Choice Theory, and Neighborhood Councils: A New Model for Civic Engagement," *University of Colorado Law Review* 79 (2008): 137.

130. Lobel, "Renew Deal," 467, 469.

131. Quoting first Lobel, "Renew Deal," 384; and second, Holly Kruse, "An Organization of Impersonal Relationships," *First Monday* 12 (2007), http://first monday.org/htbin/cgiwrap/bin/ojs/index.php/fm/rt/printerFriendly/2028/1893.

132. The 1990s Community Economic Development Movement represents a spatial shift to decentralization that gave people "a sense of place." See Elaine L. Edgcomb and Joyce A. Klein, *Opening Opportunities, Building Ownership: Fulfilling the Promise of Microenterprise in the United States* (Aspen, CO: Aspen Institute, 2005).

133. In 2010 Tennessee and Delaware received grants first. See Kenneth Jost, "Revising No Child Left Behind: Can Obama's Blueprint Fix Bush's Education Policies," *CQ Researcher* 20, no. 19 (April 16, 2010).

134. Lobel, "Renew Deal," 401.

135. Ibid., 402–3.

136. Gary Orfield, *Schools More Separate: Consequences of a Decade of Resegregation* (Harvard Civil Rights Project, 2001), http://www.law.harvard .edu/groups/civilrights/publications/ resegregation01/schoolsseparate.pdf; Gary

Orfield and Chungmei Lee, *Why Segregation Matters: Poverty and Educational Inequality* (Harvard Civil Rights Project, 2005), http://bsdweb.bsdvt.org/district /EquityExcellence/Research/Why_Segreg_Matters.pdf; Jeff Faux, "The Democrats and the Post-Reagan Economy," *World Policy Journal* 3 (1986): 184. See also David Neumark, Junfu Zhang, and Stephen Ciccarella, "The Effects of Wal-Mart on Local Labor Markets," *Journal of Urban Economics* 63 (2008): 405; Jeff Gates, *Democracy at Risk: Rescuing Main Street From Wall Street* (New York: Basic Books, 2001); Morton Keller, "Governance and Democracy: Public Policy in Modern America," *Journal of Policy History* 20 (2008): 182; Lisa Mc-Girr, *Suburban Warriors: The Origins of the New American Right* (2001); and Julian E. Zelizer, "Reflections: Rethinking the History of American Conservatism," *Reviews in American History* 38 (2010): 367.

137. See Helene Slessarev, *Betrayal of the Urban Poor* (Philadelphia: Temple University Press, 1997). For some of the tensions, see Paul Frymer, *Black and Blue: African Americans, the Labor Movement, and the Decline of the Democratic Party* (Princeton, NJ: Princeton University Press, 2007); Victoria Hattam, *In the Shadow of Race: Jews, Latinos, and Immigrant Politics in the United States* (Chicago: University of Chicago Press. 2007); and Liza Featherstone, *Selling Women Short: The Landmark Battle for Worker's Rights at Wal-Mart* (New York: Basic Books, 2004).

138. John S. Dryzek, "A Post-Positivist Policy-Analytic Travelogue," *Good Society* 11 (2002): 32–36.

139. Charles E. Lindblom, "The Science of Muddling Through," *Public Administration Review* 19 (1959): 79.

140. Ibid. The U. S. Bureau of the Census concluded that in 1890 the American frontier had broken up.

141. Mimi Abramovitz, "Everyone Is Still on Welfare: The Role of Redistribution in Social Policy," *Social Work* 46 (2001): 299; and Harold D. Lasswell, *Politics: Who Gets What, When, How* (New York: Peter Smith, 1990, originally published 1936).

142. See Claire Colebrook, "From Radical Representations to Corporeal Becomings: The Feminist Philosophies of Lloyd, Grosz, and Gatens," *Hypatia* 15 (2000): 88; Genevieve Lloyd, *Spinoza and the Ethics*, 61 (London: Routledge, 1996); and Duane R. Patterson, "Michelle Obama's Vision of America," *Townhall .com*, February 15, 2008, http://townhall.com/tipsheet/duanerpatterson /2008/02/15/michelle_obamas_vision_of_america.

143. Fourth Part, Proposition 35, in Spinoza, *Ethics*, rev., trans., and ed. G. H. R. Parkinson (London: J. M. Dent & Sons, 1989), 163; Adams, "At the Table with Arendt," 1, 27; and O'Brien, *Bodies in Revolt*, 66.

144. Obama, *Audacity of Hope*, 294.

145. Adams, "At the Table with Arendt."

146. Ibid., 15; and Obama, *Audacity of Hope*, 294.

147. Susan Rose-Ackerman, "Progressive Law and Economics—And the New Administrative Law," *Yale Law School Legal Scholarship Repository* 1 (1988): 1; David B. Spence, "Public Choice Progressivism, Continued," *Cornell Law Review* 87 (2001–2002), 397.

148. David M. Trubek and Louise G. Trubek, "Hard and Soft Law in the

Construction of Social Europe," Law School and Center for European Union
Studies, University of Wisconsin–Madison, "Opening the Open Method of Co-
ordination," European University Institute, Florence Italy, July 2003.

149. Wolffe, *Revival*, 200.

150. Barack Obama, "State of the Union Address" (January 24, 2012),
http://www.whitehouse.gov/the-press-office/2012/01/24/remarks-president
-state-union-address.

151. Annie Lowrey, "White House Offers Plan to Lure Jobs to America,"
New York Times, February 2, 2012.

152. Sean Wilentz, *The Age of Reagan: A History 1974–2008* (New York:
Harper, 2008). Different political affiliations and outlooks in the debate over
women working and day care make third-wave feminism particularly incoher-
ent. See Ruth O'Brien, "Introduction: Women's Work, Writing Politics, Sharing
Stories," in *Telling Stories Out of Court: Narratives about Women and Workplace Discrimination* (Ithaca, NY: ILR, Cornell University Press, 2008), 9–11.

153. Lobel, "Renew Deal," 363–64; Barack Obama, "Stimulus Speech"
(George Mason University, Fairfax, VA, January 8, 2009), http://www.nytimes
.com/2009/01/08/us/politics/08text-obama.html?pagewanted=all.

154. Lobel, "Renew Deal," 375–77. For examples of how executive action
can be thwarted, see Elizabeth Sanders, "The Presidency and the Bureaucratic
State," in *The Presidency and the Political System*, ed. Michael Nelson, 2nd ed.
(Washington, DC: Congressional Quarterly Press, 1989), 409–42.

CHAPTER FIVE

1. Barack Obama, "Speech Delivered in Kabul, Afghanistan" (May 1, 2012);
David S. Cloud and Alex Rodriguez, "The CIA Steps Up Pakistan Drone Strikes;
Tired of Islamabad's Refusal to Crack Down on Militants in Cross-Border At-
tacks, the U.S. Is Changing Tack," *Los Angeles Times*, June 8, 2012.

2. David Miliband, "We Are Losing Our Balance. A Left Hand Will Steady
Us," *The Times.co.uk*, May 8, 2012; Christi Parsons and Don Lee, "G-8 Shifts
to Growth over Austerity; The Leaders Also Emphasize that Greece Should Stay
in the Eurozone," *Los Angeles Times*, May 20, 2012; "G20 Leaders Push Jobs,
Growth Mantra," *New Zealand Herald*, June 20, 2012.

3. Daniel Klaidman, "Drones: The Silent Killers: The Obama Campaign Outs a
Commander in Chief Who Never Flinches, but the Truth Is More Complex: How
the President Came to Embrace a New Way of War," *Newsweek*, June 11, 2012;
and David Sanger, *Confront and Conceal: Obama's Secret Wars and Surprising
Use of American Power* (New York: Crown Books, 2012), preface. See Aaron Wil-
davsky, "The Two Presidencies," *Trans-action* 4 (1966); and Lee Sigelman, "A Re-
assessment of the Two Presidencies Thesis," *Journal of Politics* 41 (1979): 1195.

4. Barack Obama, "Renewing American Leadership," *Foreign Affairs*, July
/August 2007; Barack Obama, "UN General Assembly Speech" (September 23,
2009); Obama, "Speech Delivered in Kabul"; Sanger, *Confront and Conceal*;
and Cloud and Rodriguez, "CIA Steps Up Pakistan Drone Strikes."

5. Obama, "Renewing American Leadership"; and Obama, "UN General
Assembly Speech."

6. Hendrik Hertzberg, "Nobel Surprise," *New Yorker*, October 19, 2009, http://www.newyorker.com/talk/comment/2009/10/19/091019taco_talk _hertzberg#ixzz1yAcrtrp7; and George Packer, "Peace and War," *New Yorker*, December 21, 2009, http://www.newyorker.com/talk/comment/2009/12/21 /091221taco_talk_packer#ixzz1yAdaRLrF.

7. See Debra B. Bergoffen's feminist sifting of the just war and just peace traditions in "The Just War Tradition: Translating the Ethics of Human Dignity into Political Practices," *Hypatia* 23 (2008): 72, especially her application of Sara Ruddick, "The Rationality of Care," in *Women, Militarism, and War: Essays in Politics and Social Theory* (Boston: Beacon Press, 1990); Luce Irigaray, "Wonder: A Reading of Descartes' 'The Passions of the Soul,'" in *An Ethics of Sexual Difference* (Ithaca, NY: Cornell University Press, 1993); Elaine Scarry, *The Body in Pain: The Making and Unmaking of the World* (New York: Oxford University Press, 1985); and Simone de Beauvoir, *The Ethics of Ambiguity*, trans. B. Frechtman (New York: Citadel Press, 1991, originally published 1947). Bergoffen concludes that "the only legitimate objective of war is in defense of a just peace . . . [and] requires states to submit to principles of justice grounded in the idea of our *common humanity*, we have the roots of a human rights global order that curtails state sovereignty in the name of the common good" (my italics).

8. Obama, "Renewing American Leadership"; Obama, "UN General Assembly Speech." Sanger's preface to *Confront and Conceal* confirms Ryan Lizza's reporting on Obama's "rebalancing" of the United States and Asia, rather than allowing the Middle East to dominate, a position taken by his national security advisors. Ryan Lizza, "The Consequentialist: How the Arab Spring Remade Obama's Foreign Policy," *New Yorker*, May 2, 2011, http://www.newyorker.com/reporting /2011/05/02/110502fa_fact_lizza; and *Confront and Conceal*, xviii.

9. Obama, "UN General Assembly Speech."

10. See Obama, "UN General Assembly Speech"; Barack Obama, "Address to the Nation on Libya" (speech, National Defense University, Washington, DC, March 28, 2011), http://www.huffingtonpost.com/2011/03/28/obama -libya-speech-_n_841311.html#text; Obama, "Speech Delivered in Kabul"; and Sanger, *Confront and Conceal*, chap. 1. Clinton and George W. Bush gave General Pervez Musharraf of Pakistan financial support without altering his support of, or his incapacity to control, terrorist organizations. See *International Security* 33 (2008), especially articles by S. Paul Kapur, Mette Eilstrup-Sangiovanni, Calvert Jones, Arthur A. Goldsmith, Norrin M. Ripsman, and Jack S. Levy. See also Thomas E. Ricks, "Covert Wars, Waged Virally," review of *Confront and Conceal*, by David Sanger, *New York Times*, June 5, 2012.

11. Obama, "UN General Assembly Speech"; Obama, "Address to the Nation on Libya"; Stephen Eliot Smith, "Definitely Maybe: The Outlook for U.S. Relations with the International Criminal Court during the Obama Administration," *Florida Journal of International Law* 22 (2010): 158, 162; and Tai-Heng Cheng and Eduardas Valaitis, "Shaping an Obama Doctrine of Preemptive Force," *Temple Law Review* 82 (2009): 737; Barack Obama, "Remarks at Strasbourg Town Hall Meeting" (April 3, 2009) (my italics).

12. Georg Geismann, "Spinoza—Beyond Hobbes and Rousseau," *Journal of the History of Ideas* 52 (1991): 42.

13. Bergoffen, "The Just War Tradition," 72–79, 84–90 (note her use of Maurice Merleau-Ponty, "Dialogue and the Perception of the Other," in *The Prose of the World* [Evanston, IL: Northwestern University Press]); "Security Council Resolution 1325," PeaceWomen, http://www.peacewomen.org/themes _theme.php?id=15; and "Obama's Speech on Libya Sparks Off Wave of Republican Rhetoric," *International Business Times*, March 29, 2011, http://www .ibtimes.com/articles/127945/20110329/barack-obama-speech-libya-sarah -palin-donald-trump-republican-presidental-polls-2012-hopefuls-john-b.htm. See also Mona Eltahawy, "Why Do They Hate Us? The Real War on Women Is in the Middle East," *Foreign Affairs*, May/June 2012, http://www.foreignpolicy .com/articles/2012/04/23/why_do_they_hate_us. Quoting Obama, "Address to the Nation on Libya."

14. Fourth Part, Propositions 17 and 57, in Spinoza, *Ethics*, rev., trans., and ed. G. H. R. Parkinson (London: J. M. Dent & Sons, 1989).

15. See Geismann, "Spinoza," 52–53.

16. Barack Obama, "On a New Beginning" (speech delivered at Cairo University in Cairo, Egypt, June 4, 2009), http://www.whitehouse.gov/the-press -office/remarks-president-cairo-university-6-04-09; Smith, "Definitely Maybe," 155–58; Geismann, "Spinoza," 43–52; and Aaron David Miller, "Barack O'Romney," *ForeignPolicy.com*, May 23, 2012.

17. Obama, "UN General Assembly Speech."

18. Ibid.

19. Ibid.; Benedict de Spinoza, *The Chief Works of Benedict de Spinoza, Tractatus-Theologico-Politicus*, trans. R. H. M. Elwes (London: George Bell and Sons, 1891), vol. 1, chap. 9, *Tractatus-Politicus*, vol. 2, chap. 2, parts 5, 8, http:// oll.libertyfund.org/index.php?option=com_staticxt&staticfile=show.php%3 Ftitle=1710&layout=html#chapter_202671; Fourth Part, Propositions 35–36, in Spinoza, *Ethics*, 162–63.

20. Spinoza, *Ethics*, 158; Obama, "Renewing American Leadership"; Obama, "On a New Beginning"; Obama, "UN General Assembly Speech"; and Obama, "Remarks at Strasbourg Town Hall Meeting."

21. Obama, "UN General Assembly Speech" (my italics).

22. Barack Obama, "State of the Union Address" (January 27, 2010); "Too Much Power for a President," editorial, *New York Times*, May 30, 2012; Fourth Part, Proposition 37 in Spinoza, *Ethics*.

23. Barack Obama, "AIPAC Speech" (March 4, 2012).

24. Geismann, "Spinoza," 46; Spinoza, *Tractatus-Theologico-Politicus*, vol. 1, chap. 3; Fourth Part, Propositions 35–36 in Spinoza, *Ethics*, 163.

25. Geismann, "Spinoza," 43–46.

26. Barack Obama, "State of the Union Address" (January 27, 2010); Barack Obama, "AIPAC Speech" (March 4, 2012); Geismann, "Spinoza," 10–12.

27. Obama, "UN General Assembly Speech" (my italics); quote from Geismann, "Spinoza," 37, explaining "There is no cause from whose nature some effect does not follow," First Part, Concerning God, Proposition 36, in Spinoza, *Ethics*, 70.

28. Fourth Part, Proposition 35, in Spinoza, *Ethics*, 163.

29. Smith, "Definitely Maybe," 157.

30. Andrew Sullivan, "Obama Purrs Softly, Then—Flash—His Claws Kill," *Sunday Times of London*, May 8, 2011.

31. My italics. Katie Couric, "Obama: 'Capture Or Kill' Bin Laden," *ABC News*, February 11, 2009, http://www.cbsnews.com/stories/2009/01/14/eveningnews /main4722185.shtml; and Sullivan, "Obama Purrs Softly."

32. Tom Cohen, "Obama Tells Families of 9/11 Victims that 'Justice Has Been Done,'" *CNN*, May 2, 2011.

33. See Ray Rivera and Carlotta Gall, "Is One-Eyed Taliban Leader Mullah Omar Dead? Taliban Says No," *New York Times*, May 23, 2011; Nappy Rippa, "U.S. Envoy Reportedly Eyes Introduction to Taliban Leader," *FoxNews.com*, June 1, 2011, http://www.foxnews.com/politics/2011/06/01/envoy-reportedly -eyes-introduction-taliban-leader.

34. Paul Koring, "U.S. Presses Pakistan to Find More Terrorists," *Globe and Mail* (Canada), May 19, 2011, http://www.cbsnews.com/stories/2009/01/14 /eveningnews/main4722185.shtml.

35. Ibid. My italics.

36. My italics. J. Samuel Barkin, "The Evolution of the Concept of Sovereignty and the Emergence of Human Rights Norms," *Millennium—Journal of International Studies* 27 (1998): 229.

37. Couric, "Obama: 'Capture Or Kill' Bin Laden."

38. Ibid.

39. Obama, "UN General Assembly Speech."

40. Couric, "Obama: 'Capture Or Kill' Bin Laden"; and Obama, "UN General Assembly Speech."

41. Obama, "UN General Assembly Speech."

42. Ibid.

43. Ibid.; and Marc Ambinder and Matthew Cooper, "'Begin Now,' Obama Tells Mubarak," *National Journal*, February 1, 2011.

44. Obama, "UN General Assembly Speech" (my italics).

45. Simon Coleman, "An Empire on a Hill? The Christian Right and the Right to Be Christian in America," *Anthropology Quarterly* 78 (2005): 653.

46. Samuel Huntington, *A Clash of Civilizations and the Remaking of the World Order* (New York: Simon & Schuster, 1996). See David A. Westbrook, "Law through War," *Buffalo Law Review* 48 (2000): 299; and for the evangelical *realpolitik* argument, see Coleman, "Empire on a Hill?"; Jason C. Flanagan, "Woodrow Wilson's 'Rhetorical Restructuring:' The Transformation of the American Self and the Construction of the German Enemy," *Rhetoric & Public Affairs* 7 (2004): 115; Charles Kurzman, "Development Theory: Waves of Democratization," *Studies in Comparative International Development* 33 (1998): 42. "This Puritan tradition resulted in . . . a realist view of human nature," writes Jonathan Monten in "The Roots of the Bush Doctrine: Power, Nationalism, and Democracy Promotion in U.S. Strategy," *International Security* (2005): 112.

47. Obama, "On a New Beginning"; Barack Obama, "A More Perfect Union" (speech, Philadelphia, March 18, 2008), http://www.politico.com/news /stories/0308/9100.html.

48. Kenneth Jost, "Human Rights Issues: Are They a Low Priority under

President Obama?," *CQ Researcher* 19, no. 38 (October 30, 2009); Obama, "UN General Assembly Speech."

49. Ibid.

50. Clinton had an entourage of 500. Roland Flamini, "U.S.-China Relations: Is a Future Confrontation Looming?," *CQ Researcher* 20, no. 18 (May 7, 2010).

51. Flamini, "U.S.-China Relations."

52. Helene Cooper and David Barboza, "Obama Wades into Internet Censorship in China Address," *New York Times*, November 16, 2009; and Flamini, "U.S.-China Relations."

53. Flamini, "U.S.-China Relations."

54. Flamini, "U.S.-China Relations." Iran supplies over 30 percent of China's oil.

55. Jost, "Human Rights Issues." The Norwegian Nobel Committee said Obama created "a new atmosphere of international politics." http://nobelprize .org/nobel_prizes/peace/laureates/2009/press.html.

56. Robert Kaplan, "The Geography of Chinese Power," *Foreign Affairs* 89, no. 3 (2010): 22–41 (my italics).

57. Jost, "Human Rights Issues"; Barack Obama, Town Hall Meeting (Shanghai, November 16, 2009), http://www.whitehouse.gov/blog/2009/11/16 /full-video-and-photos-presidents-town-hall-shanghai; "Obama's Speech Spelled a New Era in American Foreign Policy," *South China Morning Post*, November 21, 2009.

58. "Obama's Speech Spelled a New Era in American Foreign Policy."

59. Jost, "Human Rights Issues," 38.

60. Ibid. Critics emphasize that Obama "engages" with Egypt, Syria, Iran, and Myanmar, which have deplorable human rights records. Obama appointed human rights advocates Harold Hongju Koh as State Department legal advisor and Michael Posner as assistant secretary of state for human rights, democracy, and labor.

61. Eboo Patel and Brad Hirschfield, "Reflections on Obama's Speech to Muslim World," *Washingtonpost.com*, June 6, 2009, http://www.washingtonpost .com/wp-dyn/content/article/2009/06/05/AR2009060503422.html. Hirschfield argued that "what troubled him" was Obama's idea that "Islam was not part of the problem in combating religious extremism but an important part of promoting peace."

62. Obama, "On a New Beginning."

63. Jost, "Human Rights Issues."

64. Barack Obama, "2004 Democratic National Convention Keynote Address" (July 27, 2004), http://www.americanrhetoric.com/speeches/convention 2004/barackobama2004dnc.htm; Kenneth Roth, "Human Rights Watch World Report 2009," http://www.hrw.org/world-report-2009.

65. Barack Obama, "Speech Accepting Democratic Nomination for President" (August 28, 2008).

66. Jost, "Human Rights Issues." The United States did not sign the Convention on the Elimination of All Discrimination Against Women (joining Iran,

Nauru, Palau, Somalia, Sudan, and Tonga) or the Convention on the Rights of
the Child (joining Somalia). See Obama, "UN General Assembly Speech."
    67. Obama sought $51 billion, but his effort failed. See Sheryl Gay Stolberg,
"Obama Seeks a Global Health Plan Broader Than Bush's AIDS Effort," *New
York Times*, May 6, 2009.
    68. Larissa MacFarquhar, "The Conciliator: Where Is Barack Obama Com-
ing From?," *New Yorker*, May 7, 2007, http://www.newyorker.com/reporting
/2007/05/07/070507fa_fact_macfarquhar.
    69. Barack Obama, *The Audacity of Hope: Thoughts on Reclaiming the
American Dream* (New York: Crown, 2006); and MacFarquhar, "Conciliator":
"There is a running thread in American history of idealism that can express itself
powerfully and appropriately, as it did after World War II with the creation of
the United Nations and the Marshall Plan."
    70. MacFarquhar, "Conciliator." Obama relied on Reinhold Niebuhr's *The
Irony of American History* (Chicago: University of Chicago Press, 2008, originally published in 1952). Influential from the 1930s to the 1960s, Niebuhr transformed himself from a Christian Socialist to a pacifist, to an advocate of U.S. intervention in World War II, to a staunch anti-Communist, to an architect of Cold
War liberalism, to a critic of the Vietnam War.
    71. Niebuhr, *Irony of American History*, 164–65.
    72. Ibid., 73.
    73. Ibid., 3, 73.
    74. Ibid., 74.
    75. David R. Cook, "Reinhold Niebuhr," November 8, 2008, *Booktalk.org*,
http://www.booktalk.org/reinhold-niebuhr-t5583.html.
    76. Ibid.
    77. MacFarquhar, "Conciliator."
    78. Lizza, "Consequentialist"; Joe Klein, "Middle East Priority: A Regional In-
frastructure Bank," *Time*, March 17, 2011, http://www.time.com/time/magazine
/article/0,9171,2059609,00.html#ixzz1itNZDpma; and Mark Landler, "Secret
Report Ordered by Obama Identified Potential Uprisings," *New York Times*,
February 16, 2011. Countries in Eastern Europe, Latin America, and Southeast
Asia, particularly Indonesia, were included.
    79. Lizza, "Consequentialist" (my italics); and Klein, "Middle East Priority."
    80. Lizza, "Consequentialist."
    81. Lizza, "Consequentialist"; and Obama, "On a New Beginning."
    82. Klein, "Middle East Priority"; and Lizza, "Consequentialist."
    83. Lizza, "Consequentialist" (my italics).
    84. Ibid.
    85. Ibid.
    86. Gayle Smith, "Beyond Borders: American Foreign Policy Must Look Be-
yond the Nation State and Toward Human Security," *Democracy* 3 (Winter
2007): 64. The United States invested $100 billion (in 2007 dollars) in the Mar-
shall Plan.
    87. Ibid.; Klein, "Middle East Priority."
    88. Obama, "Nobel Lecture."
    89. Ibid. As Lizza notes, John Quincy Adams was the first president not to

"go abroad in search of monsters to destroy." His America was "the well-wisher to freedom and independence of all," but the "champion and vindicator only of her own." George Kennan repeated these words, in opposition to the Vietnam war, in 1966, saying, "Foreign-policy problems are always more complicated than Americans, in their native idealism, usually allow." Thirty-six years later Kennan said, "Today, if we went into Iraq, as the President would like us to do, you know where you begin. You never know where you are going to end." Obama met Zbigniew Brzezinski, President Carter's national security advisor and the Democrats' "reigning realist," in Iowa.

90. Obama, "Nobel Lecture."

91. Samantha Power, who worked as a journalist in the Balkans and Africa, wrote *A Problem from Hell: America and the Age of Genocide* (New York: Harper Perennial, 2007). Michael McFaul, a Stanford professor who became a mid-level Obama advisor, privileges democracy, and went to Russia in 2012. Lizza, "Consequentialist."

92. Obama, "On a New Beginning."

93. Ibid.

94. Ibid.

95. Barack Obama, "State of the Union Address" (January 25, 2011).

96. David E. Sanger, "As Mubarak Digs In, U.S. Policy in Egypt Is Complicated," *New York Times*, February 6, 2011.

97. Lizza, "Consequentialist."

98. Ibid.; and Sanger, *Confront and Conceal*, xviii.

99. Lizza, "Consequentialist."

100. Ibid. As Obama's NSC team rethought rudimentary assumptions about American interests, Egyptian officials warned Obama that the Muslim Brotherhood would try to take power. "My daughter gets to go out at night," Ahmed Aboul Gheit, Egypt's then foreign minister, told Secretary Clinton during one conversation. "And, God damn it, I'm not going to turn this country over to people who will turn back the clock on her rights."

101. Lizza, "Consequentialist."

102. Mohammed Abbas, of the Muslim Brotherhood, said, "Obama supported this revolution. She [Clinton] was against." "We respect Obama's attitude toward our revolution, and when we were in Tahrir Square we were following all of the leaders all over the world and what were their views," Abbas said. "His speeches were more understanding and more appreciative of what we were doing, especially his second one," el-Ghazaly Harb said, referring to Obama's demand that the transition "begin now," Richard Holbrooke, who died (December 11, 2010) in the midst of these events, left records of the discord that his wife, Kati Marton, said "tell a dramatic story of a fractured relationship between the State Department and White House." Lizza, "Consequentialist."

103. David D. Kirkpatrick, "Revolt Leaders Cite Failure to Uproot Old Order in Egypt," *New York Times*, June 14, 2012; Wendell Steavenson, "Egypt: The Army and the President," *New Yorker*, June 18, 2012, http://www.newyorker .com/online/blogs/newsdesk/2012/06/egypt-the-army-and-the-president .html#ixzz1yL03jPbH.

104. Lizza, "Consequentialist."

105. Ibid.; Tom Malinowski, "The Timeliness Paradox," *New Republic*, March 27, 2011. Lizza adds, "Was it possible that the Americans were trying to make the military options appear so bleak that China and Russia would be sure to block action?"

106. Lizza, "Consequentialist." Brzezinski complained that Obama "doesn't strategize. He sermonizes."

107. Lizza, "Consequentialist"; Barack Obama, "The War We Need to Win," (speech delivered at the Woodrow Wilson Center, Washington, DC, August 1, 2007).

108. Leon Hadar, "Obama's Right in 'Leading from Behind' in Libya," *Business Times*, August 25, 2011.

109. Ibid.; P. J. Crowley, "It's Time to Tell Assad to Go," *Washington Post*, August 23, 2011.

110. Crowley, "It's Time to Tell Assad to Go"; and David Ignatius, "The Too-Quiet President," *Washington Post*, July 17, 2011.

111. Daniel Philpott, Timothy Samuel Shah, and Monica Duffy Toft, "The Dangers of Secularism in the Middle East," *Christian Science Monitor*, August 11, 2011. Monica Duffy Toft, Daniel Philpott, and Timothy Samuel Shah wrote *God's Century: Resurgent Religion and Global Politics* (New York: W. W. Norton, 2011).

112. Obama, "On a New Beginning"; and Obama, "Nobel Lecture."

113. Obama, "On a New Beginning"; Obama, "Nobel Lecture"; and Philpott, Shah, and Toft, "Dangers of Secularism." "Let me also say this: the promotion of human rights cannot be about exhortation alone. At times, it must be coupled with painstaking diplomacy. I know that engagement with repressive regimes lacks the satisfying purity of indignation. But I also know that sanctions without outreach—and condemnation without discussion—can carry forward a crippling status quo. No repressive regime can move down a new path unless it has the choice of an open door." Obama, "Nobel Lecture."

114. Hillary Clinton, "Remarks to the U.S.-Islamic World Forum" (speech, Andrew W. Mellon Auditorium, Washington, DC, April 12, 2011), http://www.state.gov/secretary/rm/2011/04/160642.htm.

115. Ibid. The U.S. Overseas Private Investment Corporation (OPIC) allocated the $2 billion to Partners for a New Beginning, led by former secretary of state Madeleine Albright, Muhtar Kent of Coca-Cola, and Walter Isaacson of the Aspen Institute.

116. David Remnick, "Behind the Curtain," *New Yorker*, September 5, 2011; Michael Shear, "Best Political Quotes of the Weekend," *New York Times.com*, March 21, 2011.

117. Lizza, "Consequentialist"; Liz Sly, "Syrian Protesters Energized by Obama's Call for Departure of Al-Assad," *Washington Post*, August 19, 2011; and Helene Cooper, "Solution on Syria Remains Elusive for White House," *New York Times*, February 5, 2012.

118. Remnick, "Behind the Curtain"; Wilson Scott and Karen DeYoung, "Limited Intervention Contrasts Obama with Bush," *Washington Post*, October 21, 2011.

119. Remnick, "Behind the Curtain"; Scott and DeYoung, "Limited Inter-

vention"; Jonathan Rynhold, "Presenting the Obama Doctrine," *Jerusalem Post*, May 26, 2011.

120. Rynhold, "Presenting the Obama Doctrine." Obama is often accused of inconsistency because he stood by Syria until 2012. Ewen MacAskill, "Obama Tells Arab Dictators Change or Go: Warning to Syria Coupled with Call for Israel to Pull Back to Pre-1967 Borders," *Guardian*, May 20, 2011.

121. Rynhold, "Presenting the Obama Doctrine"; Arnaud de Borchgrave, "Obama Can't Wish Away the Wall; President's Plea for Boundary Overlooks Existing Partition," *Washington Times*, May 23, 2011; and MacAskill, "Obama Tells Arab Dictators."

122. Lizza, "The Consequentialist."

123. Obama, "UN General Assembly Speech."

124. Jost, "Human Rights Issues."

125. Morris Davis, "America's Much Abused Moral Authority," Guardian .co.uk, March 5, 2011; and Ari Shapiro, "Senate Panel Delves into Harsh Interrogation Methods," *Morning Edition*, National Public Radio, May 14, 2009.

126. Davis, "America's Much Abused Moral Authority," and Spencer Ackerman, "Human Rights in America," *Washington Independent*, April 27, 2009.

127. See *Getting Away with Torture: The Bush Administration and Mistreatment of Detainees*, Human Rights Watch, 2010, http://www.scribd.com /doc/59920124/Human-Rights-Watch-Getting-Away-with-Torture-The-Bush -Administration-and-Mistreatment-of-Detainees; and David P. Forsythe, "U.S. Foreign Policy and Human Rights: Situating Obama," *Human Rights Quarterly* 33 (2011): 767. The Human Rights Watch report includes "substantial information warranting criminal investigations of Bush and senior administration officials, including former vice president Dick Cheney, defense secretary Donald Rumsfeld, and CIA director George Tenet, for ordering practices such as 'waterboarding,' the use of secret CIA prisons, and the transfer of detainees to countries where they were tortured."

128. See Davis, "America's Much Abused Moral Authority."

129. Manfred Nowak, Moritz Birk, and Tiphanie Crittin, "The Obama Administration and Obligations under the Convention against Torture," *Transnational Law & Contemporary Problems* 20 (2011): 33.

130. Perry Bacon Jr., "Left, Right Press Obama on War Funds; Points of Contention Include Guantanamo Bay, Abuse Photos and Loan to IMF," *Washington Post*, June 10, 2009; and Richard Wolffe, *Revival: The Struggle for Survival inside the Obama White House* (New York: Crown Books, 2011), 219–23.

131. Tom Reifer, "Guantanamo, Torture, and the Perversion of Justice: Obama's New Executive Order," Transnational Institute of Policy Studies, March 16, 2011, http://www.tni.org/article/guantanamo-torture-and-perversion -justice-obama's-new-executive-order; Morris Davis, "America's Much Abused Moral Authority."

132. Mark Danner, *Stripping Bare the Body: Politics, Violence, War* (New York: W. W. Norton, 2011); and Reifer, "Guantanamo."

133. "Obama's Guantanamo Bay Just Like Gulag Archipelago," *Kalgoorlie Miner*, March 23, 2009; Denny LeBoeuf, "Executing the Evidence," *Blog*

of Rights, American Civil Liberties Union, http://www.aclu.org/blog/capital
-punishment-national-security/executing-evidence; "The Prison that Won't Go
Away," *New York Times,* March 9, 2011; and John T. Parry, *Understanding
Torture* (Ann Arbor: University of Michigan Press, 2010).

134. Mary Bruce, "Obama: Gitmo Likely Won't Close in First 100 Days,"
ABCNews.com, January 11, 2009.

135. John L. Mearsheimer and Stephen M. Walt, *The Israeli Lobby and
U.S. Foreign Policy* (New York: Farrar, Straus & Giroux, 2007), 191; Exec.
Order 13,567—Periodic Review of Individuals Detained at Guantánamo Bay
Naval Station Pursuant to the Authorization for Use of Military Force, avail-
able at http://www.whitehouse.gov/the-press-office/2011/03/07/executive
-order-13567-periodic-review-individuals-detained-guant-namo-bay-nava.

136. Jonathan Hafetz, *Habeas Corpus after 9/11: Confronting America's
New Global Detention System* (New York: New York University Press, 2011).
Not disguising his disregard for Bush's interrogation policy, Obama added that
many "very dangerous" prisoners at Guantanamo are in legal limbo because
"some of the evidence against them may be tainted even though it's true." "From
my view, waterboarding is torture," Obama has reiterated consistently. See
Thomas M. DeFrank, "Gitmo's a No-Go, Sez Bam," *New York Daily News,*
January 12, 2009. "Estimates run as high as 18,000 people" "held in legal black
holes": Gwynne Dyer, "Obama and the Gulag Archipelago," *Trinidad Express,*
February 6, 2011; *Rasul v. Bush,* 542 U.S. 466 (2004); Anton Antonowicz,
"Barack Obama Inauguration: Unclench Your Fist," *Mirror,* January 21, 2009;
Reifer, "Guantanamo."

137. John R. Crook, "Contemporary Practice of the United States Relat-
ing to International Law: International Human Rights and Humanitarian Law,"
American Journal of International Law 205 (2011): 594, 596–97; and Nowak,
Birk, and Crittin, "Obama Administration."

138. Obama, "Nobel Lecture."

139. George W. Bush, George H. W. Bush, former secretaries of defense
Richard Cheney and Donald Rumsfeld, and former Justice Department lawyer
John Yoo cannot travel to Spain, France, Belgium, Germany, the United Kingdom, Israel, Canada, Australia, or the Czech Republic, given universal jurisdiction and the possibility that they could be jailed for possible prosecution, as
Augusto Pinochet Ugarte, the former head of Chile, was in 1998. Under this expansive jurisdictional doctrine, a sovereign nation-state can detain and prosecute
individuals for committing "crimes against all" regardless of whether the victim
or the perpetrator resides or resided inside that country. See James Thuo Gathii,
"Torture, Extraterritoriality, Terrorism, and International Law," *Alabama Law
Review* 67 (2003): 338; and Maximo Langer, "The Diplomacy of Universal Jurisdiction: The Political Branches and the Transnational Prosecution of International Crimes," *American Journal of International Law* 105 (2011): 30.

140. Klaidman, "Drones: The Silent Killers"; and Catherine Philip, "Obama
Gives Nod for Drone Killings," *Australian,* May 31, 2012.

141. Klaidman, "Drones: The Silent Killers"; Paul Harris, "Drone Wars
and State Secrecy—How Barack Obama Became a Hardliner," *Guardian.com,*
June 2, 2012; and Justin Elliott, "Obama Administration's Drone Death Figures

Don't Add Up," *ProPublica*, June 18, 2012, http://www.propublica.org/article
/obama-drone-death-figures-dont-add-up.

142. Klaidman, "Drones: The Silent Killers"; Philip, "Obama Gives Nod for
Drone Killings."

143. Philip, "Obama Gives Nod for Drone Killings."

144. David Sanger, "Obama Order Sped Up Wave of Cyberattacks Against
Iran," *New York Times*, June 1, 2012 (excerpted from his book *Confront and
Conceal*).

145. Justin Elliott, "Dissecting Obama's Standard on Drone Strike Deaths,"
ProPublica, June 5, 2012, http://www.propublica.org/article/dissecting-obamas
-standard-on-drone-strike-deaths; Harris, "Drone Wars and State Secrecy."

146. Harris, "Drone Wars and State Secrecy"; Charles Savage, "Tracking
Leaks Is Difficult, Prosecution Is Harder Still," *International Herald Tribune*,
June 10, 2012.

147. Ivo Daalder, "A New Shield over Europe," *International Herald Tribune*, June 7, 2012.

148. Orly Lobel, "The Renew Deal: The Fall of Regulation and the Rise
of Governance in Contemporary Legal Thought," *Minnesota Law Review* 89
(2004): 342, 390. See Martha Finnemore, "Norms, Cultures, and World Politics:
Some Insights from Sociological Institutionalism," *International Organizations*
52 (1996): 325.

149. See Michael Mason, "The Governance of Transnational Environmental
Harm: Addressing New Modes of Accountability/Responsibility," *Global Environmental Politics* 8 (2008): 8–10.

150. Ibid.; Luigi Pellizzonia and Marja Ylönen, "Responsibility in Uncertain Times: An Institutional Perspective on Precaution," *Global Environmental
Politics* 8 (2008): 51; and Peter Newell, "Civil Society, Corporate Accountability
and Politics of Climate Change," *Global Environmental Politics* 8 (2008): 122.

151. See Jane Mayer, "The Predator War: What Are the Risks of the CIA's Covert Drone Program?," *New Yorker*, October 26, 2009, http://www.newyorker
.com/reporting/2009/10/26/091026fa_fact_mayer#ixzz1mI06DPVQ.

152. See Dana Priest and William Arkin, *Top Secret America* (Boston: Little,
Brown, 2011); Noah Schachtman and Spencer Ackerman, "Search Top Secret
America's Database of Private Spooks," *Danger Room*, July 19, 2010, http://
www.wired.com/dangerroom/2010/07/search-through-top-secret-americas-
network-of-private-spooks; "Top Secret America: Air and Space Operations,"
WashingtonPost.com, http://projects.washingtonpost.com/top-secret-america
/functions/air-and-space-ops/.

153. Republican Senators sponsored the 2005 Detainee Treatment Act,
which prohibited inhumane treatment of all prisoners, including those in Guantanamo Bay, and mandated that interrogations follow protocol delineated in the
U.S. Army Field Manual for Human Intelligence Collector Operations. It eliminated the federal courts' jurisdiction to consider habeas corpus petitions, and it
reduced appellate review of decisions of Combatant Status Review Tribunals and
military commissions. Yet the Supreme Court gave a 5–4 ruling in *Boumediene
v. Bush*, 553 U.S. 723 (2008), that the Military Commissions Act of 2006 uncon-
stitutionally limited detainees' access to judicial review and that detainees have

the right to challenge their detention in conventional civilian courts. Amendment no. 1977 to the Detainee Treatment Act of 2005, the so-called McCain amendment, introduced by senators John McCain, Lindsey Graham, Chuck Hagel, Gordon H. Smith, Susan M. Collins, Lamar Alexander, Richard Durbin, Carl Levin, John Warner, Lincoln Chafee, John E. Sununu, and Ken Salazar, was signed by President Bush, since ninety Senators, all told, voted for it, whereas only six were opposed. Bush issued a signing statement that "the executive branch shall construe Title X in Division A of the Act, relating to detainees, in a manner consistent with the constitutional authority of the President to supervise the unitary executive branch and as Commander in Chief and consistent with the constitutional limitations on the judicial power, which will assist in achieving the shared objective of the Congress and the President, evidenced in Title X, of protecting the American people from further terrorist attacks."

154. Mason, "Governance of Transnational Environmental Harm," 10.

155. See Tanya Roth, "Court Dismisses Nisour Square Charges against Blackwater Employees," *FindLaw Decided*, January 4, 2010; *U.S. v. Slough*, DC Circuit Court of Appeals (2011), http://blogs.findlaw.com/decided/2010/01/court-dismisses-nisour-square-charges-against-blackwater-employees.html; Carol D. Leonnig and Nick Schwellenbach, "Former Blackwater Employees Accuse Security Contractor of Defrauding Government," *Washington Post*, February 12, 2010. See also Rebecca DeWinter-Schmitt, "Holding Private Security Contractors Accountable for Human Rights Abuses," *Human Rights Now*, June 28, 2011, http://blog.amnestyusa.org/justice/holding-private-security-contractors-accountable-for-human-rights-abuses; "Blackwater Guards Pitch Manslaughter Case to U.S. Supreme Court," *Blog of LegalTimes*, October 24, 2011, http://legaltimes.typepad.com/blt/2011/10/blackwater-guards-pitch-manslaughter-case-to-us-supreme-court-.html. Finally, see *General Dynamics v. United States*, 415 U.S. 486 (2011), http://www.scotusblog.com/case-files/cases/general-dynamics-corp-v-united-states/; and *Boeing v. United States*, 537 U.S. 437 (2003), http://www.scotusblog.com/case-files/cases/the-boeing-company-v-united-states.

156. Mason, "Governance of Transnational Environmental Harm," 8–10 (my italics).

157. Ibid.

158. Fourth Part, Proposition 35, in Spinoza, *Ethics*; and Anne-Marie Slaughter, "A New Theory for the Foreign Policy Frontier: Collaborative Power," *Atlantic*, November 30, 2011. Slaughter attributes this power-with/power-over distinction to Lani Guinier, but does not look far enough. Like nesting Russian matryoshka dolls, Guinier is indebted to critical race theory, which in turn is influenced by postwar sources of critical theory such as the Frankfurt School, itself informed by Warren Montag's argument that Spinoza himself is the "first critical theorist."

159. Slaughter, "A New Theory."

160. Ibid.; and see Anne-Marie Slaughter, "Interests vs. Values: Misunderstanding Obama's Libya Strategy," *New York Review of Books Blog*, March 30, 2011, which echoes the 1990s ethic of care debate. See Carol Gilligan, *In a Different Voice* (Cambridge, MA: Harvard University Press, 1993); and Martha

Fineman, *The Neutered Mother and the Sexual Family and Other Twentieth Century Tragedies* (New York: Routledge, 1995).
   161. Lobel, "Renew Deal," 400, 440, 443.
   162. Ibid., 444.

CHAPTER SIX

   1. Epigraph: See U.S. Treasury, *FAQs: Portraits and Designs on Coins,* http://www.treasury.gov/resource-center/faqs/Coins/Pages/edu_faq_coins _portraits.aspx.
   2. Casey Gane-McCalla, "How Bob Marley's Songs of Freedom Led to Barack Obama's Message of Hope," *Huffington Post,* February 6, 2009, http://www.huffingtonpost.com/casey-ganemccalla/how-bob-marleys-songs -of_b_164476.html; Bob Marley and Curtis Mayfield, "One Love," on *Exodus* (Tuff Gong Records, 1977); "We Are One: The Obama Inaugural Celebration," *NPR Music,* January 18, 2009, http://www.npr.org/templates/story/story .php?storyId=99389770.
   3. Nicholas Philip Trist Papers, 1765–1903, Collection Number: 02104, Southern Historical Collection, Louis Round Wilson Special Collections Library, University of North Carolina, Chapel Hill, http://www.lib.unc.edu/mss /inv/t/Trist,Nicholas_Philip.html. See Personal Seal, The Jefferson Encyclopedia, http://wiki.monticello.org/mediawiki/index.php/Jefferson's_Seal.
   4. Ibid.; and Ryan, P. Jordan, "The Dilemma of Quaker Pacifism in a Slaveholding Republic, 1833–1865," *Civil War History,* 53 (2007): 5. Trist, a proslavery U.S. consul in Havana, Cuba, in 1833 "became corruptly involved in the creation of false documents designed to mask illegal sales of Africans into bondage." A pamphlet detailing this came out before the *Amistad.* Trist did not appear in the film *Amistad,* directed by Steven Spielberg.
   5. Max Weber, *The Protestant Ethic and the Spirit of Capitalism* (London: Penguin Press, 2002), 6, 33–35, and 63–105.
   6. Jefferson did use this seal on an April 4, 1790, letter to Richard Gem. Franklin published many "truisms" in his newspaper columns that he later compiled in *Poor Richard's Almanac.* "Until the Civil War amendments," political theorist Judith Shklar argues, "America was neither a liberal nor a democratic country." Judith Shklar, "Redeeming American Political Theory," *American Political Science Review* 85 (1991): 4; John Winthrop, "A Model of Christian Charity," http://history.hanover.edu/texts/winthmod.html; and Weber, *The Protestant Ethic.*
   7. Lynn Sweet, "Rev. Lowery Inauguration Benediction: Transcript," *Chicago Sun-Times,* January 20, 2009.
   8. Victor W. Turner, "Betwixt and Between: The Liminal Period in *Rites de Passage,*" *Proceedings of the American Ethnological Society,* Symposium on New Approaches to the Study of Religion (1964): 4.
   9. Barack Obama, *Dreams from My Father: A Story of Race and Inheritance* (New York: Three Rivers Press, 2004). Obama used the phrase "wrong side of history" with Senator McCain when he started exhibiting racism. For an

overview of Obama's use of this phrase from a "neo-liberal" source, see Steve Benen, "McCain Eyes the 'Right Side of History,'" *Washington Monthly*, January 30, 2011.

10. Peter Halewood, "Laying Down the Law: Post-Racialism and the Deracination Project," *Albany Law Review* (2009): 72. For a critique of this perspective, see Rogers M. Smith and Desmond S. King, "Barack Obama and the Future of American Racial Politics," *Du Bois Review* 6 (2009): 25; and Desmond S. King and Rogers M. Smith, *Still a House Divided: Race and Politics in Obama's America* (Princeton, NJ: Princeton University Press, 2011). In both works they present an institutional argument about the "current structure of racial politics" that does not include a postracial era. They divide the political discourse landscape between those who are color-blind and who want to keep race out of politics and those who are color-conscious—often a political liability. See also Cedric Merlin Powell, "Rhetorical Neutrality: Colorblindness, Frederick Douglass, and Inverted Critical Race Theory," *Cleveland State Law Review* 56 (2008): 823.

11. Karen Orren, "Standing to Sue: Interest Group Conflict in the Federal Courts," *American Political Science Review* 70 (1976): 723; Eric Biber and Berry Brosi, "Officious Intermeddlers or Citizen Experts? Petitions and Public Production of Information in Environmental Law," *UCLA Law Review* 58 (2010): 321; and "Note: Nontaxpayer Standing, Religious Favoritism, and the Distribution of Government Benefits: The Outer Bounds of the Endorsement Test," *Harvard Law Review* 123 (2010): 1999.

12. David Roediger, *Wages of Whiteness: Race and the Making of the American Working Class* (New York: Verso, 1991); Shelley Fisher Fishkin, "Interrogating 'Whiteness,' Complicating 'Blackness': Remapping American Culture," *American Quarterly* 47 (1995): 428; Bruce Baum, "Barack Obama and the White Problem," paper presented at the Annual Meeting of the Western Political Science Association, 2011; and Darryl Fears, "Hue and Cry on 'Whiteness Studies,'" *Washington Post*, June 20, 2003.

13. Charles Flint Kellogg, "The Negro in the Economy," in *Employment, Race, and Poverty*, ed. Arthur Ross and Herbert Hill (New York: Harcourt, Brace & World, 1967), 25.

14. *Brown v. Board of Education*, 347 U.S. 483 (1954). See Andrew Kull, *The Colorblind Constitution* (Cambridge, MA: Harvard University Press, 1992) for a classic interpretation.

15. Manning Marable, *Race, Reform, and Rebellion: The Second Reconstruction in Black America* (Jackson: University Press of Mississippi, 1991).

16. Helene Slessarev, *Betrayal of the Urban Poor* (Philadelphia: Temple University Press, 1997), 17, 51–52. In 1977 Hasia Diner wrote, in *In the Almost Promised Land: American Jews and Blacks, 1915–1935* (Baltimore, MD: Johns Hopkins University Press, 1995), that American Jews supported the NAACP and that anti-Semitism hit a peak just as the KKK did, in 1915, with the lynching of Leo Frank in Atlanta, Georgia. Franz Boas helped undermine eugenics and the false scientific correlation between race, ethnicity, and intelligence. See also Karen Brodkin, *How Jews Became White Folks and What That Says about Race in America* (New Brunswick, NJ: Rutgers University Press, 1999); and Emily

Budick, *Blacks and Jews in Literary Conversation* (New York: Cambridge University Press, 1998).

17. Slessarev, *Betrayal of the Urban Poor*, 39. See also Ruth O'Brien, "Duality and Division: The Development of American Labor Policy from the Wagner Act to the Civil Rights Act," *International Contributions to Labour Studies* 4 (1994): 21.

18. Kull, *Colorblind Constitution*, 186.

19. Ibid., 187–188 (my italics).

20. B. Dan Wood and Richard W. Waterman, "The Dynamics of Political Control of the Bureaucracy," *American Political Science Review* 85 (1991): 801.

21. Kull, *Colorblind Constitution*, 188; Slessarev, *Betrayal of the Urban Poor*, 36–37.

22. Ruth O'Brien, *Crippled Justice: The History of Modern Disability Policy in the Workplace* (Chicago: University of Chicago Press, 2001), 94–97.

23. Slessarev, *Betrayal of the Urban Poor*, 36–37.

24. *Griggs v. Duke Power Co.*, 401 U.S. 424 (1971). See Earl M. Maltz, "The Legacy of *Griggs v. Duke Power Co.*: A Case Study in the Impact of a Modernist Statutory Precedent," *Utah Law Review* 1994: 1353.

25. Slessarev, *Betrayal of the Urban Poor*, 36–37. See also Hugh Graham, *The Civil Rights Era* (New York: Oxford University Press, 1990). The very existence of the Voting Rights Act of 1965 underwent scrutiny during the reauthorization debate. See Chandler Davidson, *Quiet Revolution in the South: The Impact of the Voting Rights Act, 1965–1990* (Princeton, NJ: Princeton University Press, 1994).

26. Dr. E. Wayne Harris, a consultant, speaking at a public school about "Equity Then and Now: Still a Necessity" (October 5, 1999), broke this process up into four phases. Phase 3 was titled "Efforts to Integrate Lose Momentum: *Milliken v. Bradley—I* (1974); *Milliken v. Bradley—II* (1977)"; and phase 4 was titled "Efforts to Dismantle Desegregation: *Riddick v. Norfolk City, Virginia School Board* (1986); *Oklahoma Board of Education v. Dowell* (1991); *Freeman v. Pitts* (1992); *Missouri v. Jenkins* (1995); *Capacchione v. Charlotte-Mecklenburg Schools* (1999); and *Swann v. Charlotte-Mecklenburg Schools* (1999)." See also Gary Orfield, "Race and the Liberal Agenda: The Loss of the Integrationist Dream, 1965–1974" in *The Politics of Social Policy in the United States*, ed. Margaret Weir, Ann Shola Orloff, and Theda Skocpol (Princeton, NJ: Princeton University Press, 1988).

27. *Grutter v. Bollinger*, 539 U.S. 306 (2003); and *Gratz v. Bollinger*, 539 U.S. 244 (2003). See also Nicholas Lemann, *The Promised Land: The Great Black Migration and How It Changed America* (New York: Vantage Books, 1991); and Barbara A. Perry, *The Michigan Affirmative Action Cases* (Lawrence: University Press of Kansas, 2007).

28. Malcolm X, *By Any Means Necessary: Malcolm X Speeches and Writing*, 2nd ed. (New York: Pathfinder Press, 1992), 118.

29. Matt Bai, "Is Obama the End of Black Politics?," *New York Times Magazine*, August 6, 2008.

30. Slessarev, *Betrayal of the Urban Poor*, 116. Nixon signed the executive order establishing the Office of Minority Business Enterprise (OMBE). See also

Dean Kotlowski, "Black Power—Nixon Style: The Nixon Administration and Minority Business Enterprise," *Business History Review* 72 (1998): 409.

31. Slessarev, *Betrayal of the Urban Poor*, 64 and 132. My italics.

32. Ibid., 35–37.

33. "Correlation" is defined by the *Oxford Dictionary Online* as "a mutual relationship or connection between two or more things: *research showed a clear correlation between recession and levels of property crime*," or, in statistics, "interdependence of variable quantities"; "a quantity measuring the extent of such interdependence"; or "the process of establishing a relationship or connection between two or more measures."

34. Obama, *Dreams from My Father*; "Wage Gap Statistically Unchanged," *National Committee on Pay Equity* (2010), http://www.pay-equity.org/. Fifty years ago, women earned 61 percent of what men earned, according to a Census official.

35. Quoted in Halewood, "Laying Down the Law," 1047, 1049.

36. Alan Woolfolk, "The Denial of Character," *Society* 39 (March/April 2002), reprinted in Jonathan B. Imber, ed., *Therapeutic Culture: Triumph and Defeat* (New Brunswick, NJ: Transaction Publishers, 2004), 70. Woolfolk's paper was presented at a conference that evaluated Christopher Lasch's, Philip Rieff's, and Thomas Szasz's work on culture and the therapeutic state. Rieff was a sociologist and cultural critic, Lasch considered himself a social critic; originally a socialist influenced by the Frankfurt school of critical theory, he was later denounced by feminists for his "syncretic synthesis" of Freud and paleoconservatism. Thomas S. Szasz was not just a conservative, but fought for deinstitutionalization as well as human and civil rights for those with mental illness. See Thomas S. Szasz, "The Myth of Mental Illness," *American Psychologist* 15 (1960): 113; and Thomas S. Szasz, *The Therapeutic State: Psychiatry in the Mirror of Current Events* (Buffalo, NY: Prometheus Books, 1975). See also Garry Wills, *Nixon Agonistes: The Crisis of the Self-Made Man?* (New York: Houghton Mifflin, 1969), 67.

37. Gloating is the opposite of bitterness, and is defined by the *Oxford Dictionary Online* as "to contemplate or dwell on one's own success or another's misfortune with smugness or malignant pleasure."

38. See Sandra M. Gilbert and Susan Gubar, *The Madwoman in the Attic: The Woman Writer and the Nineteenth-Century Literary Imagination* (New Haven, CT: Yale University Press, 1979).

39. See Susan Gubar, *White Skin, Black Face in American Culture* (New York: Oxford University Press, 1997). Gubar references Marilyn Hacker, *Assumptions* (New York: Alfred A. Knopf, 1985); Grace Paley, "At That Time or the History of a Joke," in *The Collected Stories* (New York: Farrar, Straus & Giroux Classics, 2007); e. e. cummings, *Him* (New York: Liveright, 1927), http://www.gvsu.edu/english/cummings/Him.htm; and T. S. Eliot, "The Beating of a Drum," *Nation and the Athenaeum* 34 (October 6, 1926): 12–13.

40. Jake Tapper, "William Bennett Defends Comment on Abortion and Crime," *ABC News*, September 29, 2005; and Stephen J. Levitt and Stephen J. Dubner, *Freakonomics: A Rogue Economist Explores the Hidden Side of Everything* (New York: Harper Perennial, 2006).

41. Levitt and Dubner, *Freakonomics*.

42. This fear helps explains "adultification" of African American males starting at age 13. Nicole Hansen, "Mass Opinion, Elite Discourse, and Crime Policy—The Case of Adultification Statutes in the United States" (unpublished paper, 2010).

43. Laura J. Khoury, "Racial Profiling as Dressage: A Social Control Regime!," *African Identities* 7 (2009): 55 (italics in original).

44. Ibid., 52; Theda Skocpol and Lawrence R. Jacobs, "Reaching for a New Deal: Ambitious Governance, Economic Meltdown, and Polarized Politics," in *Reaching for a New Deal: Ambitious Governance, Economic Meltdown, and Polarized Politics in Obama's First Two Years*, ed. Theda Skocpol and Lawrence R. Jacobs (New York: Russell Sage Foundation, 2011).

45. Hope Lewis, "Defining Race: Transnational Dimensions of Race in America," *Albany Law Review* 72 (2009): 999.

46. The Ivy League, predominantly Catholic, lineage of the Supreme Court justices became a topic of discussion in the *New Yorker*, the *Nation*, and the *New Republic*. See, for example, Jeffrey Rosen, "The Case against Sotomayor," *New Republic*, May 4, 2009.

47. Bai, "Is Obama the End of Black Politics?"

48. *Regents of the University of California v. Bakke*, 438 U.S. 265 (1978).

49. David A. Hollinger, *Postethnic America—Beyond Multiculturalism* (New York: Basic Books, 1995).

50. Lewis, "Defining Race."

51. Skocpol and Jacobs, "Reaching for a New Deal," 20 (my italics).

52. Skocpol and Jacobs, "Reaching for a New Deal." This argument is similar to the line in Theda Skocpol, *Protecting Soldiers and Mothers: The Political Origins of Social Policy in the United States* (Cambridge, MA: Harvard University Press, 1992). See also Suzanne Mettler, *Soldiers to Citizens: The G.I. and the Making of the Greatest Generation* (New York: Oxford University Press, 2007); and Jonathan Alter, *The Promise: President Obama, Year One* (New York: Simon & Schuster, 2010), 49–53.

53. Skocpol and Jacobs, "Reaching for a New Deal"; Alter, *Promise*, 85–86.

54. Skocpol and Jacobs, "Reaching for a New Deal," 27, 37 (my italics).

55. See Ron Suskind, *Confidence Men: Wall Street, Washington, and the Education of a President* (New York: Harper, 2011); *Confront and Conceal: Obama's Secret Wars and Surprising Use of American Power* (New York: Crown, 2012); and Peter Baker, "The Education of a President," *New York Times Magazine*, October 12, 2010. "Overturning a law would not be unprecedented or extraordinary, as any first-year law student could tell you, but don't take my word for it. Harvard University's Laurence Tribe, one of Obama's professors and a leading liberal scholar of constitutional law, said that his former student 'obviously misspoke.'" Kathleen Parker, "Justice Roberts on Trial," *Washington Post*, May 23, 2012. For comparison, see Jack Anderson, "Education of a President," *Sarasota Herald Tribune*, January 23, 1980, who reports that Carter was slow to realize that the Soviets were lying about supporting insurgencies around the globe. This is qualitatively different than being duped by your colleagues inside the Democratic Party.

56. Slessarev, *Betrayal of the Urban Poor*, 1–5.

57. Cheryl R. Kaiser, Benjamin J. Drury, Kerry E. Spalding, Sapna Cheryan, and Laurie T. O'Brien, "The Ironic Consequences of Obama's Election: Decreased Support for Social Justice," *Journal of Experimental Social Psychology* 45 (2009): 556–59.

58. Richard Kahlenberg, "The Affirmative Action Trap," *Tapped*, April 2, 2010.

59. Stuart Hall, "Cultural Studies: Two Paradigms," *Media, Culture and Society* 2 (1980): 57–72; and Michel Foucault, *Discipline and Punish: The Birth of the Prison*, trans. Alan Sheridan (New York: Vintage Books, 1975).

60. Stuart Hall, "The Spectacle of the Other," in *Representations: Cultural Representations and Signifying Practices* (London: Sage Publications, 1997).

61. Nikolaos A. Stavrou, "The Obama Presidency in Philosophical and Historical Context," *Mediterranean Quarterly* 20 (2009): 8.

62. Cotton Seiler, " 'So That We as a Race Might Have Something Authentic to Travel By': African American Automobility and Cold-War Liberalism," *American Quarterly* 58 (2006): 1092–94.

63. Michel Foucault, *Society Must Be Defended*, ed. Mauro Bertani and Alessandro Fontana, trans. David Macey (London: Picador, 2003), 97–98.

64. Franz Boas, Ruth Benedict, Theodosius Dobzhansky, and Leslie Clarence Dunn, "armed with the powerful new tools of population thinking and genetics, lifted the veil of ideology that previously shrouded biological studies of human diversity." By 1950, "population genetics eclipsed the ideological science of race biology." See Jenny Reardon, "Decoding Race and Human Difference in a Genomic Age," *differences: A Journal of Feminist Cultural Studies* 15 (2004): 38, 41–42.

65. Gina Athena Ulysse, "She Ain't Oprah, Angela, or Your Baby Mama," *Meridians: Feminism, Race, Transnationalism* 9 (2008): 174–76; and Jane Caputi, "Character Assassinations: Hate Messages in Election 2008 Commercial Paraphernalia," *Denver University Law Review* 86 (2009): 602. Caputi also cocurated an exhibit shown at Florida Atlantic University, September 5 through November 1, 2008, titled "Political Circus: A 3-Ring Reflection on the 2008 Political Campaigns."

66. Caputi, "Character Assassinations."

67. Reardon, "Decoding Race," 38; Yasmin Gunaratnam, *Researching Race and Ethnicity: Methods, Knowledge and Power* (Beverly Hills, CA: Sage, 2003).

68. Gunaratnam, *Researching Race and Ethnicity*.

69. Holning Lau, "Identity Scripts and Democratic Deliberation," *Minnesota Law Review* 94 (2010): 926.

70. Paul C. Light, *The President's Agenda* (Baltimore, MD: Johns Hopkins University Press, 1982).

71. Richard Neustadt, *Presidential Power and the Modern Presidents* (New York: John Wiley and Sons, 1960).

72. Kate Zernike and Megan Thee-Brenan, "Poll Finds Tea Party Backers Wealthier and More Educated," *New York Times*, April 14, 2010.

73. Skocpol and Jacobs, "Reaching for a New Deal," 48.

74. See Justin Ewers, "Obama and Race Relations: Civil Rights Leaders Aren't Satisfied," *U.S. News & World Report*, April 30, 2009.

75. Dianne Avery and Marion Crain, "Branded: Corporate Image, Sexual Stereotyping, and the New Face of Capitalism," *Duke Journal of Gender Law & Policy* 14 (2007): 13.

76. Catharine MacKinnon, *Only Words* (Cambridge, MA: Harvard University Press, 1993). See also Judith Butler, "Constitutions and 'Survivor Stories': Burning Acts: Injurious Speech," *University of Chicago Law School Roundtable* 3 (1996): 199.

77. Lau, "Identity Scripts," 896–97.

78. Kimberlé Crenshaw, "Demarginalizing the Intersection of Race and Sex: A Black Feminist Critique of Antidiscrimination Doctrine, Feminist Theory, and Antiracist Politics," *University of Chicago Legal Forum* (1989): 139.

79. Lau, "Identity Scripts," 927. See also Martha Minow, "The Supreme Court, 1986 Term: Foreword: Justice Engendered," *Harvard Law Review* 101 (1987): 10.

80. Lau, "Identity Scripts," 923.

81. Lau, "Identity Scripts," 924. In an interview with Bill Moyers on *Bill Moyers Journal*, December 7, 2007, Kathleen Hall Jamieson said, "The people who are producing these products are trying to attach to a candidate what scholars call negative affect." Quoted from Caputi, 608.

82. Lau, "Identity Scripts," 924.

83. Jacquelyn Bridgeman, "Defining Ourselves for Ourselves," *Seton Hall Law Review*, volume 35 (2005) no. 4, 1261; Lau, "Identity Scripts," 925.

84. Bridgeman, "Defining Ourselves for Ourselves," 1264.

85. Caputi, "Character Assassinations," 586.

86. Obama, *Dreams from My Father*, 25; Barack Obama, "What I See in Lincoln's Eyes," *Time*, October 26, 2005, http://www.time.com/time/magazine/article/0,9171,1077287-2,00.html#ixzz1DgirS6wq.

87. Obama, *Dreams from My Father*, 85; Obama, "What I See in Lincoln's Eyes"; Saul D. Alinsky, *Rules for Radicals: A Pragmatic Primer for Realistic Radicals* (New York: Random House, 1971); and Lewis, "Defining Race."

88. Obama, "A More Perfect Union." Lani Guinier is the daughter of a Jamaican American immigrant man and a Jewish American woman, and Gates is a native-born African American whose family raised him in West Virginia. See Lewis, "Defining Race," 1018.

89. Melani McAlister, "A Virtual Muslim Is Something to Be," *American Quarterly* 62 (2010): 221; "Muslim Voters Detect a Snub from Obama," *New York Times*, June 24, 2008; Alexandra Marks, "For Blacks, a Hidden Cost of Obama's Win?," *Christian Science Monitor*, July 5, 2009; and Lau, "Identity Scripts."

90. Marks, "For Blacks, a Hidden Cost?"; "The Supreme Love and Revolutionary Funk of Dr. Cornel West, Philosopher of the Blues," *Rolling Stone*, May 28, 2009.

91. Lewis, "Defining Race," 1006–7.

92. Lewis, "Defining Race." By contrast, black immigrants have also historically been essentialized as racial radicals, along the lines of Marcus Garvey, Malcolm X, or Stokely Carmichael/Kwame Ture, and labeled as having a hyper-racial, pan-African political consciousness.

93. McAlister, "Virtual Muslim."

94. One percent of African Americans are Islamic converts. McAlister, "Virtual Muslim," 226; and Lewis, "Defining Race," 1020–21.

95. McAlister, "Virtual Muslim."

96. Nicholas D. Kristof, "The Push To 'Otherize' Obama," *New York Times*, September 21, 2008; "How the Media Covered Religion, Obama Gets Most Coverage, Much of It on False Rumor He Is a Muslim," *Pew Forum on Religion and Public Life*, November 20, 2008.

97. Gerald Horne and Malika Horne-Wells, "First Lady in Black, Michelle Obama and the Crisis of Race and Gender," in *Barack Obama and African American Empowerment: The Rise of Black America's New Leadership*, ed. Manning Marable and Kristin Clarke (New York: Palgrave Macmillan, 2009), 142; and Lewis, "Defining Race," 1020, note 89.

98. Grant Farred, "The Ethics of Colin Powell," in Marable and Clarke, *Barack Obama and African American Empowerment*, 110.

99. McAlister, "Virtual Muslim."

100. Lewis, "Defining Race," 1016. A Web research firm, Hitwise, found that of the roughly one thousand Internet search themes related to Obama, the seventh most common was "Obama Antichrist" (Obama + Antichrist; by June 7, 2011, over 2 million on Google, and September 6, 2012 it hit over 4 million). Ann Coulter linked Obama to Hitler on Fox News, and Geoff Davis, a member of Congress from Kentucky, referred to Obama as "boy." Caputi, "Character Assassinations," 596.

101. Lewis, "Defining Race," 1016.

102. Ibid., 1015.

103. Ibid., 1017.

104. Ibid., 1019; and Caputi, "Character Assassinations," 593. Similar was the phrase, "If Obama is President . . . will we still call it the White House?"

105. David A. Hollinger, "Obama, the Instability of Color Lines, and the Promise of a Postethnic Future," *Callaloo* 31 (2008): 1034.

106. Ibid.

107. Rachel L. Swarns and Jodi Kantor, "First Lady's Roots Reveal Slavery's Tangled Legacy," *New York Times*, October 8, 2009; Allison Samuels, "What Michelle Means to Us," *Daily Beast*, November 21, 2008, http://www.thedailybeast.com/newsweek/2008/11/21/what-michelle-means-to-us.html; and Brittney Cooper, "A'n't I a Lady?: Race Women, Michelle Obama, and the Ever-Expanding Democratic Imagination," *MELUS: Multi-Ethnic Literature of the U.S.* 35 (2010): 39.

108. Quoted in David A. Hollinger, "Obama, Blackness, and Postethnic America," *Chronicle of Higher Education*, February 29, 2008.

109. Hollinger, "Obama, the Instability of Color Lines," 1034; and John Skrentny, *The Minority Rights Revolution* (Cambridge, MA: Harvard University Press, 2002).

110. Lewis, "Defining Race," 1020.

111. Ibid., 1022.

112. Ibid.

113. Philip Kennicott, "Obama as the Joker: Racial Fear's Ugly Face; 'Po-

litical' Poster Turns on Violent Symbolism," *Washington Post*, August 6, 2009; *U.S. Human Rights Network ICERD Shadow Report* 2008; and Lewis, "Defining Race."

114. Lau, "Identity Scripts," 918.

115. Lau, "Identity Scripts"; Caputi, "Character Assassinations," 586.

116. Caputi, "Character Assassinations."

117. See Adam Nagourney, Elisabeth Bumiller, Marjorie Connelly, and Jeff Zeleny, "Obama: Racial Barrier Falls in Decisive Victory," *New York Times*, November 5, 2008; Kaiser et al., "Ironic Consequences of Obama's Election."

118. Patricia Williams, "A Year On, Has Barack Obama Met the Hopes of the World?," *Observer*, October 30, 2009, http://www.guardian.co.uk /commentisfree/2009/nov/01/observer-debate-barack-obama.

119. Peter Baker, "Court Choice Pushes Issue of 'Identity Politics' Back to Forefront," *New York Times*, May 31, 2009.

120. Linda Trinh Võ, "Beyond Color-Blind Universalism: Asians in a 'Post-racial America,' *Journal of Asian American Studies* 13 (2010): 331.

121. Võ, "Beyond Color-Blind Universalism," 331; and Michael Omi and Howard Winant, *Racial Formation in the United States* (New York: Routledge Press, 1994), chapter 2.

122. Võ, "Beyond Color-Blind Universalism" 331.

123. Hollinger, "Obama, the Instability of Color Lines," 1037.

CHAPTER SEVEN

1. Barack Obama, "Nobel Lecture" (Oslo, Norway, December 10, 2009), http://www.nobelprize.org/nobel_prizes/peace/laureates/2009/obama-lecture _en.html. See Jean Paul Sartre, *No Exit* (1944); and Paul Bowles, *The Sheltering Sky* (1949).

2. See Atul Gawande, "Now What?," *New Yorker*, April 5, 2010, http:// www.newyorker.com/talk/comment/2010/04/05/100405taco_talk_gawande; and Jeffrey Toobin, "Ask the Author Live: Jeffrey Toobin on Clarence and Virginia Thomas," *New Yorker*, August 22, 2011, http://www.newyorker.com /online/blogs/ask/2011/08/clarence-virginia-thomas-jeffrey-toobin.html# ixzz11PUyJnaV.

3. Ron Suskind, *Confidence Men: Wall Street, Washington, and the Education of a President* (New York: Harper, 2011). For an analysis of Aristotle's dramatic irony, see Wayne C. Booth, *The Rhetoric of Fiction*, 2nd ed. (Chicago: University of Chicago Press, 1983); Robert Scholes, James Phelan, and Robert Kellogg, *The Nature of Narrative* (New York: Oxford University Press, 2006), chap. 8; and Martha Nussbaum, *Love's Knowledge: Essays on Philosophy and Literature* (New York: Oxford University Press, 1990).

4. Richard Wolffe, *Revival: The Struggle for Survival inside the Obama White House* (New York: Crown Books, 2011).

5. Robert C. Rowland, "Barack Obama and the Revitalization of Public Reason," *Rhetoric & Public Affairs* 14 (2011): 707, 709; Jonathan Alter, *The Promise: President Obama, Year One* (New York: Simon & Schuster, 2011); Jeff Madrick, *The Case for Big Government* (Princeton, NJ: Princeton University

Press, 2008), and Madrick, "The Case for Government," lecture at the CUNY Graduate Center, 2005.

6. Alter, *Promise*, 400.

7. Jesse Lee, "A Bipartisan Meeting on Health Reform: The Invites Are Out," *White House Blog*, February 12, 2010, http://www.whitehouse.gov /blog/2010/02/12/a-bipartisan-meeting-health-reform-invites-are-out; and Wolffe, *Revival*, 17.

8. "Barack Obama's Inaugural Address," *New York Times*, January 20, 2009, http://www.nytimes.com/2009/01/20/us/politics/20text-obama.html? pagewanted=all; Ryan Lizza, "Inside the Crisis; Larry Summers and the White House Economic Team," *New Yorker*, October 12, 2009; and Rowland, "Barack Obama and the Revitalization of Public Reason."

9. Rowland, "Barack Obama," 700; and Randal Strathan, "Personal Motives, Constitutional Forms and the Public Good: Madison on Public Leadership," in *James Madison, The Theory and Practice of Republican Government*, ed. Samuel Kernell (Palo Alto: Stanford University Press, 2003), 71, paraphrasing Madison, "Federalist #10."

10. Katherine Adams, "At the Table with Arendt: Toward a Self-Interested Practice of Coalition Discourse," *Hypatia* 17 (2002): 1.

11. Obama's speechwriter Jon Favreau wrote a first draft, but Obama "handwrote nine pages of a new version, the bulk of the speech." Barack Obama, "Health Care Speech to Joint Session of Congress (September 15, 2010)," http:// en.wikipedia.org/wiki/File:Obama_Health_Care_Speech_to_Joint_Session_of _Congress.jpg; and Rowland, "Barack Obama," 694.

12. Rowland, "Barack Obama," 694, 700, 707, 709; Alter, *Promise*; and Elizabeth Drew, "Is There Life in Health-Care Reform," *New York Review of Books*, March 11, 2010.

13. Joshua Cohen, "Deliberation and Democratic Legitimacy," in *Deliberative Democracy: Essays on Reason and Politics*, ed. James Bohman and William Rehg (Cambridge, MA: MIT Press, 1997), 73.

14. Jim Sleeper, "An Unlikely Pragmatist," review of *Reading Obama: Dreams, Hope, and the American Political Tradition*, by James T. Kloppenberg, *Dissent* (Spring 2011), http://dissentmagazine.org/article/?article=3924.

15. Twin towns or sister cities stem from Sister Cities International, founded in 1956 to "promote peace through mutual respect, understanding, and cooperation—one individual, one community at a time." See Sister Cities International, http://www.sister-cities.org.

16. Benjamin Barber, *Strong Democracy: Participatory Politics for a New Age*, 2nd ed. (Berkeley: University of California Press, 2004), especially the preface.

17. See Ryan Lizza, "The Obama Memos: The Making of a Post-Post-Partisan Presidency," *New Yorker*, January 30, 2012, http://www.newyorker.com /reporting/2012/01/30/120130fa_fact_lizza#ixzz1kP5jF4uh. An oft-quoted phrase from Thomas Jefferson's first inaugural address is "Every difference of opinion is not a difference of principle. We have called by different names brethren of the same principle. We are all Republicans, we are all Federalists." http:// www.bartleby.com/124/pres16.html.

18. E. J. Dionne Jr., "A Catholic Spring?," *Washington Post*, May 24, 2012. See Adam Liptak and Allison Kopicki, "Approval Rating for Justices Hits Just 44% in New Poll," *New York Times*, June 7, 2012; and Peter Baker and Rachel L. Swarns, "Obama Uses College Speech to Push for Gender Equality," *International Herald Tribune*, May 15, 2012.

19. Matt Pearce, "Could the End Be Near for the Occupy Wall Street Movement?," *Los Angeles Times*, June 11, 2012.

20. "Reaction from Expert Bloggers," *National Journal*, February 25, 2009. Tea Partiers proposed a "Repeal Amendment" that would give two-thirds of state legislatures the power to repeal federal laws and regulations. See Randy Barnett, "The Tea Party, the Constitution, and the Repeal Amendment," *Northwestern University Law Review Colloquy* 105 (2011): 281.

21. Ewen MacAskill, "How Republicans and Tea Party Will Use Congress to Bash Barack Obama," *Guardian*, January 3, 2011, http://www.guardian.co.uk/world/2011/jan/03/republicans-tea-party-barack-obama; "Beyond the Results: House," *Washington Post*, http://www.washingtonpost.com/wp-srv/special/politics/2010-race-maps/house; Maya Srikrishnan, Jared Pliner, Jennifer Schlesinger, Joshua Goldstein, and Huma Khan, "Vote 2010 Elections: Tea Party Winners and Losers," November 3, 2010, http://abcnews.go.com/Politics/2010_Elections/vote-2010-elections-tea-party-winners-losers/story?id=12023076#.Tx793ph5HVs; and Lawrence R. Jacobs and Theda Skocpol, *Obama's Agenda and the Dynamics of U.S. Politics* (New York: Russell Sage Foundation, 2010).

22. Jill Lepore, *The Whites of Their Eyes: The Tea Party's Revolution and the Battle over American History* (Princeton, NJ: Princeton University Press, 2010), 8.

23. Ibid.; and Eugene Robinson, "Racism and the Tea Party Movement," *Real Clear Politics*, November 2, 2010, http://www.realclearpolitics.com/articles/2010/11/02/race_and_the_tea_partys_ire_107805.html. Robinson continues, "Witness the willingness of so many to believe absurd conspiracy theories about Obama's birthplace, his religion, and even his absent father's supposed Svengali-like influence from the grave."

24. LeAna B. Gloor, "From the Melting Pot to the Tossed Salad Metaphor: Why Coercive Assimilation Lacks the Flavors Americans Crave," *Hohonu* 4, no. 1 (2006), available at http://hilo.hawaii.edu/academics/hohonu/documents/Vol04x06FromtheMeltingPot.pdf.

25. Ibid.; J. D. Hayworth, "Immigrants Need to Embrace U.S. Culture," *Arizona Republic*, January 29, 2006, http://www.azcentral.com/arizonarepublic/viewpoints/articles/0129hayworth0129.html; Thomas Ricento, "A Brief History of Language Restrictionism in the United States," in *Official English? No! TESOL's Recommendations for Countering the Official English Movement in the US* (November 27, 2002; March 5, 2006), available at www.smkb.ac.il/privweb/Teachers/Chaim_Tir/nurit/OFFICIAL%20ENGLISH.doc; and Katharyne Mitchell, "Geographies of Identity: Multiculturalism Unplugged," *Progress in Human Geography* 28 (2004): 641.

26. Gloor, "From the Melting Pot."

27. Israel Zangwill's "melting pot" metaphor had rhetorical support from black nationalists such as W. E. B. Du Bois and Marcus Garvey. See William

Booth, "One Nation, Indivisible: Is It History?," *Washingtonpost.com*, February 22, 1998; and Bill Frey, "A Closer Look at the Melting-Pot Myth," *Newsday*, March 16, 2001.

28. Jackie Calmes, "In Border City Talk, Obama Urges G.O.P. to Help Overhaul Immigration Law," *New York Times*, May 11, 2011.

29. Gloor, "From the Melting Pot"; George Bornstein, "The Colors of Zion: Black, Jewish, and Irish Nationalisms at the Turn of the Century," *Modernism/modernity* 12 (2005): 380; and Israel Zangwill, *The Melting Pot* (New York: Macmillan, 1932), 203.

30. Mitchell, "Geographies of Identity." The idea that a multiethnic society can have an interdependent cohesion based on national solidarity while retaining distinct cultural histories not dependent on like-minded homogeneity existed in the early twentieth century.

31. Calmes, "In Border City Talk"; and Peter Baker and Sheryl Gay Stolberg, "Obama Exhorts Congress to Back Immigration Overhaul," *New York Times*, July 2, 2010.

32. Julia Preston and Charlie Savage, "Justice Dept. Sues Arizona over Its Immigration Law," *New York Times*, July 7, 2010; Baker and Stolberg, "Obama Exhorts Congress to Back Immigration Overhaul"; Sam Youngman and Jordy Yager, "GOP Brands Obama's Call for Immigration Reform Political," *The Hill*, May 11, 2011. The DREAM Act (read Development, Relief, and Education for Alien Minors) had been introduced in the Senate in August 2011.

33. Preston and Savage, "Justice Dept. Sues Arizona"; Jacobs and Skocpol, *Obama's Agenda*, 32; and Jacob S. Hacker and Paul Pierson, "Business Power and Social Policy: Employers and the Formation of the American Welfare State," *Politics and Society*, 30 (2002): 277. Sarah Palin, the Tea Party's supposed leader, did not even initiate the movement. A *Washington Post* poll gave Palin a 60 percent favorability rating "among those who view the tea party favorably and 71 percent among conservative Republicans." "Behind the Numbers, Sarah Palin and the Tea Party Movement," *Washington Post*, March 27, 2010, http://voices.washingtonpost.com/behind-the-numbers/2010/03/sarah_palin _and_the_tea_party.html.

34. William Yardley, "The Branding of the Occupy Movement," *New York Times*, November 27, 2011, http://www.nytimes.com/2011/11/28/business/media /the-branding-of-the-occupy-movement.html?_r=1&pagewanted=all.

35. Michael Cooper and Megan Thee-Brenan, "Disapproval Rate for Congress at Record 82% After Debt Talks," *New York Times*, August 4, 2011, http://www.nytimes.com/2011/08/05/us/politics/05poll.html; Gary C. Jacobson, "The Republican Resurgence in 2010," *Political Science Quarterly* 126 (2011): 27; Jeff Shesol, *Supreme Power, Franklin Roosevelt vs. the Supreme Court* (New York: W. W. Norton, 2010); and Peter H. Irons, *The New Deal Lawyers* (Princeton, NJ: Princeton University Press, 1982).

36. See Thomas Byrne Edsall, *The Age of Austerity: How Scarcity Will Remake American Politics* (New York: Doubleday, 2012); and Jeff Madrick, *Age of Greed: The Triumph of Finance and the Decline of America* (New York: Doubleday, 2012). The most imperiled person in the Obama administration is Attorney General Holder, and rumors abound that the Secretary of State is leaving. See

David A. Fahrenthold and Sari Horwitz, "Holder Embattled on Two Fronts," *Washington Post*, June 14, 2012.

37. Garry Wills, "Two Speeches on Race," *New York Review of Books*, May 1, 2008; Evan Thomas and Richard Wolffe, "Obama's Lincoln," *Newsweek*, November 24, 2008; see also the *New Yorker*, November 17, 2008 (the cover picturing the Lincoln Memorial at night with the "O"). See Charles R. Kesler, "The Audacity of Barack Obama," *Claremont Review of Books*, Fall 2008, for Obama's self-fashioning and historical references; and Susan Schulten, "Barack Obama, Abraham Lincoln, and John Dewey," *Denver University Law Review* 86 (2009): 808.

38. Peggy Noonan, "Conceit of Government," *Wall Street Journal*, June 29, 2005.

39. Schulten, "Barack Obama"; Obama, *Audacity of Hope*. At the Democratic National Convention, Al Gore compared Obama to Lincoln, including his lack of experience. Al Gore, "Address at the 2008 Democratic National Convention" (August 28, 2008), http://www.demconvention.com/al-gore/.

40. Robert Kuttner, "Barack Obama's Theory of Power: Why the President's Bipartisan, Detached Use of Power Hasn't Worked," *American Prospect*, May 10, 2011, http://prospect.org/article/barack-obamas-theory-power; and George Packer, "Deepest Cuts," *New Yorker*, April 25, 2011, http://www.newyorker.com/talk/comment/2011/04/25/110425taco_talk_packer#ixzz11PX1zWy5.

41. George Packer, "Foreclosed Futures," *New Yorker*, December 6, 2011, http://www.newyorker.com/online/blogs/comment/2011/12/foreclosed-futures.html#ixzz11Qtlfsw4; Packer, "Deepest Cuts"; Michelle Alexander, "Obama's Drug War," *Nation*, December 9, 2010, http://realcostofprisons.org/blog/archives/2010/12/obamas_drug_war.html; Melinda Henneberger, "Saul Alinsky Would Be So Disappointed: Obama Breaks 'Rules for Radicals,'" *Washington Post*, January 25, 2012; and Kuttner, "Barack Obama's Theory of Power."

42. Dionne, "A Catholic Spring?"; "Freedom of Religion Is Safe," *Los Angeles Times*, June 17, 2012.

43. *San Antonio Independent School District v. Rodriguez*, 411 U.S. 1 (1973).

44. Michael Paisner, "Boerne Supremacy: Congressional Responses to *City of Boerne v. Flores* and the Scope of Congress's Article I Powers," *Columbia Law Review* 105 (2005): 537.

45. Helen Hershkoff, "Positive Rights and State Constitutions: The Limits of Federal Rationality Review," *Harvard Law Review* 112 (1999): 1131, offers an excellent critique of federalism, including Morton Grodzin's classic "marble cake" or dual sovereignty thesis.

46. *City of Boerne v. Flores*, 521 U.S. 527 (1997). See also the website of the American Legislative Exchange Council (ALEC), which promotes free trade, limited government, and federalism, at http://www.alec.org/. The Center for Media and Democracy reported that ALEC drafted 800 model bills for states that corporations approved in advance (see http://www.prwatch.org/news/2011/07/10883/about-alec-exposed). A whistleblower provided the information. See "ALEC Exposed," http://alecexposed.org/wiki/ALEC_Exposed.

47. My italics. "If you look at the victories and failures of the civil rights

movement, and its litigation strategy in the court, I think where it succeeded was to vest formal rights in previously dispossessed peoples, so that I would now have the right to vote, I would now be able to sit at a lunch counter and order and as long as I could pay for it I'd be okay." Obama made these comments on January 18, 2001, in discussing "The Courts and Civil Rights" on WBEZ-FM's *Odyssey*, on National Public Radio.

48. Aaron Y. Tang, "Broken Systems, Broken Duties: A New Theory for School Finance Litigation," *Marquette Law Review* 196 (2011): 1195.

49. Patrick Welsh, "Education by the Book: Inside Look at School Reform Puts Too Much Faith in Charters," review of *Class Warfare: Inside the Fight to Fix America's Schools*, by Steven Brill, *Journal Gazette* (Fort Wayne, IN), http://www.journalgazette.net/article/20110904/ENT07/309049980/1134.

50. Achieve, "Ready or Not: Creating a High School Diploma That Counts," December 10, 2004, available at http://www.achieve.org/readyornot; Sam Dillon, "Education Secretary May Agree to Waivers on 'No Child' Law Requirements," *New York Times*, June 12, 2011.

51. Sam Dillon, "Obama Proposes Sweeping Change in Education Law: Readiness for College; Continued Testing, but Less Interference for Well-Run Schools," *New York Times*, March 14, 2010.

52. Ibid. Jennifer Allen, Congressman John Kline's spokesperson, said this Republican from Minnesota and an original backer supports giving "enhanced flexibility, believing a more streamlined federal role in education combined with reduced regulatory burdens would encourage greater innovation and higher academic achievement."

53. Ibid. See the 5–4 decision on *Knox et al. v. Service Employees International Union, Local 1000* (Slip Opinion, October 2011), 4, 17–23, http://www.supremecourt.gov/opinions/slipopinions.aspx?Term=11, curbing public sector unionism. "If the nonmembers pay too much [for lobbying], their First Amendment rights are infringed. But, if they pay too little, no constitutional right of the union is violated because it has no constitutional right to receive any payment from those employees."

54. Ibid.

55. Geoffrey Canada, credited with turning around underachievement in Harlem, said that teaching unions threaten the education secretary's reforms. Jeevan Vasagar and Allegra Stratton, "Conservative Conference 2010: Education and Defence: School Reform: Unions Block Change, Says Obama Pioneer," *Guardian*, October 6, 2010.

56. This projection is a spike from data showing that 37 percent of schools will miss the law's targets. "Four out of five schools in America would not meet their goals under [No Child Left Behind] by next year," Duncan said in his opening statement before Congress. Patrick B. McGuigan and Stacy Martin, "Schools Approach No Child Left Behind Deadline; Feds Say Nation's Schools Cannot Meet It," *CapitolBeatOK*, April 3, 2011, http://capitolbeatok.com/_webapp_3864886/Schools_approach_No_Child_Left_Behind_deadline;_Feds_say_nation's_schools_cannot_meet_it; "Duncan: Change Bush 'No Child' law," *TheHill.com*, March 9, 2011, http://thehill.com/blogs/blog-briefing-room

/news/148541-duncan-says-82-percent-of-schools-could-be-failing-under-no
-child-left-behind.

57. For some of this history, see the Carnegie Corporation's 1967 report, *Public Television: A Program for Action*, http://www.current.org/pbpb/carnegie /carnegieisummary.html. In another example, the Annie E. Casey Foundation's Juvenile Detention Alternatives Initiative (JDAI) in 1992 showed that youth are unnecessarily detained and that it is debilitating for their development and public safety; see http://www.aecf.org/MajorInitiatives/JuvenileDetentionAlternatives Initiative.aspx. See also Suzanne Perry and Grant Williams, "How the *Chronicle* Compiled Its Review of Campaign Contributions," *Chronicle of Philanthropy*, October 31, 2008, http://philanthropy.com/article/How-The-Chronicle -Compiled-Its/62938/; Lauren Foster, "Charitable Relations," *American Prospect*, May 2009.

58. Foster, "Charitable Relations."

59. "I've heard one question over and over: Can it really be reproduced? It's true that it took a leader with Canada's unique qualities and personal history to create the first Harlem Children's Zone, to inspire donors enough to expand it from a modest community organization into a nonprofit powerhouse with a $68 million annual budget." Paul Tough, "Man with a Plan," *Mother Jones* (January /February 2009). See also Paul Tough, *Whatever It Takes: Geoffrey Canada's Quest to Change Harlem and America* (New York: Houghton Mifflin Harcourt, 2008).

60. Tough, "Man with a Plan."

61. Foster, "Charitable Relations."

62. Allen Ken Easley, "Of Children's Plates, Melting Pots, Tossed Salads and Multiple Consciousness: Tales from a Hapa Haole," *UCLA Asian Pacific American Law Journal* 3 (1995): 75; Peter Kivisto, "What Is the Canonical Theory of Assimilation?," *Journal of the History of the Behavioral Sciences* 40 (2004): 153.

63. Gloor, "From the Melting Pot" (my italics).

64. J. Hector St. John de Crèvecoeur, *Letters from an American Farmer*, ed. Susan Manning (Oxford: Oxford University Press, 1997), 44.

65. Bornstein, "Colors of Zion"; and Zangwill, *Melting Pot*, 203.

66. Gloor, "From the Melting Pot"; Kivisto, "What Is the Canonical Theory of Assimilation?," 153.

67. Gloor, "From the Melting Pot"; Preston and Savage, "Justice Dept. Sues Arizona" (the American Civil Liberties Union, the Mexican American Legal Defense and Educational Fund, and other civil rights groups brought this suit, signed April 23, 2010); Jon Swaine, "Obama Offers 'Amnesty' for up to 800,000 Young Illegal Immigrants," *Daily Telegraph*, June 16, 2012; David Usborne, "Obama Lifts Deportation Threat for 800,000 Young Illegal Immigrants; President Builds on Support among Hispanic Voters in Swing States with Shock Announcement," *Independent*, June 16, 2012; and "Plouffe Defends Obama Immigration Change, Criticizes Romney," *Los Angeles Times*, June 17, 2012.

68. Richard E. Neustadt, *Presidential Power and the Modern Presidents: The Politics of Leadership from Roosevelt to Reagan*, 3rd ed. (New York: Free Press,

1990); and James David Barber, *Presidential Character: Predicting Performance in the White House*, 4th ed. (New York: Prentice Hall, 1992).

69. Barack Obama, "Remarks by the President to a Joint Session of Congress on Health Care" (Washington, DC, September 9, 2009), http://www.whitehouse.gov/the_press_office/Remarks-by-the-President-to-a-Joint-Session-of-Congress-on-Health-Care; and Wolffe, *Revival*, 14–15.

70. Wolfe, *Revival*, 9–25, 44. "His senior advisors, who were paid to care about his survival, were not enthusiastic about his commitment to a comprehensive health care package."

71. Neustadt, *Presidential Power and the Modern Presidents*; and Stephen Skowronek, *The Politics Presidents Make: Leadership from John Adams to Bill Clinton* (Cambridge, MA: Harvard University Press, 1997) for *the* most influential studies about presidential leadership.

72. Joshua Cohen, "Deliberation and Democratic Legitimacy," in *The Good Polity: Normative Analysis of the State*, ed. Alan Hamlin and Phillip Petit (New York: Blackwell, 1989); Seyla Benhabib, "The Democratic Moment and the Problem of Difference," in *Democracy and Difference: Contesting the Boundaries of the Political*, ed. Seyla Benhabib (Princeton, NJ: Princeton University Press, 1996), 3.

73. James Fishkin, "Town Halls by Invitation," *New York Times*, August 15, 2009. Fishkin proposes five easy steps for selecting a random sample of deliberators: (1) a survey "identifies the range of attitudes and demographics in the district"; (2) a random group or citizen jury is chosen; (3), the jury members receive information so that "they can each study or contemplate the issue before the deliberative meeting"; (4) "their positions are assessed, with experts polling each deliberator before and after the decision-making meeting"; and (5) "trained moderators, who have no agenda or stake in the process or the outcome, make sure that every voice is heard and that the group carefully and thoughtfully narrows in on its most pertinent and pressing policy questions."

74. Ibid.

75. Iris Marion Young, "Activist Challenges to Deliberative Democracy," *Political Theory* 29 (2001): 670; John S. Dryzek, "Deliberative Democracy in Divided Societies: Alternative to Agonism and Analgesia," *Political Theory* 29 (2005): 218; and Philip Pettit, "Freedom as Antipower," *Ethics* 106 (1996): 590–92.

76. Young, "Activist Challenges."

77. Ibid.

78. Dryzek's list of requirements for deliberation: "deliberative institutions at a distance from sovereign authority; deliberative forums in the public sphere that focus on particular needs rather than general values; issue-specific networks; centripetal electoral systems; a power-sharing state that does not reach too far into the public sphere; the conditionality of sovereignty; and the transnationalization of political influence." Dryzek, "Deliberative Democracy in Divided Societies," 239. Pettit asks "first, the question of how many contexts—electoral, parliamentary, industrial, educational, and so on—ought to be democratised. Second, the question of how many issues in any democratised context ought to

be under democratic control: just the choice of office-holders, or also the choice of policy-programs, or perhaps the choice of some detailed policies. And third, the question of how far a democratic character serves to justify or legitimate a regime and pattern of decision-making, or at least to give them a presumptive authority: to place the onus of argument on the shoulders of those who would not comply." Philip Pettit, "Deliberative Democracy and the Discursive Dilemma," *Philosophical Issues* 11 (2001): 269. Amy Gutmann and Dennis Thompson argue that moral agreements require some amount of reciprocity, which is to say seeking "fair terms" for their own sake, in *Democracy and Disagreement: Why Moral Conflict Cannot Be Avoided in Politics, and What Should Be Done about It* (Cambridge, MA: Cambridge University Press, 1996). This logic is also presented by Cass Sunstein, *Free Markets and Social Justice* (Oxford: Oxford University Press, 1997), 9. See also John Dryzek, "Discursive Democracy vs. Liberal Constitutionalism," in *Democratic Innovation: Deliberation, Representation, and Association*, ed. Michael Saward (London: Routledge, 2000); Young, "Activist Challenges"; Andrew Knops, "Delivering Deliberation's Emancipatory Potential," *Political Theory* 34 (2006): 594; Archon Fung, "Deliberation before the Revolution: Toward an Ethic of Deliberative Democracy in an Unjust World," *Political Theory* 33 (2005): 398; and Jürgen Habermas, *Between Facts and Norms: Contributions to a Discourse Theory of Law and Democracy* (Cambridge, MA: MIT Press, 1998).

79. Others call this view civic humanism, a term this book avoids, given its universal connotation. Jean-Jacques Rousseau did not approve universal intervention in the government, given the relation between the represented and the representative. To Pocock, federalism is medieval, not classical. It is also sovereign, or has concentrated power, instead of being republican. See J. G. A. Pocock, *Machiavellian Moment* (Princeton, NJ: Princeton University Press, 1975), 518; Hannah Arendt, *The Human Condition* (Chicago: University of Chicago Press, 1958); Quentin Skinner, *Liberty before Liberalism* (Cambridge: Cambridge University Press, 1998); and Philip Pettit, *Republicanism: A Theory of Freedom and Government* (New York: Oxford University Press, 2000). All of these authors regard civic virtue as part of civic humanism. The latter scope is larger, concentrating on how civic virtue helped preserve the classically Roman/Florentine ideal of political liberty. For an opposing view, see Andreas Kalyvas and Ira Katznelson, "The Republic of the Moderns: Paine's and Madison's Novel Liberalism," *Polity* 38 (2006): 447. For the civic republicanism in administrative law, see Mark Seidenfeld, "A Civic Republican Justification for the Bureaucratic State," *Harvard Law Review* 1511 (1992): 105.

80. Kurt Andersen, "The Protester," *Time*, December 14, 2011, http://www.time.com/time/specials/packages/article/0,28804,2101745_2102132_2102373,00.htm; Jacobs and Skocpol, *Obama's Agenda*, 33, 51 (my italics). In 1922 Dewey reviewed Lippmann's book *Public Opinion* favorably in the *New Republic*. In 1925 *The Phantom Public* was published. Dewey engaged it in public lectures at Kenyon College in 1926, which he published in 1927 as *The Public and Its Problems*.

EPILOGUE

1. For the half-empty/full and half-credit/blame debate, see Michael Grunwald, *The New, New Deal: The Hidden Story of Change in the Obama Era* (New York: Simon and Schuster, 2012); and Noam Scheiber, *The Escape Artists: How Obama's Team Fumbled the Recovery* (New York: Simon and Schuster, 2012). Also see Theda Skocpol and Vanessa Williamson, *The Tea Party and the Remaking of Republican Conservatism* (New York: Oxford University Press, 2012); and Theda Skocpol, *Obama and America's Political Future* (Cambridge, MA: Harvard University Press, 2012), emphasizing economics and inside-the-Beltway partisan politics, rather than the rainbow coalition and reinvigorated culture wars.

2. Chapters 3 and 4 show how Obama took advantage of mediation rather than adversarial principles underlying the Administrative Procedure Act. Another example is his reliance on the Administrative Dispute Resolution Act (ADRA), mandating that federal agencies use mediation. The legal profession has accommodated these changes, but public discussion lags behind. Ellen Joan Pollock, "Wrangles with the Feds May Get Easier to Resolve," *Wall Street Journal*, April 8, 1991; Marc Ferris, "Reaching Out to a Third Party," *New York Times*, January 27, 2002.

3. David Leonhardt, "Who Gets Credit for the Recovery?," *New York Times*, October 28, 2012; David Firestone, "Don't Tell Anyone, but the Stimulus Worked," *New York Times*, September 16, 2012.

4. Thomas J. Cleary, "A Wolf in Sheep's Clothing: The Unilateral Executive and the Separation of Powers," *Pierce Law Review* 6, no. 2 (2007): 265–97. http://works.bepress.com/thomas_cleary/1.

5. Richard Neustadt, *Presidential Power and the Modern Presidents* (New York: John Wiley and Sons, 1960); and Stephen Skowronek, *The Politics Presidents Make: Leadership from John Adams to Bill Clinton* (Cambridge, MA: Harvard University Press, 1997).

6. Matthew Dull and Patrick S. Roberts, "Continuity, Competence, and the Succession of Senate-Confirmed Agency Appointees, 1989–2009," *Presidential Studies Quarterly* 39 (2009): 432–53, adds six months to the "two-year rule." Obama preferred continuity and competence, devoting executive-action attention to labor, education, health and human services, justice, and transportation as well as the EEOC, the EPA, and the FCC. Departures from his Cabinet, though they served the first term, include Treasury, State, Interior, and Energy.

7. Lisa Jackson is "leaving after four productive years." "Time to Confront Climate Change," *New York Times*, December 28, 2012.

8. Grunwald, *The New, New Deal*, argues that Obama had no choice, downplaying the suggestion that *he* selected this Clintonesque team. What attracted Obama most about stimulus was that it could be more akin to the WPA, rebuilding infrastructure. See also Lori Montgomery and Paul Kane, "Obama, Senate Republicans Reach Agreement on 'Fiscal Cliff,'" *Washington Post*, December 31, 2012.

9. Leonard Lopate interview with presidential biographer Doris Kearns Goodwin, who said Lincoln is the subject of as many books as Jesus.

10. See Richard M. Vallely, *The Two Reconstructions: The Struggle for Black Enfranchisement* (Chicago: University of Chicago Press, 2004).

11. Micah Cohen, "Gay Vote Proved a Boon for Obama," *New York Times*, November 15, 2012.

12. "The Rise of Asian Americans," PEW Social and Demographic Trends, PEW Research Center, June 19, 2012, http://www.pewsocialtrends .org/2012/06/19/the-rise-of-asian-americans/7/#chapter-6-political-and-civic-life.

Index